The GOLD CLAUSE

What it is and how to use it profitably

Edited, and with an introduction and two chapters
By Henry Mark Holzer

BOOKS IN FOCUS INC., NEW YORK

This book is dedicated, with love, to
ERIKA HOLZER

Acknowledgement

Were it not for five people, my life would be very different. Unfortunately, two of them—my late parents, Rose and Herbert Holzer—cannot know how fruitful was their insistence that I obtain a solid education.

Years later, that education was augmented by the brilliant political philosophy of Ayn Rand, whose ideas influenced me profoundly and became the root of much that I have accomplished intellectually.

I am indebted to Allan Blumenthal, for his graciousness and aid in time of need.

Erika Holzer, to whom this book is dedicated, has enriched my life incalculably. Without her, neither this book nor a great many other things would have been possible.

Table of Contents

Foreward

The factual materials, and his own brilliant legal analyses, which Henry Holzer has brought together here, combine to make this book invaluable—to the corporation attorney, to the monetary economist, and to the interested layman.

Practically every monetary economist now agrees that, appalling as the evils of a runaway inflation may be, they cannot be corrected by deflation. The late Ludwig von Mises used to compare the belief that the damages of inflation could be undone by a corresponding deflation with the belief of a motorist who has just run over a man that to back up over his victim would correct his mistake.

The damage done by an inflation is irreversible. Even trying to bring an inflation to a halt may do additional damage—though it will be less than the evils of allowing the inflation to continue.

So it is with our government's action in 1933 in repudiating not only its own solemn printed pledges to make its currency convertible into gold, but in making it impossible for private citizens to keep their own pledges to redeem their obligations in gold.

Repudiation of the pre-1933 gold clauses cheated creditors to benefit their debtors. This amounted to a forced transfer of private property. It deeply shook confidence throughout the business world. It shook it not only in past but in future pledges. But if the pre-1933 pledges were today suddenly declared by the Congress and the courts to be valid, all degrees of new forced transfers of private property would take place. Present holders of pre-1933 bonds, who may have acquired them at the merest fraction of their new value, would get unexpected windfalls. Old corporations with such bonds outstanding would be forced into bankruptcy. And if Congress or the courts sought a compromise solution of the old gold-clause pledge that would secure "justice" in every instance, it would find the task impossible.

vii

As an economist, I must confine myself here to calling attention to the admirable way in which Professor Holzer has emphasized the enormous economic damage done by the repudiation of the gold clause, and leave it to others to judge how well he has performed his analysis of the legal consequences of the gold-clause repudiation, and how satisfactory his recommendations are regarding what the future legal status ought to be.

The aim of the law should surely be to uphold the inviolability of legal contracts in order to maintain and justify faith in those contracts. When the law in any case does the exact opposite—when it not only permits, but practically orders the breaking of pledges and the repudiation of contracts—the evil consequences are beyond measurement.

> Henry Hazlitt
>
> December, 1979
> Wilton, Conn.

Introduction

In her classic novel, *Atlas Shrugged*, author-philosopher Ayn Rand observed that:

> Whenever destroyers appear among men, they start by destroying money, for money is men's protection and the base of a moral existence. Destroyers seize gold and leave to its owners a counterfeit pile of paper. This kills all objective standards and delivers men into the arbitrary power of an arbitrary setter of values. Gold was an objective value, an equivalent of wealth produced. Paper is a mortgage on wealth that does not exist, backed by a gun aimed at those who are expected to produce it. Paper is a check drawn by legal looters upon an account which is not theirs; upon the virtue of the victims. Watch for the day when it bounces, marked: 'Account overdrawn.'

The rampant inflation of the late 1970s has been just one example of the devastating consequences flowing from the government's manipulation of paper money. In self defense, some of the victims have successfully fled from currency, finding refuge in gold, other precious metals, real estate, and even collectibles. But not everyone has been fortunate enough to escape; paper money's principal hostages are creditors. Basically, one becomes a creditor in one of two ways: by selling goods or services to be paid for later, or, like a bondbuyer, by actually lending money, to be repaid later. Either way, the creditor parts with money at today's value, but has it returned at tomorrow's.* Unfortunately, each tomorrow has seen paper money's value become less and less.

In many conventional sales transactions, payment is not due or received for at least ninety days. Short term personal loans are rarely less than six months in duration. Residential leases usually run for two or three years, commercial and industrial leases often for ten years or more. Corporate and municipal bonds extend

---

*Strictly speaking, even those who lease real or personal property to someone else—e.g., an apartment house landlord, an office copying maching company— are also creditors. The lessor parts with something of value today—an apartment, a xerography machine—and receives in exchange something else of value tomorrow.

even longer. Mortgages are not fully payable for decades. Yet in 1979, the *annual* rate of inflation in the United States was between twelve and fourteen percent.

Does this mean, then, that today's creditors are condemned to tomorrow's relentless decrease in the value of their invested capital, impotent to avoid what Rand characterized as the "arbitrary power of an arbitrary setter of values?"

Happily, the answer is that no creditor need be at the mercy of the government's manipulation of paper money—thanks to the current availability of the gold clause.

The gold clause, a contractual provision, is a security device, but not in the conventional sense. Usually, when a substantial loan is made, the creditor obtains "collateral": a legal interest in some property (normally tangible, and belonging to the debtor) which can be sold to satisfy the debt if the debtor defaults. Ironically, the gold clause, though a security device, is intended to protect the creditor not against default but against payment— against payment by the debtor of today's loan with tomorrow's money. Instead, by increasing the debtor's repayment obligation by the value that the creditor's money has depreciated during the period of the loan, the gold clause provision of a contract can assure that the debtor's repayment will be with today's money. A simple example is a contractual requirement that the repayment either be in a specified quantity of gold, or in an amount of currency equal to the value of a specified quantity of gold.

One could rightly assume that widespread use would be made of a contractual device capable of providing creditors with such substantial protection against the ravages of government-manipulated paper money. Yet, the opposite is true. Today, use of the gold clause is almost nil, principally because very little is known about it. Because it seemed surprising to me that such an important weapon in the arsenal of financial self-defense suffered from such disuse, I decided to assemble a collection of essays and other material describing the history and practical use of the gold clause in America.*

---

*When I reviewed the literature on the gold clause, I sought material that would provide the reader with a comprehensive view of America's experience with it, material which would appeal to, and be understandable by, not only professionals—lawyers, bankers, economists, investors—but also

In order to provide the reader with a contextual starting point, *The Gold Clause* begins with Professor Arthur Nussbaum's discussion of the gold clause's genesis and historical development. Professor Nussbaum then explains the precise differences between gold coin clauses, gold value clauses, and gold bullion clauses, observing that: "In a modern monetary system the greatest danger to persons contracting in terms of money lies in the fact that the monetary unit may be severed from gold, and may therefore be subjected to the unpredictable processes of depreciation and appreciation in the markets."

The danger of which Professor Nussbaum speaks had been experienced, of course, during the Civil War. In order to finance that internecine bloodletting, the government found it necessary to suspend gold convertibility and to issue a veritable torrent of unbacked paper money. The flood of currency launched a twenty-four percent inflation rate in 1862, and within two years the dollar had sunk to a third of its value against gold. America was drowning in "greenbacks," and the Supreme Court of the United States would have the final word as to their constitutionality. A crucial stage in America's monetary history had been reached. Those who today wish to plan their financial futures as intelligently as possible should discover how the Court treated the greenbacks. Chapter 2, contributed by New York attorney, Robert S. Getman, examines the Supreme Court's handling of those greenbacks in the *Legal Tender Cases*. In the chapter, Mr. Getman identifies a curious dichotomy, one which provides a clue not only to what would come nearly three-quarters of a century later, but also to what the 1980's and beyond may hold for monetary affairs: a Supreme Court which, on the one hand, continued to recognize the gold clause under certain circumstances, but which, on the other, also recognized the government as possessing "virtually unlimited powers."

Where this disequilibrium would lead, would not become apparent until Franklin Delano Roosevelt's "New Deal," and unless one understands Roosevelt's machinations concerning the gold clause, it is pointless to consider using one today. F.D.R.'s

interested laypersons. For the reader who wishes to delve even more deeply into the various aspects of the gold clause, I have included at the end of the book all of the original footnotes from each selection.

plans for America's monetary system encompassed measures never before contemplated, let alone implemented. Almost immediately after Roosevelt was inaugurated, he declared the bank "holiday," aimed, among other things, at closing the doors on the removal of currency and gold deposits. Next came confiscation of all privately owned gold bullion, gold certificates, and some gold coin. Later, by means of reducing the dollar's gold content, there would be a devaluation of the dollar against gold. Since the planned devaluation would apply not only to all future obligations, but to all existing ones as well, there was rampant speculation that the New Deal would try to nullify the gold clause, thereby wiping out countless billions of dollars in existing gold clause debt. Chapter 3 is fascinating in this regard, providing an insight into how one can often predict the government's monetary moves if one begins with the appropriate premises. Written for the *Harvard Law Review* on the eve of the New Deal's move against the gold clause, the chapter analyzes in great detail whether Congress at that time possessed the power to nullify the gold clause. The author's conclusion presaged what actually happened when the government finally did attack the gold clause.

It is widely known, at least in a general way, that on June 5, 1933, a Joint Resolution of Congress purported explicitly to abrogate the gold clause, declaring its existence in every current and future contract to be "against public policy." Not nearly as widely known are some of the details:

● the literal text, with its pronouncements that gold "affect[s] the public interest" and that gold clauses "obstruct" Congress' power "to regulate the value of the money of the United States—"

● the floor debates, with their revelation that one purpose of the legislation was to redistribute $200,000,000,000 (two hundred billion!), and on a *class* basis.

Chapter 4 is devoted entirely to the Joint Resolution. By setting forth its complete text and a sampling of the Congressional debate that enabled it to be railroaded through a compliant legislature, the reader can see first-hand just what steps the government took, and what arguments the Resolution's supporters advanced. Also included is a thorough discussion of the important constitutional questions created by the gold clause nullification. In the end, the author poses this question: "Can the recent legislation allowing all obligations, private and governmental, State and Federal, to be discharged by payment of any kind of dollars in circulation, even though the contract medium of payment be gold, be sustained as within the constitutional powers of Congress?" His answer, though not emphatic, is interesting in light of what would be the Supreme Court's decisions in the soon-to-be-decided *Gold Clause Cases*.

Among the thousands and thousands of decisions by the Supreme Court, there are probably no more than a handful which have actually changed the course of American history. Among those few are the *Gold Clause Cases*, the linchpin of the New Deal's anti-gold clause campaign. These cases must be understood by anyone who contemplates using the gold clause today. The principal case is *Norman v. Baltimore & Ohio Railway Company*.

Norman C. Norman was an investor. Apparently concerned about possible depreciation of the dollars that he had available to lend, he purchased a railroad bond containing coupons payable in gold coin "of or equal to the standard of weight and fineness existing on February 1, 1930." The coupon's face amount was $22.50. It became payable on February 1, 1934, but because the President had devalued the dollar forty percent against gold, Mr. Norman calculated the coupon's then value against gold to be $38.10. Not surprisingly, when he presented it for payment, the railroad refused to pay the amount due either in gold, or in legal tender measured by the then value of gold.

Exactly what Mr. Norman had tried to protect himself against had happened. Fearing currency depreciation, he had bought a gold clause bond. The dollar depreciated forty percent. He invoked the gold clause. The debtor refused to honor it.

Needless to say, Mr. Norman believed himself injured, and his claim for the $38.10 ended up before the Supreme Court of the United States. In deciding Mr. Norman's case, the Court would affect untold billions of dollars in existing gold clause obligations.

Because of the *Gold Clause Cases'* importance and their length (about 140 pages in the official reports), Chapter 5 begins with an outline of them. It was prepared by Mr. Angus D. MacLean, Assistant Solicitor General of the United States, who supervised all of the Government's briefs in the *Gold Clause Cases*. The outline is followed by an extensive analysis of the *Cases* by Professor John P. Dawson, who explores every aspect of each Justice's opinion. Then, using the *Cases* as a springboard, Professor Dawson speculates on what the future holds for "stable value contracts." Regrettably, when the author allows his own value judgments to invade his analysis of the Court's work, it is apparent that he sympathizes with that Tribunal's upholding of the gold clause nullification. Nevertheless, his analysis, itself, is excellent. Moreover, the literature on the *Gold Clause Cases* contains virtually no criticism of those decisions. Indeed, the only critical comment one ever hears about them is derived from Justice McReynolds' famous dissent. Bold, impassioned, dramatic, unanswerable—but ultimately useless, its final version does not appear even in the official Supreme Court report of the *Cases*. It is reprinted in full in Chapter 5. Justice McReynolds' closing sentence—"Moral and financial chaos may confidently be expected"—were the last words on the gold clause for four decades. Then, gold ownership, itself, was relegalized.

The legislative history of gold ownership relegalization in the mid-1970s unfortunately contained no reference to the gold clause, and no suggestion or indication that it was sought to be resurrected by gold ownership relegalization. The language of the relegalization statute itself was no help: "No provision of any law—and no rule, regulation or order—may be construed to prohibit any person from purchasing, holding, selling, or otherwise dealing with gold in the United States or abroad." Questions abounded, views differed, authorities speculated. Chapter 6 is devoted to the question of whether relegalization of private gold ownership retroactively resuscitated the gold clauses which had been so effectively nullified during the New Deal. This question is important not only to owners of pre-New Deal gold clause bonds who have been holding on since the 1930s, but also to countless speculators who purchased some of those old gold clause bonds after relegalization. The chapter begins with a December 9, 1974 statement of the Treasury Department. Not surprisingly, it contended that the relegalization of private gold ownership, which would become effective twenty-two days later, would not relegalize the gold clause. The chapter also contains two of Professor Gerald T. Dunne's provocative ideas on retroactivity, and four recent court decisions which held that gold ownership relegalization in no way revived the gold clause.

It was only new legislation that finally relegalized the gold clause. The major outlines of how, and through whose efforts, that legislation came into being are set out in Chapter 7. The cast of characters includes the Treasury Secretary, the Chairman of the Federal Reserve System, Senator Jesse Helms, and one of his unlikely allies, Senator William Proxmire. Perhaps most important about relegalization of the gold clause, especially as to retroactive resuscitation (again!), is the precise intent behind it. This intent, not widely known, is often misunderstood even by those few who are aware of it. Many of them had waited a long time for the relegalization victory.

It is one thing, however, to win even a major campaign like relegalization of the gold clause. It is quite another to win the war. New problems arose even as the gold clause was being revived. the major one concerning its legality in the many states having usury ("excessive" interest) laws on their statute books. Needless to say, the usury problem looms large for anyone considering the use of the gold clause, given the possible criminal penalties that exist for violating anti-usury laws, as well as the attendant denial of any interest payment at all. Chapter 8 introduces the usury problem by presenting the decisions of the two American courts that have ruled on the point, and by discussing the more important one.

How the problem of usury can be dealt with, so that the gold clause can be used profitably, is the subject of Chapter 9. It analyzes the two state court decisions which concluded that loans containing indexed principal were usurious. Emphasis is given to the courts' various errors, and the underlying policy reason for the courts' conclusion. As a means of avoiding the usury problems altogether, Chapter 9 contains a proposal for a new, hybrid form of the gold clause.

The *Gold Clause Cases*, an indispensable component of Roosevelt's war against gold, marked one of the few judicial turning points in American constitutional history, certainly as to the Government's monetary powers. Because no one can fully capture the flavor of those decisions merely by writing about them, the Supreme Court's opinions in the *Gold Clause Cases* are set forth verbatim as an appendix to this book. It is hoped that they will greatly enhance the reader's understanding of *The Gold Clause*.

ONE

The Gold Clause: Its Source and Nature*

The gold clause can be of considerable value to creditors. Its use is now legal in the United States. But because it has been illegal for the past forty years or so, not many people know much about it. Even fewer know that the gold clause's roots go as deep as the middle ages, when the same basic attributes it possesses today were first formed. Yet those roots must be understood if the modern gold clause is to be used successfully. It is also important to understand that, under the rubric "gold clause," there are actually several different kinds. All this, Professor Arthur Nussman addresses in Chapter 1.

I. Gold Clauses and Silver Clauses. The Facts[1]

In a modern monetary system the greatest danger to persons contracting in terms of money lies in the fact that the monetary unit may be severed from gold, and may therefore be subjected to the unpredictable processes of depreciation and appreciation in the markets. Before the appearance of the modern monetary systems, it was debasement or alteration in the tariffing of the coin contracted for that was feared.[2] Hence creditors have never been free from the threat of monetary changes. As far back as the latter part of the middle ages, when monetary economy began to

---

* This chapter appeared as Chapter VI, section 25, parts I-III (pages 301–310) of *Money In the Law* by Professor Arthur Nussbaum (The Foundation Press, Inc., Chicago, 1939). In *Money In the Law*, Chapter VI was entitled "Gold Clauses and Other Protective Clauses," and section 25 was subtitled "Occurrence and Types of Gold Clauses." Copyright © 1939, 1950 by the Foundation Press, Inc., Reprinted with permission. All rights reserved.

develop, creditors protected themselves against losses from such changes by appropriate contractual provisions.[3] Taeuber[4] cites the following protective provisions in French contracts of the first half of the 16th century: "25 *scuta solis*[5] *boni auri et justi ponderis;*" "25 *scuta solis auri et in auro;*" "50 *librae*[6] *in 25 scutis auri;*" "25 *scuta solis solvenda in eadem specie;*" "25 *scuta solis solvenda in pecunia eiusdem bonitatis et qualitatis*". Sometimes the monetary provisions were even more specific. While the protective clauses of early times were ordinarily articulated in terms of special coins of gold or silver,[7] under a developed monetary system they call for the payment of a definite amount of the basic unit, with the *caveat*, however, that only gold coins or silver coins of the system or either of them may be used in payments, thus excluding paper money and minor coins. Pure silver clauses are rare although they were used more frequently after the California gold rush.[8] Alternative gold-silver clauses are more frequently found. In *Dalloz Périodique*, the famous French reporter system, of 1872[9] one reads that the clause *en or ou en argent et non autrement* appears "in almost every notarial contract". In the United States, until the sixties, the requirement of payment "in specie" was very frequent[10] and in various European countries the phrase "*en espèces sonnantes,*" "*in klingender Münze* (in tingling coin)[11] was popular with draftsmen. However, it was the gold clause which had by far the greatest expansion. By this clause the debtor promises to pay a *sum of money*, gold coin or equivalent.[12] It is found chiefly in long term contracts, such as mortgage deeds, life insurance policies, and loan bonds,[13] particularly of an international character. In times of monetary troubles, however, the gold clause makes an appearance even in bills of exchange and other short term evidences of indebtedness.[14] With occasional exceptions, the clause covers both principal and interest.[15]

There is probably no country in which the gold clause has been more widely used than in the United States. Before 1933 gold obligations in this country totalled probably more than one hundred billion dollars (nominal amount).[16] The insertion of the gold clause in bonds and mortgages was a matter of routine. Memories of the Continentals, the state bank notes, and the greenbacks contributed to this result; but probably the most effective cause was the pre-war silver agitation.[17] In Germany it was doubtless the bimetallistic endeavors of powerful agrarian parties which before the World War caused the gold clause to pervade the whole field of mortgages, rural and urban. After the war something like a "gold-clause rush"[18] developed, a psychological compensation for the lack of real gold. In France the spectre of the *assignats* and the suspension of redeemability of banknotes, from 1848 to 1850,[19] were probably together responsible for the spread of gold and specie clauses.[20]

Gold clauses are not, however, a universal phenomenon. England, despite the suspension of the *Bank Act* during and after the French wars, remained aloof from them. It was an article of English commercial faith that the pound sterling was as good as gold; the addition of a gold clause to the sterling obligation was regarded as an impairment of the national currency.[21] It is significant that in the Peace Treaties at the end of the late War, England was the only victorious power which forebore to require a gold clause in the reparations provisions.[22] Pounds sterling were demanded and nothing more. It was only after that War that a solitary gold sterling clause made its appearance in English international financing.[23] In Holland[24] and Switzerland[25] also, the domestic use of gold clauses seems to have been restricted.

Judicial or legislative maintenance of gold clauses during and after depreciation is wholly different from revaluation. The difference is not merely that a gold clause, unlike revaluation, presupposes a specific agreement by the parties, but also that instead of being a restoration of an impaired debt, the gold clause safeguards the debt against impairment at all by depreciation. The aim of the gold clause is to maintain the full gold value of the debt whereas revaluation seeks the equitable apportionment between the parties of the loss caused by depreciation. Although these would appear to be obvious differences, gold clauses and revaluation are sometimes not distinguished in legal discussion.[26]

II. Gold Coin Clauses and Gold Value Clauses

The typical gold clause consists of a promise by a money debtor that the sum promised will be paid in gold coins. On the continent it has been customary to add to the nominal expression ("1000 francs"; "1000 lire") a brief phrase such as "in gold", "in gold coin",[27] or merely to express the sum to be paid as 1000 *"francs-or" (gold francs)*.[28] In the United States the clause almost universally employed is more elaborate; it reads: "to pay ... dollars in gold coin of the United States of (here is frequently added: "or equal to") the standard of weight and fineness existing on ..." (the date of contracting follows). This formula has now spread beyond the frontiers of the United States.[29]

On the other hand the clause may merely purport to require payment, in currency, of an amount equal to the value of a quantity of gold coins. This clause is rarely found by itself in explicit form, *e.g.*, "payment of the value of 1000 gold dollars".[30] In earlier American practice, however, there sometimes appear alternative provisions of this type: "in gold or its equivalent;"[31] "in gold coin ... and if said principal ... is not paid in gold coin ... then I promise ... to pay in addition thereto and as damages such further amount and percentage as may be equal to the difference in value ... between such gold coin and paper evidence of indebtedness of the States or of the United States, that are or may hereafter be made a legal tender in payment of debts by the laws of this state or the United States;"[32] "in gold or if paid in paper, the amount thereof necessary to purchase the gold at the place of payment".[33] Much more important, however, are implied promises to pay the value of a certain quantity of gold coin.[34]

Promises to pay in gold coin are spoken of as "gold-coin clauses" *[clause espèces-or; Goldmünzklausel; clausola corso oro]*, promises to pay the value of gold coin as "gold-value clauses" *[clause valeur-or; Goldwert-Klausel; clausola valore-oro]*. This terminology, continental in origin,[35] has been adopted by the Supreme Court of the United States.[36] The distinction is made with particular clarity, although not in those terms, in the Joint Resolution of June 5, 1933, abrogating the gold clauses,[37] and it has become of great importance in judicial interpretation.[38]

A further variation of minor importance is that some clauses refer merely to gold coins, while others, *e.g.*, the customary American formula, which speaks of gold coins as of the time of contracting, fix the amount of fine gold to be given in payment. The latter clause protects the creditor against later debasement of the gold coin such as occurred in the United States in 1834.[39] This aim appears quite clearly in such gold coin clauses as the following:" $1,000 gold coin *of or equal to* the standard..."[40] The words italicized differentiate the clause from alternative gold value clause which is usually phrased as follows: "$1000 gold coin *or equivalent.*"

III. Gold Bullion Clauses

After inflation the attempt is sometimes made to escape the risks of depreciation by gold clauses requiring payment in gold bullion. In *Holyoke Water Power Co. v. American Writing Paper Co.*, the plaintiff, in 1894, had executed a number of leases of water power by which the lessee promised to pay as rent "a quantity of gold which shall be equal in amount to $1,500 of the gold coin of the United States of the standard of weight and fineness of the year 1894, or the equivalent of this commodity in United States currency". This alleged gold bullion clause, however, was held by the Supreme Court of the United States, in a brilliant and forceful opinion written by Mr. Justice Cardozo, to constitute a monetary obligation with a gold clause.[41] The court pointed out that what the creditor really wanted and the debtor promised, were dollars: "Weasel words will not avail to defeat the triumph of intention when once the words are read in the setting of the whole transaction".[42] Not even the use of measures of weight to fix the quantity of gold to be given in payment[43] would protect the creditor against such realistic methods of interpretation.

In Germany, at the height of inflation, the legislature encouraged the use of sham gold-bullion clauses. By a law of June 23, 1923,[44] permission was given to record mortgage-obligations requiring payment of the value of so many kilograms and grams of fine gold despite the fact that German mortgage law required the debts secured by the mortgage to be for a sum certain expressed in marks. As a matter of fact the legislative experiment of 1923 was practically abandoned when in 1924 registration of mortgages in terms of "gold marks" was permitted.[45]

A real gold-bullion contract is that envisaged by the French Civil Code, art. 1896, which provides that the nominalistic rule of art. 1895[46] shall not apply where "the loan is made in bars" *(lingots)*. This rule has been adopted by other Codes on the French model[47] but seems to be without practical importance.

TWO

The Gold Clause Before The 1930s*

As early in our history as the Convention of 1787, which framed the Constitution of the United States of America, the fear of paper money was widespread. Indeed, the Convention's keynote speaker, Edmund Randolph, railed against "the havoc of paper money" when he attacked the Articles of Confederation, and not until President Lincoln signed the Legal Tender Act on February 25, 1862, did legal tender paper money circulate with official sanction in America. The new "greenbacks" opened at a discount, steadily dropped in value during 1862, and then seesawed in price, depending on how well the war was going for the North. Eventually the fate of the greenbacks was decided by the Supreme Court of the United States. In the decisions, the Court sowed seeds of extensive government monetary power that would be harvested at the expense of future generations. The greenback cases teach important lessons about government monetary power today, as Mr. Getman ably demonstrates in this chapter.

Prior to the Civil War, the Government had never made paper money legal tender. Treasury notes had been issued during the War of 1812, the Mexican War, and the "panics" of 1837 and 1857, but none had been forced upon unwilling obligees.[1] Indeed, even "in the darkest hour of the War of 1812, Congress decisively rejected a proposal to give this [legal tender] feature to Trea-

* This chapter appeared as part I, C ("The Civil War, Gold Clauses and Legal Tender 'Greenbacks'") of Robert S. Getman's note "The Right to Use Gold Clauses in Contracts," which appeared in Vol. XLII of the *Brooklyn Law Review* (Winter 1976), pages 479-526. The footnotes have been renumbered, but references within the footnotes to pages of the note are unchanged and appear as they did originally. Copyright © 1976 by Brooklyn Law School. Reprinted with permission of Mr. Getman, the *Brooklyn Law Review*, and Fred B. Rothman & Co.

sury notes."[2] But the incredible cost of the Civil War, both in men's lives and in their money, prompted the Government to undertake several unprecedented coercive measures. To meet the cost in men's lives, men were forced into the army by the first draft law.[3] To meet the cost in men's money, men were forced to pay the first direct federal tax on their incomes[4] and to suffer an indirect tax effected by the depreciation of new legal tender treasury notes [hereinafter referred to as greenbacks] that they were compelled to accept at face value in exchange for their property.[5]

The emergency was real. The Lincoln administration found the treasury nearly empty and the Government's credit badly shaken.[6] In July of 1861, non-legal tender notes were authorized to be issued, but, by December 30th, banks throughout the loyal States had resold scarcely one-third of these notes.[7] On that day, Representative Spaulding, Chairman of the House Ways and Means Committee, introduced a bill to retire these notes and to issue new notes; the new notes, dubbed "greenbacks," were to differ radically from the old notes in one crucial respect: the greenbacks were to be legal tender for all debts. The bill was intended as a stopgap measure[8] to sustain the Government while Congress considered Secretary of the Treasury (later Chief Justice) Salmon P. Chase's national bank plan. Amidst fears of imminent fiscal disaster, Attorney General Bates gave Representative Spaulding a hastily-prepared, informal opinion that the proposed bill was constitutional.[9] Thus, a measure of momentous consequence and of doubtful constitutionality was launched with an unofficial opinion written "with all brevity and without argument ...."[10]

In committee, the first vote to report the bill out ended in a tie. However, "one member withdrew his opposition in order that a bill might go to the house,"[11] and the bill was passed after one month's debate.[12] Although it was generally admitted that the Government could have obtained the funds it needed by selling its bonds for whatever they would have brought on the open market, this solution to the problem was rejected because it "went against the dogma that the United States ought never to sell its bonds below par."[13] So, in the name of a dogma dictating that the Government should never recognize that its difficulties might make citizens unwilling to take its promises at face value, the Government refused to take what men would freely offer in the marketplace. Instead, the Government forced its citizens to act against their economic interests and judgments. The original act and its successors[14] [hereinafter referred to as the Legal Tender Acts] forced upon the populace $450 million in greenbacks,[15] whose values subsequently dipped as low as thirty-eight cents on the gold dollar.[16]

Every aspect of the Legal Tender Acts eventually was tested in a torrent of cases[17] that came to the Supreme Court of the United States after the Civil War. The issues involved generated heated nationwide debate, unparalleled acrimony among the members of the court itself[18] and a meteoric rise in the frequency of use of gold clauses in contracts.

In the first cases involving the greenbacks, the Court construed the Legal Tender Acts narrowly in an effort to avoid ruling on their constitutionality.[19] Among these cases was *Bronson v. Rodes*,[20] a suit brought on a contract that contained a gold clause, which raised the question of the Acts' effect on such clauses' enforceability. In 1851, one Metz had borrowed $1,400 of Bronson and had executed a bond calling for repayment of the principal and interest in "gold and silver coin, lawful money of the United States."[21] The indebtedness had been secured by a mortgage that later was assumed by Rodes. In 1865, Rodes tendered and Bronson refused payment in greenbacks of sum due. At that time, $2.25 in greenbacks was equivalent in market value to one dollar in gold coin.[22] Logically, because the Legal Tender Acts had declared that all debts might be satisfied by the tender of United States notes, the Court's inquiry should have focused upon whether it was constitutional to compel a party to accept notes only nominally equal to an amount due in coin. Instead, the Court assumed *arguendo*, that the Acts were constitutional and inquired only whether, despite the express mandate that all debts be payable in greenbacks, the Acts actually had intended to allow satisfaction of contract to pay coined money by payment of paper money.

The Court began by noting that a prime function of courts was to enforce contracts according to the intent of the parties. In this case, the parties' intent had been obvious:

> It is not to be doubted, then, that it was to guard against the possibility of loss to the [obligee], through an attempt to force the acceptance of a fluctuating and perhaps irredeemable currency in payment, that the

express stipulation for payment in gold and silver coin was put into the bond. There was no necessity in law, for such a stipulation, for at that time no money, except gold or silver, had been made a legal tender.

. . . .

The intent of the parties is, therefore, clear. Whatever might be the forms or the fluctuations of the note currency, this contract was not to be affected by them. It was to be paid, at all events, in coined lawful money.[23]

The Court then pointed to various Congressional acts regulating the weight and purity of metal coins, as proof that Congress intended to have the value it assigned to coins correspond to the value of the metal comprising the coins. Given this intent, the Court reasoned that in the eyes of the law a contract calling for payment in gold coins was indistinguishable from "a contract to deliver an equal weight of bullion of equal fineness".[24] This led the Court to conclude:

We cannot suppose that it was intended by the provisions of the [Legal Tender] Acts to enforce satisfaction of either contract [for coin or for bullion] by the tender of depreciated currency of any description equivalent only in nominal amount to the real value of the bullion or of the coined dollars.[25]

After concluding that a clause calling for payment in gold coin was equivalent to a clause calling for delivery of bullion as a commodity, and apart from the fact that the value of paper dollars was only nominally equivalent to that of coined dollars, the Court reasoned, in apparent dicta, that the distinction between contractual provisions requiring payment in coin and those requiring payment in paper money had to be recognized because both coin and paper money were sanctioned by the law as legal tender. Moreover, the Court observed, the Government itself tacitly had fostered this distinction by requiring that its duties be paid in coin. Thus, requiring that contracts specifying payment in gold might be satisfied only by tender of gold was viewed as the only equitable way to reconcile the intent of Congress in creating two types of legal tender with that of parties who contracted for payment in one or the other of these types. But, whether its decision was based on the "bullion theory"[26] or on the "dual money theory,"[27] the *Bronson* Court clearly carved an exception in favor of gold clauses out of the Legal Tender Acts' mandate that greenbacks be accepted as legal tender for all debts.[28]

Subsequent to the *Bronson* decision, the High Court did come to grips with the issue of the Legal Tender Acts' constitutionality. In *Hepburn v. Griswold*,[29] the obligee on a note, which had been executed in 1860, refused a tender of greenbacks and sued to obtain payment in coin. The note had called for payment in dollars but had not specified payment in gold dollars, *i.e.*, no gold clause had been incorporated into the bargain. The Supreme Court, per Chief Justice Chase, reasoned that, although the Act had made greenbacks a legal tender "for all debts, public and private,"[30] there were strong equitable reasons for construing the Act to exclude previously contracted debts. Congress had been aware, the Court stated, that before the Act's passage only coin was lawful money, so that "[e]very such contract [was] ... , in legal import, a contract for the payment of coin."[31] Furthermore, the Court reasoned that Congress should have known of the economic laws that made depreciation of the greenbacks inevitable, so that construing the Act to encompass pre-existing contracts would have been tantamount to assuming that Congress had intended unjustly to impair the obligation of such contracts. However, examination of the legislative history of the Act and a re-examination of its literal import compelled the Chief Justice to conclude that the Act had to be construed to include pre-existing contracts. This brought the Court face-to-face with the constitutional question of whether it was within Congress' power to enact a law of such effect. The Court divided principally upon the issue of whether the Act was a legitimate exercise of congressional power under the Necessary and Proper Clause, [32] as illuminated by Chief Justice Marshall's landmark opinion in *McCulloch v. Maryland*,[33] for, even the dissenters in *Hepburn* were "not able to see in [Congress' express powers] standing alone a sufficient warrant for the exercise of [the legal tender] power ... ."[34]

Chief Justice Chase, writing for the *Hepburn* majority, emphasized certain components of Chief Justice Marshall's definition of "necessary and proper": the end must be legitimate and the means must be plainly adapted to that end and consistent with the letter and the spirit of the Constitution. The Chief Justice found the means used in the case at bar—the legal tender feature of the greenbacks—not at all adapted to any legitimate end. More importantly, he found the legal tender provision inconsistent with the spirit[35] of the Constitution. Thus, the Legal Tender Acts were declared unconstitutional, at least insofar as they applied to pre-existing debts.[36] Although it had taken the Supreme Court over four years to decide the constitutional question presented in *Hepburn*,[37] little more than one year later, following a change in its membership,[38] the Court reversed that decision.

In two cases[39] that had been consolidated and dubbed *Legal Tender Cases* by the reporter, the Court reconsidered the constitutionality of the Legal Tender Acts. The majority launched its opinion in those cases with an argument *ex necessitate:* holding the Legal Tender Acts unconstitutional would endanger "the possible continued existence of the government .... [and] cause great business derangement, widespread distress, and the rankest injustice."[40] The majority fretted over the precipitous increase in indebtedness that would result to obligors who had contracted in reliance upon the acts, were the Acts to be voided. Yet, the majority's solicitude did not extend to the obligees of pre-statute contracts, who had contracted in reliance upon payment in gold and whose claims would be as precipitously reduced, were the Acts to be upheld. No clue was provided as to why one group's plight should evoke concern, and the other's only indifference.

Apart from considering the effect its holding would have on contracting parties, the Court maintained that the judicial deference owed to Congress' judgment was such that no statute should be voided unless the Court found it unconstitutional beyond a reasonable doubt.[41] All of the powers in the Constitution were viewed as "means for a common end":[42] the establishment of a sovereign Government that was capable of self-preservation. Toward that end, a claimed power, neither granted by the Constitution expressly nor even traceable to any expressly granted power, nonetheless might be upheld as one of a group of "resulting powers, arising from the aggregate powers of the government"[43] taken as a whole. This whole was perceived somehow to be greater than the sum of its parts. In short, the Court opined that powers that could not quite be found anywhere in the Constitution somehow still might be "constitutional."[44] Accordingly, in response to the argument that the grant of power "to coin money" excluded, by negative implication, the power to make paper money, Justice Strong countered that, although the Government had specific constitutional authority to outlaw only treason, piracy, and counterfeiting, it routinely criminalized many other acts as well.[45] Additionally, in response to the dissent's assertion that the creation of legal tender paper was neither "necessary" nor "proper," Justice Strong pointed out that the Secretary of the Treasury (who had been Chief Justice Chase) had advocated the dire need for legal tender greenbacks.[46] Finally, the majority rejected the argument that the Acts violated the spirit of the Constitution. Three members of the Court had attacked this argument previously in their dissenting opinion in *Hepburn*. There, Justice Miller had written:

> This whole argument of the injustice of the law ... and of its opposition to the spirit of the Constitution, is too abstract and intangible for application to courts of justice, and is, above all, dangerous as a ground on which to declare the legislation of a Congress void by the decision of a court. It would authorize this court to enforce theoretical views of the genius of government, or vague notions of the spirit of the Constitution and of abstract justice, by declaring void laws which did not square with those views. It substitutes our ideas of policy for judicial construction, an undefined code of ethics for the Constitution, and a court of justice for the National Legislature.[47]

Nowhere in this burst of anti-philosophical judicial abstention was it explained how "courts of justice" could function if they found arguments of injustice too "abstract and intangible for application." Nor did its authors make clear how a Constitution that established a certain system of government based upon a specific philosophy of man's rights could be expounded without reference to "theoretical views of the genius of government" or to the code of ethics implicit in the concept of inalienable rights. Thus, the protectors of the Constitution and its philosophy, while borrowing some principles from Chief Justice Marshall's opinion in *McCulloch v. Maryland*,[48] ignored others that were as applicable here as they had been there, *i.e.*, "that it [was] *a constitution* [they were] expounding"[49] and that it was the duty of the Court to expound it.[50]

It was not individual rights that the majority of the Court in the *Legal Tender Cases* viewed as the soul of the Constitution, but the sovereignty and powers of the Federal Government. Justice Strong's reply to contentions that the Acts impaired the obligations of contracts and operated to deprive persons of property in violation of the fifth amendment's guarantee of due process was that any "covenant [is] undertaken in subordination to the *paramount right of the government*"[51] and, arguably begging the question, that the "property of a citizen *or subject* is ownership subject to the lawful demands of the sovereign ...."[52] In the face of the Constitution, which had delegated limited powers to the Government so that the Government might protect its citizens' inalienable rights, the Court spoke of the "paramount right of the Government." In the face of the Declaration of Independence, so often invoked during the recent Civil War, which had rejected a sovereign and his form of government in favor of the rights of men— not the privileges of subjects—a majority of the Court spoke of property as a privilege subject to the demands of a sovereign.

The basic premises of the majority's holding stood out even more clearly in Justice Bradley's concurring opinion. After stating that the legal tender power was "incidental to the power of borrowing money,"[53] Justice Bradley revealed that he was speaking of "forced" loans: "[T]he Government simply *demands* that its credit be accepted.... Every government has a right to demand this when its existence is at stake."[54] Lest anyone underestimate the staggering breadth of the powers to which he regarded the Government entitled when it deemed its existence endangered, Justice Bradley proclaimed: "In certain emergencies government must have at its command, not only the personal services—the bodies and lives—of its citizens, but the lesser, though not less essential, power of absolute control over the resources of the country."[55] It may well be asked just what emergencies were to trigger such sacrifices and who was to be the final arbiter on the question of their existence. Surely a Government that considered the bodies and lives of its citizens expendable but its own existence inviolate could not have been the Government "of the people, by the people, and for the people,"[56] that the Civil War was supposed to have preserved.

Despite the potential for harm inherent in the majority's rationale of virtually unlimited governmental powers, the *Legal Tender Cases* did not necessarily expose future contracting parties to the vicissitudes of a paper money economy. Only contracts that did not expressly require payment in gold dollars were to be construed to permit payment in paper dollars. Because *Bronson v. Rodes* had not been overruled, gold clauses still could serve to preserve the sanctity of contract for those wary enough to use them.

THREE

Could Congress Nullify The Gold Clause?*

Almost immediately after his inauguration as President of the United States on March 4, 1933, Franklin Delano Roosevelt's administration attacked gold. On March 6, 1933, F.D.R.'s "holiday" closed America's banks. On March 9, Congress enacted the Emergency Banking Act, granting the President absolute power over gold. Executive Orders, Presidential Proclamations, rules, regulations, decrees, all followed, and by mid-May 1933, steps had been taken to confiscate virtually all privately owned gold and to devalue the dollar against gold. What had not yet occurred, however, was any overt move against the gold clause. Although it had existed for years in most long-term debt obligations, the gold clause was wholly antithetical to the New Deal's gold policies. Speculation about its fate was intense. Interestingly, the principal question was not whether the Roosevelt administration would attempt to nullify the gold clause—that was pretty much taken for granted. The real question was whether Congress actually possessed the power—or, more precisely, whether the Supreme Court would *say* that Congress possessed the power. The following chapter, written during the New Deal's early moves against gold, but before the gold clause, itself, was attacked, provides an interesting insight—not only into how the gold clause situation appeared in early 1933, but

---

* This chapter, by Russel L. Post and Charles H. Willard, originally entitled "The Power of Congress to Nullify Gold Clauses," appeared in Vol. XLVI of the *Harvard Law Review*, 1933, pages 1225-1257. Copyright © 1933 by the Harvard Law Review Association. Reprinted with permission. All rights reserved.

also into how easily one can predict what government will do about monetary affairs, if certain of its basic premises are identified and understood.

The financial panic of 1933 has brought actively into the foreground of legal and economic issues the question of the validity of the gold clause.[1] The large number of May I maturities of principal and interest of funded obligations[2] payable in New York[3] did not produce any declaration of policy by the financial community, and much uncertainty and lack of agreement prevails on the exact nature and essential value of the obligation. This uncertainty takes the form of speculation whether the courts will enforce the obligation as it is written, and also whether Congress has the power to enact legislation[4] nullifying the gold clause in outstanding contracts and preventing its inclusion in contracts to be made in the future.[5]

We believe—and we shall attempt to show—that the question of the constitutionality of such a supposed Act resolves itself into the question whether the existence of gold clauses, and the power to make them, is such an interference with the legitimate functions of the government, that Congress has the power to abolish them. That question will be answered, one way or the other, by the Supreme Court, depending upon whether or not that Court thinks that the gold clause does constitute such an interference, and that the real purpose of the legislation is to remove it. This means that in order to decide such a case, the Court will have to consider in detail, as a practical question of fact, the effect that gold clauses have on the government's position as a borrower and as an issuer of currency.

No attempt has been made to fit this article to the Thomas amendment to the Farm Bill,[6] which was approved May 12, nor to any other currency legislation pending in Congress. The Thomas amendment contains no provision dealing specifically with gold clauses, and any questions of constitutionality that may arise from it are beyond the scope of this study. It is, however, closely related to the issues of fact upon which the issues of law we are discussing seem to turn. What the administration may do under the amendment, as the delegate of Congress,[7] or how it may construe and effectuate its purposes, cannot be predicted with any accuracy. But among the purposes avowed by its sponsors are the relief of debtors[8] and the revival of interstate and foreign commerce through an increase in the price level.[9] There is no doubt that Congress has some power to change the currency, but the policy behind a change, in regard to matters which are not directly affected, may be of vital importance. Congress may or may not be able, by its power over the currency, to make it operate as a just medium of exchange, uniform in purchasing value over a period of years. If the Thomas amendment should be held constitutional on the basis of such objectives, the effect of such a decision would be to increase, to that extent, the scope of the government's powers.[10] The effect of gold clauses, as a possible obstruction to the accomplishment of these purposes, would then become a question of fact.

The answer to most of these questions falls with more propriety in the field of the monetary specialist than in the field of the lawyer. Our purpose, therefore, in this article is to set out briefly what we understand to be the present state of the authorities on the points of law which would become relevant on the argument of the question whether Congress has power to nullify the gold clause.

A. Validity of the Gold Clause

Gold clauses have been held enforceable by the courts of this country since the decision of the Supreme Court in *Bronson v. Rodes.* [11] The mortgage note there in controversy, made in 1851, contained the promise to pay 1400 "dollars payable in gold and silver coin, lawful money of the United States". In 1865 Rodes, the mortgagor, tendered Bronson, the mortgagee, United States notes (greenbacks) to the amount of $1507, the nominal amount of principal and interest. At the time of the tender these notes were equivalent in market value to 670 gold dollars. Bronson refused the tender, whereupon Rodes deposited the tendered notes in a bank to the credit of Bronson, and filed his bill in equity to relieve the premises from the lien of the mortgage, and to compel Bronson to deliver a satisfaction piece. The Court of Appeals of New York held that the tender was a good one, since the obligation fell within the Legal Tender Act.[12] This was reversed by the Supreme Court, principally on the ground that an obligation to pay in gold coin was not a "debt," as that word was used in the Legal Tender Act.[13] In holding that Rodes' tender was ineffective to discharge the obligation, the Court necessarily held that the gold clause was valid and enforceable.[14] The Court rested this latter conclusion squarely on the intent of the parties:

> Our conclusion, therefore, upon this part of the case is, that the bond under consideration was in legal import precisely what it was in the understanding of the parties, a valid obligation to be satisfied by tender of actual payment according to its terms, and not by an offer of mere nominal payment. Its intent was that the debtor should deliver to the creditor a certain weight of gold and silver of a certain fineness, ascertainable by count of coins made legal tender by statute; and this intent was lawful.[15]

Bronson v. Rodes has been consistently followed by the Supreme Court since its decision.[16] The important point which it decided was that there was nothing in the existing statutes which, either as a matter of statutory construction or of public policy, required the Court to treat gold dollars and paper dollars as equivalents.[17] The Court recognized that this was the central issue, for it said that there were "two kinds of money, essentially different in their nature, but equally lawful."[18] Since 1868, a policy of recognizing the actual or potential difference between gold and currency, and consequently of respecting the intent of gold clauses, has been firmly embedded in the federal statutes.[19]

Bronson v. Rodes upheld the gold clause against a currency depreciation. The standard form in use today also purports to safeguard against a decrease in the gold content of the dollar, by specifying that the gold coins are to be "of the present standard of weight and fineness." The effect of these additional words has never been tested,[20] but we see no reason why *Bronson v. Rodes* should not be followed in such a case. The intent of the parties, on which the validity of the clause was upheld in that case, is just as clearly to guard against a devaluation of the gold dollar, as is the intent of the parties in using the words "in gold coin," to guard against a depreciation of the paper dollar.[21] No new public policy seems to be introduced.[22]

Recently the English Courts, in *In re Société Intercommunale Belge d'Electricité—Feist v. The Company*,[23] have reached a conclusion exactly contrary to that reached in *Bronson v. Rodes*. They have held that a gold clause in a sterling bond is ineffective, and that the bond can be discharged by payment of the nominal amount of pounds in depreciated currency.

The question, which had apparently never been passed on before by an English court, concerned a bond for £100 containing a clause to pay in gold coin "of or equal to" the standard of weight and fineness existing on the date the bond was issued.[24] Feist, the holder, asked in the alternative for a declaration that he was entitled to the gold coins themselves, or to their market value in depreciated currency on the date of maturity.

Mr. Justice J. Farwell, in the Chancery Division, construed the promise as one "to pay £100 in gold coins,"[25] but concluded that this promise could be fulfilled by paying £100 in depreciated currency.[26] He recognized that, in so doing, he was nullifying the gold clause.[27] Though much of the language of the opinion deals with the construction of the obligation,[28] the basis of the decision must be that such a clause violates public policy, by interfering with the power of the sovereign to declare what shall be money and legal tender. Mr. Justice Farwell seemed to find such a policy expressed in section 6 of the Coinage Act of 1870.[29]

This decision was unanimously affirmed by the Court of Appeal. Lord Justice Lawrence[30] thought that the Coinage Act of 1870, by express provision, made such a stipulation unenforceable. Lord Justice Romer came to a similar conclusion,[31] basing his decision on the same construction of the obligation as Mr. Jusice Farwell's—that it was to pay 100 gold sovereigns.[32]

If the *Feist* case means that the Coinage Act of 1870 nullifies gold clauses, it is not material to our problem. If the case does not mean that, it must mean that, as a rule of common law, or as a matter of public policy expressed in the Coinage Act of 1870, persons cannot contract in one kind of legal tender to the exclusion of all others. If this is the correct interpretation of the case, it is directly opposed to the rule of *Bronson v. Rodes,* as that rule is set out in the passage which we have quoted. It is difficult to see, therefore, how an American court could follow the *Feist* case, unless the Supreme Court should overrule *Bronson v. Rodes,*[33] either expressly or by fortuitous distinction, the possibility of which is, of course, beyond the limits of permissible speculation.[34]

B. The Obligation of the Gold Clause

In that part of this article which deals with the constitutional aspects of the question, we conclude that the power of Congress will probably depend on whether or not the Supreme Court considers gold clauses an interference with the proper exercise of the money and borrowing powers of Congress. The extent of such interference, if there is any, will depend, in turn, on the exact nature of the obligation of a gold contract.

A contract made January 1, 1933, to pay $100 in gold coin of the United States of the present standard of weight and fineness, seems to be subject to five possible reasonable constructions: (1) that it is a pure bullion contract, constituting a single obligation to deliver 2580 grains of gold nine-tenths fine; (2) that it is a single obligation to deliver gold coins containing the same amount of gold, of the same fineness, as is now contained in, say, ten gold eagles; (3) that it is an alternative obligation, with an option in the obligee to decide, at maturity, whether he will take that amount of gold coins or the value in paper dollars of the gold contained in them;[35] (4) that it is an alternative obligation, with the option in the obligor to decide whether he will pay that amount of gold coins, or paper dollars equal to the market value of the gold contained in them; and (5) that it is a single obligation to pay one hundred legal tender paper dollars. This last alternative, which is the one adopted by the Court of Appeal in the *Feist* case, is not really a construction of the gold clause, for it nullifies it. Since it was expressly rejected in *Bronson v. Rodes*, it need not be considered further. The other possible constructions set out above will be considered in order.

The Supreme Court, at the beginning, leaned heavily to the view that the contract is a pure bullion contract, which could, presumably, be satisfied by the delivery of uncoined gold. In *Bronson v. Rodes*, it made its classic declaration that such a contract is, "... in legal import, nothing else than an agreement to deliver a certain weight of standard gold, to be ascertained by a count of coins ... It is not distinguishable ... in principle, from a contract to deliver an equal weight of bullion of equal fineness."[36] A tendency to depart somewhat from this strict view was shown in *Trebilcock v. Wilson*[37] where it was said that the words *"in specie"* were "merely descriptive of the kind of dollars in which the note is payable." The dangerous implication in the above-quoted statement from *Bronson v. Rodes* was corrected in *Thompson v. Butler.*[38] In rejecting the appellant's argument that a judgment for $5000 "in coin" was a judgment for more than $5000, and so was reviewable by the Supreme Court, the Court, after referring to the statement from *Bronson v. Rodes* which we have quoted above, said, "... but, notwithstanding this, it is a contract to pay money, and none the less so because it designates for payment one of the two kinds of money which the law has made a legal tender in discharge of money obligations."[39]

This must be correct. All the judges who heard the *Feist* case dismissed, without discussion, the suggestion that the bond was a bullion or commodity contract. The mere use of the dollar sign, or of the word "dollars,"[40] to say nothing of the plain purpose of the parties to deal in, and get the advantages of money, should be enough to defeat the commodity construction.[41] Although the point seems never to have been passed on, it is hard to see how an instrument to deliver a specified amount of gold, as bullion, could be negotiable.[42]

Real difficulty is presented by the choice between the next three alternatives. The second, that the contract consists of a single obligation to pay gold coins equivalent to ten present gold eagles to the exclusion of all other kinds of legal tender, may represent the present state of the Supreme Court cases.[43] This conclusion might be rested on the decision in *Thompson v. Butler,* from which we have quoted. It finds support also in the line of cases which hold that a gold clause creditor is entitled to a judgment for the specified amount of gold coins, and that it is error to enter judgment for the amount of legal tender paper money equal, at the date of maturity, to the market value of the gold.[44] Notable among these cases is *Trebilcock v. Wilson,*[45] where the Court sought to defend this rule on the ground that the possibility that the value of gold might fluctuate between the date of judgment (or maturity of the obligation)[46] and the date of actual payment by the judgment debtor, was a burden that should not be borne by the creditor. Referring to the provision in the Legal Tender Act of February 25, 1862,[47] that duties on imports must be paid in coin, the Court said:

> It is obvious that the requirement of coin for duties could not be complied with by the importer, nor could his necessities for the purchase of goods in a foreign market be answered, *if his contracts for coin could not be specifically enforced,* but could be satisfied by an offer to pay its nominal equivalent in note dollars.[48]

To the same effect is the statement in *Butler v. Horwitz* that "the obvious intent" in gold contracts, is "that such contracts should be satisfied, *whether before or after judgment,* only by tender of coin."[49]

If these cases are to be taken literally to hold that a gold clause is as single an obligation as a contract to deliver coal of a certain grade and specification, then, it seems that the Supreme Court has not adhered to its original policy of discovering and enforcing the intention of the parties.[50] The gold clause is inserted in contracts for the benefit of the obligor as well as the obligee, in order to make the instrument attractive by assuring the obligee that, in case of currency depreciation, the obligor will take the loss, and not the obligee. The gold creditor, when he makes the contract, has no intention of committing himself entirely to payment in gold coin, thereby putting it in the power of the debtor, in case of a shortage of gold or an embargo, to raise the defense of impossibility of performance.[51]

As an incidental objection to this construction, there would be some difficulty in the case of every gold obligation that is for an amount of gold that cannot now, or in the future, be specified exactly in multiples of five dollars.[52]

The only practicable construction seems to be that the obligation is alternative, with an option in the obligee to decide, at maturity, whether he will demand, on his gold claim for $100, gold coins equivalent to ten present gold eagles or the number of paper dollars necessary to buy 2580 grains of gold in the market.[53] This construction gives to the contract the primary effect the parties intended, which is to protect the creditor against fluctuations in the value of money. The Supreme Court has recognized this to be the primary purpose of the gold clause.[54] What the creditor wants is not gold coins, but gold values.[55]

The Supreme Court has never, in the case of an action directly on the obligation, expressly approved this construction. As we have seen, in the "gold judgment" cases[56] the Court reversed judgments for the dollar equivalent of the gold. But in all of these cases either the creditor demanded the gold judgment, or, apparently, the debtor both demanded it and could satisfy it. But we do not believe that, under these cases, it would be error to enter a judgment for the dollar equivalent of the gold, if the creditor asked for such a judgment, and if the debtor could not satisfy a gold judgment.[57] In the "gold judgment" cases the choice between a judgment for gold coins and a judgment for their currency value, was a fairly narrow one. The rule was established to give full protection to the gold creditor. It could not consistently be applied to preclude the creditor from asking for the currency value of the gold at a time when a demand for the gold itself could be met with the defense of impossibility.

The construction suggested finds some affirmative support in *Gregory v. Morris*,[58] and appears in many of the pre-*Bronson v. Rodes* state cases,[59] both in the claims made by gold creditors, and in verdicts of trial courts.[60] If this construction is correct, and a gold creditor chooses to take the equivalent of the gold coins in paper dollars, in satisfaction of the debt, that choice will be binding on him, as the exercise of an option which he has reserved.

The only difference between the fourth construction and the one discussed in the preceding paragraphs is that it would put the option in the obligor to decide at maturity whether he would pay in gold coins or in the amount of dollars necessary to buy them.[61] The American cases do not seem to sanction this construction.[62] It is, in our view, directly in the teeth of the language we have quoted from *Trebilcock v. Wilson* and *Butler v. Horwitz*. It was rejected by all the judges who passed on the *Feist* case on the sensible ground that it would make the obligation not one for £100 which was impressed all over the instrument, but one for an indeterminate amount, in terms of legal tender generally.

It probably is not of great importance whether the option is held to be in the obligee or in the obligor. The principal reason for preferring the former construction is that it is obviously more in accord with the intent of the parties. Under the Negotiable Instruments Law,[63] the instrument would probably be equally negotiable under either construction. If there is any doubt about the effect of that statute, the instrument would stand a better chance of being held negotiable, if the option as to the medium of payment is in the obligee rather than in the obligor.[64]

We conclude, therefore, on this branch of the question, that the obligation of a gold clause contract to pay $100 is either to pay gold coins equivalent to ten present gold eagles or so much legal tender paper money as will, on the date of maturity, equal the market value of the gold in ten present gold eagles, at the option of the creditor.

CONSTITUTIONAL QUESTIONS

We have concluded in the preceding part of this article that the ordinary gold clause is probably, under the existing authorities in this country, valid and enforceable according to its plain intent. This conclusion suggests the question whether or not Congress could, by statute, abrogate it.

No decided cases have been found which determine this question. The nearest approach to an authority is what Justice Bradley said in his concurring opinion in *Knox v. Lee:*

> I do not understand the majority of the court to decide that an act so drawn as to embrace, in terms, contracts payable in specie, would not be constitutional. Such a decision would completely nullify the power claimed for the government. For it would be very easy, by the use of one or two additional words, to make all contracts payable in specie.[65]

The overruling, in *Bronson v. Rodes,* of the state decisions which held that the Legal Tender Act included gold debts and was, at the same time, constitutional,[66] is not authority against the validity of the kind of statute we are here discussing, since the ground of reversal was that such debts were not included in the word "debts" in that Act.

There are, for purposes of analysis, two aspects of the constitutional problem. The first is the question whether or not the government has the affirmative power to accomplish the objective for which the legislation may be enacted and the second is the question whether the due process clause prohibits such legislation. The distinction, in other words, is between the question of a lack of power and the question of a lack of due process in the exercise of a power.[67] But it will be seen that the due process clause defines the scope of the affirmative powers by limiting their exercise to measures reasonably designed to accomplish the ends for which the powers were conferred. Necessarily, therefore, the two aspects shade into each other, the distinction not being one between a true affirmative and a true negative.[68]

A. Affirmative Powers

Article I, Section 8 of the Constitution provides that Congress shall have power, among other things:

(1) To lay and collect Taxes, Duties, Imposts, and Excises, to pay the Debts and provide for the common Defence and general Welfare of the United States;

(2) To borrow Money on the credit of the United States;

(3) To regulate Commerce with foreign Nations, and among the several States, and with the Indian Tribes;

(4) To establish ... uniform Laws on the subject of Bankruptcies throughout the United States;

(5) To coin Money, regulate the Value thereof, and of foreign coin, and fix the Standard of Weights and Measures; ...

(18) To make all laws which shall be necessary and proper for carrying into Execution the foregoing powers, and all other Powers vested by this Constitution in the Government of the United States, or in any Department or Officer thereof.

Obviously, none of these provisions includes in terms a power to nullify gold clauses.[69] In ascertaining whether Congress has power to enact such legislation, it is necessary to determine the nature of the delegated powers, to examine the doctrines of composite powers and implied powers, and to analyze the scope of the pertinent express powers.

The Doctrine of Composite Powers. This doctrine is illustrated in *Knox v. Lee,* in which the Supreme Court, overruling its two-year-old decision in *Hepburn v. Griswold,*[70] held Congress had power to issue irredeemable paper money and to constitute it a legal tender for private debts under a symposium of the enumerated powers, with special reference to the war power, the power to borrow money and the power to coin money. The Court, after stating that the government has the "capability of self-preservation," went on to say:

> And here it is to be observed it is not indispensable to the existence of any power claimed for the Federal government that it can be found specified in the words of the Constitution, or clearly and directly traceable to some one of the specified powers. Its existence may be deduced fairly from more than one of the substantive powers expressly defined, or from them all combined. It is allowable to group together any number of them and infer from them all that the power claimed has been conferred. Such a treatment of the Constitution is recognized by its own provisions.[71]

The doctrine has general approval except when confused with the renounced theory of inherent sovereignty.[72] Power may therefore exist in Congress as an incident to the accomplishment of an objective which several powers collectively embrace.[73]

The Implied Powers.[74] The 18th clause of Article I, Section 8 extends to Congress power "to make all laws which shall be necessary and proper for carrying into execution the foregoing powers ..." Logically, this subjects to the power of Congress anything which interferes with the exercise of the express powers.[75] In other words, it makes those powers effective to carry out the purposes for which they werre designed. The leading case on the subject is *M'Culloch v. Maryland,* in which the Supreme Court held that the Federal government had power to create a bank, incident to the accomplishment of the objects entrusted to the government in the several powers of taxation, of borrowing money, of commerce, of war, and of the support of armies and navies. Chief Justice Marshall established for all time the criteria upon which the power in each case rests:

> Let the end be legitimate, let it be within the scope of the constitution, and all means which are appropriate, which are plainly adapted to that end, which are not prohibited, but consist with the letter and spirit of the constitution, are constitutional.[76]

So too in *Knox v. Lee,*[77] after the Court had determined that the objects sought to be attained in the war power, the power to borrow money, the power to coin money and regulate its value, together with other express powers cited in the opinion, disclosed the objective of self-preservation, it held that the government had implied power to accomplish that object by means appropriate to the end. The conclusion is that the Federal government has implied power to effect the objects entrusted to it, whether such objects are embraced in the separate express powers or in a composite of powers.

The Express Powers. The particular powers which it seems most likely the courts would consider in questioning the constitutionality of an act abrogating or nullifying gold clauses are those which provide that Congress may "borrow money on the credit of the United States" and may "coin money [and] regulate the value thereof."[78]

These powers received considerable judicial interpretation in three important cases decided by the Supreme Court. The most illuminating authority on the subject of the money power is *Veazie Bank v. Fenno,*[79] in which the Supreme Court upheld the constitutionality of a tax on state bank notes used for circulation. The avowed purpose of the act was to drive the circulating notes out of existence in order to create a uniform currency, but the court held the power to "coin money, [and] regulate its value" is tantamount to a power to establish "a currency, uniform in value and description, and convenient and useful for circulation,"[80] and therefore comprehends power to destroy state bank notes which undermine the national currency. Here is the full expression of the implied power—the enactment of legislation "necessary and proper for carrying into execution" the express coinage power by removing an interference with the accomplishment of the objective embraced in the power conferred. In the language of the Supreme Court:

> Having thus, in the exercise of undisputed constitutional powers, undertaken to provide a currency for the whole country, it cannot be questioned that Congress may, constitutionally, secure the benefit of it to the people by appropriate legislation. To this end, Congress has denied the quality of legal tender of foreign coins, and has provided by law against the imposition of counterfeit and base coin on the community. To the same end, Congress may restrain, by suitable enactments, the circulation as money of any notes not issued under its own authority. Without this power, indeed, its attempts to secure a sound and uniform currency for the country must be futile.[81]

This case was followed by *Knox v. Lee,* in which the Supreme Court held that the Constitution "was designed to provide the same currency, having a uniform legal value in all the States." The Court went on to explain why the currency powers were taken away from the states:

> In view of this it might be argued with much force that when it is consi-
> dered in what brief and comprehensive terms the Constitution speaks,
> how sensible its framers must have been that emergencies might arise
> when the precious metals (then more scarce than now) might prove
> inadequate to the necessities of the government and the demands of the
> people—when it is remembered that paper money was almost exclu-
> sively in use in the States as the medium of exchange, and when the
> great evil sought to be remedied was the want of uniformity in the
> current value of money, it might be argued, we say, that the gift of
> power to coin money and regulate the value thereof, was understood as
> conveying general power over the currency, the power which had
> belonged to the States, and which they had surrendered.[82]

In *Juilliard v. Greenman*, after the fiat money had been
redeemed and reissued, the Supreme Court determined the constitutionality of the enabling legal tender act under the power of
Congress to borrow money and to establish a national currency.
Of the two powers under consideration, the Court said:

> Under the power to borrow money on the credit of the United States,
> and to issue circulating notes for the money borrowed, its power to
> define the quality and force of those notes as currency is as broad as the
> like power over a metallic currency under the power to coin money and
> to regulate the value thereof. Under the two powers, taken together,
> Congress is authorized to establish a national currency, either in coin or
> in paper, and to make that currency lawful money for all purposes, as
> regards the national government or private individuals.

These cases determine the scope and objectives of the money
powers as they exist today, the coinage power being the power to
establish a sound and uniform national currency and the power to
borrow money comprehending power to effect the purpose
implied. It remains to be seen whether or not legislation nullifying
gold clauses could be upheld as a way of accomplishing these
purposes, within the limits imposed on the exercise of these powers by the Fifth Amendment.

B. The Limitations of the Fifth Amendment

The only pertinent limitation imposed by the Constitution on
the exercise of the delegated powers is the Fifth Amendment.[84] A
proper understanding of this Amendment requires that its separate

provisions be distinguished and analyzed severally. For purposes of such analysis, these provisions will be reversed in the order of consideration; the due process clause, being the more troublesome aspect, will be undertaken after disposing of the requirement that no property be taken for public use without just compensation.

The Supreme Court has clearly defined this provision of the Constitution and has held in many cases that the Federal government must compensate for the direct appropriation of private property for public use. But the distinction is drawn between direct appropriation and indirect destruction of property.[85] This is clearly illustrated in the cases of *Monongahela Navigation Co. v. United States*[86] and *Omnia Commercial Co., Inc. v. United States*.[87] In the first of these cases, following condemnation proceedings instituted by the United States to appropriate a lock and dam on the Monongahela River under the commerce power, the plaintiff sought to recover the value of a franchise to collect tolls which had not been included in the reported valuation. The Supreme Court held that the value of the franchise should have been included, saying:

> Congress has supreme control over the regulation of commerce, but if, in exercising that supreme control, it deems it necessary to take private property, then it must proceed subject to the limitations imposed by this Fifth Amendment, and can take only on payment of just compensation.[88]

In the second of the cases mentioned, the distinction is made clear. Plaintiff had acquired by assignment of a contract the right to purchase a large quantity of steel plate from the Allegheny Steel Company at a price under the market. Subsequently the Federal government requisitioned the entire production of the latter company for the year 1918 and ordered the company not to carry out the contract with the plaintiff. An action was commenced by the plaintiff in the Court of Claims to recover losses resulting from the alleged appropriation of private property for public use. The demurrer of the United States was sustained and the petition dismissed. The Supreme Court, affirming, recognized that the contract in question was property within the meaning of the Fifth Amendment and that the government would be liable if it were taken for public use. However, the Court said: "In the present case the effect of the requisition was to bring the contract to an end, not to keep it alive for the use of the Government."[89] Clearly the nullification of gold clauses and the declaration that all money contracts shall be solvable in legal tender currency would not constitute a direct appropriation of the contracts for public use, but would constitute, rather, a destruction of them.

It is established that the due process clause does not necessarily inhibit the impairment of contract obligations in the exercise of the delegated powers. This, of course, is of the first importance to the problem since the nullification of gold clauses would involve the destruction of contract obligations. Thus in *Knox v. Lee*[90] the Supreme Court summarily disposed of the argument that the Fifth Amendment prohibited the impairment of the contract, by reducing the actual quantum of it, since the government was acting in the exercise of its express and implied powers. It said:

> Nor can it be truly asserted that Congress may not, by its action, indirectly impair the obligation of contracts, if by the expression be meant rendering contracts fruitless, or partially fruitless. ... It is, then, clear that the powers of Congress may be exerted, though the effect of such exertion may be in one case to annul, and in other cases to impair the obligation of contracts. And it is no sufficient answer to this to say it is true only when the powers exerted were expressly granted.[91]

Another case involving the deprivation of property in the exercise of the coinage power is *Ling Su Fan v. United States*,[92] in which the Supreme Court held valid the Philippine law prohibiting the exportation of silver coin from the Philippine Islands. The law was passed by the Philippine Commission pursuant to the acts of Congress authorizing the Philippine government to establish a mint, and to enact laws for its operation and for the striking of certain coins. It was designed to maintain the value of the silver peso at the rate of one gold peso, the bullion value of the coin being at the time some nine per cent greater than its face value. The Court held that the power to coin money, "a prerogative of sovereignty,"[93] included the power to prevent its outflow from the country of its origin; that such an act is not an arbitrary or unreasonable interference with private rights of contract or property and hence is not lacking in due process; and that the wisdom of such legislation is not relevant to the question, of power. Answering the argument that the statute was a violation of due process, the Supreme Court said:

> To justify the exercise of such a power it is only necessary that it shall

appear that the means are reasonably adapted to conserve the general public interest and are not an arbitrary interference with private rights of contract or property. The law here in question is plainly within the limits of the police power, and not an arbitrary or unreasonable interference with private rights. If a local coinage was demanded by the general interest of the Philippine Islands, legislation reasonably adequate to maintain such coinage at home as a medium of exchange is not a violation of private right forbidden by the organic law.[94]

Of course, these cases do not answer the question whether Congress has power to nullify gold clauses. They recognize no general power to impair a contract by legislation aimed directly at it.[95] They merely indicate that in the exercise of the coinage power, or other powers, the limitations of due process may in certain circumstances be satisfied even though contracts be incidentally impaired or destroyed. In order to ascertain what these circumstances are and their relation to the gold clause question, we refer to a case involving the impairment of the obligation of a contract in the lawful exercise of the commerce power. In *Louisville & Nashville R.R. v. Mottley*,[96] the Supreme Court denied the right of the plaintiff to the specific performance of a contract for free transportation for life in view of the act of Congress prohibiting carriers from receiving a different compensation than that specified in their published tariffs, despite the fact that the contract was valid when entered into many years prior to the passage of the act and constituted a settlement of the plaintiffs' claim for injuries incurred on the defendant railroad. In so holding, the Court said:

> The agreement between the railroad company and the Mottleys must necessarily be regarded as having been made subject to the possibility that, at some future time, Congress might so exert its whole constitutional power in regulating interstate commerce as to render that agreement unenforceable or to impair its value. That the exercise of such power may be hampered or restricted to any extent by contracts previously made between individuals or corporations, is inconceivable. The framers of the Constitution never intended any such state of things to exist.[97]

This statement, it is submitted, is applicable to any contract which interferes with the accomplishment of the objectives embraced in the delegated powers.[98] To hold otherwise would render the government impotent; it would, in fact, make the due process clause a true negative and would result in the nullification of the granted powers. Such is not the proper conception of the due process limitation. Under the nineteenth century philosophy, re-appearing periodically, due process is a concept of fundamental rights;[99] today it is more generally a requirement that the end be permissible (one within the purview of the Federal government) and that the means bear some fairly adequate relation to the end.[100] It prohibits the unreasonable and arbitrary deprivation of property, but the prohibition gives way, as we have seen, where the public interest is involved, where the legislation is designed to obviate an interference with the accomplishment of one or more of the objectives embraced in the delegated powers.[101]

The basis of decision lies in the particular purpose Congress seeks to serve in each case, dependent upon the two questions, (1) whether that purpose is comprehended in the objectives of the delegated powers and (2) whether the means employed bear a fair relation to such lawful objective. It is, therefore, all-important to bear in mind the objective of Congress, both in ascertaining whether there is the affirmative power to accomplish it and in determining whether legislation is so unreasonable and arbitrary as to be confiscatory.

It begs the question to say that the nullification of gold clauses would be unreasonable, even unconscionable, because it would redistribute property just as would a statute scaling or cancelling debts. The cases we have discussed illustrate instances in which property has been redistributed under the enumerated powers.[102] If Congress should attempt to nullify gold clauses merely to accomplish a redistribution of property, it might be unconstitutional for lack of an affirmative power which has as its objective the redistribution of property.[103] If, on the other hand, Congress should endeavor to accomplish an arbitrary redistribution of property by forbidding all gold bond creditors who insist upon payment in gold to use the facilities of interstate commerce, or should raise the rates for such persons, such legislation might well be held unreasonable within the meaning of the Fifth Amendment, since it would apparently not bear a fair relation to a lawful objective. It is quite another story, however, if gold contracts interfere with the exercise of any of the delegated powers. In that case, Congress may accomplish the purpose for which the power was conferred even though contracts are impaired and property is incidentally redistributed.

C. Judicial Review of Congressional Act

The question of the reasonableness of legislation is, in the last analysis, for the Supreme Court.[104] Reasonableness, however, being the test of the relation of means to end which the due process clause requires, it seems that the Supreme Court would sustain an act of Congress nullifying gold clauses if the Court were persuaded that it was designed to obviate an interference with an objective embraced in the delegated powers. Of course the attainment of such objectives may be more difficult in periods of emergency than in normal times. The scope of the powers may be enlarged accordingly.[105]

But whether the court reviews legislation as an emergency measure or otherwise, the fundamental question for its consideration is that of the appropriateness of such legislation to the objects embraced in the delegated powers.[106] In determining this question, the Supreme Court has indicated that it will be guided by the findings of Congress. Illustrating this, the Supreme Court upheld the Grain Futures Act in *Board of Trade v. Olsen*,[107] accepting the findings of Congress that transactions in grain futures obstruct interstate commerce. The Court said:

> It is clear from the citations, in the statement of the case, of evidence before committees of investigation as to manipulations of the futures market and their effect, that we would be unwarranted in rejecting the finding of Congress as unreasonable, and that in our inquiry as to the validity of this legislation we must accept the view that such manipulation does work to the detriment of producers, consumers, shippers and legitimate dealers in interstate commerce in grain and that it is a real abuse.

This indicates how important it is that whatever Congress does, should be done only after a thorough investigation of the necessity for action and the effect that it will have. If Congress should, however, determine upon due consideration that the gold clause obstructs the ability of the Federal government to borrow money or if it should find that the gold clause interferes with its ability to maintain a sound and uniform currency,[109] the Court probably would be largely guided by such findings.[110]

CONCLUSIONS

Having analyzed the scope of the money powers and the due process limitations, we may attempt to summarize our views. Under the Legal Tender Acts,[111] paper currency was made a legal tender for "debts," but the Supreme Court held that the acts were intended to include only simple debts, excluding contracts in which the medium of payment was specified.[112] It is noteworthy that in upholding the act in *Knox v. Lee,* the Court stated that Congress has power to impair contracts in the exercise of its lawful powers[113] but avoided a finding of impairment by holding that money contracts are made subject to regulation of the currency.[114] The Court made it clear that it was referring only to contracts in which the medium of payment had not been specified. It follows that there is no precedent that the money power, *per se,* is the power to declare the paper currency a legal tender for obligations expressly limited to payment in gold.[115] The sovereign money power of the English government apparently is so extensive. Possibly the Court would uphold a statute nullifying gold clauses, without considering the question of an interference with the government's lawful objectives, on the ground that *all* money contracts, notwithstanding express words of limitation, are made subject to the exercise of the power of Congress to declare what constitutes money. We hazard no opinion on this question. It, of course, shades into the question of interference.[116] There is, however, room for certain conclusions based on the decided cases. We have seen that the money powers include power to establish a sound and uniform national currency and to destroy that which competes with and thereby discredits such currency. This applies alike to the power to coin money and the power to borrow money, to the end that the currency system may be controlled and that the government may finance itself. So far the scope of the two powers has been determined, so far their objectives have been defined. Therefore, if the gold clause does in fact constitute an interference with the ability of the government to perform these functions, or to accomplish the objectives embraced in a composite of powers, then under the doctrine of implied powers and the cases discussed in connection with the due process clause it is subject to the exercise of the powers with which it interferes. The determination of this question of fact must be left to students of money and its phenomena.

FOUR

The New Deal Attacks The Gold Clause*

The New Deal's frontal assault on the gold clause began with a Joint Resolution of Congress on June 5, 1933. Unequivocally answering the question of whether the Roosevelt administration would attempt to nullify the gold clause, the Joint Resolution condemned it as being "against public policy" and simply expunged the gold clause from all existing contracts. Although this much is generally known, there was considerably more to the legislative attack on the gold clause which is not widely known. A particularly revealing example is the *explicit* congressional intent to use nullification of the gold clause as a means of transferring hundreds of billions of dollars worth of assets from America's "haves" to its "have nots." This intent, as well as other examples of what motivated F.D.R.'s Congress (all found in Chapter 4), reveals the pervasive anti-gold animus of many legislators. More importantly, this chapter exposes Congress' basic view of how far its money powers actually extend.

Text of the Statute

The Joint Resolution of Congress dated June 5, 1933,[1] undertakes to nullify any clauses contained in contracts, private or

---

* This chapter, by George A. King, originally entitled "The Gold Clause—Can It Constitutionally Be Abrogated by Legislation?", appeared in Vol. II of *The George Washington Law Review*, 1934, pages 131-154, Reprinted With The Permission of *The George Washington Law Review* © 1934.

governmental, which provide for payment in gold coin of the weight and fineness existing at the time the contract was made. It reads as follows:—

Joint Resolution to assure uniform value to the coins and currencies of the United States.

Whereas the holding of or dealing in gold affect the public interest, and are therefore subject to proper regulation and restriction; and

Whereas the existing emergency has disclosed that provisions of obligations which purport to give the obligee a right to require payment in gold or a particular kind of coin or currency of the United States, or in an amount of money of the United States measured thereby, obstruct the power of the Congress to regulate the value of money of the United States and are inconsistent with the declared policy of the Congress to maintain at all times the equal power of every dollar, coined or issued by the United States, in the markets and in the payment of debts. Now therefore be it

Resolved by the Senate and House of Representatives of the United States of America in Congress assembled, That (a) every provision contained in or made with respect to any obligation which purports to give the obligee a right to require payment in gold or a particular kind of coin or currency, or in an amount in money of the United States measured thereby, is declared to be against public policy; and no such provision shall be contained in or made with respect to any obligation hereafter incurred. Every obligation, heretofore or hereafter incurred, whether or not any such provision is contained therein or made with respect thereto shall be discharged upon payment, dollar for dollar, in any coin or currency which at the time of payment is legal tender for public and private debts. Any such provision contained in any law authorizing obligations to be issued by or under authority of the United States, is hereby repealed, but the repeal of any such provision shall not invalidate any other provision or authority contained in such a law.

(b) As used in this resolution, the term 'obligation' means any obligation (including every obligation of and to the United States, excepting currency) payable in money of the United States; and the term 'coin or currency' means coin or currency of the United States, including Federal Reserve notes and circulating notes of Federal Reserve banks and national banking associations.

Sec. 2. The last sentence of paragraph (1) of subsection (b) of section 43 of the Act entitled 'An Act to relieve the existing national economic emergencyby increasing agricultural purchasing power, to raise revenue for extraordinary expenses incurred by reason of such emergency, to provide emergency relief with respect to agricultural indebtedness, to provide for the orderly liquidation of joint-stock land banks, and for other purposes,' approved May 12, 1933, is amended to read as follows:

All coins and currencies of the United States (including Federal Reserve notes and circulating notes of Federal Reserve banks and national banking associations) heretofore or hereafter coined or issued, shall be legal tender for all debts, public and private, public charges, taxes, duties, and dues, except that gold coins, when below the standard weight and limit of tolerance provided by law for the single piece, shall be legal tender only at valuation in proportion to their actual weight.

What the Gold Clause Is

I have before me a bond of a public service corporation promising to pay the interest at its respective dates and ultimately the principal at maturity of the bond "in gold coin of the United States of America of or equal to the present standard of weight and fineness." This clause occurs in practically all bonds issued by railroad companies, other public utilities, industrial corporations, states and their subordinate municipalities, such as towns, cities and sanitary districts.

The bonds issued by the United States contain a clause of similar purport. We have also international obligations to other countries payable in gold as well as far larger obligations of foreign governments to our government likewise payable in gold. According to the legislation just quoted every one of these obligations, private or public, whether by its terms payable in gold or in "dollars" generally may now be discharged in any coin or currency which is at the time of payment legal tender for any debt.

Object of the Legislation

As to what is intended to be accomplished by this legislation its proponents leave us in no doubt. Senator Thomas of Oklahoma in advocating the proposition introduced by him made this statement as to its object and effect.[2]

> Mr. President, the amendment, in my judgment, is the most important proposition that has ever come before the American Congress. It is the most important proposition that has ever come before any parlimentary body of any nation of the world. Saving the single issue of the World War, there has been no issue joined in 6,000 years of recorded history as important as this issue pending here to-day.
>
> Mr. President, it will be my task to show that if the amendment shall prevail it has potentialities as follows. It may transfer from one class to another class in these United States value to the extent of almost $200,000,000,000. This value will be transferred, first, from those who

own the bank deposits. Secondly, this value will be transferred from those who own bonds and fixed investments.

I want to make that statement clear. No issue in 6,000 years save the World War begins to compare with the possibilities embraced in the power conferred by this amendment. Two hundred billion dollars now of wealth and buying power rests in the hands of those who own the bank deposits and fixed investments bonds and mortgages. That $200,000,000,000 these owners did not earn, they did not buy it, but they have it, and because they have it the masses of the people of this Republic are on the verge of starvation—17,000,000 on charity, in the bread line.

If the amendment carries and the powers are exercised in a reasonable degree, it must transfer that $200,000,000,000 in the hands of persons who now have it, who did not buy it, who did not earn it, who do not deserve it, who must not retain it, back to the other side—the debtor class of the Republic, the people who owe the mass debts of the Nation.

The above frank statement of the purpose of this Joint Resolution leaves no doubt of what was intended to be accomplished. A larger quantity of wealth is now in the hands of persons described as "those who own the bank deposits and fixed investments, bonds and mortgages." Many billions of this wealth are to be transferred to people described as "the debtor class of the Republic, the people who owe the mass debts of the Nation." All this is on the ground that those who now hold this wealth did not earn it and have no right to it, and that it should be transferred to another class of people who are regarded as its rightful owners.

The far-reaching extent of the proposition is also clearly shown by the report of the House Committee on Banking and Currency, which gives in more precise form the grounds of this legislation:[3]

The occasion for the declaration in the resolution that the gold clauses are contrary to public policy arises out of the experiences of the present emergency. These gold clauses render ineffective the power of the Government to create a currency and determine the value thereof. If the gold clause applied to a very limited number of contracts and security issues, it would be a matter of no particular consequence, but in this country virtually all obligations, almost as a matter of routine, contain the gold clause. In the light of this situation two phenomena which have developed during the present emergency make the enforcement of the gold clause incompatible with the public interest. The first is the tendency which has developed internally to hoard gold; the second is the tendency for capital to leave the country. Under these circumstances no currency system, whether based upon gold or upon any other foundation, can meet the requirements of a situation in which many billions of dollars of securities are expressed in a particular form of the circulating medium, particularly when it is the medium upon which the entire credit and currency structure rests.

There can be no substantial question as to the constitutional power of Congress to make this legislation applicable to all obligations, public and private, both past and future. The power of Congress to issue a currency and determine the value thereof and to provide for the borrowing of funds by the Government is express and undoubted. It is also undoubted that Congress has all powers necessary to make the exercise of these two express powers effective. Contracts of private individuals, past or future, are valid and enforceable only insofar as they do not conflict with public policy as enunciated by Congress in the exercise of its constitutional powers. When, therefore, as is declared in this resolution, the enforcement or making of gold-clause provisions obstructs the proper exercise of the congressional powers such provisions must yield. Nor does the fact that outstanding obligations of the Government are expressed as payable in gold coin impose a limitation, under the circumstances obtaining, upon the exercise of the powers conferred by the Constitution. The Government cannot, by contract or otherwise, divest itself of its sovereign power. All contracts of the Government are made in the light of this inalienable power to legislate as the public interest may demand. It is too well settled to admit of controversy that contracts or provisions of contracts, even though not inconsistent with public policy when made, may subsequently become contrary to public policy, as authoritatively announced by the legislative branch of the Government, and that, in such event, they become invalid and unenforceable.

Grounds of Opposition

These are best stated in a minority report from the same committee by Mr. Luce of Massachusetts.[4] This states as follows:

This proposal has two elements. First, it renounces obligations of the United States. Secondly, it prohibits future obligations of the same sort.

The second of these elements calls for no protest here. If in the judgment of the Treasury future borrowings or issuance of currency would better not be subject to payment or redemption in gold, very well. Questioning of such judgment need not distract attention from the far more important issue, that of the public faith.

In 1869 it was enacted (remember that 'equivalent' means 'equal worth'):—

The faith of the United States is solemnly pledged to the payment in coin or its equivalent of all the obligations of the United States not bearing interest, known as United States notes, and of all the interest-bearing obligations of the United States, except in cases where the law authorizing the issue of any such obligations has expressly provided that the same may be paid in lawful money or other currency than gold and silver.' (Act March 8, 1869, 16 U.S. Statutes at Large, page 1.)

Yet we are now asked to declare that because such provisions 'obstruct the power of Congress to regulate the value of the money of the United States,' the faith that we solemnly pledged 64 years ago is to be repudiated. What emergency can justify breaking the solemn pledge of a nation? Do 'solemn' and 'pledge' mean nothing?

When the first Liberty bond law was enacted in April of 1917, it said of the bonds:

The principal and interest thereof shall be payable in United States gold coin of the present standard of value.' (Act of April 24, 1917, 40 U.S. Statutes at Large, page 35.)

The same provision appears in the second, third and fourth Liberty Loan Acts and in other loan laws since then.

Millions of our people bought these bonds with this pledge. Whether all gave equal weight to it is irrelevant where honor is involved. The pledge alone counts though no more than one man gave it heed.

As a matter of fact this pledge has been a vital consideration not alone with public securities but also with a great number of corporate borrowings. Their total has been estimated at a hundred billions in par value. Importance has been attached to the gold promise by countless treasurers of universities, colleges, other educational and philanthropic institutions, by all sorts of men who are entrusted with investing the resources that support work for humanity. This includes the officers of our mutual savings banks with their nine billion and more of deposits, the life-insurance companies with more than 120,000,000 policies outstanding, and all other officials who must think of safety first when exercising their trusts. Shall the solemn pledge to them be broken?

The good faith of a nation is its greatest asset. We have boasted that in this no nation is our superior. Upon it we have relied in our international relations. On the very eve of a conference that bids fair to be of supreme consequence to the welfare of the world, we are asked to replace good faith with bad faith, to tell those with whom we confer that whatever agreements we make may be repudiated next day or next year. If we break solemn pledges to our own, what may be expected of those to others?

We are asking sundry nations to pay us what they owe. Will they be more likely to make good their promises if we set them the example of repudiation?

That is the right name for it, repudiation, and this bill ought to be known throughout history as 'The Repudiation Bill of 1933.'

We are making huge loans to our own people, to States, to cities, to various kinds of governmental agencies. If we repudiate, shall we expect them to pay?

It is true that legal casuistry, in England and in one of our own subordiate courts, has recently perverted the plain meaning of language in order to give a color of defense to repudiation. Not all the subtleties of all the lawyers in the world can change the fact that both parties to these contracts understood the words to mean what they said, what it has been hitherto accepted that they meant.

Our Constitution forbade the States to impair the obligations of contracts. For some unknown reason the fathers did not impose the same prohibition on the Nation. But the moral principle involved is the same. The sanctity of contracts is the cornerstone of our civilization. To violate that sanctity is to invite ruin.

Question of Constitutionality

We have seen what this legislation is and the reasons authoritatively given for and against it by its proponents and opponents, respectively, in Congress.

Congress is empowered "to coin money, regulate the value thereof and of foreign coin, and fix the standard of weights and measures." It has power "to borrow money on the credit of the United States." It has power "to make all laws which shall be necessary and proper for the carrying into execution the foregoing powers, and all other powers vested by this Constitution in the Government of the United States or in any department or officer thereof."

Congress in the height of the Civil War passed acts authorizing the issuance of a paper currency not redeemable in gold which should constitute a legal tender for the payment of all debts, public or private, except duties on imports and interest on the public debt.

The constitutionality of the legal tender acts was violently attacked before the courts.[5] The Supreme Court, after once holding the acts invalid as in violation of the Constitution, later decided in favor of their validity.[6] Still later in 1884, it sustained the power of Congress to reissue the same notes and make them legal tender even long after the Civil War emergency had passed.[7]

These were promises to pay "dollars" generally. These legal tender decisions held that where the promises are for "dollars" any dollars which are legal tender at the time the obligation becomes due are sufficient to satisfy the obligation. The court in deciding the last *Legal Tender Case* in 1884, said:[8]

> A contract to pay a certain sum of money, without any stipulation as to the kind of money in which it shall be paid, may always be satisfied by payment of that sum in any currency which is lawful money at the place and time at which payment is to be made.

Contracts by their terms payable in gold raise a different question. Such contracts are to be paid in the medium of payment stipulated in the contract.

The question first came before the Supreme Court in 1869 in a case arising before the Civil War on a bond for money lent and stipulated to be repaid in gold and silver coin. One thousand, five hundred and seven dollars ($1,507) was due and the debtor sought to discharge his liability by payment of that amount in paper money worth in the market at that time $670 in coin. The court held the contract payable in gold and silver.[9]

In *Trebilcock v. Wilson*,[10] decided by the Supreme Court simultaneously with their legal tender decision, the court held that an obligation payable "in specie" is payable in coin and not in irredeemable Treasury notes. The court said:—

> If we look to the act of 1862, in the light of contemporaneous and subsequent legislation of Congress, and of the practice of the Government, we shall find little difficulty in holding that it was not intended to interfere in any respect with existing or subsequent contracts payable by their express terms in specie; and that when it declares that the notes of the United States shall be lawful money, and a legal tender for all debts, it means for all debts which are payable in money generally; and not obligations payable in commodities, or obligations of any other kind.

Along with *Bronson v. Rodes*,[11] they decided another case involving a ground rent in Baltimore for "the yearly rent or sum of £15, current money of Maryland, payable in English golden guineas, weighing five pennyweights and six grains, at thirty-five shillings each, and other gold and silver at their present established weight and rate." The court stated that the obvious intent of the contract was to secure payment of a certain rent in gold and silver and thereby avoid fluctuations in the currency. They said that the contract was in substance to deliver a certain weight of gold and silver of a certain fineness; that it was equivalent to a contract to deliver bullion. The judgment of the court might either be paid in coin—gold or silver money of the United States—or such kind of legal tender notes as would be equal to the corresponding amount of gold and silver.[12]

The decision was reaffirmed in 1878 long after the constitutionality of the legal tender acts had been settled. The purchaser of a large quantity of cattle made the price of them payable in gold. The vendor retained a lien on them for the purchase. The Supreme Court held that the vendor was entitled to his price in gold coin or in such amount of currency as would purchase the gold coin called for by the contract. The court made the following clear statement on the effect of the contract:[13]

> But the court did say to the jury, that, if they found the contract on the part of the plaintiff was to pay a certain sum of money in gold, they should compute the difference between gold and currency, and render their verdict in dollars and cents in currency; and in this we see no error. While we have decided that a judgment upon a contract payable in gold may be for payment in coined dollars, we have never held that in all cases it must be so. While gold coin is in one sense money, it is in another an article of merchandise. Gregory was required to discharge his debt in gold before he could rightfully take the property into his possession under the replevin. If the payment had been so made, Morris would have had his coin at that time to use as money or merchandise, according to his discretion. But it was not made; and Gregory by his wrongful act in taking the property subjected himself to damages. If the contract had been in terms for the delivery of so much gold bullion, there is no doubt but the court might have directed the jury to find the value of the bullion in currency, and bring in a verdict accordingly. But we think, as was thought in *Bronson v. Rodes*, such a case is not really distinguishable from this.

These decisions sustain the validity of clauses in contracts making them payable in gold coin or its equivalent. Persons were left free to make their own contracts payable in gold. The creditor is entitled to enforce the payment of that contract in gold or its equivalent value in paper. The agreement to pay in gold is a contract to deliver so much gold in coin or bullion. Payment had to be made in gold dollars or their equivalent in legal tender money.

Congress has now by legislation of 1933 enacted that all contracts payable in gold of the present standard of weight and fineness, whether already in existence or hereafter made, are contrary to public policy as far as they are required to be paid in any particular kind of money. All of them, public or private, individual or corporate, national or international, may be discharged by payment of the number of dollars therein stipulated in any kind of money now or hereafter declared by Congress to be legal tender.

Private Obligations

The opinion of the court in the legal tender cases[14] limits its decision to contracts payable in dollars generally and holds that a contract to pay in gold is different:—

> It is true that under the acts, a debtor, who became such before they were passed, may discharge his debt with the notes authorized by them, and the creditor is compellable to receive such notes in discharge of his claim. But whether the obligation of the contract is thereby weakened can be determined only after considering what was the contract obligation. It was not a duty to pay gold or silver, or the kind of money recognized by law at the time when the contract was made, nor was it a duty to pay money of equal intrinsic value in the market. (We speak now of contracts to pay money generally, not contracts to pay some specifically defined species of money.) The expectation of the creditor and the anticipation of the debtor may have been that the contract would be discharged by the payment of coined metals, but neither the expectation of one party to the contract respecting its fruits, nor the anticipation of the other constitutes its obligation. There is a well-recognized distinction between the expectation of the parties to a contract and the duty imposed by it.

The Fifth Amendment provides "No person shall be deprived of life, liberty, or property, without due process of law; nor shall private property be taken for public use without just compensation."

The provision against depriving any person of life, liberty, or property, without due process of law relates entirely to the United States. In 1870 a similar prohibition was laid upon the several States by the Fourteenth Amendment to the Constitution, which provides "nor shall any State deprive any person of life, liberty, or property, without due process of law." Section 4 of the Fourteenth Amendment contains a clause which may also bear on this question: "The validity of the public debt of the United States, authorized by law, including debts incurred for payment of pensions and bounties for services in suppressing insurrection or rebellion, shall not be questioned."

There have been very few decisions on the provision of the Fifth Amendment that "no person shall be deprived of life, liberty, or property, without due process of law"—that is, by the United States,—but many on the same proposition as applying to the States by the Fourteenth Amendment.

Fifth Amendment Limiting Federal Power

In *Monongahela Navigation Company v. United States*,[15] it was held that an act of Congress providing for the taking of property, a bridge, but which excluded from consideration fixing the value of the franchise to take tolls on that bridge was unconstitutional in denying the full value of the bridge to its owner.

Explaining the object of the first ten amendments to the Constitution, the court said:—[16]

> The first ten amendments to the Constitution, adopted as they were soon after the adoption of the Constitution, are in the nature of a bill of rights, and were adopted in order to quiet the apprehension of many, that without such declaration of rights the government would assume, and might be held to possess, the power to trespass upon those rights of persons and property which by the Declaration of Independence were affirmed to be unalienable rights.

In *Adair v. United States*,[17] an act of Congress making it a criminal offense for a railroad company to discharge an employee on account of his being a member of a labor organization was held to be an arbitrary and unconstitutional deprivation of the right of contract. The court said:—[18]

> The provision of the statute under which the defendant was convicted must be held to be repugnant to the Fifth Amendment and as not embraced by nor within the power of Congress to regulate interstate commerce, and under the guise of regulating interstate commerce and as applied to this case it arbitrarily sanctions an illegal invasion of the personal liberty as well as the right of property of the defendant Adair.

In *Adkins v. Children's Hospital*,[19] an act of Congress providing a minimum wage for women engaged in certain occupations in the District of Columbia was held unconstitutional as in conflict with the Fifth Amendment. In reaching this conclusion the court made these remarks which are very pertinent to the present case:—[20]

The statute now under consideration is attacked upon the ground that it authorizes an unconstitutional interference with the freedom of contract included within the guaranties of the due process clause of the Fifth Amendment. That the right to contract about one's affairs is a part of the liberty of the individual protected by this clause, is settled by the decisions of this court and is no longer open to question.

Within this liberty are contracts of employment of labor. In making such contracts, generally speaking, the parties have an equal right to obtain from each other the best terms they can as the result of private bargaining.

There is, of course, no such thing as absolute freedom of contract. It is subject to a great variety of restraints. But freedom of contract is, nevertheless, the general rule and restraint the exception; and the exercise of exceptional circumstances.

To sustain the individual freedom of action contemplated by the Constitution, is not to strike down the common good but to exalt it; for surely the good of society as a whole cannot be better served than by the preservation against arbitrary restraint of the liberties of its constituent members.

Fourteenth Amendment Limiting State Power

Decisions under the Fourteenth Amencment providing that no *State* shall deprive any person of life, liberty, or property, without due process of law are quite numerous. They are strictly applicable to legislation by Congress because the same prohibition against depriving any person of life, liberty, or property, without due process of law applies to the United States under the Fifth Amendment the same as it does to the States under the Fourteenth Amendment.

To take only a few typical cases the following decisions of the Supreme Court hold State legislation of various kinds to be unconstitutional and void under the clause of the Fourteenth Amendment providing against any State depriving any person of life, liberty, or property, without due process of law.

In *Allgeyer v. Louisiana*,[21] a statute of Louisiana which prohibited the making of a contract for marine insurance with any company not complying with the requirements of Louisiana law as to registration and license was held void as a restriction of the right of contract. The court said:[22]

The act done within the limits of the State under the circumstances of this case and for the purpose therein mentioned, we hold a proper act, one which the defendants were at liberty to perform and which the state legislature had no right to prevent, at least with reference to the Federal Constitution. To deprive the citizen of such a right as herein described without due process of law is illegal.

In *Coppage v. Kansas*,[23] a State law was considered making it unlawful for any officer of a corporation to coerce or even influence any person to enter into an agreement not to join, become, or remain a member of a labor organization as a condition for such person securing employment or continuing in the employment of such corporation. A superintendent in the service of a railway company called upon a switchman to agree to withdraw from the switchmen's union. The court relied upon the *Adair* case, decided in 1908, holding a similar act of Congress under the Fifth Amendment void, and stated that it equally prohibited a State from interfering with the liberty of contract under the Fourteenth Amendment. They said:—[24]

> Unless it is to be overruled, this decision is controlling upon the present controversy; for if Congress is prevented from arbitrary interference with the liberty of contract because of the 'due process' provision of the Fifth Amendment, it is too clear for argument that the States are prevented from the like interference by virtue of the corresponding clause of the Fourteenth Amendment; and hence if it be unconstitutional for Congress to deprive an employer of liberty or property for threatening an employee with loss of employment or discriminating against him because of his membership in a labor organization, it is unconstitutional for a State to similarly punish an employer for requiring his employee, as a condition of securing or retaining employment, to agree not to become or remain a member of such an organization while so employed.

The Kansas law was therefore held unconstitutional as an arbitrary attempt to interfere with the freedom of contract just as the act of Congress considered in the *Adair* case was held unconstitutional for the same reason.

In *Adams v. Tanner*,[25] a statute of Washington State forbidding the taking of fees by an employment agency for finding a job for a worker was held unconstitutional on the ground that it "is arbitrary and oppressive, and that it unduly restricts the liberty of appellants, guaranteed by the Fourteenth Amendment, to engage in a useful business. It may not therefore be enforced against them.[26]

In *Wolff Packing Co. v. Industrial Court*,[27] a State statute giving an administrative authority the power to fix minimum wages in the meat packing business was held to be void as an arbitrary interference with the freedom of contract. The court said:—[28]

> These qualifications do not change the essence of the act. It curtails the right of the employer on the one hand, and of the employee on the other, to contract about his affairs. This is part of the liberty of the individual protected by the guaranty of the due process clause of the Fourteenth Amendment. *Meyer v. Nebraska, 262* U.S. 390. While there is no such thing as absolute freedom of contrtact and it is subject to a variety of restraints, they must not be arbitrary or unreasonable. Freedom is the general rule, and restraint the exception. The legislative authority to abridge can be justified only by exceptional circumstances.

In *Tyson v. Banton*,[29] the legislature of New York was held to be without authority to limit the price for re-sale of theatre tickets by a middleman:—[30]

> The first of these is that the right of the owner to fix a price at which his property shall be sold or used is an inherent attribute of the property itself, and, as such, within the protection of the due process of law clauses of the Fifth and Fourteenth Amendments. The power to regulate property, services, or business can be invoked only under special circumstances; and it does not follow that because the power may exist to regulate in some particulars it exists to regulate in others or in all.

These cases show how far the Supreme Court has gone in protecting the liberty of contract as a right of which persons may not constitutionally be deprived.

English Decisions

An English case, *Feist v. Societe Intercommunale Belge D' Electricite*, was referred to in the debates in Congress.[31] This was a case of a Belgian electric company which issued debentures payable in England "in sterling in gold coin of the United Kingdom of or equal to the standard of weight and fineness existing on the 1st of September, 1928." The House of Lords has just (December 15, 1933) held, reversing two lower courts, that even since England has gone off the gold standard the holders of these debentures are entitled to be paid as provided in the contract, that is, in gold coin of the value existing at the date of the contract, or in so much legal tender money as will provide the amount of gold provided for by the contract.

Lord Russell in announcing the judgment said:

> I think that in clauses 1 and 2 of the bond the parties are referring to gold coin of the United Kingdom of a specific standard of weight and fineness not as being the mode in which the company's indebtedness is to be discharged, but as being the means by which the amount of that indebtedness is to be measured and ascertained.
>
> I would construe clause 1 not as meaning that £100 is to be paid in a certain way, but as meaning that the obligation is to pay a sum which would represent the equivalent of £100 if paid in a particular way: in other words, I would construe the clause as though it ran thus (omitting immaterial words) 'pay ° ° ° in sterling a sum equal to the value of £100 if paid in gold coin of the United Kingdom of or equal to the standard of weight and fineness existing on the 1st day of September, 1928.

This decision is the more striking in its application to the present situation from the fact that the British Parliament is not, as is our own Congress, under any constitutional restriction. England is not governed by a written Constitution and whatever the British Parliament enacts is law.

In *Broken Hill Proprietary Company v. Latham*[32] certain Australian debentures were made payable, principal and interest, at various places in Australia or in London at the option of the holder. The obligations of the company were payable in so many "pounds." The Australian pound was at a heavy discount as compared with the English pound when the due date of payment arrived.

The question was whether a holder, exercising his option to ask for payment in London was entitled:—

1. To the amount in pounds sterling, or
2. So much sterling as would purchase the stipulated number of Australian pounds.

It was held by the Court of Appeal that the word "pound" while generally meaning English pound does not necessarily have the meaning, but that it was whatever the parties intended by their contract. Australian pounds were meant by the contract. Even if the holder demanded payment in London where Australian money is not legal tender, he was obliged to take such a number of English pounds as the Australian money of the contract was worth. As £125 of Australian currency was worth only £100 sterling, it was held that the creditor was entitled to demand only

£100 sterling for every £125 of Australian money. This was put on the ground that "the obligation of the debtor must be discharged by paying the sum in the currency in which it was contracted to be paid."

Comparison With American Decisions

This closely corresponds to the decision of our own Supreme Court in *Thorington v. Smith*,[33] where it was held that a contract between persons residing in the Confederate States during the war and contracting for payment in "dollars" were contracting with reference to the existing state of affairs and referred to Confederate dollars and hence the judgment must be rendered, not for the same number of dollars in lawful money of the United States, but in United States money corresponding at the date of the transaction to the value of the Confederate money for which the parties bargained.

These distinctions carry out the intention of the parties as expressed in their contracts. Where gold is stipulated in an American contract, it must be paid in gold or its equivalent in paper. Where the agreement was made with reference to Confederate money, that money though unlawful, is the yardstick by which the right of the creditor is to be measured by its conversion into lawful United States money. Where a foreign company makes a contract to pay a sum in England in gold pounds of the present standard of weight and fineness it can only be discharged by payment in gold of the agreed medium. Where the contract is made in Australia and the promise is to pay £125, the contract is made with reference to Australian currency. If payment is demanded in London the creditor is only entitled to £100 in English currency as that would purchase £125 Australian currency. These decisions recognize the sanctity of contracts. There seems to be little difference on this point between the decisions in England and here, except that we have a Constitution defining fundamental rights while England has none.

Still another question has recently come up. Bonds have been issued by several companies payable, respectively, in a certain amount of "dollars" or another amount in pounds sterling, or still a third in Dutch guilders. The question has been raised whether

American bondholders are entitled to payment only in "dollars," which according to the resolution before us means any kind of dollars issued by the United States Government, or at their option in English pounds or Dutch guilders. This question is now pending before the courts. It is here mentioned only to show the many unexpected angles involved in the construction of this gold clause legislation.

National Obligations

From 1869 down to 1933, as shown by the excerpts previously given from the minority report on the Joint Resolution, the faith of the Government of the United States was solemnly pledged to the payment in coin or its equivalent of all the obligations of the United States, both interest-bearing and noninterest-bearing. All this is done away with by the Joint Resolution of June 5, 1933, which permits all obligations to be discharged by the payment of any money which may at the time be legal tender.

The law on the obligations of the Government, national, state, or municipal was stated by Alexander Hamilton:—[34]

> When a Government enters into a contract with an individual it it deposes, as to the matter of the contract, its constitutional authority and exchanges the character of a legislator for that of a moral agent with the same rights and obligations as an individual.

This principle was applied in *Murray v.Charleston*,[35] where it was said:—

> The truth is, States and cities, when they borrow money and contract to repay it with interest, are not acting as sovereignties. They come down to the level of ordinary individuals. Their contracts have the same meaning as that of similar contracts between private persons. Hence, instead of there being in the undertaking of a State or city to pay, a reservation of a sovereign right to withhold payment, the contract should be regarded as an assurance that such a right will not be exercised. A promise to pay, with a reserved right to deny or change the effect of the promise, is an absurdity.
>
> The inviolability of contracts, and the duty of performing them as made, are foundations of all well-ordered society, and to prevent the removal or disturbance of these foundations was one of the great objects for which the Constitution was framed.

The same principle has repeatedly been applied to the contracts of the United States. In *United States v. Bank of the Metropolis*,[36] the court said:—

> When the United States, by its authorized officer, become a party to negotiate paper, they have all the rights, and incur all the responsibility of individuals, who are parties to such instruments.

In *United States v. State Bank*,[37] the court said:—

> In these cases, and many others that might be cited, the rules of law applicable to individuals were applied to the United States. Here the basis of the liability insisted upon is an implied contract by which they might well become bound by virtue of their corporate character. Their sovereignty is in no wise involved.

The principle is most emphatically stated in *Corliss Company v. United States:*[38]

> When the Government assumes the position of a contractor with a citizen, it comes under all the obligations and liabilities of an individual, and must abide by its own acts and agreements, with the added obligation, because it is a government and more powerful than any individual, to deal with the individual in the strictest fairness and justice.

This decision was affirmed by the Supreme Court on the same ground.[39]

In *Hollerbach v. United States*,[40] it was said:—

> A Government contract should be interpreted as are contracts between individuals, with a view to ascertaining the intention of the parties and to give it effect accordingly, if that can be done consistently with the terms of the instrument.

In *Reading Steel Casting Company v. United States*,[41] it was said:—

> The contract is to be construed and the rights of the parties are to be determined by the application of the same principles as if the contract were between individuals."

Enough has been said to show that the Government when it makes a contract assumes the same obligations as an individual and can not rightfully claim immunity by virtue of its sovereign power.

International Obligations

In 1903 we entered into a treaty with the new Republic of Panama for "the use, occupation and control of a zone of land and land under water for the construction, maintenance, operation," etc., of a canal. The price to be paid was stipulated by Article XIV:—[42]

> The United States agrees to pay to the Republic of Panama the sum of ten million dollars ($10,000,000) in gold coin of the United States on the exchange of the ratification of this convention and also an annual payment during the life of this convention of two hundred and fifty thousand dollars ($250,000) in like gold coin beginning nine years after the date aforesaid.

Up to the present time these payments have been made in gold coin as provided in the treaty. Have we a right, legal or moral, national or international, to meet this payment by delivering to Panama $250,000 in money from the printing press not redeemable in coin? The Joint Resolution we have before us provides that we may so discharge the payment. It does not fulfill the international obligation into which we have entered.

Conclusion

The preamble of the Resolution declares a state of emergency. It is contrary to public policy to make contracts payable in anything but legal tender money of the United States or to discharge existing obligations in any other kind of money.

How far these emergency clauses would be sustained were the question to come before the courts for decision and ultimately before the Supreme Court of the United States it is impossible to say in advance. The idea that the Constitution may be suspended by the existence of national emergencies or even in time of war was repudiated by the Supreme Court in a famous decision arising out of the Civil War in 1867, *Ex parte Milligan*.[43] In an eloquent passage the court said:

> The Constitution of the United States is a law for rulers and people equally in war and in peace, and covers with the shield of its protection all classes of men, at all times, and under all circumstances. No doctrine, involving more pernicious consequences was ever invented by the wit of men than that any of its provisions can be suspended

during any of the great exigencies of government. Such a doctrine leads directly to anarchy and despotism, but the theory of necessity on which it is based is false; for the government within the Constitution has all the powers granted to it, which are necessary to preserve its existence; as has been happily proved by the result of the great effort to throw off its just authority.

The country is undoubtedly at the present time confronted by an emergency. Whether its existence justifies legislation chang-changing the obligations of contracts and perhaps having billions of dollars transferred from one class to another in opposition to the terms of their contracts is something that remains for the courts to decide.

The decisions under both the Fifth and Fourteenth Amendments have all made freedom of contract the rule, and its restriction the exception.

Can the recent legislation allowing all obligations, private and governmental, State and Federal, to be discharged by payment of any kind of dollars in circulation, even though the contract medium of payment be gold, be sustained as within the constitutional powers of Congress? This is a question which only the highest court can answer. An affirmative answer would involve a new construction of the rights of parties over their property and over their own power to make contracts.

In *Wilson v. New*,[44] an eight-hour day with a standard minimum of wages on railroads was held constitutional and was enforced. The act was passed to deal with an extreme emergency. A complete tie-up of all the railroads of the country was threatened. The act was passed to put an end to a dangerous situation. As such it was sustained. The emergency was thus treated:—[45]

> Although an emergency may not call into life a power which has never lived, nevertheless emergency may afford a reason for the exertion of a living power already enjoyed.

In 1921 the Supreme Court sustained as an emergency measure an act of Congress forbidding a landlord to reenter upon the leased premises even though the lease had expired, provided the tenant paid the rent and complied with the other conditions of the lease.

Even the rent might be reduced if deemed unreasonable by the Commission organized to pass upon that question. Active hostilities of the war were over in 1919, when the statute was enacted.[46] The life of the Commission was by subsequent legislation extended to May 22, 1922, and from that date for another two years to May 22, 1924, when it expired. In both 1922 and 1924 the war [was] not only actually but legally at an end, so the extension acts could only be sustained as a peace-time emergency measure. This the Supreme Court did but only conditionally upon the emergency being shown to have continued existence.[47]

At the same time a New York statute enacted as late as 1920, allowing tenants to hold over after the expiration of their leases was sustained as an emergency measure.[48]

This decision was reaffirmed in 1922 in *Edgar A. Levy Leasing Company v. Siegel.*[49] Here rent legislation was sustained on the ground that "the acts involved are 'emergency' statutes," and "that there existed in the larger cities of the state a social emergency, caused by an insufficient supply of dwelling houses and apartments, so grave that it constituted a serious menace to the health, morality, comfort and even to the peace of a large part of the people of the State."

How far this "emergency" doctrine can be successfully invoked to sustain the legislation now before us is a question that can only be answered by the highest court.

The quotation of the statute at the opening of this paper shows the strongest possible declaration of an "existing emergency" as well as that of public policy. Such declarations while not conclusive on the court may exert a powerful influence on the judicial mind and may conceivably be the determinative factor in the final decision.

This article has served its purpose if it points the way to a solution of the question in the light of authoritative decisions made down to the present time.

FIVE

The Gold Clause In F.D.R.'S Supreme Court

Although it took legislation by Congress to launch the New Deal's war on the gold clause, it would be in the Supreme Court of the United States that the major battle would be fought.

In our system of government, the United States Constitution is the supreme law of the land, and the Supreme Court is the ultimate interpreter of the Constitution. During its nearly two hundred years of existence, the Court has decided thousands of cases, many of them interpreting the Constitution, and of those, many of great importance. However only a few mark crucial turning points in America's constitutional history.

The *Gold Clause Cases* are among them.

The *Cases* are of obvious importance because of the crucial role they play in Roosevelt's entire anti-gold program. They constitute the linchpin of his anti-gold clause campaign. But the wider significance of the Gold Clause Cases transcends both the New Deal's war on gold, and the fate of the gold clauses themselves. The majority decision in the Cases provides a rarely seen example of rank judicial pragmatism at work in one of the areas of congressional power most dangerous to individual liberties: money and monetary affairs. Many of the financial and economic problems which have beset this Nation for the past forty years have been engendered by the premises which made possible the majority decisions in the Gold Clause Cases. Much that will heppen to money and monetaryaffairs in the future will come from the same premises. Accordingly, an understanding of the Gold Clause

Cases is essential not only for anyone who contemplates using the gold clause today, but for anyone concerned with the kind of monetary problem that the gold clause is designed to solve.

The *Gold Clause Cases* cover about 140 pages in the official reports of the Supreme Court. There are majority opinions and dissents, and there is much to be said about every aspect of the *Cases*. Accordingly this chapter contains three separate sections. First, an overview of the *Cases* is presented by a lawyer with first-hand experience with them: Angus D. MacLean, Assistant Solicitor General of the United States when the *Cases* were litigated; he had primary responsibility for the government's briefs in all of the *Cases*. Next, Professor John P. Dawson provides an extensive analysis of every aspect of the *Cases,* which should leave the reader with no unanswered questions about what the Court did, or why. Lastly, this chapter contains the legendary but rarely seen dissent by Justice McReynolds, scathingly attacking not only the majority decisions, but also the underlying political, economic, and legal values which made the majority decisions possible. In any contemporary planning involving the gold clause, those values must be considered and then dealt with.

Outline of the Gold Clause Cases*

The Gold Clause Cases, four in number, consumed three days in argument, January 8, 9 and 10, 1935, and were decided on February 18, 1935. Two of them,[1] decided together, the Norman case, which came from the Court of Appeals of New York, and the Missouri Pacific case, which the Supreme Court, on the Government's petition, took directly from the District Court in Missouri without awaiting decision by the Circuit Court of Appeals—a procedure rarely adopted—involved the gold clause in private obligations; specifically, in the Norman case, a coupon for $22.50 attached to a bond issued by the Baltimore & Ohio Railroad, and in the Missouri Pacific case, in which the Government intervened, an issue of bonds by the St. Louis, Iron Mountain and Southern Ry., part of the Missouri Pacific system. The other two, the Perry[2] and Nortz[3] cases, involved the gold clause in government or national obligations, or payment in gold coin or its equivalent; in the Perry case, a Liberty Loan Bond for $10,000, and in the Nortz

---

* Footnote appears on next page.

case, "yellow backs" or gold certificates for $106,300. These two suits were instituted against the United States in the Court of Claims at Washington and the controlling questions in them were certified by that Court to the Supreme Court for answer, a practice permitted when the question is of sufficient importance. All four cases, and others similar in different parts of the country which never reached the Supreme Court, arose out of Public Resolution No. 10 of the 73d Congress, entitled "Joint Resolution to assure uniform value to the Coins and Currencies of the United States"[4] and certain other legislation, Executive orders, proclamations and Treasury rulings or regulations relating to legal tender, the hoarding and surrender of gold and gold certificates, and kindred subjects.

This Joint Resolution, approved June 5, 1933, not only declared all gold clauses to be void, but enlarged the legal tender provisions of the Agricultural Adjustment Act of May 12, 1933, so as to make them inclusive of all coins and currencies of the United States and of all kinds of debts and obligations, public and private.

It is said that gold clauses, such as we are considering here, have been in use for many years, and grew out of the differences in value of different kinds of money circulating at the same time, but the legal tender acts of the Civil War period, which made greenbacks or paper money legal tender for all purposes, with certain immaterial exceptions, stimulated their use and made it general.

This Resolution also, it will be noticed, not only declared gold clauses contrary to public policy, but prohibited their further use, a prohibition, it turns out, which has not been strictly observed. On that point, which is beside our present discussion, it is interesting to learn that some recent issues were found to contain such clauses—due to an oversight of the lawyers, it was said—and Wall Street was puzzled to know what to do about them, wondering whether their insertion would make the bonds invalid, but concluded that it would be sufficient to add a clause or rider calling attention to the prohibition. Although not disturbing to many of us, some idea of the potential significance of these clauses may at

* Angus D. MacLean's † outline of the *Gold Clause Cases* appeared in Vol. 15 of the *North Carolina Law Review*, 1937, pages 249–254. Reprinted with permission from the *North Carolina Law Review* and with the permission of Dennis & Co., Inc. Copyright © 1937 by the University of North Carolina Press.

once be gathered from the fact that the total of private obligations containing them was estimated at 75 to 80 billion dollars and of public or government obligations at 20 to 25 billion, a conservative aggregate of one hundred billion, while gold coin, in which they were all payable, was actually 4 billion in this country, much of it in hiding, and eleven billion in the world. Devaluation of the dollar or reduction in its gold content to the extent proposed by the President meant in effect that every dollar of indebtedness payable in gold, or its equivalent, would be increased to $1.69, if gold clauses were maintained, and practically this meant bankruptcy on a national scale. This was the situation which impelled Congress, confronted by a deep depression, a banking collapse and a money panic, to adopt the Joint Resolution annulling all such clauses. It was also the background of the Government's legal position. Its brief, while strongly supported by authority, reviewed the economic and monetary crisis and to an unusual extent employed graphs and tables to demonstrate that complete financial disaster was likely to ensue unless the Resolution was upheld, not only to strengthen the presumption of constitutionality by showing that the action of Congress was not capricious, but to establish affirmatively a reasonable basis for Congressional determination that the gold clause is contrary to public policy, inconsistent with our present monetary system, under which all coins and currency are legal tender and of relatively equal value, and an obstruction to the exercise by Congress of its monetary and other powers. So impressive were the facts and figures that I convinced myself, at any rate, that the Supreme Court was virtually obliged to sustain the action of Congress, if adequate legal ground could be assigned, in order to save the country; and, from the narrow decisions in the Nortz and Perry cases, adopting the Government's secondary rather than its primary position, I am satisfied the argument *in terrorem* to some extent prevailed. This is by no means to admit, however, that the Government's position did not rest on broad constitutional and legal ground. In these cases, the attack on the Resolution did not deny the power of Congress to control the currency, to declare what should be legal tender, to call in the gold, to prevent hoarding in the flight from the dollar by prohibiting its export; but those who attacked the Resolution contended that they were entitled to be paid in lawful money the equivalent in value of what their contracts called for, and that the Resolution denied them due process, took their property without compensation, the right to payment in gold being a property right, and in part impaired the public debt, all contrary to the Constitution, which not only did not authorize, but prohibited these things. It is recognized that these are formidable positions and they were argued with great force and earnestness, particularly in support of the sanctity of the Government's wartime Liberty Bonds. But the Government's main position was stronger, in my opinion. We relied, of course, on a broad interpretation of the power of the Congress to coin money and regulate the value thereof, and of foreign coin, and gathered much support from certain of the Legal Tender Cases, of which there were several and which, in their day, were as important as the Gold Clause Cases became sixty years later. The Legal Tender Acts, which it is said saved the country in the Civil War, when the notion of coin or hard money was much stronger than it is today, made greenbacks legal tender for private debts and other purposes, with some exceptions. We had difficulty in distinguishing the case of *Bronson v. Rhodes,*[5] which rested on the difference in the kinds of money then in circulation. This case was followed by *Hepburn v. Griswold,*[6] which held that the Legal Tender Act was invalid as to debts created prior to its passage, but *Hepburn v. Griswold* was overruled by the later Legal Tender Cases,[7] in which the Court fully sustained the Legal Tender Acts and made use of the expression "Whatever power there is over the currency is vested in Congress. If the power to declare what is money is not in Congress, it is annihilated."[8] The distinction was also pointed out that the declaration against laws which impaired the obligation of contracts, as the Resolution expressly did, applied only to the States and not to Congress and that the plenary power of Congress over currency could not and should not be diminished by provisions in private contacts; further, that this power could not be curtailed or surrendered by similar provisions in public obligations.

The opinion of the Court by Mr. Justice Strong in the *Legal Tender cases* and the concurring opinion of Mr. Justice Bradley, as well as the later opinion of Mr. Justice Gray in *Juilliard v. Greenman,* suggested that the Government's power in money matters was not only plenary, by virtue of the Constitution, but inherent, and this led to the taking by us of the advanced position that power over coinage and currency is an attribute of sovereignty, as much so in this country as any other.

Secondary positions were also taken, such as impossibility of performance, it being contended that the clauses in suit called for the payment in gold coin, an impossibility—it could not be had, none was available, and its possession would be unlawful since Congress had exercised its undoubted power of calling in all the gold and prohibiting its circulation. In the Nortz and Perry cases, it was also contended that no damage had been sustained or could be shown since legal tender currency would buy just as much and pay as many debts as gold coin—one dollar being equal to every other in value—and if a man had to give up a gold bond or gold certificate for other lawful money he was equally as well off as before, at least in this country, export of gold to any other being prohibited.

Among the cases cited against us were the Feist case,[9] decided on appeal by the House of Lords, and the Serbian and Brazilian bond cases,[10] decided by the Permanent Court of International Justice, in which gold clauses were held to require payment of an equivalent in value, but the decisions in these cases, as we pointed out to the Court, turned entirely upon the construction to be placed on these clauses in the absence of any statute intended to abrogate them, it appearing that the parties contracted in terms of a measure of value and not a mode of payment.

It was also pointed out, of course, that these cases conflicted with no legislative policy or prohibition such as that declared in the Joint Resolution of Congress, and that no question of power was involved. It was shown in the Government's brief that since 1928 Great Britain and various other leading countries had gone off the gold standard before this country; that, at the end of 1932, over thirty countries had adopted measures for the control of their foreign exchange, and that their power to do so was unquestioned. For what it was worth, we were able to cite later the decision of a Netherlands Court upholding the validity of the Congressional Resolution.

The result has now passed into history, so far as gold clauses are concerned, but the decision of the Court was awaited in Washington and elsewhere with great anxiety. When the opinions were delivered, the famous little Supreme Court room was overflowing with Senators, officials and others interested, and I understand that the President himself, at the White House, followed the opinions closely.

The Chief Justice delivered the majority opinions with great vigor and was followed by Mr. Justice McReynolds, who opened his dissenting opinion with the ominous statement that "The Constitution is gone."

In the Norman and Missouri Pacific cases, the power of Congress to strike down gold clauses was fully sustained, the Chief Justice declaring at the close of the opinion: "We think that it is clearly shown that these clauses interfere with the exertion of the power granted to the Congress, and certainly it is not established that the Congress arbitrarily or capriciously decided that such an interference existed."

In contrast, the dissenting opinion begins with the declaration that "If given effect, the enactments here challenged will bring about confiscation of property rights and repudiation of national obligations."

In the Perry case, however, the Court took a different view as to government bonds, holding that the provision of the 14th Amendment that the validity of the public debt of the United States should not be questioned applied to bonds issued after, as well as before, the Amendment, and that the Joint Resolution was unconstitutional as to pre-existing Liberty Loan gold bonds. The Court, nevertheless, sustained the Government's secondary position and denied any recovery to the plaintiff, who was seeking, so the Court said, "not a recoupment of loss in any proper sense, but an unjustified enrichment."

A short concurring opinion by Mr. Justice Stone in this case also aroused great interest, because of his statement that it was unnecessary and undesirable for the Court to say that the obligation of the gold clause in government bonds was greater than in the bonds of private individuals, and because of his suggestion that all doubts might be transferred to the realm of speculation if Congress simply exercised its undoubted power of withdrawing the right to sue. This suggestion, it should be added, was soon followed by Bills withdrawing this right, but they evoked much criticism and were so modified as to permit the right if exercised by a set future date.

The main questions having been discussed in the bond cases, the Nortz case, on gold certificates, was disposed of in harmony with the government's contention that since its power of control over coin and currency was admitted and since Nortz had shown no actual damages and the Court of Claims was not authorized to award nominal damages only, he could recover nothing and the demurrer should be sustained; the Court laying aside the questions whether the government had ever consented to be sued upon its own currency as upon an express contract and whether the suit could be maintained in the Court of Claims as a taking of property without just compensation.

Mr. Justice McReynolds concluded his lugubrious dissent in all these cases with the prediction that "Loss of reputation for honorable dealing will bring us unending humiliation; the impending legal and moral chaos is appalling." It is too close to the event to appraise future consequences, but so far it can fairly be replied that no such chaos has occurred and that even now the three great democracies of the world have turned toward monetary stabilization. What has been decided is that in a conflict between the obligation of private contracts and the power of Congress over the monetary system of the country, the private right must give way to public policy.

Analysis of the Gold Clause Cases*

The gold clause decisions of February 18, 1935, have already taken their place among the great landmarks of American constitutional history. They have given a partial answer to some basic questions of constitutional law. Directly they have disposed of claims amounting to a total of many billions of dollars. But their further implications, both for public and private law, are of even greater magnitude; it may be many years before these wider implications are more fully understood.

* Professor John P. Dawsons article, originally entitled "The Gold Clause Decisions," appeared in Vol. 33 of the *Michigan Law Review*, 1935, pages 648-684. In the article, the author acknowledged that "Mr. James W. Coultrap of the senior class of the University of Michigan Law School has greatly assisted in the preparation of this article." Copyright © 1934-1935 by Michigan Law Review Association. Reprinted by permission. All rights reserved.

The five cases, decided by the Supreme Court on the same day, all involved the constitutionality of the Congressional joint resolution approved by the President on June 5, 1933. The purpose of the resolution, as declared in its title, is "to assure uniform value to the coins and currencies of the United States." It recites, first, that "the holding of or dealing in gold affect the public interest, and are therefore subject to proper regulation and restriction," and, second, that "the existing emergency has disclosed" that obligations calling for payment "in gold or a particular kind of coin or currency of the United States, or in an amount in money of the United States measured thereby, obstruct the power of the Congress to regulate the value of the money of the United States, and are inconsistent with the declared policy of the Congress to maintain at all times the equal power of every dollar, coined or issued by the United States, in the markets and in the payment of debts." The operative language of the resolution is as follows:[1]

(a) Every provision contained in or made with respect to any obligations which purports to give the obligee a right to require payment in gold or a particular kind of coin or currency, or in an amount in money of the United States measured thereby, is declared to be against public policy; and no such provision shall be contained in or made with respect to any obligation hereafter incurred. Every obligation, heretofore or hereafter incurred, whether or not any such provision is contained therein or made with respect thereto, shall be discharged upon payment, dollar for dollar, in any coin or currency which at the time of payment is legal tender for public and private debts. Any such provision contained in any law authorizing obligations to be issued by or under authority of the United States, is hereby repealed, but the repeal of any such provision shall not invalidate any other provision or authority contained in such law.

(b) As used in this section, the term 'obligation' means an obligation (including every obligation of and to the United States, excepting currency) payable in money of the United States; and the term 'coin or currency' means coin or currency of the United States, including Federal Reserve notes and circulating notes of Federal Reserve banks and national banking associations.

The five cases may be divided for purposes of discussion into two groups, (1) two cases involving the public obligations of the United States, and (2) three cases involving gold clause contracts between private parties.

I
Public Obligations

The case of *Nortz v. United States*[2] came up to the Supreme Court on certified facts from the Court of Claims. The plaintiff sued the United States Government, claiming as holder of $106,300 in gold certificates issued by the Treasury. These certificates were in the usual form, reciting that a specified sum in gold coin had been deposited at the Treasury and would be paid to the holder on demand. Plaintiff alleged that he presented the certificates and demanded payment on January 17, 1934; that the demand was refused; and that, to avoid the penalties for the possession of gold certificates imposed by the regulations of the President and the Secretary of the Treasury, he surrendered the certificates under protest and received instead currency of the United States, which was not redeemable in gold, to the amount of $106,300. Plaintiff sued for $64,334.07 damages, representing the difference between the currency so received and the value of the gold coin described in the certificates. The Supreme Court held that the plaintiff had shown no substantial damages through the refusal to pay gold coin and that the action therefore could not be maintained.

In *Perry v. United States*[3] the plaintiff likewise sued in the Court of Claims. He claimed as the owner of a $10,000 Fourth Liberty Loan bond. He alleged that the bond was issued in 1918, was payable "in United States gold coin of the present standard of value," was called for redemption on April 15, 1934, and was presented for payment by him on May 24, 1934. Plaintiff then alleged a demand for delivery of the quantity of gold represented by $10,000 in gold coin at the time the bond was issued or, in the alternative, for payment of $16,931.25 in legal tender currency. On the refusal of the Government to pay more than $10,000 in legal tender currency the plaintiff sued for $16,931.25 damages, "the value of the defendant's obligation." As in the gold certificate case the Supreme Court held that the action could not be maintained, since no substantial damages were shown as a result of the Government's refusal to pay more than the nominal sum fixed in the bond.

The decisions denying recovery in both these cases rest initially on one basic assumption. All the opinions (including the dissenting opinion of Mr. Justice McReynolds[4]) proceed on the assumption that the legislation withdrawing gold coin from circulation and prohibiting the domestic possession or the export of gold coin or gold bullion constituted a valid exercise of the power to regulate the currency.[5] Neither plaintiff in fact contested its validity; the plaintiff in *Nortz v. United States* expressly admitted the power of the Government to appropriate outstanding gold coin, gold bullion, and gold certificates and to compel all residents of the country to surrender them. Chief Justice Hughes, speaking for the majority, went further and declared that "these powers could not be successfully challenged."[6] The constitutionality of the gold-hoarding legislation had already been affirmed by the Federal District Court for the Southern District of New York and an appeal from this decision had been dismissed by the United States Supreme Court.[7] The power of the territorial legislature to prohibit the export of silver coin had been strongly asserted in an earlier case arising from the Philippine Islands, and been explained as a by-product of the broad power to coin money and maintain its parity with other media of exchange.[8]

The denial of recovery in both cases proceeds from this point along lines which appear at first sight narrowly legalistic and which have provoked most of the adverse comment the decisions have received. The argument is that the plaintiffs in both cases, if they had been paid in gold coin, would have been required to surrender it immediately to Treasury officials. They could not have transferred it within the United States or exported it to foreign countries without violating the law and subjecting themselves to fine or imprisonment. It is therefore impossible to say that they have suffered damage, even if the non-payment of gold coin is considered a breach of contract. Accordingly, the argument is that the Court of Claims has no jurisdiction. The want of jurisdiction is not rested on the ground that the obligations in the two cases are not "contracts" on which the Government has consented to be sued; it is due rather to the fact that the damages at most are nominal. The jurisdiction of the Court of Claims extends only to cases where substantial damages can be proved.[9] The net effect of this is—the Government cannot escape liability on its gold clause obligations, but *prima facie* its promise to pay gold is met by payment of currency.

The opinion of Mr. Justice McReynolds, apart from its insistence on the immorality of the Government's conduct, suggests only two arguments by which this logic might be evaded. The first argument is this: "Congress brought about the conditions in respect of gold which existed when the obligation matured. Having made payment in this metal impossible, the government cannot defend by saying that if the obligation had been met the creditor could not have retained the gold." And the opinion later suggests the analogy of a private debtor who seeks "to annul or lessen his obligation by secreting or manipulating his assets with the intent to place them beyond the reach of his creditors." Both the argument and the analogy are unconvincing. If the legislation prohibiting the possession or export of gold is valid, as the dissenting opinion apparently assumed, this exercise of the sovereign power over the currency will inevitably have the effect on private claims against the Government that is attributed to it by the majority. The second argument of Mr. Justice McReynolds, however, is more impressive. Agreeing with the majority that the gold-coin clause carries with it by implication a gold-*value* clause, he argued that the value in currency of the coin promised could be readily ascertained. He pointed out that the Government itself buys newly mined gold bullion at the rate fixed by Presidential proclamation, 15⁵/₂₁ grains to the dollar.[10] It was also urged by the claimant in *Nortz v. United States*, though the dissenting opinion does not do so, that the value of gold coin or gold bullion on foreign markets could be used as a measure of value if the court were anxious to find a basis for recovery.

The possibility of ascertaining the value of gold either by reference to the limited internal market or to foreign markets raised special difficulty in *Perry v. United States*, the Liberty Loan bond case. The court construed the gold clause there involved as creating a secondary obligation to pay *the paper-money equivalent* of gold, in the event that gold coin was withdrawn from circulation. The gold certificates involved in *Nortz v. United States* were evidently not thought to indicate the broader purpose of protecting the holder against subsequent depreciation or devaluation of the currency. By finding that the gold-coin clause in *Perry v. United States* carried with it by implication a gold-*value* clause, the court was led to some of its most interesting and important remarks.

Chief Justice Hughes, speaking in this instance for himself and three of his colleagues, announced the sweeping proposition that the promise of the Government to pay the paper-money equivalent of the gold coin specified could not be repudiated or impaired by this exercise of the currency power. A clear distinction was declared to exist between the emancipation of private obligors from their duty to pay in gold coin or its paper-money equivalent, and a discharge of the Government from its own obligation. The power of the Government to contract against subsequent repudiation or impairment of its obligation was derived by implication from its constitutional power to "borrow money on the credit of the United States" (Art. I, sec. 8). Unless that credit could be so pledged as to preclude any subsequent act of the Government altering the substance of the obligation, the pledge would be illusory. Some support for this conclusion was found in the fourth section of the Fourteenth Amendment, providing that "The validity of the public debt of the United States, authorized by law shall not be questioned." But the essential basis was shortly stated in the sentence: "The right to make binding obligations is a competence attaching to sovereignty." This was true although the obligations so assumed might interfere with a subsequent exercise of another sovereign power, the power "To coin Money, [and] regulate the Value thereof. . . ."

The notion that the sovereign has power to bind itself by contract is no novelty in political theory.[11] In American law it had been asserted in several cases.[12] The attitude of Chief Justice Hughes and his associates in these cases was foreshadowed in *Lynch v. United States*, involving an attempted abrogation of war risk insurance policies.[13] The importance of the dicta in *Perry v. United States* lies in the application of this central idea in a case where the power to contract conflicts with the exercise of an independent substantive power conferred by the Constitution. This conflict is resolved, by eight out of the nine justices,[14] in such a way that the power to contract is made paramount. The implications of this suggestion reach far beyond the scope of the gold clause cases.[15]

A different attitude toward the issues of *Perry v. United States* appears in the concurring opinion of Mr. Justice Stone. He begins by declaring his concurrence in the Court's construction of the gold-coin clause, as containing by implication a secondary obligation to pay the paper-money equivalent of the coin promised. He then says that the only default in performance by the Government has resulted from "the regulation by Congress of the use of gold as currency." While deploring this partial repudiation of the Government's promise, he finds himself unable to say that the exercise of the currency power which is valid and effective as to private debts is any less effective as to the Government's own obligations. To hold otherwise is to assert that the power to borrow money can be so exercised as to restrain a subsequent exercise of the power to regulate the currency.[16]

This remarkably acute opinion presents still other reasons why the majority should have withheld the views expressed in *Perry v. United States*. Not only is it no comfort to the particular litigant to be assured that he has a constitutional right to relief at some future date, but the jurisdiction of the Court of Claims may be withdrawn by Congress before substantial damages have accrued. The practical consequences of these remarks as to the Government's continued liability are still more important. For the time being it becomes impossible for the Government to restore a free gold market and resume specie payments without an automatic addition of some billions of dollars to the national debt.[17]

The opinion of Chief Justice Hughes seems at first sight to be strangely inconsistent. An opportunity is seized to announce a proposition in constitutional law whose meaning is distinctly doubtful, and which has no bearing on the immediate decision. On the other hand, a close and technical analysis of the plaintiff's cause of action for damages leads to a denial of relief, in spite of the strong moral claim which the opinion emphatically asserts. But the inconsistency disappears on more careful examination. A broader strategy must have shaped the opinion of the Chief Justice and secured the concurrence of Justices Brandeis, Roberts, and Cardozo. The moral and political effect of the language in *Perry v. United States* should be tremendous and salutary. On the other hand, the denial of substantial damages to the claimants in *Nortz v. United States* and *Perry v. United States* has its own moral justification. The sharp rise in the value of gold is the result merely of a governmental manipulation of exchange rates. To allow the holders of public gold-clause obligations to profit by this artificial price-rise, production by the Government itself, would indeed result, as the Chief Justice said, in their "unjust enrichment." The sponsors of the Government's gold-buying program anticipated a prompt and spontaneous response of internal prices to the rise in the value of gold. Contrary to their expectations (and in accordance with the predictions of most economists), no such spontaneous response has occurred. The devaluation of the dollar represented in itself an effort to readjust the purchasing power of the dollar after a drastic fall of the world price-level. Until that effort succeeds and the purchasing power of money has been brought down to the pre-depression level, it would be outrageous for one class of creditors to receive an unmerited advantage—to secure a free gift of purchasing power through governmental action taken in the public interest.

The gold-clause decisions will have an immediate and important effect on the monetary policies of the Government. On the one hand, if an attempt is made in the near future to stabilize at the present rate of devaluation and a free gold market is restored, the holders of gold obligations of the Government would automatically become entitled to substantial damages.[18] The present restrictions on private ownership, sale, and export of gold must therefore be maintained unless the Government decides to adopt one of three alternatives. (1) The dollar can be revalued to the old gold content; (2) the Government can compensate holders of gold-clause obligations, as the Supreme Court has said it is morally bound to do, and thereby add approximately three billion dollars to the national debt; (3) the repudiation of the gold clause can be made complete by withdrawing the government's consent to be sued in the Court of Claims on gold-clause obligations.[19] Any one of these alternatives contains the materials for a major political explosion. For some time to come we must expect to remain as we now are, on a gold-bullion standard, with a government monopoly of the gold supply and with free export and import of gold only on the Government's account.

On the other hand, the maintenance of the present restrictions on private ownership and sale of gold will not in itself guarantee an immunity of the Government from suit. The opinion of the Chief Justice in *Perry v. United States* contains some significant language on this point. In demonstrating that the plaintiff in that case had suffered no substantial damage, the opinion argues that the value of the gold coin to which the plaintiff was entitled could only be determined by "a consideration of the purchasing power of the dollars which the plaintiff could have received. Plaintiff has not shown, or attempted to show, that in relation to buying power he has sustained any loss whatever. On the contrary, in view of the adjustment of the internal economy to the simple measure of value as established by the legislation of Congress, and the universal availability and use throughout the country of the legal tender currency in meeting all engagements, the payment to the plaintiff of the amount which he demands would appear to constitute, not a recoupment of loss in any proper sense, but an unjustified enrichment."[20]

The reference to the purchasing power of the dollar as a standard for the measurement of damages opens up some important possibilities. In the first place, it promises to project the courts much further than any American court has yet gone into calculations of monetary value on the basis, presumably, of commodity-price indices. In this respect it lends some weight to the proposal later made in this article, for a general adoption of price-indices in private contracts. In the second place, the risk of liability on outstanding gold-clause bonds should impose a drastic check on purely monetary devices, used for the purpose of securing a general rise in prices. In so far as a fall in the purchasing power of the dollar is traceable to monetary factors there will be the prospect of an automatic and proportionate increase in the national debt (unless the jurisdiction of the Court of Claims is withdrawn).

It is precisely on the issue of causation, however, that the greatest difficulty will arise. Most of the agencies of the Government are now engaged in activities that aim to produce, directly or indirectly, a rise in commodity prices. The production-control and wage policies of the NRA administration, the crop-restriction program of the Department of Agriculture, the expenditures of the Federal Government on relief and public works, the credit policies of the Federal Reserve System, all form part of an impressive program, not consistent in all its details but aimed broadly at the same general objective. As a result of these efforts and of other co-operating factors a rise in wholesale commodity prices has already occurred since March 1933, in the ratio of about 31 percent.[21] The devaluation of the dollar has contributed some share to this price-rise, particularly through its effect on foreign trade, on the speculative markets, and on public psychology; and through the broader base it has supplied for financing government expenditure. Through the other activities of the Government, however, and through the accident of a major drought in agricultural areas, a considerable rise in prices could have been achieved without devaluation and without further additions to the supply of currency and credit. Will it be enough for the holder of a Liberty Bond to show that the purchasing power of the dollar is less than it would have been if the concerted program of the Roosevelt Administration had not been undertaken? If it is enough merely to compare the purchasing power of the dollars lent to the Government with the purchasing power of the dollars repaid, should the holders of bonds issued before 1929 recover anything? Ordinary principles of causation would seem to require that the reduction in purchasing power of the dollars received should be traceable to the devaluation policy, or, more specifically, to the Government's refusal to pay in gold coin of the former standard. In short, the Supreme Court will be faced soon with the necessity for isolating the influence of purely monetary factors on the quantum of damages for breach of contract. The distinction thus required is difficult enough as a matter of general monetary theory; in the practical administration of judicial remedies it will lead to intolerable confusion and debate. More than any other factor involved in the gold-clause decisions, it may make the Supreme Court regret the entirely laudable but premature remarks of the Chief Justice in *Perry v. United States.*

II
Private Obligations

The cases involving the validity of the gold clause in private obligations came to the Supreme Court on two appeals, one from the Court of Appeals of New York in *Norman v. Baltimore and Ohio R.R.*,[22] and one from the Federal District Court for the Eastern District of Missouri, *In re Missouri Pacific R.R.*[23]

The action in *Norman v. Baltimore and Ohio R.R.* was brought to enforce payment of an interest coupon for $22.50, payable February 1, 1934, on a $1000 bond issued by the railroad February 1, 1930. The bond provided that principal and interest should be payable "in gold coin of the United States of America of or equal to the standard of weight and fineness existing on February 1, 1930." The bond and mortgage for $1000 involved in *In re Missouri Pacific R.R.* was issued May 1, 1903. It was payable May 1, 1933, in "gold coin of the United States of the present standard of weight and fineness." Writs of certiorari were granted by the United States Supreme Court to review the judgments rendered below, which were based on the conclusion that the obligations in each case could be discharged by payment in legal tender currency, dollar for dollar, of the nominal amounts due. In both cases the judgments were affirmed.[24]

Chief Justice Hughes, delivering the majority opinion, first reviews the currency legislation of which the Joint Resolution of June 5, 1933, forms an integral part. He considers the meaning and purpose of the gold clauses in suit. Contrary to the contention of the obligors in both cases that the clauses were exclusively "gold coin" clauses which became inoperative when payment in coin became impossible, the opinion declares (p. 413) that their purpose was "to afford a definite standard or measure of value, and thus to protect against a depreciation of the currency and against the discharge of the obligation by a payment of lesser value than that prescribed." That this was the meaning of the parties hardly admits of doubt.[25] Against this construction of the contracts there were only two points that could be urged. First, as the obligors here contended, the instruments would hereby be rendered nonnegotiable, since they would not call for "a fixed sum of money" but for a sum that would fluctuate with the value of gold coin. The Court's opinion does not definitely answer this objection. Whether its construction would affect the negotiability of the bonds is not stated. It was enough for the immediate purpose to hold that in any event the gold clause revealed an overriding intent to protect the obligee against the risk of monetary depreciation.[26] The second obstacle to the construction adopted was the language of earlier Supreme Court decisions, describing similar provisions as promises to deliver, not the specified sum in gold coin, but a certain weight of gold bullion, viewed as a commodity.[27] The Court had no difficulty in disposing of this language. It had been unnecessary to the decisions and had been repudiated in later Supreme Court Cases.[28] It appears then, that neither of these points controverts the Court's interpretation of the terms of the contracts, and the Court's construction seems unquestionably correct.

The second and third branches of the Chief Justice's opinion discuss the constitutional power of Congress over the currency and its power to invalidate contractual provisions that interfere with currency control. The powers of Congress over the monetary system had already been recognized by the decisions in exceedingly broad terms. The *Legal Tender Cases* had decided that Congress could create a non-metallic medium and attach to it the legal-tender quality, in spite of the frustration of the intent of private parties that might result.[29] Even earlier it had been held in Veazie Bank v. *Fenno* that a tax could be imposed on bank notes for the purpose and with the effect of discriminating against such currency and insuring freer circulation of the national currency.[30] In *Juilliard v. Greenman*, the last of the *Legal Tender Cases*, the power of Congress to declare paper money legal tender even in times of peace had been derived from the aggregate of the broad powers to lay and collect taxes, to pay the debts and borrow money on the credit of the United States, and "To coin Money, [and] regulate the Value thereof, and of foreign Coin."[31] More recently the power of the Government to control the use and especially the export of the precious metals, for the purpose of regulating currency values, had been asserted in strong terms.[32] Finally, there was in other fields abundant authority to the effect that contracts between private parties could not stand in the way of the exercise of an acknowledged governmental power.[33]

The main issue was thus narrowed to the single question discussed in the fourth branch of the Chief Justice's opinion. Should the Court accept the finding of Congress that the gold clause in private contracts interfered with the exercise by Congress of its power to regulate the currency? It was on this point that the Court divided. In order to demonstrate that there was some foundation in fact for this finding, the Chief Justice considered first the effect of a literal enforcement of such contracts through payment in gold coin. He declared[34] that their literal enforcement "would be calculated to increase the demand for gold, to encourage hoarding, and to stimulate attempts at exportation of gold coin." The power of Congress to conserve the gold resources of the Treasury by withdrawing gold coin from circulation and prohibiting its export was reasserted at this point, as it was in connection with the public obligations of the Government. In determining whether the enforcement of gold-coin clauses would endanger the monetary resources of the Government, it was entirely proper for Congress to take account of the enormous volume of debts containing the gold clause. The finding that danger existed could not be described as unreasonable and accordingly the legislation in this respect was valid.

But this line of argument would not dispose of the problem raised by the alternative obligation to pay gold *value* when the payment of gold *coin* was forbidden. The Court had already declared that a promise to pay the value in currency of the gold coin was to be implied in gold-clause obligations. Here it could not be argued that the enforcement of the gold clause would deplete the supply of precious metals or violate the emergency restrictions on ownership, sale or export of coin. The argument took a different form. On June 5, 1933, the date of the resolution abrogating gold clauses, devaluation of the dollar had not yet occurred but it was in prospect. Although the precise point at which the new gold content would be fixed was as yet not determined, Congress could anticipate a discrepancy between the values of paper money and gold coin defined by the old standard. The economic consequences of preserving the old standard as a measure of value for paper money debts were declared to justify a general leveling down of all gold-clause obligations. The language of Chief Justice Hughes is significant:

> The devaluation of the dollar placed the domestic economy upon a new basis. In the currency as thus provided, states and municipalities must receive their taxes; railroads, their rates and fares; public utilities, their charges for services. The income out of which they must meet their obligations is determined by the new standard. Yet, according to the contentions before us, while that income is thus controlled by law, their indebtedness on their 'gold bonds' must be met by an amount of currency determined by the former gold standard. Their receipts, in this view, would be fixed on one basis; their interest charges, and the principal of their obligations, on another. It is common knowledge that the bonds issued by these obligors have generally contained gold clauses, and presumably they account for a large part of the outstanding obligations of that sort. It is also common knowledge that a similar situation exists with respect to numerous industrial corporations that have issued their 'gold bonds' and must now receive payments for their products in the existing currency. It requires no acute analysis or profound economic inquiry to disclose the dislocation of the domestic economy which would be caused by such a disparity of conditions in

which, it is insisted, those debtors under gold clauses should be required
to pay $1.69 in currency while respectively receiving their taxes, rates,
charges, and prices on the basis of $1 of that currency.

In analyzing the reasons of the majority for sustaining the legislation it seems important first to consider the general scope of the
currency power.[36] The Constitution grants to Congress the power
"To coin Money, regulate the Value thereof, and of foreign Coin,
and fix the Standard of Weights and Measures" [Art. I, sec. 8 (5)].
It has frequently been observed that the contrast between the
power to "regulate the Value" of money and the power to "fix the
Standard" of weights and measures implies a power to alter the
monetary standard and control the fluctuations in the value of
money. How far may Congress go in regulating the value of
money? First, it seems clear that Congress has plenary power to
decide what commodity shall constitute the monetary medium.
Thus, it could now impress the quality of money on wampum,
wheat, or tobacco, and even, perhaps, make them a legal tender.[37]
Second, if paper money remains the basic medium of exchange,
Congress can select the standard in terms of which the nominal
par of the currency will be fixed. Thus, it is believed, Congress
has a wide discretion in fixing or altering the *quantity* of gold,
silver, wampum, wheat, or tobacco which would be represented
by the currency dollar.[38] If more than one commodity were used
as a standard, as in a period of bi-metallism, Congress could
undoubtedly alter the relations between the commodities used by
changing the quantity of either one which the "dollar" would
represent.[39] Finally, there would seem to be no constitutional
objection to expressing the value of the dollar in terms of commodity-price indices.[40]

In addition to such changes in the monetary *medium* and the
monetary *standard*, there are numerous devices by which Congress can determine *indirectly* the purchasing power of money.
The power to pledge the credit of the United States can be used to
issue paper promises to pay. If issued in excessive quantities, and
especially if the legal tender quality is attached, such promises
may circulate as the standard money and produce a drastic shift in
the level of prices.[41] The machinery now developed for influenc-
ing the credit policies of commercial banks also provides an indirect but effective means for continuous control of monetary

values. In an economic system where deposit credit has become the principal medium of exchange, governments can scarcely be expected to ignore so promising an avenue for indirect regulation.[42] Nor is this list exhaustive. New avenues may be developed. The gold-clause decisions themselves suggest that any commodity or credit mechanism which becomes invested with the quality of money and which vitally affects the foundations of the financial structure may thereby become subject to Congressional control.

Does it follow that Congress can by legislation determine *the value at which money shall circulate?* Literally construed, the power to "regulate the value of money" would include the power to fix its purchasing power in terms of commodities. This of course is another way of saying that Congress may set a general legislative scale of prices. In periods of rapid monetary depreciation a price scale has occasionally been attempted through legislation.[43] Of the great modern industrial countries the only one in which such legislation could hope to succeed is Soviet Russia. In our own country "price-fixing" has lost some of the ominous implications that it possessed until very recently. But the caution shown by the Supreme Court in extending the limits of price-regulation by the states is a sufficient index of its views toward Congressional regulation of prices under the currency power.[44]

On a narrow view the gold-clause resolution of June 5, 1933, could be described as a special form of price-fixing. It applies in terms only to "obligations...payable in the money of the United States." It invalidates any clause in such obligations which requires payment "in gold or a particular kind of coin or currency, or in an amount of money of the United States measured thereby." Contracts for the delivery of a specified quantity of gold bullion (in other words contracts dealing with gold as a commodity) would clearly fall outside the scope of the resolution.[45] But in obligations for the payment of "money," it is now impossible to contract either for payment in gold coin or for the value in paper money that such gold coin may possess. Even if gold coin is returned to general circulation, no person can ask more for gold coin promised in "money" obligations than the nominal value affixed to that coin by the monetary authorities.

But this is far from a recognition of a general power to fix the value of money in terms of commodities, that is to say, a power to fix a scale of commodity prices. The objective of the gold-clause legislation is to ensure complete parity in value between two kinds of *United States currency,* and to preserve their equality in debt-discharging power. To understand the extension of the currency powers of Congress that is involved in the gold-clause decisions, it is necessary to approach them from still another point of view, by considering the scope of prior legal-tender legislation.

The legal-tender acts of the Civil War period were in a sense an attempt to "regulate the value" of money. They provided in substance that the Treasury notes there authorized were to be a legal tender for the discharge of all "debts," public and private (with enumerated exceptions).[46] All "debts" expressed in fixed sums of money, either through private contract, statute, or judgment, could then be discharged by payment of the nominal sum fixed in legal tender notes. The economic effect of the legislation, in the special field where it applied, was equivalent to a "regulation of the value" of money. Creditors were obliged to accept paper money in payment of "debts" arising through the sale of land, goods or services, in spite of the loss they might suffer through the intervening depreciation. But it must be emphasized that the legal tender acts in themselves had no effect on the processes by which the quantum of any "debt" would be determined. Where the debt arose out of express agreement the amount that would be paid was left for free negotiation between the parties. Mr. Justice Strong, speaking for the majority in the second legal tender case,[47] repudiated the contention that the legal tender acts had anything to do with the "regulation of the value" of money. In *Julliard v. Greenman,* the last of the legal tender cases, the Supreme Court made it abundantly clear that the legal tender acts were not an exercise merely of the currency power. The power to make paper money a legal tender for the discharge of "debts" was derived from an *aggregate* of constitutional powers: to lay and collect taxes, to pay the debts of the United States, to provide for the common defense and general welfare, to borrow money, to regulate interstate and foreign commerce, and to coin money and regulate the value thereof.[48]

In none of the cases of the greenback period was it suggested that the derived power to issue legal-tender notes would justify the leveling to a single nominal sum of debts expressed in different amounts. Suppose, for example, that the same parties entered into two separate contracts, one for the payment of $100 and the other for the payment of $169. Congress did not provide in the legal tender acts, and clearly could not have provided, that both debts should be satisfied on tender, in each case, of $100. This, however, is substantially the effect of the gold-clause resolution, in view of the Court's implication of gold value obligations as alternative to gold coin obligations. Suppose, for example, that in 1930 two parties entered two separate contracts, one for the payment of $100 and one for the payment of $100 "in gold coin of the present standard of weight and fineness." By the Court's construction the second of these obligations was, after January 31, 1934, an obligation for the payment of $169. But both may now be discharged on payment of $100.

It appears from the majority's treatment of the public obligations of the Government that this alteration in the amount specified in paper-money debts is an exercise of the currency powers of Congress only in a secondary sense. The gold certificates involved in *Nortz v. United States* were evidently not construed by the majority to contain a gold-*value* clause, which could still survive a change in the gold content of the dollar. There is a strong suggestion in the opinion of Chief Justice Hughes that the devaluation of the dollar was an exercise of the sovereign power over the currency, which would override even an express contract to pay a specified quantity of gold coin.[49] The question would then arise— is not the repudiation of the gold clause in Liberty Bonds an exercise of the currency power which emancipates the Government from all legal obligation? It was precisely on this ground that Mr. Justice Stone found himself unable to concur in the reasoning of the Chief Justice in *Perry v. United States*.[50] On grounds of strict logic the position of Mr. Justice Stone seems unassailable. The solution to the riddle seems to lie in a conviction of the Chief Justice and his associates that the gold-*value* clauses interfere only indirectly with the devaluation policy and that this interference is not so clear as to justify repudiation of the Government's own obligations.

The question would become more acute if Congress should try to prevent the reference by private parties to some standard of value which was not impressed with the quality of money.

Suppose, for example, that an obligor agreed to pay the sum of money necessary to purchase, at the maturity of the debt, one hundred bushels of wheat. If the positions so far taken are correct, Congress could not, under its power to "regulate the value of money," fix the value which paper money shall possess in terms of wide groups of commodities. In the absence of some special ground for price-regulation (such as the regulation of interstate commerce), Congress cannot fix the sum which will be paid for a particular commodity on a cash sale. No more can it fix the quantum of damages which shall be paid for breach of a contract to deliver the particular commodity. Nor, it is believed, can Congress under the currency power provide that a promise to pay a sum of money, measured by the value of a non-monetary commodity, shall be discharged by the payment of any particular sum of money. This would appear to be true (though here our footing becomes more precarious) even if the commodity in question (e.g., wheat) were widely used as a standard of value, and although the forces of supply and demand had driven up its market value and thereby increased the real weight of a large mass of money obligations.[51]

The joint resolution of June 5, 1933, must therefore be understood as an effort to preserve parity in value between different types of United States currency. This purpose is written large over the text of the resolution itself. It clearly appears from the opinion of Chief Justice Hughes that he so understands its purpose and effect.[52] He describes at some length the economic consequences of maintaining gold clauses in force, but in this description attention is directed throughout to the effects of preserving two distinct *monetary* standards in domestic transactions. It is true that the resolution invalidates all references to "gold" as a standard of value, and thus includes gold bullion as well as United States gold coin. The broad sweep of its provisions at this point is justified by the fact that gold, whether in the form of coin or bars, is still the basic monetary medium and standard of reference of most of the world's currency systems.

In holding that devaluation policies are hampered by the use of gold clauses in private contracts, the Supreme Court has not only recognized a perfectly apparent fact but has reached the conclusion which a number of foreign countries at various times have reached. In spite of the hardship to creditors and in spite of the destruction of private rights entailed, foreign legislatures have not hesitated to strike down the gold clause, for the purpose of maintaining the parity of devalued currency.[53] The experience of foreign countries is not decisive on a question of American constitutional law, though it serves to cast some light on the purposes and the fairness of Congressional policies. Even more persuasive is the impressive body of state court decisions at the time of the legal tender acts, holding that gold clauses were *by implication* invalidated by the legislation of Congress making paper money legal tender. The strongest courts in the country, with almost perfect unanimity, struck down the gold clause without the aid of express legislation.[54] The contrary decisions of the United States Supreme Court enforcing specie contracts by way of judgment for gold or silver coin were, at the time, a real innovation.[55]

The economic situation in which we now find ourselves provides a further moral justification for the Court's decision. The devaluation policy has not resulted in a prompt and spontaneous rise of internal commodity prices. Until a corresponding rise has occurred the enforcement of the gold clause in private contracts would result, as in the case of public obligations in the creditor's "unjust enrichment." The value of the gold has been deliberately and artificially raised by the Government, in the course of a concerted effort to induce a general rise in prices. The argument of Chief Justice Hughes is chiefly directed to the effects on debtors of enforcing payment of $1.69 for every dollar promised, when their incomes and assets are measured in dollars whose purchasing power is unchanged. On the converse side, the gain to creditors would represent an increment owed not to their own industry or to an equivalent value contributed by them, but to governmental action undertaken in the public interest.

The gold clause is now invalidated in private contracts for the long future, and not merely for the time being. If and when internal prices rise above their present level, the holders of private gold-clause obligations cannot hope for compensation, as can the holders of government gold-clause bonds. But no real hardship to them will result unless and until internal prices rise above the world price of gold, as defined in terms of the old standard. If they rise to exactly that point, the gold that creditors demand will be worth no more to them than the currency they receive and debtors will presumably be willing to pay gold coin rather than paper money. If internal prices rise *beyond* that point some hardship may arise. But so long as the national currency remains tied to gold, this hardship will be traceable to reliance by creditors on a commodity whose world price is subject to all the influences of ordinary supply and demand and is subject also to political control.[56] It is only in the event that the gold standard is wholly abandoned that the claims of such creditors should provoke sympathy and initiate a movement for their protection.

The outlawry of the gold clause in private obligations seems, then, to be fully justified by considerations of expediency. Nor need there be regret on account of its immediate effects on money obligations. Monetary history has provided no basis for the widespread faith in gold as a stable index of value. The events of the last decade have done much to shake that faith. To insist now upon strict enforcement of gold-clause obligatons would not only place an intolerable restraint on governmental control of the monetary system but would preserve a legal device that can no longer perform its economic function. In England and the United States metallic coin has been largely displaced as a medium of exchange by bank credit. In countries where paper currency still serves as the principal monetary medium, an increasing governmental control of the financial structure makes possible a more effective control of monetary values. Within the framework of the gold standard great fluctuations in the value of money are possible. Against these fluctuations the gold clause can provide no protection. The gold-clause decisions of 1935 are significant, then, for two main reasons: (1) they mark out an important but inevitable extension of the currency powers of Congress;[57] and (2) they may stimulate the development of new devices for protecting money obligations against the risk of monetary fluctuation.

The lines along which such development may occur will be considered briefly in the concluding section of this article.

III
Remaining Possibilities for Stable Value Contracts
I. *Clauses Referring to Monetary Media*

The joint resolution of June 5, 1933, does not restrict its attack to contracts calling for payment in gold coin. By its terms it invalidates any provision for payment "in gold or a particular kind of coin or curency or in an amount in money of the United States measured thereby." The broad language used by the Supreme Court in sustaining the legislation indicates that any express reference to a particular kind of United States coin or currency, either as a medium of payment or as a standard of value, is now precluded.

Gold bullion deserves special attention. It has been suggested above that a contract for the delivery of a specified quantity of gold bullion is not a "money obligation" within the language of the resolution. When the present restrictions on the ownership and sale of gold coin and gold bullion are removed, there should be no obstacle to "commodity" contracts involving gold bullion. The same would be true if a quantity of gold *coin* were sold by weight. Here, however, great care would have to be exercised in describing the coin by weight rather than by its nominal value as money, to avoid crossing the line into "money" obligations.[58]

If gold bullion were referred to *as a standard of value* in a "money" obligation, the language of the joint resolution would apply. The Supreme Court has not been asked to decide whether the legislation in this respect is constitutional. In the gold-clause cases gold *coin* was provided primarily as the medium of payment and secondarily as the measure of value. It would be altogether unsafe to rely on this fact element as indicating a limit to the constitutional powers of Congress. The almost universal use of gold as a standard of value in international transactions impresses it to a peculiar degree with the quality of money. The power to maintain the parity of all kinds of United States currency would need only a slight extension to include this regulation of parity with gold bullion, the basic international standard.

Silver bullion, on the other hand, falls entirely outside the scope of the joint resolution. Not only would it be permissible to contract for delivery of silver bullion as a commodity, but a "money" obligation could refer to it as a standard of value. The objections to the use of silver bullion for the purpose of stabilizing values are economic, not legal. The abandonment of the bimetallic standard by the great industrial countries has left silver free for its wild gyrations on world markets in recent years. The efforts of the United States Government to stabilize its value have had some effect, but its future is still dark.[59]

One other important possibility is to be found in foreign currencies, which can be used in domestic debts both as media of payment and as standards of value.[60] But political and economic risks threaten the currencies of Europe quite as greatly as they do our own. It is not to be expected that private persons in this country will willingly stake their fortunes on the stability of any monetary system in so confused and troubled a world.

Accordingly, we feel justified in confiding that neither through the precious metals nor through the official currency of any country can we now attain the security that the gold clause was intended to provide.

2. *Clauses Referring to Particular Commodities*

The gold-clause resolution would clearly not prevent the adoption of particular commodities or groups of commodities as standards of value in money obligations. In an earlier section of this article it was argued that Congress would exceed the limits of the currency powers if it undertook to level down such obligations to a single basic standard. Nor does it seem that Congress could directly prohibit the resort to *non-monetary* standards of performance, even as the measure of money obligations. If this argument is mistaken, it is enough to say that Congress has not undertaken to do so and is unlikely to do so, unless the widespread use of such devices clearly interferes with Congressional control of money.

The obstacle to the use of particular commodities for this purpose is the instability in market value resulting from uncontrolled conditions of demand and supply. The survival of gold as the foundation for modern monetary systems is not due merely to historical accident. Not only can gold be handled conveniently in small quantities (this is true of iron and copper), but the limited world supply gives some assurance against a sudden flooding of world markets and wide fluctuations in its price. There have been such fluctuations in the past. But with commodities that enter more widely than gold into general consumption, there would be not only the risk of excessive increase in supply, but also wider variations in demand.

The adoption of particular commodities as a measure of

money obligations would not be a novel experiment. Some American colonies, indeed, made wampum, tobacco, wheat, and corn their basic monetary media and in some instances impressed them with the legal tender quality.[61]The depreciation of paper currency during the American Revolution led Massachusetts to issue a tabular standard, based on the value of four commodities, for computing the wages of soldiers.[62] In the period after the Revolution there are records of private contracts adopting a similar device for measuring the sum due in private debts.[63]

More recent monetary disasters have had the same effect in stimulating resort to commodity prices as a more stable index of value than the monetary medium.[64] The richest experience with this device is that of Germany in the great inflation of 1918-1923. A great variety of commodities and services were there used at various stages of the inflation—rye, wheat, iron, wood, coal, potash, and electric light.[65] Also by express legislation in the later stages mortgages were authorized whose amount would be measured by the value of rye, wheat, potash, and coal.[66] At the same time legislation authorized the issue of negotiable drafts in which the principal sum due could be defined by any standard expressed in the instrument itself.[67] Even before this legislation, "rye-mortgage" banks had been organized and "rye mortgages" were executed in enormous volume.[68] The difficulties in translating the values in defined terms of rye into a rapidly depreciating currency made this device wholly unsatisfactory for use by large credit institutions.[69] The fluctuations in the value of the commodities used and the extreme inconvenience in calculating money values by such standards led finally to legislation which redefined these mortgages simply in terms of money.[70]

A recent analysis of price movements has led to the conclusion that for an adequate index of the general level of prices, no less than 50 commodities must be taken into account.[71] It is clearly impracticable for private contracts to provide so formidable a list, with the necessary details as to weight and volume of each commodity involved. Even if this recital were made, the difficulties in fixing the relative weights to be given price-changes in each commodity group and the physical labor of collecting current market prices would present insuperable obstacles and provoke dispute.[72] The costs of litigating these complicated questions of fact would greatly exceed the saving to the parties through the adoption of such multiple standards of value.

Any reference to the general level of commodity prices for stabilization of contracts must therefore adopt a more simplified device for registering changes. It is believed that this device must be developed through the commodity price index, some form of which must apparently be adopted if private contracts are to be adequately protected against monetary fluctuation.

3. *Commodity Price Indices*

The modern commodity price index is merely a more scientific and exact method of recording movements in the commodity prices selected for study. The method chosen for the purpose results primarily from the difficulty of comparing the prices of different commodities directly. If butter is 40 cents a pound and wheat is $1.00 a bushel, one must make a comparison with previous prices before one can judge which of these is relatively high or low. Discrepancies due to differences in quantity and price can be eliminated, however, if the *percentage* in the rise or fall can be measured for a given quantity of the same commodity at different periods of time. Professor Irving Fisher, the most prominent modern protagonist of the index system of calculation, has defined the index number as a "figure which shows the average percentage change in the prices of a number of representative goods from one point of time to another."[73] By combining the percentages of change in the prices of numerous commodities into an average, some notion may be secured of the movement of prices over a fairly wide area. By selecting the prices of the chosen commodities on a given date as a base, the relative change over long periods of time (both forward and backward) may be described.

The device of the index number is not a new invention. It first appeared in economic literature over 170 years ago.[74] The price fluctuations of the nineteenth century produced an increasing interest in the causes of this phenomenon and an increasing resort to the index method of calculation. The theoretical bases of modern systems were well laid before the end of the nineteenth century and some regular series of index numbers had reached the stage of publication. But it was not till the twentieth century that price-indices were subjected to prolonged and intensive study and a variety of different series were continuously maintained. An enormously complicated statistical apparatus has been devised for the construction of price-indices. This should not disguise the fact that the ultimate standard of reference is the current price of specified commodities.

It seems plain that there is nothing in the language of the gold-clause resolution to prohibit the use of this device in private contracts for the payment of money. It has been urged in the earlier sections of this article that the currency power of Congress could not be used to invalidate a clause adopting price indices as a basis for calculation or to prohibit altogether the adoption of this device. If the price-index method of contracting could be shown to a practicable method for adjusting money obligations to changes in the purchasing power of money, any legislature would be convicted of an arbitrary and destructive purpose in attacking such contractual provisions.[75]

The regulation of currency is a subject withdrawn from the competence of the states and committed to the federal Government.[76] For this reason the attitude that the Supreme Court of the United States might adopt toward contracts of this type is especially important. The Supreme Court has in the past asserted a broad power to review state decisions on currency questions, not only as to the form of judgment which should be rendered on money obligations,[77] but as to the construction of contracts calling for payment in money.[78] But there is nothing in the gold-clause decisions or in prior Supreme Court cases to indicate that the sum due in a money debt cannot be made to fluctuate with the purchasing power of money. In one case it was assumed that a contract providing for such fluctuation was perfectly valid.[79]

The adoption of price-indices for the measurement of money obligations involves serious technical difficulties. There are important classes of debts for which this device is wholly unsuitable. For its successful application the co-operation of lawyers and economists will be required, and a new technique must be developed. It is believed, however, that the difficulties are not insurmountable.[80]

The abrogation of the gold-clause has coincided with a new and more determined search for monetary stability. The gold clause was struck down in an effort to dethrone gold from its high place as an international standard of value. It is too soon to say what new standards will emerge, or what new devices will be found for deliberate governmental control of currency values. The "commodity dollar," with its automatic adjustment of the gold content to the movement of commodity prices, seems as yet too hazardous an experiment. Until order has been restored in the monetary systems of the world and we are better able to see where these new paths will lead, a whole economic system should not be exposed to the risk of continued shift in currency values. In a money economy built on the essential foundation of long term credit, an imperative need for monetary stability cannot await the results of political action. And in the end, if political action should achieve the grand objective, the stabilization of money values through private contract would promote and not defeat its purpose.[81] By turning energies in new directions the elimination of the gold clause in private contracts may contribute in a wholly unexpected manner to the achievement of monetary stability.

Justice McReynolds' Corrected Dissent in the Gold Clause Cases*

Mr. Justice Van Devanter, Mr. Justice Sutherland, Mr. Justice Butler, and I do not accept the conclusions announced by the Court. The record reveals a clear purpose to bring about confiscation of private rights and repudiation of national obligations. To us these things are abhorrent. We cannot believe the wise men who

---

* Justice McReynolds corrected dissent in the *Gold Clause Cases* appears in Vol. 18 of the *Tennessee Law Review,* 1945, pages 768–771. It is introduced there as follows:

"In reply to the Editor's request for a contribution for publication in the *Tennessee Law Review,* Mr. Justice James C. McReynolds submitted a revised report of his oral dissent in the *Gold Clause Cases,* [citation in footnote omitted] with the following comment:

A while ago I corrected a badly reported account of my oral dissent in the Gold Clause Cases. I send herewith a copy which you may feel free to publish if you so wish.

It was the position of the bondholders in these cases that the private corporations which had issued "Gold Clause" bonds were obligated to pay in gold coin of the standard of weight and fineness existing when the promise was

framed the Constitution intended to authorize them. On the contrary, adequate words of inhibition are there.

Our views are in print and after a little will be available. I assume those of you who wish to understand will examine them. I will not read them. It may be well, however, to speak of the results to follow the conclusions reached.

I will narrate the situation, unobscured, I hope, by a superabundance of words.

It is impossible fully to estimate the result of what has been done. The Constitution as many of us have understood it, the instrument that has meant so much to us, is gone. The guarantees heretofore supposed to protect against arbitrary action have been swept away. The powers of Congress have been so enlarged that now no man can tell their limitations. Guarantees heretofore supposed to prevent arbitrary action are in the discard.

That statement is not overdrawn; you may expect an unfolding unhappy panorama.

The particular situation: There are three classes of cases; one involves private obligations, another solemn promises by the Government to pay, the third perhaps are still more solemn undertakings.

In harmony with policy sanctioned for many years, individuals entered into contracts which they expected would protect them against a fluctuating currency—a depressed currency, if you will. Such currency is not new; it has been known for centuries. Nero used it. Long ago it was familiar in France.

Many men entered into contracts, perfectly legitimate, and

---

made. Congress passed a joint resolution on June 5, 1933, declaring such clauses void and all obligations containing them dischargeable in any current legal tender, dollar for dollar. The holding of the Supreme Court (4 Justices dissenting) to the effect that the resolution was constitutional as an exercise of Congress' constitutional power to regulate the value of money was significant from the standpoint of popular interest and the financial magnitude of the issues involved and evoked considerable comment from economists, lawyers, and others throughout the country.

There was no official stenographic report of Justice McReynold's oral remarks in the *Gold Clause Cases,* and the newspaper versions of his remarks varied. The following is an accurate report of what he actually said:"

undertook to protect themselves. The lender against depreciated currency, the borrower possibly against an appreciated one. Under these obligations millions were loaned. Railroads, canals, many great enterprises were begun and their bonds sold throughout the world. With them went solemn promises that takers would receive in payment money like that furnished by them. Now we are told Congress can sweep all this away; declare such payments against public policy!

Government bonds: Congress in 1900 enacted a statute declaring that money value should depend upon the Gold Dollar —25.8 grains of gold. Later, that all Government bonds should contain a contract to pay in gold. Billions went out with that solemn obligation in every one of them.

During the World War men stood on the street corners and proclaimed the advantage of such bonds. "We are offering you the finest investment known, the solemn promise of the United States to pay you in Gold Dollars. Our country is in danger, freedom is at stake, your assistance is needed; buy that we may survive." Billions were bought on such assurances. On May 2, 1933, after the Government had commandeered all gold, it nevertheless sold five hundred millions of bonds, containing this same solemn promise!

In 1900 the Government began to receive on deposit Gold Dollars and issue certificates therefor. The Treasury accepted the gold coin. Certificates acknowledged the receipt of gold and promised to return like coin upon demand. Millions of such certificates went out; every one bore that assurance.

In April 1933, under threat of heavy penalties, Congress declared all gold within the United States must be brought to the Treasury and directed the Treasurer to issue for this some form of currency. Millions came in. We left the Gold Standard and refused to recognize obligations. Our currency was depreciated, for all gold bullion received, only paper was offered.

That was not enough. Notwithstanding the five hundred million gold bonds sold on May 2, Congress on the 12th declared its duty to raise the price of commodities and lower the value of securities. Also, that every dollar obligation, whatever the form, should be equal to every other one. And it gave the President power to depreciate the gold content of the dollar to fifty cents.

If in that state of affairs the President had reduced the dollar to fifty cents, the holders of gold securities might have been entitled, under their contracts, to the value of the thing contracted for. But that would not have produced the end desired; so another act undertook to destroy all contracts for payment in gold.

Later the dollar was depreciated to less than 60 cents, and we were told that for all obligations, only 60 percent of the thing contracted for must be accepted.

To that condition our Government came. These suits followed. Not an agreeable situation; certainly not a thing of which I like to speak. But there are responsibilities which attach to a position here—to reveal in all its nakedness what has been decreed is obligatory.

The owner of private bonds demands payment. His debtor replies, 'I have no gold with which to pay. I am prohibited by Congress from carrying out my contract; here is a paper dollar, you must take it.' And this Court holds Congress may sanction that very thing.

The holder of a Government bond, which promises payment in gold, presents it. The Treasurer replies, "Here is a paper dollar which you must accept; we are prohibited from paying gold, and you are prohibited from accepting it." The holder insists, "But my contract provides for payment in gold, or its equivalent." The Treasurer replies, "Take this paper dollar."

This Court, in one breath, declares Congress has no power to repudiate Government obligations; that the Constitution grants the right to bind the Government to pay bonds in coin. In the next it is said, a creditor can get only sixty cents for a promise to pay one hundred, but Congress, although without authority to repudiate debts, has declared unlawful the acceptance of what it agreed to pay. It being unlawful now for him to accept the thing contracted for, he is not damaged! This gives with one hand, takes with the other.

Such argumentation, I submit, is at war with logic and suggests unconscious, though dominant, wishing.

The gold certificates: All gold certificaters recite upon their face that gold has been deposited and promise to repay this metal upon presentation of the certificate. What is he told? "For each dollar, we offer sixty cents; you must take it." "But," he says, "in the Treasury are gold dollars which I placed there upon the solemn promise of return upon demand." The Treasurer declares, "Congress has made payment of gold unlawful; has made it unlawful to receive or keep gold, therefore you are not hurt. True, I do not return what you left here, but I give you a promise to pay something else in the indefinite future; that is now full value." Such reasoning seems to us mere verbiage—a conclusion without regard to fact.

We are told that all this is possible because under the provisions of the Constitution granting power to coin money and regulate its value, Congress may adopt any monetary system and effectuate this by destroying whatever interferes.

It is well to observe the point at issue. Mere generalities with many words avail nothing. None deny the power of Congress to adopt a monetary system. But because Congress may adopt a system, it does not follow that this may be enforced in violation of existing contracts. Congress may not arbitrarily undo what it has sanctioned.

What was the purpose of the grant? Obviously to fix standards and establish a circulating medium; not to cover up repudiation under the guise of law. Congress has full power to provide for honest obligations. Such was the holding in the Legal Tender cases. Here we have a supposed monetary system intended to effectuate plain repudiation.

First, the President is granted power to depreciate the dollar. He fixed sixty cents. Next, attempt is made to destroy private obligations by "A Statute to Regulate the Currency of the United States." Also to destroy Government obligations. The same language —the same section—covers both. Having put out five hundred million Gold Clause bonds in May, Congress declares in June that these promises so to pay in gold are illegal and contrary to existing public policy, although this had been consistently observed for many years and had been approved by the courts.

After this effort to destroy the gold clause, the dollar is depreciated to sixty cents. Prices are to be estimated in deflated dollars. Mortgages, bank deposits, insurance funds, everything that thrifty men have accumulated, is subjected to this depreciation! And we are told there is no remedy!

We venture to say that the Constitution gives no such arbitrary power. It was not there originally; it was not there yesterday; it is not properly there today.

We are confronted by a dollar reduced to sixty cents, with the possibility of twenty tomorrow, ten the next day, and then one.

This thing we utterly abhor. We have earnestly tried to prevent its incorporation into our system without success.

It is said the National Government has made by these transactions $2,800,000,000 and that all gold hypothecated to the Treasury now may be used to discharge public obligations! If the dollar be depreciated to five cents or possibly one, then, through fraud, all Government obligations could be discharged quite simply.

Shame and humiliation are upon us now. Moral and financial chaos may confidently be expected.

SIX

Private Gold Ownership, and the Gold Clause

For forty years, the owners of pre-New Deal gold clause debt obligations did not receive their payments in gold coin, gold bullion, or currency measured by the ever increasing value of gold. Instead, for those forty years, they received their payments in a fixed amount of constantly depreciating paper money. For forty years, they waited for something to happen that would check the relentless depreciation of their assets.

Then, in the mid-1970s, private gold bullion ownership was relegalized, and hope was rekindled for investors who held gold clause obligations. Indeed, some speculators began acquiring pre-New Deal gold clause bonds, hoping that relegalization of private gold bullion ownership would somehow affect the calculus of payment on those bonds.

Chapter 6 first sets forth the anti-gold clause statement issued by the Treasury on the eve of relegalization. Next, Professor Gerald T. Dunne speculates on the question of whether relegalization resuscitated the gold clause. The four court decisions that complete the chapter leave no room for doubt about the answer to that question, nor about the attitude of the Supreme Court.

Important parts of those four decisions sound strikingly similar to the Gold Clause Cases decided four decades earlier.

Statement on
Gold Clause Resolution

DEPARTMENT OF THE TREASURY
WASHINGTON, D.C.

December 9, 1974

The repeal of the restrictions on private ownership of gold effective December 31, 1974, has prompted a number of inquiries on the continuing validity of the Gold Clause Joint Resolution enacted by Congress on June 5, 1933. This statement is issued by the Treasury Department, after consultation with other concerned Government agencies, to help clarify the application of this law.

The Gold Clause Joint Resolution (31 U.S.C. 463) provides that "every provision contained in or made with respect to any obligation which purports to give the obligee a right to require payment in gold or a particular kind of coin or currency, or in an amount in money of the United States measured thereby, is declared to be against public policy...." This law mandates that such provisions shall be discharged upon payment, dollar for dollar, in the current legal tender. It is Treasury's view that the Gold Clause Joint Resolution continues to apply after the lifting of restrictions on bullion ownership.

Under the Resolution a contract clause providing for payment in gold, or in United States dollars equivalent to a certain amount of gold, is not enforceable if the subject of the contract is something other than gold, so that gold as a commodity has no relationship to the business being transacted. In such a case, gold would be used solely for the purpose of establishing the value of the obligation. This view is based on judicial decisions which held unenforceable a lease providing for payment in gold bullion as one method of rent settlement, since the intention of the parties by using gold in the contract was solely to stabilize the dollar value of the rent. *Holyoke Water Power Co. v. American Writing Paper Co.*, 300 U.S. 324 (1937); *Emery Bird Thayer Dry Goods Co. v. Williams*, 107 F. 2d 965 (1939). Similarly, loans or certificates of deposit repayable in gold, or in an amount of dollars measured in terms of gold, would be unenforceable.

In contrast, if gold as a commodity is the subject matter of the contract, then the Resolution would not bar enforcement according to its terms. For example, a present sale of gold bullion or coins and a sale of gold for future delivery (*i.e.*, a gold futures contract) fall outside the Resolution. A similar conclusion has been reached with respect to a contractual provision giving a shareholder, in an organization with assets consisting of gold, the right to redeem his equity, either in those assets, or in an equivalent amount of dollars at the then current market price.

Contracts containing multiple currency clauses, as in the past, are unenforceable under the Resolution. The reason for this is that in the late 1930's the Supreme Court construed the Resolution to prohibit enforcement of multi-currency contracts.

Multi-currency clauses are now common in contracts in international financial markets. For example, bonds are issued and denominated in "Eurcos" which provide for payment in a number of European currencies in an amount measured by an index composed of these currencies. The Secretary of the Treasury has indicated that consideration of a change in the law at the next session of Congress to allow American businessmen to deal in this kind of instrument would be desirable.

The United States law making gold clauses unenforceable has been in effect solely during the period in which private ownership of gold by United States citizens was prohibited. Nonetheless, there is nothing inconsistent between private ownership of gold and the Gold Clause Joint Resolution.* Canada, France and Germany, for example, have for some years allowed private ownership of gold while prohibiting gold clauses.

Finally, this area of the law is subject to varying legal interpretations as in other cases of statutory construction, the final arbiter must be the courts.

Gold Clauses: Dead or Well?**

Toward the close of the historic Hundred Days, Congress passed and President Roosevelt signed a joint resolution which declared "against public policy" every provision in any obligation purporting to give the obligee a right to require payment in gold or a particular kind of coin or currency, or in an amount in money of [the] United States measured thereby.[1]

---

* More than one government agency entertained this view. 4 *CCH Banking L. Rep.* ¶56 *(1975)* reported that the Administrator of National Banks, Banking Circular No. 58 (December 9, 1974) stated that: "Even though United States citizens may own gold after December 31, 1974, they are still bound by the Joint Resolution of June 5, 1933 (31 U.S.C. 463)."

** Footnote appears on next page.

Indeed, it was no coincidence that the gold clause prohibition was the finale of the complex sequence of actions outlawing private gold ownership nor that it became the focal point of litigation in which that outlawry was tested before the Supreme Court.[2]

Singularly, Congress did not expressly repeal the gold clause prohibition in the recent restoration of the right of private gold ownership.[3] Also singularly, the monetary and bank supervisory bureaucracy spoke with a united voice by insisting that the prohibition continued with all vigor and as part of a remarkable effort calculated to undo, at least psychologically, the congressional relaxation of the forty-year-old constraint.[4] Nonetheless, we have Dr. Parkinson's warning that a governmental agency's word may be the last one to take where power and jurisdiction may be involved, and perhaps further analysis may be in order.

The black letter law that repeals by implication are not favored still, of course, obtains. But beyond it, Coke's dictum of *cessante ratione legis, cessat et ipsa lex*[5] can find modern restatement in expressions from the Supreme Court itself. One from the pen of Mr. Justice Sutherland might be summarized as the "arch" doctrine— that the adjuncts fall with the keystone or "that purpose failing, the remaining portions of the act, seeming merely to facilitate or contribute to the consummation of that purpose, must likewise fail."[6]

Also applicable is the doctrine of "chilling effect"[7] which suggests that any action which may numb or inhibit the exercise of a guaranteed right falls under the same prescription as an out-and-out constraint. And here, such is the specific language of the congressional relaxation—that "no provision of any law in effect on the date of this enactment and not any rule, regulation or order ... *may be construed* to prohibit any person from purchasing, holding, selling or otherwise dealing with gold in the United States or abroad." [Emphasis supplied.][8] "Chilling effect" has a special application here. Indeed, "to construe" the gold clause prohibition so as to ban the historic range and sanction of such provisions could well refrigerate the newly given freedom to purchase, hold,

** These observations, by Professor Gerald T. Dunne, appeared as an Editor's Headnote in Vol. 92, Number 9, of the *Banking Law Journal*, 1975, pages 927-929. (Professor Dunne is Editor-in-Chief of the *Banking Law Journal*). Copyright © 1975 by Warren, Gorham & Lamont, Inc. Reprinted with permission. All rights reserved.

sell, or deal into unrecognizability.

Given the conventional tests of regulation constitutionality, it is difficult to see what rational purpose the gold clause prohibition could possibly serve *solo* in its new policy context. As Justice McReynolds' volcanic dissent in *Norman v. Baltimore and Ohio Railroad Company*[9] notes, the clause is neither new, nor obscure, nor "discolored by any sinister purpose." Surely, it cannot be compared to polygamous marriage "in violation of social duties or subversive of good order."[10]

Given the shaky legal base on which the prohibition now rests, bank counsel should be alert for judicial or legislative development which would formally legitimate the mechanism of value stability and be prepared to put it to use once the latter event has come to pass.

Gold Clause Prohibitions— Alive and Well*

Notwithstanding intimations to the contrary in these pages,[1] recent judicial decisions suggest that the demise of the gold clauses has been grossly exaggerated. Indeed, recent decisions out of Pennsylvania [2] and Tennessee[3] suggest that the half-forgotten Joint Resolution of June 5, 1933 is so fortified by Mr. Justice Black's hard-lining opinion in *Guaranty Trust v. Henwood*[4] that any effort to use indexation as an anti-inflationary device in a loan agreement presents the unwary with all the perils of a rusty bear trap in the high grass.

Indeed, this is so, notwithstanding the obviously troubled effort of the Supreme Court of Tennessee to dispel the logical implications of its own decision (notably, the controverted obligation was also scotched as usurious) by asserting that "indexing is a current and very legitimate concept in modern business transactions,"[5] perfectly proper in payment formulas for the transfer of labor and leased property but *not* for money. With all deference, however, and as shown by the quotations of the Court itself, the unmistakable stamp of illegality like a mark of Cain rests on "contractual provisions designed to require payment in a frozen money value

* This Editor's Headnote by Professor Dunne appeared in Vol. 93, Number 2, of the *Banking Law Journal*, 1976, pages 131-132. Copyright ©1976 by Warren, Gorham & Lamont, Inc. Reprinted with permission. All rights reserved.

rather than of a dollar in legal tender current at the date of payment."[6] In brief, the illegality rests upon the calculus, and not the object of the payment, and a word to the wise should indeed suffice.

Decisions

The Equitable Life Assurance Society
of the United States, Plaintiff,

v.

Charles Niles Grosvenor III et al., Defendants. *

Ruling on Motions for Judgment

McRae, District Judge.

Plaintiff, The Equitable Life Assurance Society of the United States (hereinafter called "Equitable" or "plaintiff"), filed its Complaint for a Declaratory Judgment herein seeking an adjudication of the rights of the parties under a certain written lease agreement. The particular controversy at issue relates to whether Equitable as lessee must pay rent to the defendants in the amount of $1,500 a month in currency of the United States or whether it must pay such rent in gold coins of the standard weight and fineness as of May 1, 1927, or the equivalent thereof in currency of the United States. Defendants have demanded payment of the $1,500 rental in currency equivalent to $1,500 in gold coin of the standard weight and fineness as of May 1, 1927. According to defendants, $1,500 in gold coin of the standard weight and fineness as of May 1, 1927, equals 72.5625 troy ounces of fine gold. The rental demand for the month of January 1975 was for the sum of $13,469.63, or 72.5625 troy ounces of fine gold multiplied by $186.00, which was the price of one troy ounce of gold on January 2, 1975. This rental sum will change monthly as the market price of gold fluctuates.

---

* This case was decided on October 27, 1976, by a federal trial-level court, the United States District Court for the Western District of Tennessee. It is reported at 426 F. Supp. 67 (1976). The case is interesting not only because it squarely presents the "resuscitation" issue, but because it does so not in the context of a bond, but in the context of a land lease. After they lost in the district court, the landlords appealed to the United States Court of Appeals for the Sixth Circuit. That court, on July 6, 1978, affirmed the lower court's decision without even writing an opinion. Undaunted, the landlords next attempted to obtain review in the Supreme Court of the United States. Early in January, 1978, that Court declined even to hear the case.

Equitable seeks the Judgment of this Court that its obligation to pay rent is dischargeable by the payment each month of $1,500 in currency.

Jurisdiction is founded upon diversity of citizenship between Equitable and the defendants and the fact that the action arises under the laws of the United States concerning the monetary system of the United States. The matter in controversy exceeds, exclusive of interest and costs, the sum of $10,000.

The defendants are all the parties who have an interest, either vested or in expectancy, in certain real property in Memphis, Tennessee, upon which a multi-story office building known as the Sterick Building is situated. All of the defendants are properly before the Court. Guardians *ad litem* have been appointed to represent unborn children who upon their birth would have an interest in the real estate involved herein, and to represent the defendants who are minors.

All of the defendants have filed Answers. All of the defendants except Memphis Bank & Trust Company, Trustee, have filed a Counter-Claim for Declaratory Judgment. An Answer to such Counter-Claim has been filed by Equitable. Simply stated, the Counter-Claim seeks a Declaratory Judgment that would have the opposite effect of the Declaratory Judgment sought by plaintiff.

Plaintiff filed a Motion for Judgment on the Pleadings based upon the allegation that there is no genuine issue as to any material fact as shown by the pleadings and plaintiff is entitled to a Judgment as a matter of law.

Subsequently a Motion for a Summary Judgment was filed in behalf of all the defendants. The case has been thoroughly briefed and an oral argument was presented on the respective Motions. The Court is of the opinion that there is not a disputed material issue of fact and that the case may be determined on the present record as a matter of law.

By lease dated May 1, 1927, the predecessors in title to the defendants of the land upon which the Sterick Building is situated leased such land to the predecessors in interest of the plaintiff herein. The original lessee and its successors in interest have constructed, and there is now maintained, improvements of substantial value upon the subject real estate. Section Two of said lease provides as follows:

Term, Rental and Taxes

TO HAVE AND TO HOLD the same for the full term of ninety-nine years, beginning on the first day of May, Nineteen Hundred and Twenty-Six (1926) and ending on the Thirtieth day of April, Two Thousand and Twenty-Five (2025) at noon, at which last mentioned date and time, the term hereby created shall be fully and absolutely completed and terminated. The said Lessee hereby agrees and covenants with the said Lessor to pay as and for the rent of the above described premises each year during the full ninety-nine years, being the full term of said lease, the sum of Eighteen Thousand ($18,000.00) Dollars per annum, without any deduction or abatement whatever, in equal monthly installments of Fifteen Hundred ($1,500.00) Dollars each, in advance, one monthly installment to be paid on the first day of each and every month of each and every year during the full term of this lease; *all of which rent and each monthly installment shall be paid by the Lessee to the Lessor in gold coin of the United States of America of the present (the date of the execution of this instrument) standard weight and fineness, or its equivalent to be determined at the time of the payment of each separate monthly installment of rent.* (Emphasis supplied)

Plaintiff contends that the underlined provision of said Section Two, relative to payment in gold or its equivalent, was abrogated and made null and void when Congress enacted the law set out below by Joint Resolution of June 5, 1933, which law sometimes will be referred to hereinafter as the "Joint Resolution" and that said Joint Resolution remains in full force and effect to the present date:

Resolution

To assure uniform value to the coins and currencies of the United States. Whereas the holding of or dealing in gold affect the public interest, and are therefore subject to proper regulation and restriction; and
Whereas the existing emergency has disclosed that provisions of obligations which purport to give the obligee a right to require payment in gold or a particular kind of coin or currency of the United States, or in an amount of money of the United States measured thereby, obstruct the power of the Congress to regulate the value of the

money of the United States, and are inconsistent with the declared policy of the Congress to maintain at all times the equal power of every dollar, coined or issued by the United States, in the markets and in the payment of debts. Now, therefore, be it

Resolved by the Senate and House of Representatives of the United States of America in Congress assembled, That (a) every provision contained in or made with respect to any obligation which purports to give the obligee a right to require payment in gold or a particular kind of coin or currency, or in an amount in money of the United States measured thereby, is declared to be against public policy; and no such provision shall be contained in or made with respect to any obligation hereafter incurred. Every obligation heretofore or hereafter incurred, whether or not any such provision is contained therein or made with respect thereto, shall be discharged upon payment, dollar for dollar, in any coin or currency which at the time of payment is legal tender for public and private debts. Any such provision contained in any law authorizing obligations to be issued by or under authority of the United States, is hereby repealed, but the repeal of any such provision shall not invalidate any other provision or authority contained in such law. (b) As used in this resolution, the term "obligation" means an obligation (including every obligation of and to the United States, excepting currency) payable in money of the United States; and the term "coin or currency" means coin or currency of the United States, including Federal Reserve notes and notes of the Federal Reserve banks and national banking lating associations.

Plaintiff has paid monthly rent of $1,500 in currency since June 1973, when it succeeded to the interest of lessee under said lease. In ¶11 of the Answer, defendants state that such payment fulfilled plaintiff's obligation as lessee with regard to the payment of such rent for payments made prior to January 1, 1975, but not thereafter.

Plaintiff contends that the Joint Resolution is still in effect; that "gold clauses" are still against the public policy and of no effect; and that plaintiff is entitled to a Judgment or Decree of this Court that its obligations to pay rent under the subject lease are dischargeable by the payment of $1,500 per month in currency of the United States.

Public Law 93-110 (87 Stat. 352) and Public Law 93-373 (88 Stat. 445), both of which became effective December 31, 1974, and which are sometimes hereinafter referred to as the "Repealing Act," provide in relevant part:

Sec. 3(a) Section 3 and 4 of the Gold Reserve Act of 1934 (31 U.S.C. 442 and 443) are repealed.

(b) No provision of any law in effect on the date of enactment of this

Act, and no rule, regulation, or order in effect on the date subsections
(a) and (b) become effective may be construed to prohibit any person
from purchasing, holding, selling, or otherwise dealing with gold in
the United States or abroad.

(c) The provisions of subsections (a) and (b) of this section shall take
effect either on December 31, 1974, or at any time prior to such date
that the President finds and reports to Congress that international
monetary reform shall have proceeded to the point where elimination
of regulations on private ownership of gold will not adversely affect
the United States' international monetary position. Public Law 93-110
(87 Stat. 352) as to subsection (a) above and Public Law 93-373 (88
Stat. 445) as to subsections (b) and (c) above.

Simply stated, it is the position of the defendants that the
above quoted statutes repealed the Joint Resolution.

The reasoning of the defendants is that subsection (a) of the
Repealing Act expressly repealed sections 3 and 4 of the Gold
Reserve Act of 1934 (31 U.S.C. Sections 442 and 443), these
being the laws which gave to the Secretary of the Treasury the
authority to issue regulations prescribing conditions under which
citizens could acquire, hold, transport, melt, treat, import,
export or earmark gold for industrial, professional and/or artistic use (31 U.S.C. Section 442) and which provided heavy penalties for the violation of such regulations (31 U.S.C. Section 443).
Until the Repealing Act was passed, ownership of gold except in
accordance with the regulations of the Secretary of the Treasury
was prohibited.

Defendants contend that if all Congress intended to do by
enactment of the Repealing Act was to remove restrictions from
citizens purchasing, holding, selling and dealing in gold as a
commodity, that such could have been accomplished simply by
specifically repealing 31 U.S.C. Sections 442 and 443; but
defendants contend that it was also the intent of Congress to
remove *every* restriction of any kind on citizens as related to
gold, including the restriction on "gold clauses"; and that subparagraph (b) of the Repealing Act was a catchall which
repealed the Joint Resolution. Defendants assert that the legislative history of the Repealing Act supports their position that the
Joint Resolution was repealed by such Act.

The Joint Resolution was held to be constitutional soon after
its passage in *Norman v. Baltimore and O. R. Co.*, 294 U.S. 240,
55 S.Ct. 407, 79 L.Ed. 885 (1935) and *Holyoke Water Power
Company v. American Writing Paper Company, Inc.*, 300 U.S.

324, 57 S.Ct. 485, 81 L.Ed. 678 (1936) as to private obligations and in *Nortz v. United States*, 294 U.S. 317, 55 S.Ct. 428, 79 L.Ed. 907 (1934) and *Perry v. United States*, 294 U.S. 330, 55 S.Ct. 432, 79 L.Ed. 912 (1934) as to governmental obligations.

A primary issue in this case is whether the language of the Repealing Act repealed the Joint Resolution.

In order for a subsequent statute to repeal an earlier statute, the earlier one must either be expressly repealed or repealed by implication. A statute is expressly repealed when the later law designates the statute repealed in such manner as to leave no doubt as to what statute is intended.

Neither the Joint Resolution nor the codification thereof in 31 U.S.C. Section 463 is expressly mentioned in the Repealing Act. Only "Sections 3 and 4 of the Gold Reserve Act of 1934 (31 U.S.C. 442 and 443)" were mentioned.

As the Joint Resolution was not expressly repealed, the issue is whether it was repealed by implication.

Defendants contend that subsection (b) of the Repealing Act was enacted to repeal the Joint Resolution or otherwise there would have been no reason for its insertion in the Repealing Act. Defendants argue that Congress, by expressly repealing Sections 3 and 4 of the Gold Reserve Act of 1934 (31 U.S.C. Sections 442 and 443), removed all restrictions upon private citizens dealing with gold except those contained in the Joint Resolution. In other words, defendants say that except for 31 U.S.C. Sections 442 and 443 there were no other laws, rules, regulations or orders in effect in 1974 that prohibited citizens from dealing with gold and thus Congress must have been directing subparagraph (b) of the Repealing Act at the Joint Resolution.

However, on the date of the Repealing Act there were in full force and effect other laws, rules, regulations and orders that prohibited or conditioned the rights of citizens of the United States with regard to gold; for example, Title 31 of the *Code of Federal Regulations*, Part 53, entitled "Instructions of the Secretary of the Treasury Concerning Wrongfully Withheld Gold Coin and Gold Bullion Delivered After January 17, 1934," and Part 54 thereof entitled and containing "Gold Regulations".

Merely expressly repealing Sections 3 and 4 of the Gold Reserve Act of 1934 (31 U.S.C. Sections 442 and 443) would not have repealed these other pronouncements that had the force of law.

In considering whether earlier statutes are repealed by implication, this Court must be guided by the cardinal rule recently
reiterated by the Supreme Court in *Morton v. Mancari,* 417 U.S.
535, 549, 94 S.Ct. 2474, 41 L.Ed.2d 290 (1974); namely, that
repeals by implication are not favored.

As the Court also stated in *Morton v. Mancari,* at page 551, 94
S.Ct. at page 2483:

> The Courts are not at liberty to pick and choose among congressional
> enactments, and when two statutes are capable of co-existence, it is
> the duty of the courts, absent a clearly expressed congressional inten-
> tion to the contrary, to regard each as effective. "When there are two
> acts upon the same subject, the rule is to give effect to both if possible
> .... The intention of the legislature to repeal 'must be clear and mani-
> fest.'" Citations omitted.

The principles expressed above, when applied to the case at
bar, indicate that the Repealing Act did not impliedly repeal the
Joint Resolution.

Congress only meant to remove restrictions upon United
States citizens "purchasing, holding, selling or otherwise dealing
with gold" as a *commodity.* There is no showing that Congress
specifically intended to repeal the Joint Resolution and allow
obligations to be valued in gold.

The Joint Resolution did not prohibit the purchasing, holding,
selling or otherwise dealing with gold. It only prohibited obligees from demanding payment of obligations in gold. Laws
enacted prior to the Joint Resolution prohibited citizens generally from purchasing, holding, selling and dealing with gold.

The Repealing Act is a statute which was intended to again
allow citizens to buy, sell, hold and deal with gold as a commodity but not to use it as an index of value to measure obligations.
The two statutes are not irreconcilable. Citizens may now deal
with gold as a commodity—buying, selling and holding it, contracting on futures and generally dealing with it as they would
cotton or other commodities. However, Congress did not repeal
the prohibition against its use as an index of value to measure
obligations unrelated to their dealings in it.

The position of the defendants is that the words "or otherwise
dealing with gold" as contained in the Repealing Act were meant
to include such "dealing" as was prohibited by the Joint Resolu-

tion, i.e., using gold as an index of value to measure obligations; thus the Repealing Act was meant to repeal the Joint Resolution and again allow this type of "dealing".

There is a distinction between gold as a commodity and gold as an index of value. *Holyoke Water Power Company v. American Paper Writing Company, Inc.*, 300 U.S. 324, 57 S.Ct. 485, 81 L.Ed. 678 (1936). The Joint Resolution prohibited the use of gold as an index of value.

The defendants assert a second theory, namely, that if the Court should decide that the first theory of plaintiff is correct and that the Joint Resolution was not impliedly repealed by the Repealing Act, then the Joint Resolution is unconstitutional in the light of the provisions of the Repealing Act which allow dealing in gold. Defendants say that to construe the Joint Resolution as prohibiting the payment of rent in gold causes it to become unconstitutional, under either or both the Fifth and Tenth Amendments to the Constitution of the United States.

Defendants would reason that it was only because gold was prohibited to private citizens in 1933 and used as a monetary base or related to the monetary system that Congress could prohibit "gold clauses". However, the Joint Resolution was not upheld on this basis. *Norman v. Baltimore & Ohio Railroad Co.*, 294 U.S. 240, 55 S.Ct. 407, 79 L.Ed. 885 (1935) is the leading case in this field. In the *Norman* opinion the Supreme Court discussed at some length the power of Congress to establish a monetary system as one basis for upholding the validity of the Joint Resolution. In that opinion the Court said:

> The Constitution "was designed to provide the same currency having a uniform legal value in all the States." It was for that reason that the power to regulate the value of money was conferred upon the Federal government, while the same power, as well as the power to emit bills of credit, was withdrawn from the States. ... Or, as was stated in the *Juilliard* Case, *supra*, [*Juillard v. Greenman*, 110 U.S. 421, 4 S.Ct. 122, 28 L.Ed. 204] the Congress is empowered "to issue the obligations of the United States in such form, and to impress upon them such qualities as currency for the payment of merchandise and the payment of debts, as accord with the usage of sovereign governments." The authority to impose requirements of uniformity and parity is an essential feature of this control of the currency. The Congress is authorized to provide "a sound and uniform currency for the country," and "to secure the benefit of it to the people by the appropriate legislation."

294 U.S., pages 303-04, 55 S.Ct. at page 414.

... It requires no acute analysis or profound economic inquiry to disclose the dislocation of the domestic economy which would be caused by such a disparity of conditions in which, it is insisted, those debtors under gold clauses should be required to pay one dollar and sixty-nine cents in currency while respectively receiving their taxes, rates, charges, and prices on the basis of one dollar of that currency. 294 U.S., pages 315-16, 55 S.Ct. page 419[1]

The holding of the Supreme Court in *Norman* may be summarized as follows: (1) Congress has the right to establish the monetary system of this country and to establish a uniform currency; and (2) a valid reason for the Joint Resolution was to establish a uniform currency and to make that currency dollar for dollar, legal tender for the payment of all debts. Congress struck down gold clauses with the Joint Resolution because they interfered with its power to establish a uniform currency.

For the foregoing reasons this Court concludes that the Repealing Act of 1974 did not repeal the Joint Resolution of June 5, 1933. The basis upon which the United States Supreme Court held the Joint Resolution constitutional in 1934 still exists today in that Congress still has the power to insure that all obligations shall be paid in one uniform currency. There is no material fact in dispute in this case and the plaintiff is entitled to a Declaratory Judgment as a matter of law that its obligation to pay rent under the lease involved herein was, and in the future shall be, dischargeable by the payment of $1,500 per month in currency of the United States, which at the time of payment is legal tender. Wherefore the Clerk is hereby directed to enter a Judgment in favor of the plaintiff consistent with this ruling.

Anne T. Henderson and Helen T.
Wilkes, Plaintiffs and Appellants,
v.
Mann Theaters Corporation of California,
a Corporation, Defendant and Respondent.*

Wood, Presiding Justice.

In 1929 the owners of vacant land on Hollywood Boulevard

* Footnote appears on next page.

leased the property for a term of 99 years. Plaintiffs are successors in interest to the lessors; and defendant is the successor in interest to the lessee. Plaintiffs seek a declaration that a provision in the lease that the rent be paid in gold coin of the United States of America is valid. The trial court concluded that the provision for payment of the rent in gold coin is prohibited by the "Joint Resolution of 1933" enacted by Congress (31 U.S. Code, § 463); that the Joint Resolution was not repealed, expressly or impliedly, by the 1973 Amendment of the Par Value Modification Act (Pub. Law 93-110, Cong., H.R. 6912), and that defendant is not obligated to pay the rent in gold coin.

Plaintiffs (lessors) appeal from the judgment. They assert that said Joint Resolution was repealed by said 1973 Act, effective December 31, 1974, and the repeal revived the gold clause in the lease, effective on that date. They assert further if the 1973 Act did not repeal the Resolution, the Resolution violates due process of law. Appellant also makes other contentions, which relate to the contractual doctrines of "Impossibility" and "Illegality."

The case was submitted to the trial court on an agreed statement of facts. There is no controversy as to the facts. Appellants assert that the findings of fact and conclusions of law provide no basis for the judgment; and that the 1973 Amendment of the Par Value Modification Act "mandates that judgment be granted" in favor of plaintiffs. The facts (and findings) are in substance as follows:

On October 8, 1929, the predecessors in interest to the parties herein entered into a written ground lease whereby the property was leased by the lessors to the lessee for a period of 99 years, commencing November 1, 1929. A provision of the lease was: The rental for such 99-year term shall be $1,457,500, which sum the lessee agrees to pay the lessors in installments as follows: $750 on the first day of each calendar month of said term commencing November 1, 1929, to and including May 1, 1934; $1,250

---

* This case was decided on December 28, 1976, by the California Court of Appeal, an appeals court hierarchically one step below the California Supreme Court. The case is reported at 65 Cal. App. 3d 397 and 135 Cal. Reptr. 226. In October, 1977, the Supreme Court of the United States declined even to hear the *Henderson* case. Like the *Equitable Life* case, this case also involves a land lease.

on the first day of each calendar month of said term commencing June 1, 1934, to and including October 1, 2028. "The lessee agrees to pay said rentals to the lessors in gold coin of the United States of America of the present standard of weight and fineness (one dollar containing twenty-five and eight-tenths grains of which twenty-three and twenty-two hundredths grains are fine gold) or its equivalent in lawful money of the United States of America, at such place in the City of Los Angeles, California, as the lessors may, from time to time, in writing, designate as the place for the payment of the rent. But the lessee may make such rental payments by bank check in accordance with prevailing business practices, and the place for the payment of the rent shall be at the Hollywood Office of California Bank in the City of Los Angeles, California, until otherwise specified by the lessors as aforesaid."

A theatre building was constructed on the land; and, through mesne conveyances, the plaintiffs are the lessors, and the defendant is the lessee, of the ground lease.

In June 1933, Congress enacted the Joint Resolution of 1933 as the result of the monetary change referred to as "going off the gold standard." Said Joint Resolution was thereafter codified in section 463 of Title 31 of the United States Code, as follows:

"Provision for payment of obligations in gold prohibited; uniformity in value of coins and currencies

"(a) Every provision contained in or made with respect to any obligation which purports to give the obligee a right to require payment in gold or a particular kind of coin or currency, or in an amount in money of the United States measured thereby, is declared to be against public policy; and no such provision shall be contained in or made with respect to any obligation hereafter incurred. Every obligation, heretofore or hereafter incurred, whether or not any such provision is contained therein or made with respect thereto, shall be discharged upon payment, dollar for dollar, in any coin or currency which at the time of payment is legal tender for public and private debts. Any such provision contained in any law authorizing obligations to be issued by or under authority of the United States, is repealed, but the repeal of any such provision shall not invalidate any other provision or authority contained in such law.

"(b) As used in this section, the term 'obligation' means an obligation (including every obligation of and to the United States, excepting currency) payable in money of the United States; and the term 'coin or currency' means coin or currency of the United States, including Federal Reserve banks and national banking associations. June 5, 1933, c. 48, § 1, 48 Stat. 113."

Since the enactment of said Joint Resolution in 1933, the lessee has paid and is presently paying the rent due under the herein lease in legal tender of the United States, including payment of $1,250 for the month of January 1975 and $1,250 for the month of February 1975.

In September 1973, the Congress enacted Public Law 93-110 (93rd Cong., H.R. 6912), which provides in part as follows:

"An Act to amend the Par Value Modification Act, and for other purposes ...

"Sec. 3. (a) Sections 3 and 4 of the Gold Reserve Act of 1934 (31 U.S.C. 442 and 443) are repealed.

"(b) No provision of any law in effect on the date of enactment of this Act, and no rule, regulation, or order under authority of any such law, may be construed to prohibit any person from purchasing, holding, selling, or otherwise dealing with gold."

In July 1974, Congress enacted Public Law 93-373 (93rd Cong., S.2665, 88 Stat. 445) which provides in part as follows:

"Sec. 2. Subsections 3(b) and (c) of Public Law 93-110 (87 Stat. 352) are repealed and in lieu thereof add the following:

"(b) No provision of any law in effect on the date of enactment of this Act, and no rule, regulation, or order in effect on the date sub-sections (a) and (b) become effective may be construed to prohibit any person from purchasing, holding, selling, or otherwise dealing with gold in the United States or abroad.

"(c) The provisions of subsections (a) and (b) of this section shall take effect either on December 31, 1974, or at any time prior to such date that the President finds and reports to Congress that international monetary reform shall have proceeded to the point where elimination of regulations on private ownership of gold will not adversely affect the United States' international monetary position." Said provisions became effective on December 31, 1974.

The trial court's conclusions of law were in substance as follows: Enforcement of the gold clause provision of the lease pertaining to payment of the rent in gold coin of the United States is prohibited by the provisions of the Joint Resolution of 1933. Defendant is not obligated to make payment in gold coin of the weight and fineness in effect on October 8, 1929, or its equivalent in lawful money of the United States. The Joint Resolution of 1933 was not repealed, either expressly or by implication by the 1973 Amendment of the Par Value Modification Act. The gold clause provision of the lease was not and is not a contract for payment in gold coin or gold bullion as a commodity, but was and is a contract for the payment of money. Defendant has fully performed all conditions of the lease to be performed on its part and has fully discharged its obligation to pay rent to plaintiffs for the months of January and February 1975.

(As hereinabove stated, defendant paid $1,250 as rent for each of those months. Plaintiffs alleged in their complaint that the rental due for those months in gold coin or its equivalent was $19,300.)

As above stated, appellants assert that the trial court erred in concluding that the 1973 Act did not repeal the Joint Resolution of 1933, expressly or impliedly.

As above shown, section 3, subdivision (a) of the 1973 Act expressly repealed sections 3 and 4 of the Gold Reserve Act of 1934 (31 U.S.C. §§ 442, 443). No provision of the 1973 Act expressly repealed the Joint Resolution of 1933. A recognized rule of statutory construction is that the expression of certain things in a statute necessarily involves exclusion of other things not expressed— *expressio unius est exclusio alterius.* (See *Gilgert v. Stockton Port District,* 7 Cal.2d 384, 387, 60 P.2d 847.)

Appellants argue that subdivision (b) of section 3 of said 1973 Act impliedly repealed the Joint Resolution of 1933. Subdivision (b), as heretofore stated, provides that "No provision of any law in effect on the date of enactment of the Act, and no rule, regulation, or order under authority of any such law, may be construed to prohibit any person from purchasing, holding, selling, or otherwise dealing with gold."

Appellants assert that subdivision (b) "effectively repealed all laws restricting transactions in gold," and that legislative intent to repeal "all laws which prohibit the private purchase or dealing with gold" is shown by cited statements of a congressional committee that analyzed the bill from which the Act arose and by a cited statement by Representative Windall. One of the cited statements of the committee (H.R. Rep. No. 93-203, 93rd Cong., 1st Sess., 2 U.S.Code Cong. and Adm.News 1973, pp. 2050, 2052) is that said section 3 of the Act "would repeal the statutory and regulating provisions now applying to the ownership of gold ... [s]pecifically, this section would repeal sections 3 and 4 of the Gold Reserve Act of 1934, and all other laws, rules and regulations and orders which prohibit any person from purchasing, holding, selling, or otherwise dealing in gold." The other cited statement by the committee (H.R.Rep. No. 93-203, *supra*, p. 2062) is that "... we approved an amendment repealing Sections 3 and 4 of the Gold Reserve Act, which provides ... that regulations now in effect prohibiting purchase, sale, holding or other dealing in gold shall be repealed. ..." The cited statement by Representative Windall is, "... Americans should be able to own or deal in gold as they do in any other commodity." (119 Cong.Rec. H. 16970 (2d Col.) May 29, 1973.)

As respondent states, those cited statements in effect relate to the purchase, sale, and holding of gold as a commodity. Respondent concedes that the 1973 Act abrogated statutory or regulatory provisions relating to *ownership* of gold as a *commodity;* but respondent does assert that the 1973 Act was not intended to affect the Joint Resolution of 1933, which denied gold monetary standing, e.g., for payment of debts in gold.

Contrary to appellants' assertion that the intent of the 1973 Act was to "effectively repeal all laws restricting transactions in gold," some sections of Title 31 of the United Stated Code remain in effect, for example, section 315b thereof which discontinues gold coinage, and section 446 thereof which provides that all acts inconsistent with said section 315b are repealed. As respondent asserts, appellants are arguing in effect that the gold monetary standard was reinstated by the 1973 Act.

Congressional intent regarding the 1973 Act was stated by the chairman of the subcommittee which handled the bill, as follows: "I want to emphasize that this would not mean that we intend to allow the writing of contracts in gold, or otherwise change the joint resolution on gold. Our intention is merely to allow individuals to buy, sell and own gold if and when it is possible to do this without sacrificing our national interest."[1] (119 Cong.Rec. 16968 [May 29, 1973].) A representative sponsoring the bill stated: "It is essential that the language be quite clear, that what we are proposing is simply the elimination of any impediment upon American citizens from *ownership* of gold." (Italics added.) (119 Cong.Rec. 16980 [May 29, 1973].)

Governmental agencies have interpreted the 1973 Act as not repealing or modifying the Joint Resolution of 1933.[2] Administrative interpretation of a statute will be afforded great respect by the courts. (*Noroian v. Department of Administration*, 11 Cal. App.3d 651, 655, 89 Cal.Rptr. 889.)

In *Holyoke Water Power Co. v. American Writing Paper Co.* (1937), 300 U.S. 324, 57 S.Ct. 485, 81 L.Ed. 678, a lease entered into prior to the Joint Resolution of 1933 provided for payment of rent in "a quantity of gold which shall be equal in amount to fifteen hundred dollars ($1500) of the gold coin of the United States of the standard of weight and fineness of the year 1894, or the equivalent of this commodity in United States currency." In 1934 (after Congress passed the Joint Resolution of 1933), the lessor contended that the rent was payable in fine gold as provided in the lease, and the lessee contended that by force of the Joint Resolution the rent was payable dollar for dollar, in the then prevailing currency. The district court and the circuit court of appeals held in favor of the lessee. The Supreme Court affirmed the judgment, and said (p. 335, 57 S.Ct. p. 487): "The obligation was one for the payment of money, and not for delivery of gold as upon the sale of a commodity."

It was also said therein (300 U.S. at p. 337, 57 S.Ct. at p. 488): "A contract for the payment of gold as the equivalent of money, and a fortiori a contract for the payment of money measurable in gold, is within the letter of the Joint Resolution of June 5, 1933, and equally within its spirit." The court also rejected (pp. 340-341, 57 S.Ct. 485) an argument that the Joint Resolution, although made for protection of the monetary system, arbitrarily suppressed the rental covenant and was inconsistent with the Fifth Amendment.

The court therein concluded (p. 341, 57 S.Ct. p. 490): "In last analysis, the case for the petitioner amounts to little more than this, that the effect of the Resolution in its application to these leases is to make the value of dollars fluctuate with variations in the weight and fineness of the monetary standard, and thus defeat the expectation of the parties that the standard would be constant and the value relatively stable. Such, indeed, *is* the effect, and the covenant of the parties is to that extent abortive. But the disappointment of expectations and even the frustration of contracts may be a lawful exercise of power when expectation and contract are in conflict with the public welfare. 'Contracts may create rights of property, but, when contracts deal with a subject-matter which lies within the control of the Congress, they have a congenital infirmity.' *Norman v. Baltimore & Ohio R. Co., supra,* 294 U.S. 240 at pages 307, 108, 55 S.Ct. 407, 416, 79 L.Ed. 885, A.L.R. 1352. To that congenital infirmity this covenant succumbs."

In the *Norman* case *(Norman v. Baltimore & O.R. Co.,* 294 U.S. 240, 55 S.Ct. 407, 79 L.Ed. 885), cited in the *Holyoke* case, *supra,* the Supreme Court discussed (pp. 295 et seq., 55 S.Ct. 407.) the background and purposes of the Joint Resolution of 1933—in essence the purposes of establishing a monetary system not based upon gold and removal of gold as legal tender; discussed clauses of contracts providing for payment in gold, and held (p. 302, 55 S.Ct. 407) that the gold clauses in the bonds in that case were not contracts for payment in gold coin as a commodity but were contracts for payment of money; discussed (pp. 306-311, 55 S.Ct. 407) the power of Congress to regulate currency and to establish the monetary system for the country, and held (p. 311, 55 S.Ct. 407) that such gold clauses interfered with the policy of Congress in exercising that authority. The court noted (p. 315, 55 S.Ct. 407) that according to appellants' contentions, the indebtedness of governmental and industrial obligors under gold clause provisions must be met by an amount of currency determined by the former gold standard, whereas the receipts of such obligors would be determined under the new (non-gold) standard, and that dislocation of the domestic economy would be caused by such a disparity of conditions. Then it was said (p. 316, 55 S.Ct. p. 419):

"We are not concerned with consequences, in the sense that consequences, however serious, may excuse an invasion of constitutional right. We are concerned with the constitutional power of the Congress over the monetary system of the country and its attempted frustration. Exercising that power, the Congress has undertaken to establish a uniform currency, and parity between kinds of currency, and to make that currency, dollar for dollar, legal tender for the payment of debts. ... The contention that these gold clauses are valid contracts and cannot be struck down proceeds upon the assumption that private parties, and states and municipalities, may make and enforce contracts which may limit that authority. Dismissing that untenable assumption, the facts must be faced. We think that it is clearly shown that these clauses interfere with the exertion of the power granted to the Congress, and certainly it is not established that the Congress arbitrarily or capriciously decided that such an interference existed."

In the present case, the trial court did not err in concluding that the Joint Resolution of 1973 was not repealed. The Joint Resolution is not unconstitutional. (See *Holyoke Water Power Co. v. American Writing Paper Co., supra,* 300 U.S. 324, 57 S.Ct. 485, 81 L.Ed. 678; *Norman v. Baltimore & O. R. Co., supra,* 294 U.S. 240, 55 S.Ct. 407, 79 L.Ed. 885.)

Appellants' contentions regarding the contractual doctrines of "Impossibility" and "Illegality" are to the effect that if it is impossible or illegal to pay the rent in gold coin, then it should be payable in gold bullion.[3] A similar argument was rejected in the *Holyoke* case, *supra,* 300 U.S. at pp. 334-335, 57 S. Ct. 485. The trial court herein did not err in concluding that the gold clause provision of the lease was not a contract for payment in gold coin or gold bullion, but was a contract for the payment of money.

The judgment is affirmed.
LILLIE and HANSON, JJ., concur.

RALPH FELDMAN AND MARK LOREN, INDIVIDUALLY, AND FOR THE BENEFIT OF OTHERS SIMILARLY SITUATED, PLAINTIFFS,
v.
GREAT NORTHERN RAILWAY COMPANY ET AL., DEFENDANTS.*

Opinion,
MacMahon, District Judge.

These cross-motions for summary judgment on stipulated facts,

---

* Footnote appears on next page.

under Rule 56, Fed.R.Civ.P., present the question of whether recent congressional enactments,[1] repealing the long-standing prohibition on private ownership of, and speculation in, gold, also repealed the "Gold Clause Resolution"[2] which prohibited enforcement of any contractual clause providing for payment of an obligation in gold or any amount of money measured by gold. We conclude that the Gold Clause Resolution has not been repealed and that it is still in full force and effect.

Facts

Plaintiffs are the holders of Great Northern Railway Company General Mortgage 4½% Gold Bonds, Series D ("the bonds"). The bonds were issued under a trust indenture, dated January 1, 1921, and provided for semi-annual interest payments until maturity on July 1, 1976, when the principal amount of $1,000 per bond would become payable. Both principal and interest were payable "in gold coin of the United States of America of or equal to the standard of weight and fineness as it existed on the first day of July, 1921. ..."

Defendant, Burlington Northern Inc. (successor obligor of the bonds),[3] has offered to pay plaintiffs the $1,000 face amount of each bond, dollar for dollar, in currency of the United States. Plaintiffs have refused to accept the face amount of the bonds in dollars, contending that they are entitled to the market value, as of the maturity date, of the quantity of gold represented by the gold coin specified in the bonds as the medium of payment.

The parties stipulate that due to inflation, $6,523.94 was the market value on July 1, 1976 of the quantity of gold represented by $1,000 in gold coin of the standard of weight and fineness specified in the bonds. Thus, if plaintiffs' contention is correct, holders of these bonds would be entitled to more than six and one-half times the face amounts.

---

* This case was decided on March 16, 1977, by the United States District Court for the Southern District of New York. It is reported at 428 F.Supp. 979. Unlike the *Equitable Life* and *Henderson* cases, this one does involve a bond. Notwithstanding this difference, it is interesting how the courts' opinions in those cases are paralleled in Judge MacMahon's opinion in this one.

It appears that the subject bonds are the first "gold clause" bonds to mature since the lifting of restrictions on private gold ownership. Two other courts, however, have recently considered the application of the Gold Clause Resolution to lease obligations, and both share our conclusion that the Resolution is still in effect. See *Equitable Life Assur. Soc. v. Grosvenor*, 426 F.Supp. 67 (W.D.Tenn., 1976); *Henderson v. Mann Theatres Corp.*, 65 Cal. App. 397, 135 Cal.Rptr. 266 (1976).

Discussion

An initial problem is presented by the fact that the actual medium of payment specified in the bonds is no longer available. The bonds call for payment in gold coin of the United States, but the United States has not issued gold coin for more than forty years, all gold coin has been officially withdrawn from circulation and converted to bullion, and currency of the United States is no longer redeemable in gold.[4] Plaintiffs apparently assume that, since the specified gold coin is unavailable, they are entitled to an equivalent amount of *any* legal tender, calculated on the weight and relative value of the quantum of gold contained in 1921 gold coin. Another possibility not suggested by either party is that, if payment in gold were enforced literally according to the terms of the bonds, defendants would be entitled to gold coin, presumably available to some extent, and probably at great expense, in the numismatic market. In view of our conclusion that the Gold Clause Resolution is still in force, we need not pass on either of these possibilities.

The Gold Clause Resolution

When Congress enacted the Gold Clause Resolution (set out in full in the margin),[5] it plainly intended to make gold clauses unenforceble. In the preamble to the Resolution, Congress found that such clauses requiring payment in gold or a particular kind of coin "obstruct the power of the Congress to regulate the value of the money of the United States, and are inconsistent with the declared policy of the Congress to maintain at all times the equal power of every dollar. ..." The Resolution declared any such provisions to be against public policy and provided:

Every obligation, heretofore or hereafter incurred, whether or not any such provision is contained therein or made with respect thereto, shall be discharged upon payment, dollar for dollar, in any coin or currency which at the time of payment is legal tender for public and private debts.

In response to the expected constitutional challenge to the Resolution, the Supreme Court, in *Norman v. Baltimore & O. R. R.*, 294 U.S. 240, 55 S.Ct., 407, 79 L.Ed. 885 (1935), discussed extensively the historical prelude to the Gold Clause Resolution and upheld the power of Congress, based on its constitutional authority over the monetary and currency system, to enact the Resolution and invalidate private contracts for payment in gold or any amount of money indexed to gold. The Court in *Norman* held invalid and unenforceable a gold clause with language identical to that here.[6]

It is clear, therefore, that the gold clause contained in these Great Northern Bonds is invalid and unenforceable if the Gold Clause Resolution is still in effect. The saga, however, does not end there.

Restrictions on Private Gold Ownership and Use

Subsequent to the Gold Clause Resolution, along with numerous other Depression-era measures designed to reduce the monetary and speculative importance of gold,[7] Congress enacted the Gold Reserve Act of 1934.[8] Section 3 of the Gold Reserve Act, 31 U.S.C. § 442, directed the Secretary of the Treasury, with approval of the President, to promulgate regulations prescribing the conditions under which gold could be acquired and held, for certain permissible uses only, *e.g.*, "industrial, professional, and artistic use." Purchasing, holding, selling or dealing in gold for investment or speculation was specifically forbidden by regulations issued pursuant to Section 3. See, *e.g.*, 31 C.F.R. §§ 54.14 (b), 54.15 (1974). Section 4 of the Gold Reserve Act, 31 U.S.C. § 443, provided for forfeiture of any gold held or used in violation of the Act or regulations issued under it, along with certain specified penalties for such violation. This ban on private ownership and use of gold remained in effect for nearly forty years.

Repeal of the Restrictions

In 1973 and 1974, Congress enacted what we will refer to as the

"Gold Ownership Amendments,"[9] in which the prohibitions on gold ownership were lifted, by repealing Sections 3 and 4 of the Gold Reserve Act, and by further providing that no law, rule, regulation or order "may be construed to prohibit any person from purchasing, holding, selling, or *otherwise dealing with gold in the United States or abroad*" (emphasis added).

The first of the Gold Ownership Amendments, Pub.L. 93-110,[10] was to become effective when the President reported to Congress that "elimination of regulations on private ownership of gold will not adversely affect the United States' international monetary position." The second of the Amendments, Pub.L. 93-373,[11] adopted minor changes in phrasing and provided for automatic effectiveness of the Amendment on December 31, 1974, if the President did not so report before that date. There was no such report, and the Amendment thus became effective December 31, 1974.

Effect of the Gold Ownership Amendments
on the Gold Clause Resolution

Plaintiffs contend that the Gold Ownership Amendments revive the enforceability of pre-1933 gold clauses since no law, rule, regulation or order may now be construed to prohibit any person from purchasing, holding, selling or otherwise dealing with gold. According to plaintiffs, obligors on pre-1933 bonds containing gold clauses must therefore pay in gold or an amount of money indexed to gold!

We conclude, however, that by enacting the Gold Ownership Amendments, thereby permitting a general range of activities and uses of gold as a commodity, Congress did not intend to supplant its earlier Resolution specifically proscribing the use of gold as a medium or measure of payment of contractual obligations.

We note at the outset that there is no explicit repeal, or even mention of the Gold Clause Resolution anywhere in the Gold Ownership Amendments. Yet, Congress did manifest the clearest possible intention to repeal the gold *ownership* provisions of the Gold Reserve Act, using the following specific language: "Sections 3 and 4 of the Gold Reserve Act of 1934 (31 U.S.C. 442 and 443) are repealed."[12] Having adopted such explicit language to repeal one aspect of gold regulation (private ownership of gold), we do not believe Congress intended to repeal yet another aspect (use of gold clauses in contracts) by silence.

The question remains, however, whether the declared congressional intention to lift the prohibition against persons "dealing with gold" repeals the Gold Clause Resolution by implication. We conclude that it does not.

Repeal by implication is not favored, *Morton v. Mancari*, 417 U.S. 535, 549-50, 94 S.Ct. 2474, 41 L.Ed.2d 290 (1974); *United States v. Philadelphia Nat'l Bank*, 374 U.S. 321, 350, 83 S.Ct. 1715, 10 L.Ed.2d 915 (1962); *Wood v. United States*, 41 U.S. (16 Pet.) 342, 363, 10 L.Ed. 987 (1842), and before finding that an earlier statute is impliedly repealed by a later one, courts insist upon a clear expression of a congressional purpose to do so. As the Supreme Court said in *Morton v. Mancari, supra:*

> The courts are not at liberty to pick and choose among congressional enactments and when two statutes are capable of co-existence, it is the duty of the courts, *absent a clearly expressed congressional intention to the contrary*, to regard each as effective." 417 U.S. at 551, 94 S.Ct. at 2483 (emphasis added). See also *United States v. Borden Co.*, 308 U.S. 188, 198, 60 S.Ct. 182, 84 L.Ed. 181 (1939).

A later statute will be construed as impliedly repealing an earlier one only in cases of plain repugnancy between them. *Morton v. Mancari, supra*, 417 U.S. at 550, 94 S.Ct. 2474; *Georgia v. Pennsylvania R. R.*, 324 U.S. 439, 456-57, 65 S. Ct. 716, 89 L.Ed. 1051 (1945).

We see no basic inconsistency or positive repugnancy in granting persons general permission to purchase, sell, hold or otherwise deal with gold, while denying them the right to demand payment of obligations indexed to a certain value of gold. These statutes thus can coexist.

Standing together, the Gold Ownership Amendments and the Gold Clause Resolution permit the general range of activities incident to ownership of gold as a commodity, while denying the one specific use which has long since been declared against public policy. In addressing just such a situation, the Supreme Court recently reaffirmed another principle of statutory construction, that "a statute dealing with a narrow, precise and specific subject is not submerged by a later-enacted statute covering a more generalized spectrum." *Radzanower v. Touche Ross & Co.*, 426 U.S. 148, 153,

96 S.Ct. 1989, 1992-1993, 48 L.Ed.2d 540 (1976) (citing *Morton v. Mancari, supra*). Viewed in this light, *absent a clear congressional intention* to undercut the dominant congressional purpose of nullifying gold clauses in contractual obligations, we do not consider the general permission conferred by the Gold Ownership Amendments to have "submerged" the specific prohibition of the Gold Clause Resolution.

Not content to rest on wooden application of these familiar canons of statutory construction, we have searched the legislative history of the Gold Ownership Amendments for an expression of congressional intent respecting the Gold Clause Resolution. We have found only sparse references to the Gold Clause Resolution, none of which manifest an intention to repeal it.

On May 1, 1973, in the Senate hearings considering private ownership of gold,[13] the following brief colloquy took place between Senator Johnston, Chairman of the subcommittee, and Jack F. Bennett, Deputy Under Secretary of the Treasury:

> Senator JOHNSTON. ••• If we permitted the possession of gold, would it make any further difference if we permitted its use for payment of contracts, as legal tender?
>
> Mr. BENNETT. ••• Well, there could be technical difficulties once we permitted private trading in gold, and futures trading and so sorth [sic]; there might be technical difficulties in continuing restrictions on the freedom of individuals to contract in gold as they can contract in pork bellies. I think that the question, however, ought to be looked at carefully as to whether some restrictions on indexing dollar contracts in gold should be retained.[14]

Pursuant to Senator Johnston's suggestion, Bennett did consider the question further and wrote to Senator Johnston on May 16, 1973, saying in part:

> Any decision to repeal the Gold Clause Resolution would have to be based on consideration of its effect on our economy from both a domestic and international viewpoint. Repeal would also have to be reviewed in the light of its effect on the ability of Congress to regulate the value of money of the United States—the original reason for the adoption of the Resolution.
>
> * * *
>
> Consequently based on these preliminary concerns, repeal of the Gold Clause Resolution should not be undertaken by the Congress without a thorough consideration of all the issues and consequences involved. Since neither the hearings before your Subcommittee nor the

debates on other gold legislation pending in the Senate have focused on the gold clause issue, we believe that it would be inadvisable to include the Joint Resolution among the gold laws which are proposed to be repealed by Congress.

*   *   *

As we interpret them, the bills now before Congress on private gold ownership, although broadly phrased, are limited to holding and dealing in gold *and do not affect the Gold Clause Joint Resolution.* It would be helpful if the report of your Subcommittee explaining the objectives of these bills made this interpretation explicit through a statement to the effect that the proposed gold legislation would in no way affect the continuing validity of the Joint Resolution of June 5, 1933.

While the committee did not respond to the suggestion that the report explicitly reaffirm the continuing validity of the Gold Clause Resolution, there was no indication anywhere else in the hearings or committee reports that Bennett's interpretation was rejected or even questioned. The matter was not explicitly addressed either way.

Over a year and a half later, on December 4, 1974, Secretary of the Treasury Simon testified before a House subcommittee considering delaying the effective date of the Gold Ownership Amendments:

Contracts payable alternatively in gold or in an amount of money measured thereby are both against public policy and unenforceable in our courts under the provisions of the Congressional Gold Clause Joint Resolution of 1933. *This clause continues to apply after the lifting of restrictions on bullion ownership.*[16]

Here again, there is no indication of congressional rejection of the Secretary's interpretation, or even any discussion of it.

While neither the Deputy Under Secretary's nor the Secretary's interpretation of the Gold Ownership Amendments is binding on us, the fact that the issue was raised and Congress chose to remain silent persuades us that Congress did not manifest the requisite "clear intention" to repeal the Gold Clause Resolution.

Absent some positive expression of a clear intent to repeal the Gold Clause Resolution, we must conclude that it remains in effect. Manifestly, the economic, social and political consequences of repealing the Gold Clause Resolution dictate judicial caution and a more thorough legislative examination and explicit statement indicating an intention to repeal the resolution than we have found in the Gold Ownership Amendments or their histories.[17] In view of the serious consequences noted in the margin, we are especially reluctant to conclude readily that Congress intended that result, where there is nowhere in the legislative history any discussion of these possible consequences, nor any declaration of a congressional purpose to bring about that result.

Furthermore, it is clear to us from our examination of the history that Congress was focusing solely on the Treasury regulations issued under authority of the Gold Reserve Act and was intending only to restore to the public the panoply of activities incident to commodity ownership. The hearings and committee reports on the various gold ownership bills are replete with references to "ownership" and "possession" of gold by private citizens and to the "regulations" then proscribing such use, with no indication of intent to affect the Gold Clause Resolution, nor any discussion of the wisdom of reviving long-dormant gold obligations.[18]

Subsequent Legislation

Since the enactment of the Gold Ownership Amendments, numerous measures have been introduced in Congress by the sponsors and drafters of the Amendments, all designed to repeal explicitly the Gold Clause Resolution and restore the right to use gold clauses in obligations. See H.R. 8234, 94th Cong., 1st Sess. (1975) (Rep Crane); S. 3563, 94th Cong., 2d Sess. (1976) (Sen. Helms); H.R. 14792, 94th Cong., 2d Sess. (1976) (Rep. Conlon); S. 79, 95th Cong., 1st Sess. (1977) (Sen. Helms). Introducing the most recent of these bills in the current session, Senator Helms said:

> The bill I am introducing today would make the Federal code consistent with the action Congress took in 1974 to legalize gold ownership. Right now, contracts can be made specifying payment in any commodity—*except* gold. In this day and age, such a prohibition is anachronistic. 123 Cong.Rec. at S 280 (daily ed. Jan. 10, 1977) (emphasis added).

Senator Helms suggested that "Congress should remove all doubt about this issue by a simple amendment to the present law." *Id.* at S 281. We note in addition that S. 79 would be prospective in application only and would not revive existing obligations barred by the Gold Clause Resolution.

While no one Senator or Representative, or even a group of them, can, by introducing legislation, declare Congress' intent when it enacted prior legislation, the court may take into account a drafter's opinion of the effect of his prior bill. *Schwegmann Bros. v. Calvert Distillers Corp.*, 341 U.S. 384, 391-92, 394-95, 71 S.Ct. 745, 95 L.Ed. 1035 (1951). Viewed in this light, these attempts to clarify the statutory record support our conclusion that Congress did not address and deal with the Gold Clause Resolution in the Gold Ownership Amendments. If Congress had "clearly intended" to revive gold obligations by enacting the Amendments, "it was strange indeed that [it] omitted the one clear provision that would have accomplished that result." *Id.* at 392, 71 S.Ct. at 749.

The Bonds as Commodity Contracts

Plaintiffs argue further that, since gold is now traded like any other commodity, the gold clause in these bonds should be enforced in the same fashion as, for example, a contract providing for payment in cotton (or any other commodity) on which there would be no restriction whatsoever. We disagree.

The bonds do not call for payment of a mere commodity of a certain weight or bulk. They call for payment in "gold coin of the United States", that is, "a particular kind of coin or currency," a coin no longer issued or redeemed by the United States. See Note 4, *supra*. Secondly, while there may be no restrictions on contracts for payment in cotton (or even peanuts), it is clear that gold, of all the commodities, has traditionally possessed a special *monetary* significance. This is a role that Congress specifically addressed and found to be contrary to public policy.

While there may be sentiments to the effect that no public policy objective is *now* being served by the prohibition of gold clauses—see, *e.g.*, the letters of Secretary Simon and Federal Reserve Board Chairman Burns at 123 Cong.Rec.S 282 (daily ed. Jan. 10, 1977)—it is Congress' prerogative, not ours, to find and legislate that the public policy declaration of the Gold Clause Resolution is no longer operative.

Accordingly, we conclude that plaintiffs are entitled only to payment of the principal amount of the bonds, dollar for dollar, in legal tender of the United States. Plaintiffs' motion for summary judgment is denied, defendant's motion for summary judgment is granted, and the action is dismissed as to all defendants.

So ordered.

Southern Capital Corporation, Appellant,

v.

Southern Pacific Company,
Southern Pacific Transportation Company,
Morgan Guaranty Trust Company of New York,
Appellees. *

Before Van Oosterhout, Senior Circuit Judge,
Lay and Stephenson, Circuit Judges.

Stephenson, Circuit Judge.

Southern Capital Corporation is the owner of 175 of Southern Pacific Company's $10,000 bonds due on March 1, 1977. The bonds were issued under and pursuant to a mortgage and deed of trust dated March 1, 1927, between Southern Pacific Company and The National Bank of Commerce in New York, as trustee. Southern Pacific Transportation Company is the successor in interest to Southern Pacific Company. Morgan Guaranty Trust Company of New York is the successor trustee. The bonds contained a "gold clause" which provides for all interest and principal payments to be made "in gold coin of the United States of America of or equal to the standard of weight and fineness existing on March 1, 1927 * * *." On May 28, 1976, appellant Southern Capital brought this action below seeking a declaratory judgment to the effect that the appellees are obligated to satisfy the remaining interest and principal payments according to the express language

---

* This case was decided on January 11, 1978, by the United States Court of Appeals for the Eighth Circuit. It is reported at 568 F.2d 590. Just as in *Equitable Life* and *Henderson,* the Supreme Court of the United States declined even to hear *Southern Capital* (on May 30, 1978). Like *Feldman,* it is a bond case, and in reaching the same conclusion as *Feldman* did, it relies on that case and on *Equitable Life* as well.

of the gold clause in the bonds. Upon the appellees' motion, the district court, [1] in light of 31 U.S.C. § 463, dismissed Southern Capital's complaint for failure to state a clame upon which relief could be granted. Southern Capital appeals from that dismissal. We affirm.

The Joint Resolution of June 5, 1933, 31 U.S.C. § 463, was one of a series of congressional measures relating to the currency arising out of a banking and monetary crisis. In the Joint Resolution Congress declared that "gold clauses" were against the public policy. Furthermore, Congress provided that all such obligations "shall be discharged upon payment, dollar for dollar, in any coin or currency which at the time of payment is legal tender for public and private debts." Shortly after its passage, the Supreme Court upheld the Joint Resolution's constitutionality as to private obligations in *Norman v. Baltimore & O. R. R.*, 294 U.S. 240, 55 S.Ct. 407, 79 L.Ed. 885 (1935).[2] *Accord, Holyoke Water Power Co. v. American Writing Paper Co.*, 300 U.S. 324, 57 S.Ct. 485, 81 L.Ed. 678 (1937). Thus, it would appear that the Joint Resolution bars the relief sought by Southern Capital.

Southern Capital contends, however, that because the economic circumstances that justified the passage of the Joint Resolution no longer exist, the enactment fails of its essential purpose and must fall before the substantive due process requirements of the Fifth Amendment. It cannot be questioned that the Joint Resolution of June 5, 1933, arose out of a banking and monetary crisis. The Supreme Court in *Norman v. Baltimore & O. R. R., supra*, however, did not rely solely on the economic circumstances of the depression to uphold the constitutionality of the Joint Resolution. The Court instead discussed at some length the power of Congress to establish a uniform monetary system as an independent constitutional basis for the Joint Resolution. Several years following the *Norman* decision, the Supreme Court again in *Guaranty Trust Co. v. Henwood*, 307 U.S. 247, 259, 59 S.Ct. 847, 853, 83 L.Ed. 1266 (1939), highlighted the congressional power to enact the Joint Resolution when it stated:

> These bonds and their securing mortgage were created subject not only to the exercise by Congress of its constitutional power "to coin money, regulate the value thereof, and of foreign coin," but also to "the full authority of the Congress in relation to the currency." The extent of that authority of Congress has been recently pointed out: "The broad and

comprehensive national authority over the subjects of revenue, finance and currency is derived from the aggregate of the powers granted to the Congress, embracing the powers to lay and collect taxes, to borrow money, to regulate commerce with foreign nations and among the several States, to coin money, regulate the value thereof, and of foreign coin, and fix the standards of weights and measures, and the added express power 'to make all laws which shall be necessary and proper for carrying into execution' the other enumerated powers."

Under these powers, Congress was authorized—as it did in the Resolution—to establish, regulate and control the national currency and to make that currency legal tender money for all purposes, including payment of domestic dollar obligations with options for payment in foreign currencies. Whether it was "wise and expedient" to do so was, under the Constitution, a determination to be made by the Congress. [Footnote omitted.]

We are persuaded that the congressional power to establish a uniform monetary system which existed in 1933 and provided a basis upon which the Supreme Court upheld the constitutionality of the Joint Resolution in 1934 still exists today. Accordingly, we reject Southern Capital's first argument.

Southern Capital's remaining arguments center around two congressional enactments in 1973 and 1974 which eliminated limitations on the right of United States citizens to purchase, hold, sell or otherwise deal in gold. It is Southern Capital's position that this legislation has repealed the Joint Resolution. Additionally Southern Capital contends that this legislation is inconsistent with the Joint Resolution and thus causes that enactment to fail of its essential purpose.

In the Act of Sept. 21, 1973, Pub.L.No. 93-110, § 3, 87 Stat. 352, Congress specifically repealed sections 3 and 4 of the Gold Reserve Act of 1934, 31 U.S.C. §§ 442 and 443. We note, however, that neither the Joint Resolution or its codification in 31 U.S.C. § 463 is expressly mentioned. In the subsequent Act of Aug. 14, 1974, Pub.L.No. 93-373, § 2, 88 Stat. 445, Congress provided that no provisions of any law may be construed to prohibit any person from purchasing, holding, selling or otherwise dealing with gold in the United States or abroad. As it is clear that the Joint Resolution was not expressly repealed by either Act, the question remains whether it was repealed by implication.

In *Morton v. Mancari*, 417 U.S. 535, 550, 94 S.Ct. 2474, 2482, 41

L.Ed.2d 290 (1974), the Supreme Court stated that "[i]n the absence of some affirmative showing of an intention to repeal, the only permissible justification for a repeal by implication is when the earlier and later statutes are irreconcilable." We are not persuaded in the instant case that Congress intended to repeal the Joint Resolution by the two enactments in 1973 and 1974.[3]

We note that in the Act of Oct. 28, 1977, Pub.L.No. 95-147, 91 Stat. 1229, Congress has now specifically made the Joint Resolution nonapplicable to obligations issued on or after October 28, 1977. If Congress had earlier intended to implicitly repeal the Joint Resolution, it is highly doubtful that the Act of October 28, 1977, would have been necessary. Additionally, this recent Act clearly expresses the congressional intent to make the Joint Resolution nonapplicable to obligations issued *on or after* October 28, 1977. We are unable to find an earlier congressional intention to repeal the Joint Resolution.

Furthermore, the Joint Resolution and the two enactments of 1973 and 1974 are not irreconcilable. The Joint Resolution prohibited obligees from demanding payment of obligations in gold. The two latter enactments were concerned with the removal of restrictions imposed on the acquisition, holding and disposition of gold as a commodity. Thus, it appears that the Joint Resolution was not implicitly repealed by the enactments of 1973 and 1974. *Feldman v. Great Northern Ry.*, 428 F.Supp. 979, 984-86 (S.D. N.Y.1977); *Equitable Life Assurance Soc'y of the United States v. Grosvenor*, 426 F.Supp. 67, 71-72 (W.D. Tenn.1976).

We further reject Southern Capital's contention that the 1973 and 1974 legislation is inconsistent with the Joint Resolution. In our view there is no basic inconsistency in granting persons permission to purchase, sell, hold or otherwise deal with gold, while denying them the right to demand payment of obligations indexed to a certain value of gold. The statutes can coexist.

We affirm the district court's dismissal of Southern Capital's complaint for failure to state a claim upon which relief could be granted.

Affirmed.

Seven

Relegalizing the Gold Clause Clause*

The story of the gold clause's relegalization is both interesting, and important.

Interesting, because it is an all-too-infrequent illustration of how principle and free market economics can triumph over pragmatism and statist monetary theory even though, to achieve relegalization, skilled political operators had to work the legislative system for all it was worth.

Important, because although relegalization of the gold clause does provide creditors with a powerful anti-inflation weapon, relegalization does not go as far as some of its partisans think. The question of relegalization's *scope* is second in importance only to the fact of relegalization itself.

The first serious attempt to relegalize the gold clause began on June 26, 1975, when Congressman Philip M. Crane introduced legislation in the House of Representatives "To declare the public policy of the United States and to remove all legal obstacles to the use of gold clauses." Short and to the point, Mr. Crane's bill (H.R. 8324) provided as follows: "*Be it enacted by the Senate and House of Representatives of the United States of America in Congress assembled,* That the joint resolution of June 5, 1933, entitled "Joint resolution to assure uniform value to coins and currencies of the United States (31 U.S.C. 463) is hereby repealed, and nothing shall

---

* This chapter was written especially for *The Gold Clause in America* by the editor.

prohibit any contractual provision which gives the obligee the right to require payment by the obligor in gold, in gold coin, or in an amount of currency measured by the value of gold or gold coins." Referred to the House Committee on Banking, Currency and Housing, Congressman Crane's bill languished there.

About nine months later, Senator Jesse Helms queried then Treasury Secretary William E. Simon and Fed Chairman Arthur F. Burns, in writing, about their official positions concerning relegalization of the gold clause.

Simon answered first, making quite clear his hostility toward the gold clause:

THE SECRETARY OF THE TREASURY

Washington, May 6, 1976.

Hon. Jesse Helms
U.S. Senate
Washington, D.C.

Dear Jesse:

Thank you for your letter of March 30 in which you enclosed a paper by Professor Gerald Dunne on the Joint Resolution of June 5, 1933. I have given considerable thought to the matters raised in your letter and in Professor Dunne's article. My own feeling is that the Joint Resolution is not inconsistent with the legalization of the private ownership of gold.

In recent years, we have taken a series of steps to eliminate gold from the U.S. monetary system and to reduce the role of gold in the international monetary system. Consistent with that policy, U.S. citizens can now purchase, sell, and deal in gold as a commodity. The Joint Resolution by making unenforceable contract provisions for the payment of the obligation in gold or in an amount of dollars measured in gold, helps to assure that gold will not again assume a monetary role through widespread use in private transactions. I am also concerned that the emergence of gold clauses, which might result from repeal of the Joint Resolution, could call into question the strength of the dollar and undermine our efforts to control inflation and maintain confidence in our currency. In my view, the Joint Resolution therefore continues to have a substantial and important rationale, and its repeal at this time would be unwise.

In addition to gold clauses, you mentioned in your letter the removal of legal strictures against multiple currency clauses which would result from repeal of the Joint Resolution. As you pointed out, I have in the past expressed the view that consideration of a change in the law in this regard would be desirable. Multiple currency clauses do not raise the same concern as gold clauses, and removal of the legal strictures against multiple currency clauses could be accomplished without repealing in full the Joint Resolution.

Although we might approach the subject from different perspectives I'm hopeful that we both can agree that the policy of reducing the monetary role of gold is sound. There are so many areas in which our views are the same because we share a common philosophy. Let's work to maintain our joint views on the subject of gold. Ed Yeo, Under Secretary for Monetary Affairs and his staff are meeting with your staff. I look forward to the results of this conference.

Sincerely yours,

William E. Simon

Burns responded about a month later:

FEDERAL RESERVE SYSTEM
WASHINGTON, D.C.

June 2, 1976.

Hon. Jesse Helms
U.S. Senate
Washington, D.C.

Dear Senator Helms:

I am pleased to respond further to your letter of March 31, 1976, asking for the Board's views on a paper by Professor Gerald Dunne on gold clause contracts.

In December 1974, I testified on behalf of the Board in favor of a bill that would have postponed the date when U.S. citizens would be permitted to deal in gold without a Treasury license. While the Board favored restoring to U.S. citizens the right to deal in gold, it was concerned that removal of restrictions on private trading in gold at that time might have an adverse impact on an already strained financial situation. Fortunately, this did not happen. In the past year and a half our financial institutions and markets have strengthened markedly, and economic recovery is well under way.

In light of the changed circumstances, I personally would not object to legislative action that would permit private citizens to make contracts containing legally enforceable gold clauses. However, the Board is split on the advisability of such action. Our discussions have suggested that opinions on this subject may vary widely, and that hearings could be helpful in fully exploring the advantages and disadvantages of permitting the use of gold clauses. The Federal Reserve would be pleased to assist the Congress in this deliberation.

Sincerely yours,

Arthur F. Burns

On June 14, 1976, Helms took the floor in the United States Senate and introduced a bill (S. 3563) "To declare the public policy of the United States and to remove all legal obstacles to the use of gold clauses." In support of his measure, he said the following:

Mr. President, when Congress restored the freedom of Americans to own gold, it neglected to restore the freedom to enter into contracts which require payment in gold or dollars measured in gold. It is time this oversight is rectified.

Contracts containing "gold clauses" have as a basic purpose: to protect the maker of a loan or the seller of merchandise from having to accept a depreciated medium of exchange. In some ways, it is a form of indexing and a way to avoid the effects of inflation. Congress has long recognized the hardships which inflation causes, and it has adopted legislation which increased the incomes of certain groups as inflation increases the cost of living. These groups include social security recipients, civil service employees, military pensioners, and members of the U.S. House of Representatives and Senate.

The pertinent law on the books is the joint resolution of June 5, 1933, 31 U.S.C. 463, which prohibited gold ownership and gold clause contracts, "to assure uniform value to coins and currencies of the United States." Since we have no gold coins or currencies, it is doubly anachronistic to keep this provision on the books.

I have corresponded on this issue with both Secretary of the Treasury, William Simon, and Dr. Arthur Burns, Chairman of the Federal Reserve Board. Chairman Burns has no objection to the repeal. The Secretary, on the other hand, finds his feelings remain unchanged that the gold clause prohibition should not be repealed.

*   *   *

On August 14, 1974, the President signed into law a bill which contained the repeal of that section of the joint resolution concerning the ownership of gold. In a news release dated December 9, 1974, the Treasury declared that repeal of the prohibition against gold ownership did not affect the prohibition against contracts containing gold clauses.

*   *   *

Secretary Simon states that gold clauses "could call into question the strength of the dollar and undermine our efforts to control inflation and maintain confidence in our currency." Some discussion of his comment is in order.

First, we must assume that the Secretary is referring to international exchange markets when he refers to "the strength of the dollar." But, as most economists agree, the strength or relative value of the dollar in these markets is dependent, in the long run, on the relative rates of inflation in other nations and whether or not the United States is inflating faster or slower—or not inflating at all—compared to other major nations. The strength of the dollar is therefore not related to contracts Americans may enter into, but to relative rates of inflation.

When the Secretary refers to "our efforts to control inflation," he perhaps refers to the administration or the entire Federal Government. In the scheme of things, Congress starts the inflation ball rolling with deficit spending. The Treasury is Congress agent and is responsible for selling Federal securities in order to finance the Federal debt. The Federal Reserve Board then acts to ameliorate the effects massive Treasury borrowing has on the economy and pumps money into the system. This causes inflation. If so, the major forces which can undermine efforts to control inflation are the Federal Reserve Board and the big-spending Congress, which requires the Treasury to finance debt. Inflation is not caused by any sort of contract—be it in gold or any other commodity.

Finally, the Secretary refers to the maintenance of "confidence in our currency." Confidence in the currency is undermined by its debasement. Debasement is caused by too much money pumped out by the Federal Reserve Board, an action initiated by big-spending Congresses. Confidence in the currency is reflected in the ways people use to cushion themselves from the effects of inflation. Various forms of indexing, including the indexing of congressional salaries, are indications that people—including Members of Congress—do not have a lot of confidence in our currency.

Secretary Simon touches on an important issue, however, when he discusses the "confidence in our currency," since gold clauses, along with other inflation-hedging arrangements, provide an indication of the health of our currency. Gold clauses can give a warning signal that can tell us that Government must cut back and restore balance to the budget.

If the Government is inflating, and people seek a refuge, they will adopt this type of device. It is far better to have no inflation and no such devices, but since we have inflation, we should have freedom to cushion its effects.

One of the major indictments against the present prohibition is that it is simply an unreasonable infringement on the rights of Americans. We have been allowed to own gold since 1974, but we are not allowed to use it as we do with other commodities. Anyone can enter into agreements which state that a sum of dollars will be paid on a certain date measured in the value of pork-bellies or any other commodity. But, because of this archaic provision on the books, we could not use gold as a measure of payment.

The contradictory aspects of the present situation has attracted the attention of legal experts. For example, Prof. Gerald Dunne, editor of *The Banking Law Journal,* is of the opinion that the present prohibition of gold clause contracts is legally inconsistent with the present right to own gold. In his paper, "Gold Clause Prohibition: Derelict of the Law" Professor Dunne states that a court ruling made in Williams against Standard Oil would require that the gold clause prohibition be declared void. In that case, the court stated:

> The remaining portions of the act, seeming merely to facilitate or contribute to the consummation of that purpose must also fail.

In other words, once Congress repealed the prohibition against gold ownership, gold clauses cannot consistently be prohibited.

* * *

There are other legal opinions, of course, and litigation on such an issue would be costly as well as time consuming. Congress should remove all doubt about this issue by a simple amendment to the present law. Professor Dunne's arguments and the court's past ruling are clear and their validity should encourage Congress to act.

Another aspect of this issue is that the prohibition against using gold clauses applies only for Americans dealing with Americans. As a result, rich individuals with foreign dealings or multinational corporations can make contracts abroad containing gold clauses, but the average American and the average domestic company cannot. Recently, the Great Western Corp., a Dallas based firm, concluded a long-term contract with a Panamanian firm to pay in gold or silver bullion. The company obtained a $150 million credit arrangement with several financial institutions which will purchase the needed amount of bullion.

According to the *Wall Street Journal:*

> Great Western said the hard-currency clause provides sugar producers with potential protection from inflation and a decrease in the value of paper currencies.

* * *

Gold clauses in contracts, bonds, and other loan instruments, would be extremely attractive to some borrowers and lenders. For example, it is fully possible that a bond with a gold clause could be sold at 5-percent interest, while one without would require a 10-percent rate of interest.

If, for example, the U.S. Treasury were to offer notes which were redeemable in dollars, measured by a quantity of gold, it would mean a great savings to the taxpayer. Interest rates on such notes would be far less than presently prevailing rates. Those investors who recognize gold as a standard of value would not demand an inflation cushion in the interest rate they would require for an investment. Next year, debt servicing costs are expected to total $41 billion. If this total could be reduced by only a small percentage, the savings to the taxpayer would be great. Such a savings would result if Treasury bills containing gold clauses were to be issued.

What the Treasury Department appears to object to is the concept that gold represents a standard of value against which the dollar can be measured. Gold has obvious faults in this regard, but many people regard it as a good measure; and it is an arbitrary and excessive exercise of power for our democratic Government to deprive people of the right to such a standard, whatever it might be.

As I mentioned, the Congress itself has adopted legislation which inflation-proofs its own salaries, and thus protects itself in a very concrete way. It seems strangely inconsistent for Congress to deny private individuals a right to avoid the effects of inflation in ways of their own choosing.

Supporters of the gold clause prohibition in the bureaucracy of the Treasury Department seem to forget that our common enemy is inflation—not gold, gold clauses, pork-belly prices, peanut futures, or the price of any other commodity.

What is difficult to determine is whether the bureaucrat and the supporters of the prohibition are afraid of gold clauses, pork-belly prices, peanut pie. Regardless, that fear has only one basis, and that is that a standard of value—be it gold or some other commodity or index—will indicate when the Government is debasing the currency.

Mr. President, I send to the desk a bill proposing to repeal the joint resolution of June 5, 1933, and I ask unanimous consent that the text of the bill be printed at this point of the RECORD.

There being no objection, the bill was ordered to be printed in the RECORD, as follows:

S. 3563

Be it enacted by the Senate and House of Representatives of the United States of America in Congress assembled,

SEC. 1. *That the Congress finds and determines that:*

    (a) the prohibition from entering into contracts requiring payment in currencies of other nations, gold or gold coin, is an unreasonable infringement upon the rights of Americans.

    (b) such prohibition inequitably prevents Americans from exercising this right to protect themselves against inflation, and thus:

        (1) is inconsistent with Acts of Congress mandating inflation-related income increases for Social Security

recipients, Federal employees, Members of Congress, and others;

(2) is inconsistent with the right of Americans to enter into private financial agreements, including labor contracts providing for automatic salary increases;

(c) such prohibition does not significantly affect the stability of the value of the dollar in foreign exchange markets; such value being rimarily determined in the long run by domestic fiscal and monetary policies, the financial and monetary conditions within the United States and its major trading partners, and changing patterns of international trade;

(d) such prohibition is inconsistent with the freedom of Americans to hold, sell and deal in gold, as established by Public Law 93-373.

(e) such prohibition, by preventing Americans from exercising the aforementioned rights to protect themselves from the results of imprudent monetary policies, has reduced needed incentives to monetary authorities to adopt policies which would preserve the value of the dollar.

SEC. 2. That the joint resolution of June 5, 1933, entitled "Joint resolution to assure uniform value to coins and currencies of the United States" (31 U.S.C. 463) is hereby repealed.

In late August, 1976, Helms offered an amendment to his bill, one which would later have great significance for those attempting to resuscitate pre-nullification gold clause obligations:

Today, I submit an amendment which would add a new section to the bill to repeal the joint resolution of June 5, 1933. I feel that this reform is long overdue. It would simply finish the job begun in 1974 when Congress amended the joint resolution to allow gold ownership. The present amendment would allow individuals to enter into gold clause contracts—contracts which called for payment in gold or in dollars measured in gold.

It is a simple matter. Presently, any American can enter into an enforceable contract which specifies payment in any commodity except gold, or in dollars measured in that commodity. The gold clause contract prohibition is anachronistic. It is a simple financial freedom that should be restored.

Before the freedom to own gold was restored, the Treasury Department and others predicted that there would be a mad rush to buy gold. This in turn would depress the value of the dollar. That would, in turn, force up the price of imports and inflation would accelerate and confidence in the dollar would be undermined.

Well, everyone knows that the average American does not keep a gold ingot under his bed, and every economist will point out that buying gold abroad for dollars has the same foreign exchange effect of buying anything else abroad. Yet, Treasury did not propose that we prevent people from owning Volkswagens.

Today, there is a parallel situation. The Treasury Department contends that gold clause contracts would undermine the value of the dollar, hinder the fight against inflation and lower confidence in the dollar. Those arguments just do not hold water. Inflation undermines the value of the dollar, and inflation is not caused by the kind of contracts in to which people enter. Inflation is caused by the Federal Reserve Board pumping too many dollars into the economy in an effort to regulate the economy or ameliorate the effects of whopping Federal deficits.

In a letter I received from the Treasury Department on this issue, the telling argument against repeal of the joint resolution of 1933 is that the resolution, by prohibiting gold clause contracts, "helps to assure that gold will not assume a monetary role through widespread use in private transactions." It seems, therefore, it is not the economics of the matter that is of concern to Treasury Department folks, it is the particular material affected. Imagine the Treasury Department saying that they wanted to make sure that "peanuts will not assume a monetary role through widespread use in private transactions."

Treasury's argument rests on two shaky assumptions. The first is that gold clauses in contracts would be "widespread." The only reason for gold clauses in contracts is that they provide a hedge against inflation. Much like the indexing of salaries—such as Congressmen and civil servants now enjoy. The only reason people seek a hedge against inflation is when there is inflation, and the value of the dollar is declining. If that is the case, people should be free to try to protect themselves in any way they see fit. But, will gold clause contracts be "widespread?" I doubt it. Just as good [sic] ownership isn't particularly widespread. Or, for that matter, no single inflation-hedge is particularly widespread. In 1974, the Treasury feared the freedom of gold ownership would result in mass purchases of gold ingots. They now seem to fear that gold clause contracts would result in mass amendments to contracts.

Second, the Treasury seems to view the existence of gold clause contracts as a return of gold to the monetary system. But money must serve as a stable store of value, and a commodity freely traded and subject to the vagaries of the market does not serve as an absolutely stable store of value. The only reason people would choose gold clause contracts is that the gold market might—just might—provide a better store of value than dollars. That is a subjective judgment. And, people should be free to exercise their judgment in the marketplace. They should be free to hedge against the declining value of the dollar in any medium they choose. As long as gold is subject to market swings, and to the sort of market manipulations such as the sales of gold by the International Monetary Fund, it is stretching things to say that gold would be used as money. It is a further reach to say that gold clauses in contracts means gold is assuming a monetary role.

I believe that reasonable men would agree with the arguments.

Chairman of the Federal Reserve Board Arthur Burns states that he personally has no objection to the repeal of the prohibition against gold clause contracts.

The Treasury Department officially opposes repeal of the gold clause prohibition, just as it opposed repeal of the gold ownership prohibition, but Secretary Simon has been quoted as personally not opposing the repeal. I have not spoken with him on this subject, but his staff says his official position is unchanged.

Since I introduced my bill on this subject, S. 3653, none of my arguments have been contested. I am afraid that the status quo is the main thing that the gold clause prohibition has going for it. The other thing is the unnatural fear of gold that all midlevel bureaucrats in the Treasury Department seem to have.

The text of my amendment is slightly different from that of the bill I have introduced on this topic. My amendment, if approved, would make enforceable, gold clause contracts entered into after the enactment of the amendment. It is intended to stand neutral with regard to the enforceability of gold clause obligations issued in the past. It has come to my attention that there is at least one case pending in the courts which would require gold clause bonds issued before the 1933 resolution, be paid in gold. Since this matter is in the court, I would not want any legislation to prejudice the case one way or the other.

Mr. President, I ask unanimous consent that my amendment be printed in the RECORD at this point.

There being no objection, the amendment was ordered to be printed in the RECORD, as follows:

> At the end of the bill add the following new section:
>
> SEC. —. The joint resolution entitled "Joint resolution to assure uniform value to the coins and currencies of the United States", approved June 5, 1933 (31 U.S.C. 463), shall not apply to obligations issued on or after the date of enactment of this section.

The new section proposed by Helms was the death notice for the aspirations of those persons trying to resuscitate pre-nullification gold clause obligations. The legislative intent could not have been clearer: relegalization was not supposed to retroactively revive gold clauses.

A month later, Secretary Simon changed his mind about relegalizing the gold clause:

THE SECRETARY OF THE TREASURY
WASHINGTON 20220

Sep 21, 1976

Dear Jesse:

In my letter to you of May 6, I mentioned several concerns I have had with a proposal to repeal the Joint Gold Clause Resolution. I fully agree that gold should be treated like any other commodity and that, at an appropriate time, the legal restriction on gold clauses in contracts should be repealed. I had some question, however, whether this is the best time to repeal the Joint Resolution.

In my earlier letter, I indicated my concern that the monetary role of gold not reemerge upon repeal of the Joint Resolution through possible widespread use of gold clauses in private transactions. Second, since gold clauses in contracts call into question the strength of the dollar, their widespread use in contracts might undermine our efforts to control inflation.

Upon reflection, I believe this in fact may be a good time to repeal the Joint Gold Clause Resolution. We are well on our way in our efforts to restore stability to the U.S. economy. With a clear U.S. Government commitment to sound fiscal and monetary policies and with a substantially-reduced level of inflation, the widespread use of gold clauses by U.S. citizens in their contracts appears unlikely. Moreover, the demonstrated volatility in the price of gold over the last several years makes even more unlikely its use as a measure of value in private transactions.

Therefore, in my view, repeal of the Joint Resolution at this time should not have any undesirable monetary and economic efforts.

Sincerely yours,

William E. Simon

Secretary Simon was not the only convert. As the months dragged on, others came forward to co-sponsor the Helms bill, and to provide other support. Slowly, legislative machinations moved the bill through the Congressional labyrinth. Helms told part of the story to the 1977 meeting of the National Committee for Monetary Reform:

> In the course of Congressional consideration on the International Monetary Fund bill—a $3 billion giveaway slush fund for overpaid international bureaucrats—I saw an outside chance to repeat what was done in 1974 when gold ownership was won. That is, put a good conservative piece of legislation on a liberal bill which was going to be signed into law.
>
> Well, toward the end of the 94th Congress, it became very clear that there was not enough time to have a very long debate on the Senate floor over the IMF bill. In other words, if some Senators wanted to talk about the bill for a few days, it simply would not be passed before adjournment. It was, however, clear that if the bill were brought up again in January, the advocates had the votes to cut off debate and pass the bill.
>
> The Treasury Department wanted the bill very badly, however, and after a small amount of explanation, they came to understand that the gold clause freedom bill should go on the bill.
>
> On the very last day of the session, we found out that if the Senate changed the bill at all, the House would not be able to clear it and send it to the President before adjournment. As a result, the Senate had to pass the bill as approved by the House and send it to the White House.
>
> Treasury Secretary Bill Simon was in Manila, and he called from the IMF meeting there. We were in somewhat of a difficult situation, so we talked things over and obtained a promise from the Senate leadership that assistance would be given in the 95th Congress to pass this bill. As a result, the IMF bill was allowed to pass without the gold clause freedom bill.
>
> When, on October 11 of this year, the Senate took up H.R. 5675, I walked over to Senator William Proxmire who was managing the bill. I reminded him of our agreement of last year about the gold clause bill. In a few minutes, the Senate approved my amendment, and then passed the bill.
>
> My able associate, Howard Segermark, then contacted the staff of the members of the House of Representatives and notified them of the action. It was agreed that the House leadership would attempt to take up the bill under a unanimous consent agreement, pass it, and send it to the President. On Friday, October 14, that is exactly what happened.

After four decades, the gold clause was legal again—at least as to all obligations entered into after October 28, 1977. And at least as far as the federal government was concerned.

Eight

Is the Gold Clause Really Legal?*

The gold clause has traveled a long and hard road in America. It had only a limited use before the war between the states. Then, during the Civil War, in reaction to the government's seemingly ceaseless printing of paper money, the gold clause was widely adopted. For the next three-quarters of a century, the gold clause flourished. At the hands of F.D.R. and his New Deal, it was nullified, and for the next forty years, the gold clause was illegal. Relegalization of private gold bullion ownership fueled the hope that the gold clause had, by implication, been resuscitated retroactively, but the courts flatly refused to go along. Finally, a few years later, the gold clause was expressly relegalized. Once again, the door was opened to creditors who wished to utilize virtually the only tool that could protect the value of their long term debt.

Under the circumstances, it is more than a little troubling that the gold clause's potential users should have to clear yet another hurdle—this time, at the hands of the states.

At least two state courts have found that anti-usury laws are a barrier to certain forms of indexed principal. This chapter presents those cases, as well as an essay discussing the usury problem. It is a problem that a creditor must thoroughly understand

---

* The article entitled "*Aztec Properties* Discussed," which follows that case in this chapter, was originally entitled "Inflation and Indexing—Usury in Commercial Loans: *Aztec Properties, Inc. v. Union Planters National Bank*". Written by Mildred B. Dodson, it appeared in Vol. 11 of the *Tulsa Law Journal*, 1976, pages 450-458. Copyright © 1976 by the *Tulsa Law Journal*. Reprinted with permission of the copyright owner and Fred B. Rothman & Co.

145

before attempting to use the gold clause.*

Decisions
Jessie H. Olwine, Plaintiff-Appellee,
v.
A. Madeleine Torrens, Defendant-Appellant.**

Hoffman, Judge.

Appellant contends that the lower court erred when it found the repayment provision in appellant's loan usurious under the version of the Pennsylvania usury law[1] applicable at the time of the loan.

On November 19, 1958, appellant made a loan to the appellee and her husband for the principal sum of $7000.00 plus 6% interest, and a bond and mortgage were executed. The bond and mortgage provided that the amount of principal to be repaid should be increased or decreased by a percentage equal to the difference between the average purchasing power of the dollar for the months of July, August and September, 1958, and the average purchasing power of the dollar for the three months immediately preceding repayment, if the difference was greater than five points. The average purchasing power of the dollar was to be measured by the consumer price index. The consumer price index for the 1958 period was 100.00, and for the period immediately preceding payment was 150.80. Under the loan provision, therefore, the appellee owed an additional $3,556.00.

On May 21, 1973, the appellee filed a complaint in equity seeking to force the settlement of the mortgage and bond. During the proceedings, the lower court raised the issue of whether the provision violated the Pennsylvania usury law, *supra*, and the appellee

---

* Normally, the usury problem will arise only in conventional lending situations, where a creditor advances money to a debtor at a stated rate of interest and also attempts to index the principal. The problem is unlikely to arise in credit sale and lease transactions.

** This case was decided on September 22, 1975, by the Superior Court of Pennsylvania, a court of that Commonwealth hierarchically below the Pennsylvania Supreme Court. It is reported at 344 A. 2d 665. One interesting aspect of *Olwine*, unlike the *Aztec Properties* case which begins on page 149, is that the court found it unnecessary to hold that the indexed principal violated the Joint Resolution. Thus, *Olwine* rests exclusively on a violation of state usury law.

was permitted to file an amended reply to new matter raising this issue. In November of 1974, the lower court certified the case from the equity side of court to the law side of court, pursuant to Rule 1061 of the Pennsylvania Rules of Civil Procedure. On November 22, 1974, the lower court found that the repayment clause violated the Pennsylvania usury law, *supra*, and ordered the mortgage be marked satisfied. This appeal followed.

At the time the mortgage was executed by the parties, the Pennsylvania usury law, *supra*, provided: "The lawful rate of interest for the loan or use of money, in all cases where no express contract shall have been made for a less rate, shall be six per cent, per annum ...." *Black's Law Dictionary* (4th ed.1957) defines interest as "the compensation allowed by law or fixed by the parties for the use or forbearance or detention of money." See also, *Bair v. Snyder County State Bank*, 314 Pa. 85, 171 A. 274 (1934); *Mack Paving & Construction Co. v. American Pipe & Construction Co.*, 283 Pa. 449, 129 A. 329 (1925); *McDermott v. McDermott*, 130 Pa.Super. 127, 196 A. 889 (1938). Since usury is often accompanied by subterfuge and circumvention to present the color of legality, it is the duty of the court to examine both the substance and form of a transaction. *Richman v. Watkins*, 376 Pa. 510, 103 A.2d 688 (1954); *Simpson v. Penn Discount Corporation*, 355 Pa. 172, 5 A.2d 796 (1939).

Appellant asserts that the principal of the loan is 7000 "1957 dollars". That is, because inflation has reduced the "value" of each dollar, the extra sum charged does not give him a return on his money. Rather, he claims that the additional charge maintains the "1957 dollar" value of the principal, and therefore, the extra sum is principal. Although somewhat novel, appellant's argument ignores economic reality.

"Perhaps the mostly widely recognized consequence of inflation is its effect on contractual relationships stated in monetary terms. As a class, debtors gain during periods of inflation and creditors lose. The longer the period of time to which the contractual commitment applies, the greater is the exposure to loss or gain." Whittlessey, Freedman and Herman, *Money and Banking: Analysis and Policy*, at 380 (2d ed.1968). Thus, inflation plays an important role in determining the interest rates to be charged by a creditor. "[T]he 'nominal' interest rate—the contract, or stated, interest rate—reflects expectations about future price level behavior. If prices are rising, and are expected to rise further, the expected rate of inflation is added to the interest rate that would have prevailed in the absence of inflation to adjust for the decline in purchasing power represented by price increases." Weston and Brigham, *Managerial Finance*, at 685 (4th ed. 1972). "As people come to anticipate a steady rate of inflation, they build into their interest-rate supply and demand schedules an allowance for inflation." Samuelson, *Economics*, at 607 (9th ed.1973). In the instant case, appellant's effort to keep the "1957 dollar" value of the principal was an attempt to avoid the effects of inflation. The extra sum due, therefore, represents a charge in the nature of interest. Because the stated interest rate of the loan was the maximum allowed under the Pennsylvania usury law, *supra*, this extra charge was usurious.

Appellant further contends that even if the repayment provision provides for the payment of additional interest, the repayment provision is a contingent obligation and therefore not violative of the Pennsylvania usury law. This rule is stated in the *Restatement of Contracts*, section 527, as follows: "A promise, made as the consideration for a loan or for extending the maturity of a pecuniary debt, to give the creditor a greater profit than the highest permissible rate of interest upon the occurrence of a condition, is not usurious if the repayment promised on failure of the condition to occur is materially less than the amount of the loan or debt with the highest permissible interest unless a transaction is given this form as a colorable device to obtain a greater profit than is permissible. In that case it is usurious." The risk must be substantial, however, for a mere colorable hazard will not prevent the charge from being usurious. Courts have held that a loan is contingently repayable only if the lender has subjected himself to some greater hazard than the risk that the debtor might fail to repay the loan or that security might depreciate in value. 14 *Williston on Contracts* § 1692 (3d ed.1972). The comment to § 527 of the Restatement states: "If the probability of the occurrence of the contingency on which diminished payment is promised is remote, or if the diminution should the contingency occur is slight as compared with the possible profit to be obtained if the contingency does not occur, the transaction is presumably usurious."

In the instant case, the repayment contingency was based on the relative purchasing power of the dollar: if the purchasing power of the dollar fell, then the appellee would be required to repay more dollars to compensate for this fall. on the other hand, if the purchasing power of the dollar rose, the appellee would be required to repay fewer dollars. The appellant, therefore, was protecting himself against any depreciation in the value of the dollar. This is a risk to which all individuals are subject and which is an incident of every loan. Because this is a risk normally incident to every loan and not especially hazardous, the interest contingency rule does not apply. Even if we were to hold that risk is especially hazardous, "the probability of the occurrence of the contingency on which diminished payment is promised is remote." Therefore, the interest contingency rule is inapplicable.

Finally, the appellant contends that the appellee waived the benefit of the Pennsylvania usury law, *supra*, by failing to raise usury as an affirmative defense in his reply to new matter. In *Richman v. Watkins*, 376 Pa. 510, 551, 103 A.2d 688 (1954), our Supreme Court, quoting *Simpson v. Penn Discount Corporation et al.*, 355 Pa. 172, 5 A.2d 796 (1939), stated: "... The statute against usury forms a part of the public policy of the state and cannot be evaded by any circumvention or waived by the debtor."

Order affirmed.

Aztec Properties, Inc., Appellant,

v.

Union Planters National Bank of Memphis, Appellee.[*]

Opinion

Brock, Justice.

This is an action to recover on a promissory note. The facts are stipulated.

On July 12, 1974, Aztec Properties, Inc., executed a promissory note payable to Union Planters National Bank of Memphis in

---

[*] This case was decided on October 27, 1975, by the Supreme Court of Tennessee, that state's highest court. It is reported at 530 S.W. 2d 756. Significantly, the unanimous court of five justices expressed the opinion that the note's indexed principal could not withstand the Joint Resolution of 1933.

exchange for a $50,000.00 loan. The promisor agreed to pay the promisee $50,000.00, "in constant United States Dollars adjusted for inflation (deflation)" with interest at ten percent per annum. The adjusted principal was to be calculated according to a formula contained in the note, to wit:

> Amount of principal due shall equal the amount of original principal multiplied by the consumer price index adjustment factor. This adjustment factor shall be computed by dividing the consumer price index on date of borrowing. Said consumer price index numbers shall be for the most recent month available preceding borrowing and maturity dates. This consumer price index shall be the index not seasonably adjusted for all items as reported by the United States Department of Labor.

On maturity of the note Aztec Properties repaid to the bank $50,000.00, with discounted interest at the rate 9.875 percent, in the amount of $419.35 (which is an effective yield of 9.96% per annum), but the borrower refused to pay the additional "indexed principal" of $500.00, based on the inflation adjustment formula.

Whereupon, the bank sued Aztec Properties in Chancery Court for the "indexed principal" together with interest from maturity at the rate of ten percent per annum. Both parties filed Motions for Summary Judgment, the Chancellor holding in favor of the bank. Aztec Properties now appeals to this Court alleging that the Chancellor erred in granting the bank's Motion and in denying its own.

The first issue to be resolved is whether this note is usurious, *i. e.*, whether it charges interest in excess of the legal rate of ten percent per annum. T.C.A. § 47-14-104. A defendant sued for money may avoid the excess over legal interest, by a plea setting forth the amount of the usury. T.C.A. § 47-14-112. Interest includes *all* compensation for the use of money. "Any payment to the lender in addition to the rate of interest legally permissible, whether called by the name of bonus or commission or *by any other name*, is usurious." (Emphasis added.) *Restatement, Contracts*, § 526. Compensation is determined not by what the borrower pays but by what the lender receives; thus, if the borrower is the beneficiary of a payment it will not be interest. *Silver Homes, Inc. v. Marx & Bensdorf, Inc.*, 206 Tenn. 361, 333 S.W.2d 810 (1960). Nor are expenses incident to making a loan and furnishing the lender with satisfactory security for its repayment compensation or interest. *Silver Homes, Inc. v. Marx & Bensdorf, Inc., supra*.

The note executed by Aztec Properties bears ten percent interest on its face; that interest has been paid and is not in issue here. The borrower claims that the "indexed principal" constitutes additional interest. The bank argues that the "indexed principal" equals the difference in value between the principal lent and returned, and is not extra compensation.

There being no Tennessee case law directly on point, both parties attempt to analogize the long series of "exchange of money" cases.

One of the earliest of these cases was *Lawrence v. Morrison,* 9 Tenn. 444 (1830). In that case the borrower gave a note to Sullivan for $607.87½ in Tennessee bank notes, payable on December 25, 1825. Sullivan assigned the note to Lawrence. On December 24, 1825, the borrower executed a second note in exchange for the first note for the same sum payable in gold and silver on August 1, 1825 [sic]. After the second note fell due a suit was instituted to which the borrower plead usury averring that that $607.00 in bank notes was worth only $456.00 specie. The Court set guidelines for determining usury:

> A jury in trying the case before us would ... first enquire what was the value of the bank notes on the day the second note was given. If the sum found, compared with the amount of the note given for specie, fell so far short as to show that more than the rate of six per cent per annum had been reserved, they might then infer that the whole amount was a device to cover usury .... In short, it would be for the jury to ascertain whether under all the circumstances, it was intended by the parties under color of supposing depreciated paper equal to specie, to cover a corrupt bargain against the statutes concerning usury. *Id.* at 446.

In *Weatherhead v. Boyers,* 15 Tenn. 545 (1835), Weatherhead borrowed a sum in Tennessee bank notes from Boyers and agreed to repay an equal nominal amount in specie or notes on the Bank of the United States. The latter were equal to gold or silver while the former were greatly under par. The Court looked beyond the devices and disguises of the parties to the substance of the transaction and found usury.

The Court reached the opposite result in *Turney v. State,* 24 Tenn. 407 (1844). In that case a contractor with the post office had an arrangement with the bank whereby he deposited eastern funds and gold and silver and received Tennessee bank notes of equal face value in exchange. The later were only worth 92-93% of the former. The contractor also had the privilege of borrowing additional money from the bank up to twice the amount of his funds. Although the difference in value between the eastern funds and specie, on one hand, and the Tennessee bank notes, on the other, exceeded the legal maximum interest at that time (6%), the Court found no usury because the parties had no corrupt intentions. It pointed out that the notes received by the contractor "were notes of specie-paying banks, as sound or available, perhaps, to him and to others, in ordinary transactions, as eastern funds." *Id.* at 409.

The Court in *Turney v. State, supra,* relied heavily upon *United States v. Waggener,* 9 Pet. 378, 9 L.Ed. 163 (1835). In *Waggener,* the borrower executed a promissory note for $5,000.00 in Kentucky bank notes. At the time of the loan the Kentucky bank notes were circulating at a rate of thirty-three to forty percent depreciation below their nominal amounts. In response to the claim of usury the United States Supreme court stated, "to constitute usury within the prohibitions of the law, there must be an intention knowingly to contract for or to take usurious interest; for if neither party intend it, but act bona fide and innocently, the law will not infer a corrupt agreement." *Id.* at 171. The Court concluded that the loan in *Waggener* was not per se illegal because the Kentucky bank notes might have been worth more to the parties than their marketable value at the time of the loan. If the parties bona fide estimate equivalent values in the credits or commodities they are exchanging, there is no usury, said the Court.

In *Hamilton v. Moore,* 26 Tenn. 35 (1846), the complainant borrowed a sum of money in Alabama bank notes and sometime afterwards bound himself by a bill single to repay the face value of the loan in Tennessee bank notes. He later claimed that the bill single was usurious because Alabama bank notes were worth less than those of Tennessee. The parties agreed that they did not intend to commit usury and that the borrower said at the time that Alabama notes would be as valuable to him as Tennessee money. The Court relying on *Turney v. State, supra,* found no usury. It stated that "usury is not an inference of law, to be drawn from the mere inequality of value between the currency loaned and that stipulated to be paid for it, but, on the contrary, is a question of intention, to be made out by the proof of facts." *Id.* at 36.

In *Finely v. McCormick*, 53 Tenn. 392 (1871), the complainant lent the borrower $200.00 in gold, $150.00 in silver, and $200.00 in greenbacks or United States currency, and the latter agreed to pay back the gold and silver or to pay $1.50 for every dollar in gold, and the difference in value of silver. The borrower argued that this was usurious. The Court concluded that it could "not judicially know the value of 'greenbacks,' so called, and for ought that appears on the face of the bill, the parties may have fairly estimated the difference in value between them and gold and silver, and the contract is, *prima facie*, lawful." *Id.* at 394.

Finally in *In re Mansfield Steel Corporation*, 30 F.2d 832 (E.D.Mich. 1929), a Canadian resident lent a Michigan corporation $88,000.00, primarily in Canadian money. The corporation in exchange executed a promissory note for that amount in American funds plus the maximum legal interest in Michigan. At the time of the loan Canadian money was worth less than American money, but the parties anticipated they would be at par by the time of repayment. Evidence of the parties' expectations was an important factor in the court's decision that they lacked the intention to lend money at usurious interest.

In our view these cases are fundamentally different from the case under consideration here. With the exception of the last case all occurred in a very particular historical context; they were decided at a time when different kinds of money with different values were in circulation. Faced with the problem of the interchange of this money the court concluded that usury should be ascertained according to the parties' intentions; thus, when the moneys exchanged pursuant to a loan are *different in kind* but *equal in value* in the honest judgment of the parties, the courts will not assume that a difference in their market value is hidden interest. It is important to note that except for *Mansfield, supra*, equality of value was evaluated in these cases as of the time of the loan or agreement to repay; in no case was the sum owing adjusted at the time of repayment according to fluctuations in value of the principal after it was lent. And in *Mansfield* the parties merely considered the projected fluctuation in value of the currency of repayment, not appreciation or depreciation in value of the principal loaned.

We have found no case holding that an intentional increase in the face value of the principal to account for inflation does not constitute interest. In practice the lender has long borne the risk of inflation in this state. The interest charged by a lender is not profit, strictly speaking, but compensation for the use of money and for bearing the risk that the borrower might not repay or the principal might depreciate in value. We accordingly hold that the "indexed principal" constitutes usurious interest.

The next question raised is whether the defense of usury, provided in T.C.A. § 47-14-112, is available to *corporate* borrowers. The usury statutes of many states exempt corporations from their protection. See Hershel Shanks, *Practical Problems in the Application of Archaic Usury Statutes*, 53 Va.L.Rev. 327 at 346 *et seq.* (1967). Tennessee, however, has never adopted such a statute nor have its courts recognized a corporate exclusion. But the Bank argues that the Legislature has granted corporations organized under Tennessee law the right to borrow at whatever interest rate they choose. T.C.A. § 48-402 provides:

> Each corporation shall have power:
> "(g)To make contracts and, subject to such limitations, if any, as may be contained in the charter, to incur liabilities, *borrow money at such rates of interest as the corporation may determine*, issue its notes, bonds and other obligations, and secure any of its obligations by mortgage, pledge or otherwise. (Emphasis added.)

In our opinion this statute merely enables corporations to borrow money at such rates as are *permitted by law*. The Legislature has no power to authorize corporations to lend or borrow at any interest rate exceeding the uniform and equal rate fixed by general law. *McKinney v. Memphis Overton Hotel Company*, 59 Tenn. 104 (1873). Nor can this rate exceed ten percent per annum. *Constitution of Tennessee*, Article 11, § 7.

Aztec Properties executed a written waiver of the defense of usury at the time the note was signed, and the Bank relies upon this waiver. We find no merit in this argument because the consent or cooperation of the one paying the usurious interest is immaterial. *Providence A. M. E. Church v. Sauer*, 45 Tenn.App. 287, 323 S.W.2d 6 (1958).

Even if the "indexed principal" were not considered to be interest, we are of the opinion that as employed in this case the device of an "indexed principal" could not withstand analysis under the

Joint Congressional Resolution of June 5, 1933, popularly referred to as the "Gold Clause" Resolution. Congress made its intention extremely clear in this resolution, in which it stated:

> Every obligation, heretofore or hereafter incurred, whether or not any such provision is contained therein or made with respect thereto, shall be discharged upon payment, dollar for dollar, in any coin or currency which at the time of payment is legal tender for public and private debts. 31 U.S.C.A. § 463.

We are not concerned in this case with the exchange of currencies upon an international market, nor does the case involve the sale of any commodity. In this case a domestic customer borrowed funds from a national bank in a principal amount expressed in and repayable in United States dollars. It would be contrary to the national policy, as expressed by the Congress and as interpreted in several cases by the United States Supreme Court, to permit a lender to require of a borrower a different quantity or number of dollars from that loaned, insofar as the principal amount is concerned. In *Guaranty Trust Company, Trustee v. Henwood, Trustee et al.,* 307 U.S. 247, 252, 59 S.Ct. 847, 850, 83 L.Ed. 1266 (1939), the United States Supreme Court said:

> Having thus unmistakably stamped illegality upon both outstanding and future contractual provisions designed to require payment by debtors in a frozen money value rather than in a dollar of legal tender current at date of payment, Congress—apparently to obviate any possible misunderstanding as to the breadth of its objective— added, with studied precision, a catchall second sentence sweeping in 'every obligation', existing or future, 'payable in money of the United States', irrespective of 'whether or not any such provision is contained therein or made with respect thereto.' The obligations hit at by Congress were those 'payable in money of the United States.' All such obligations were declared dischargeable 'upon payment, dollar for dollar, in any coin or currency [of the United States] which at the time of the payment is legal tender for public and private debts.

See also *Norman v. Baltimore & Ohio Railroad Company,* 294 U.S. 240, 55 S.Ct. 407, 79 L.Ed. 885 (1935); *Holyoke Water Power Company v. American Writing Paper Company,* 300 U.S. 324, 57 S.Ct. 485, 81 L.Ed. 678 (1937).

Accordingly, even if the reserved interest in the present case were only five percent, or some other rate clearly free from any question of usury, we are of opinion that a national or state banking institution would not be authorized to "index" the principal amount of money loaned to a domestic customer on a promissory note, so as to vary the number of dollars which may be required to be paid in satisfaction of the debt.

It is recognized, of course, that "indexing" is a current and very legitimate concept in modern business transactions. Nothing in this opinion should be taken to suggest that there is an impropriety in measuring future rentals by a consumer price index, or some comparable standard, in leasing agreements. Nor is there anything improper in computing future wages or salaries by such an index in collective bargaining or employment contracts. As long as there is a national currency, however, which by law is legal tender for the payment of public and private debts, we hold that the indexing device cannot properly be applied to the principal of a debt evidenced by a promissory note payable in that currency.

Accordingly, the judgment of the Chancellor is reversed, all costs taxed against the appellee, Union Planters National Bank of Memphis.

Fones, C. J., and Cooper, Henry and Harbison, J J., concur.

"Aztec Properties" Discussed

Aztec Properties, Inc. negotiated a $50,000 loan from Union Planters National Bank at the Tennessee statutory maximum 10 percent interest rate.[1] The promissory note called for the loan principal to be adjusted for inflation (deflation) according to a formula based on the consumer price index.[2] A written waiver of the defense of usury was executed at the signing of the note by the promisor corporation. On maturity of the note Aztec Properties repaid the $50,000 plus interest but refused to pay the "indexed principal" of $500, claiming a usury defense. The bank sued for the $500 plus interest from maturity and chancery court granted summary judgment for the bank. On appeal, the Tennessee Supreme Court reversed the lower court releasing Aztec Properties from any obligation to pay the "indexed principal." The court held that the indexing device was usurious interest exceeding the constitutional rate and that, apart from the usury question, indexing the principal of a debt is improper for contravention of the national currency policy.[3]

Because of the novelty of this attempt at circumvention of the usury law, there was no case law directly on point. The plaintiff bank argued that the indexed principal was the difference in value between the principal lent and returned rather than being extra compensation. The court concluded that an intentional increase in the face value of the loan was usurious interest because interest includes *all* compensation for the use of money. "Any payment to the lender in addition to the rate of interest legally permissible, whether called ... *by any other name,* is usurious."[4] The lender has traditionally borne the risk of inflation and interest compensates him for this risk, the court explained.[5]

Waiver of the defense was immaterial to the court since consent of the one paying the usurious interest is irrelevant in Tennessee.[6] Nor did the fact of incorporation deprive the appellant of the defense, as is the case in other states.[7] Answering the bank's assertion that corporations have the power granted legislatively "to borrow money at such rates of interest as the corporation may determine,"[8] the court held that the legislature has no power to grant any rate but a uniform and equal rate applicable to all and not exceeding 10 percent because of constitutional mandate.[9]

Indexing is a legitimate business concept which the court approved for such uses as lease agreements, employment contracts and collective bargaining.[10] Relying heavily on the United States Joint Congressional "Gold Clause" Resolution of 1933,[11] however, the court concluded that indexing the principal of a loan violates the national policy of debt repayment "dollar for dollar" in legal tender.[12] Quoting the United States Supreme Court in *Guaranty Trust Co. v. Henwood,*[13] the court found

> illegality upon both outstanding and future contractual provisions designed to require payment by debtors in a frozen money value rather than in a dollar of legal tender current at date of payment. ...[14]

Thus, indexing the principal of a loan so that the number of dollars to be repaid varies from the number of dollars loaned was held to violate federal law.

Money Market Price Ignores Usury Rate

Aztec Properties portrays the dichotomy between the moral and economic aspects of usury laws.[15] The framers of the Tennessee constitution felt it was, perhaps, immoral to charge a borrower more than 10 percent interest.[16] The court speaks of "protection" regarding the usury statute. Legal scholars, on the other hand, urge legislatures to view usury in its economic setting so that the mischief it does can be perceived correctly.[17] Ryan, in his treatise *Usury and Usury Laws,* illustrates that moral usury (exacting of unreasonably high interest by taking advantage of the borrower) cannot be prevented by statutory maximum usury laws.[18] Usury laws "were enacted in ignorance of the economic laws of interest and without taking the trouble to study lenders' costs."[19]

"There is a marked difference between the making of a large commercial or investment loan and a small loan to an industrial worker," Ryan points out.[20] The price of money in commercial transactions is fixed nationally. There is less need for protection of commercial borrowers because they tend to be more sophisticated,[21] and commercial borrowers can often avoid personal liability when individuals cannot.[22] These differences are not reflected in the Tennessee constitution and cases interpreting it; the interest rate is required to be equal for all.[23] Ironically, an industrial worker in Tennessee may pay 18 percent annual interest on his credit purchase,[24] but Aztec Properties may not pay over 10 percent for a $50,000 loan.

States surrounding Tennessee recognize the differing needs and ability to pay of business borrowers. These states offer a higher interest rate to lenders than does Tennessee and thus siphon away Tennessee funds.[25] Business borrowers with credit outside the state find a source of capital there when the market rate is above Tennessee's 10 percent limit.[26] Those without outside credit may be forced to participate in one of the many subterfuges to avoid the usury law such as fees, penalties, compensating balances, etc.[27] to compensate the lender for his alternative use costs.[28] These devices have the twofold result of promoting disrespect for the law and raising the cost of money to the borrower.[29] The borrower who needs funds will find them and will pay at least the market price, regardless of the usury ceiling.

A committee of the Tennessee General Assembly in 1859 [reported] that the state usury law was then "defeating its own object" by driving money out of the state where it could earn more money.[30] In 1974 Congress recognized the severity of the restriction on commerce caused by usury laws in the states of Tennessee, Arkansas and Montana.[31] Passage of a three-year increase in the interest rate ceiling followed testimony by bankers that loans "are becoming unavailable, liquidity of financial institutions is adversely affected, small borrowers are disadvantaged with competing with national corporations and there is an outflow of funds from the states."[32] This legislation took effect after the note in Aztec Properties was signed and may be superseded by state law at any time at the state's option.[33]

Legislative Alternatives

The Tennessee Supreme Court, by terming the indexed principal additional interest, refused to give relief to the lender who was trapped between the usury ceiling and a higher market rate. It reaffirmed the rigidity of the Tennessee constitution. Now, the only possible relief is a constitutional amendment such as Oklahoma passed in 1968.[34] If an amendment were passed, supplemental laws would be necessary in Tennessee to distinguish between classes of borrowers and amounts borrowed. Four distinct alternatives exist.

The first alternative is to except corporations from the defense of usury as twenty-six states have done,[36] but the better view is to include noncorporate partnerships and associations as well as businesses in general so as to broaden the opportunities of all commercial borrowers.[36] A variation of the corporate exception is to raise the corporate ceiling above the legal and contract rate, as nine states have done, and allow a corporate usury defense subject to this rate.[37] The advantage of the corporate exception is to open sources of capital to the commercial borrower while continuing to regulate loans to individuals. The major disadvantage of this method is that some persons can be forced to incorporate to get the higher rate.[38]

A second alternative is the enactment of the Uniform Consumer Credit Code (UCCC).[39] The UCCC produces uniformity and protection of borrowers of amounts up to $25,000. Above $25,000 there is no ceiling on loans and all borrowers are free of restrictions.[40] The United States District Court for the Western District of Oklahoma, in *Stricklin v. Investors Syndicate Life Insurance &*

Annuity Co., held that the UCCC cannot be invoked by the large-scale commercial borrower since the Code applies only to consumer credit transactions up to $25,000.[41] Presumably then, in view of *Stricklin* the UCCC must be supplemented by other specific legislation to remove the ceiling in large commercial loans. Oklahoma has provided for such specific supplemental legislation.[42]

A third alternative is the English system whereby a loan with interest in excess of 48 percent is presumed excessive unless proved otherwise.[43] The English courts have the power to reopen any loan transaction in order to reduce the rate if the charge is found to be harsh and unconscionable. This system has the advantage of allowing the market rate and judgment of the parties to control yet sanctioning the overreaching party.[44] English courts are free to assess attorneys' fees as well as costs. Therefore, the borrower's threat of suit carries weight.[45] The English system assures that high-risk capital is available from licensed, regulated lenders so that loan sharking is unnecessary.[46] It has the further advantages of avoiding (1) a hodgepodge of classification laws, (2) a plethora of judicial exceptions and (3) private circumvention.[47] A variant, adding more certainty to loan transactions, is the enactment of a reasonable interest ceiling with the provision that violations are only prima facie usurious and that equity will determine if there has been overreaching.[48] The English system and the other three alternatives operate most efficiently with a comprehensive definition of interest which includes points, premiums, fees and all other subterfuges.[49]

An innovative fourth alternative is the variable interest rate tied to a reliable index.[50] A high usury ceiling or none at all is necessary for this alternative method to function. This system allows the interest rate to fluctuate with the money market and has met with some acceptance in residential real estate transactions.[51] It has the advantages of profitability to the lender and assurance of a supply of capital to meet borrower demand. However, it has the disadvantages of uncertainty to the borrower, doubtful negotiability under the Uniform Commercial Code[52] and improper notice under the Truth in Lending Act.[53] Commentators have suggested methods of avoiding each of these problems.[54]

Indexing as a Stabilizer

The indexing concept was the heart of the *Aztec Properties* case. The court's decision that principal indexing is violative of federal law was dictum, since it was not necessary to the court's resolution of the case, and further, it may be harmful to the general concept of indexing as a method of buying power stabilization. Did Congress intend in 1933 to set down the maxim that every debt must henceforth be repaid with the identical number of dollars of principal borrowed?[55] The *Congressional Record* and cases interpreting the Gold Clause Resolution of 1933 are persuasive authority for a different conclusion. The purpose of the Resolution was to insure that there was "only one currency"[56] the value of which was to be controlled by Congress, and not by the international value of gold.[57] In that historical setting, contracts and bonds calling for alternative payment in gold were causing $1.69 of currency to be repaid for $1.00 of gold.[58] Gold was being hoarded and leaving the country in great quantities.[59] The emergency was national bankruptcy; it was a crisis of gold value versus dollar value.[60] *Guaranty Trust*, relied on by the court, is largely irrelevant to indexing as a stabilization tool because the case referred only to provisions requiring "payment in (1) gold; (2) a *particular kind of coin or currency* of the United States; or (3) in an amount of United States money measured by gold or a *particular kind of United States coin or currency*."[61] *Guaranty Trust* referred to a "frozen money value"[62] whereas an index clause fluctuates continually with changes in the prices of commodities and services.[63] Gold clauses attempted to stabilize the underlying value of currency; index clauses merely seek to stabilize the buying power of currency.[64]

Commentators believe the Gold Clause Resolution was not intended to affect obligations including index clauses.[65] They argue that the prerogative of the government to control the value of currency remains intact with index clauses.[66] Without the Gold Clause Resolution argument there is little impediment to the future use of index clauses, as applied to either principal or interest. Indexing remains a viable alternative to the crippling statutory maximum interest rate, assuming public education and acceptance occur.[67]

Conclusion

The effects of the *Aztec Properties* case are devastating upon the Tennessee businessman. Federal legislation is a temporary solution, but eventually the people of Tennessee must recognize the needs of commerce by amending their rigid constitutional usury ceiling. They have many alternative directions to select for supportive legislation. Indexing, despite the court's condemnation of it, is one of these viable alternatives. Until the citizens act, other borrowers are free to enter loan transactions, promise to pay the market rate and than later hide behind the "protection" of a usury statute which has, since 1859, defeated its own object by driving money out of the state.[68]

Nine

How to Use the Gold Clause Profitably*

The author of the previous chapter characterizes the practical consequences of *Aztec Properties* as "devastating" for Tennessee businessmen. If there is any merit to that decision (or to *Olwine*), the consequences for creditors using the gold clause in other states with anti-usury laws could be no less devastating. Therefore, it is important to know whether *Olwine* and *Aztec Properties* were correctly decided.

The courts in *Olwine* and *Aztec Properties* reached the same conclusion, in virtually the same language: "the extra sum due, therefore, represents a charge in the nature of interest" *(Olwine)*; "... the 'indexed principal' constitutes ... interest" (*Aztec Properties*).** This conclusion was predicated on certain premises which

---

* This chapter was written especially for *The Gold Clause* by the editor.

** The court really meant not that the indexed principal itself was interest, but that any additional principal payable to the creditor as the result of indexed principal constituted additional interest. The *Aztec Properties* court's observation that indexed principal, even if not interest, "would be contrary to the national policy" as expressed in the Joint Resolution of 1933 and in the *Gold Clause Cases,* was unnecessary and of no legal significance: the court had already concluded that the indexed principal in the case violated Tennessee's own constitutional ceiling on interest. Moreover, after *Aztec Properties* was decided, the Joint Resolution was effectively repealed for all gold clauses created after October 28, 1977, so that even if there was merit to the *Aztec Properties* court's *dictum* about principal indexing and the Joint Resolution, the *dictum* would be wholly inapplicable to all gold clauses created after October 28, 1977.

were stated in the cases, and it depends for its validity on whether it follows logically from those premises.

In *Olwine*, there were two explicit premises which led to the court's conclusion:

- interest represents compensation for the use of money and "inflation plays an important role in determining the interest rates to be charged by a creditor";

- the creditor's "effort to keep the '1957 dollar' value of the principal was an attempt to avoid the effects of inflation."

In *Aztec Properties*, there was only one explicit premise:

- interest compensates for the use of money, for the risk of non-payment, and/or inflation.

From *Olwine's* two premises and from *Aztec Properties'* one, it is not logically possible to reach the conclusion that any additional principal payable to the creditor as the result of indexed principal constituted additional interest. This conclusion, reached by each court, is nothing more than a *non sequitur*. As such, it is invalid and not entitled to any weight.

Ordinarily, an illogical conclusion would be sufficient reason to justify no further consideration of a case. However, because *Olwine* and *Aztec Properties* are still "good law" in Pennsylvania and Tennessee, they could be used as precedent elsewhere, thereby posing a potential problem for users of the gold clause. Further analysis of the two cases is therefore warranted.

In addition to being a *non sequitur*, the courts' conclusion is based on mere assertion. In neither case does that conclusion rest on even a single legal precedent—which means that it lacks any legal roots whatever. In neither case can any reasons be found.

The *Aztec Properties* court observed (and the *Olwine* court implied) that "the lender has long borne the risk of inflation in this state." This statement is hardly a reason supporting the court's conclusion, and in no way explains *why* the creditor should be forced to accept the unwanted *certainty* (not the "risk") of inflation. Indeed, the court's observation merely begs the question.

And, historically, the facts are otherwise. Prior to the New Deal, hundreds of millions of dollars worth of gold clause obligations existed, indexing the principal of countless loans and placing the inflation risk squarely on the *debtor,* not the creditor. The New Deal's fierce efforts to nullify the gold clause were designed to relieve *debtors* of a large part of what they owed.

Another fatal mistake of *Olwine* and *Aztec Properties* was their misunderstanding of just what "principal" and "interest" really are. To begin with, when judges simply assert that principal and interest are the same, they erase all distinctions between the two. Obviously, there is a big difference—as anyone who has ever loaned or borrowed money knows.

According to *Webster's,* "principal" is the "amount of a debt". Therefore, to index principal is to calculate the amount of a debt at the time of repayment based upon a formula which takes into account whether the true value of the principal has changed during the period of the loan. The creditor's obvious motive in indexing principal is to protect its value from inflation, as the consumer-price-index formulas found in *Olwine* and *Aztec Properties* make clear, and as the courts in those cases recognized. Indexing principal seeks to assure that inflation during the course of the loan will be neutralized by requiring repayment in an amount equal to what the principal's purchasing power was when the loan was made. In short, indexing principal seeks to assure the stable value of the money loaned.

On the other hand, *Webster's* defines "interest" as "money paid for the use of money." In this sense, interest is akin to rent. Just as a tenant pays for the use of a landlord's apartment, and a tourist pays for the use of a Hertz car, a debtor pays for the use of a creditor's money.

Therefore, for a court to say that principal is interest, is for it to say that the "amount of a debt" is the same as "money paid for the use of money." In other words, the sum owed is the same as the rent for that sum; the apartment and the car are the same as the rent for them. And for a court to say that the increased payment attributable to indexed principal is interest, is for it to say that a creditor seeks to protect the value of a large amount of principal against inflation by relying on a small amount of interest. This is tantamount to saying that to protect a one-year, $1,000,000 loan, against $100,000 depreciation caused by 10% annual inflation, the creditor relies on only a few percentage point of interest (perhaps 2% or 3%, amounting to $20,000 or $30,000) on top of the interest

attributable to the rent. Such an idea is *prima facie* absurd. A creditor could never charge sufficient interest both to compensate for
the money's use, *and* to preserve the principal's value. For example, if on the $1,000,000 loan, 9% ($90,000) was a fair interest-rental
figure, and inflation was at 10% ($100,000), the creditor would have
to charge 19% ($190,000) interest in order to be both compensated
and protected. Common sense dictates that no matter how high an
interest rate, it is necessarily insufficient by itself to prevent inflation from ravaging the creditor's principal. The only way that
loaned capital can be (or ever has been) fully insulated from inflation, is by protecting the *capital*, not by charging high interest
rates (even if one could).

The display of ignorance about economics in *Olwine* and *Aztec
Properties* was not limited to the principal-interest distinction. As
Ms. Dodson has shown in Chapter 8, the two courts also misunderstood just how counter-productive anti-usury laws are. Because of
the anti-usury laws, there are two prices for the rental of money;
the market price, set by supply-demand forces, and the legal
price, set by the anti-usury laws. When money (like anything else)
becomes scarce, its price goes up, and creditors lend at the highest
price they can get. But when that market price exceeds the legal
price, during periods of "tight money," for example, the creditor
will not lend at the legal price. Instead, the creditor will look for an
investment which can be made at the market price, free of the
legal price established by the anti-usury laws. The result is that the
anti-usury laws deny needed capital to everyone supposedly "protected" by those laws.

For example, in 1969, housing starts in New York had fallen off
considerably because mortgage money had become very difficult
to obtain. Savings banks in Manhattan and the Bronx had about
sixty-nine percent of their mortgage money invested out of the
state as of June 30, 1969. The figure for pending mortgage com-
mitments was even higher: 80.8%. The reason was obvious. Lending institutions could receive higher returns elsewhere.[1] Obviously,
such counterproductive aspects of anti-usury laws made no impression on the *Olwine* and *Aztec Properties* courts.*

---

* It is interesting to observe that when the anti-usury laws pinch too tight to
suit even the government, legal steps are quickly taken to ameliorate the laws
effect. Some fascinating examples are found in Chapter 8.[2]

The last, and most fundamental, criticism of the *Olwine* and *Aztec Properties* decisions relates not to what the courts misunderstood, but to what they understood only too well: political-economic *policy*. Consider the scenario of a simple contemporary loan transaction. The creditor (whose business is to make loans) is asked to lend $100,000 for one year. By year's end, twelve percent inflation will reduce the $100,000's value to $88,000, guaranteeing a $12,000 loss. Hemmed in by a legislative ceiling on interest rarely exceeding ten or eleven percent, and judicial decisions holding that indexed principal produces illegal gain, the creditor loses from the instant the loan is made. The state's anti-usury laws have removed from the bargaining table the creditor's chance to negotiate away the consequences of inevitable inflation.

Taking money from creditors and giving it to debtors in this way, because the former have it and the latter need it, is nothing more than "legalized" theft. This is the actual basis of the *Olwine* and *Aztec Properties* decisions.

Given this recognition, and all the other reasons why *Olwine* and *Aztec Properties* were wrongly decided, it should be clear that the cases are aberrant. As such, neither should rightfully present any obstacle to successful and profitable use of the gold clause. However, the cases do exist, and other courts are, at least theoretically, capable of repeating what was done in Pennsylvania and Tennessee.

If, because of this possibility, the creditor wishes to eliminate even the remotest chance of a usury allegation, then it is probably better to abandon the traditional gold clause. Instead, the creditor can turn to a somewhat different anti-inflation device, which can afford better protection, as a comparision of the two devices will show.

Basically, as Professor Nussbaum shows in Chapter 1, there are three types of traditional gold clauses. The Joint Resolution of June 5, 1933, which nullified all three, characterized them as obligations purporting "to give the obligee a right to require payment (1) in gold or (2) a particular kind of coin or currency, or (3) in an amount in money of the United States measured thereby ..."

In the first, "a gold bullion clause," the creditor lends currency dollars and receives in payment a quantity of gold bullion equal to the actual value of the dollars when they were loaned, plus interest.

Not dissimilar is the "gold coin clause," which Professor Nussbaum describes as "a promise by a money debtor that the sum promised will be paid in gold coins." Prior to 1933, according to Professor Nussbaum, "the clause almost universally employed" in the United States promised to pay a specified amount of dollars, in gold coin of the United States, of or equal to the standard of weight and fineness existing on the day the obligation was incurred.

The third type, the "gold value clause," is different from the other two. It requires payment not in gold bullion or gold coin, but in currency dollars which have been indexed against gold during the period of the loan.

There is one crucially important element common to each type of the gold clause *and* to the loans in *Olwine* and *Aztec Properties*. If that element is present in a loan, it could enable any court to refuse to effectuate any traditional indexing device. That element is: *denomination of the debt in currency dollars.**

If, as F.D.R., his Congress, and his Court, so often reminded the American people, the government possesses absolute power over money, it is safe to say that legislatures and courts can exercise substantial control over currency dollars. (An example of this control is *Olwine* and *Aztec Properties* where each court operated on the implicit assumption that money was the government's business, and therefore government could simply ignore inflation's depreciation of the creditor's currency dollars.) Recognizing this, it seems clear that to avoid government's power over money, a successful anti-inflation device must avoid any connection with money. The idea is not as farfetched or as complicated as it might appear.

Let us assume that a debtor wishes to borrow $3,000 when gold is selling at $300 per ounce. Fearing inflation, the creditor insists on some form of protection against it. The debtor is willing to provide that protection. The loan agreement makes no reference to currency dollars. Instead, the creditor lends and the debtor repays 10 ounces of gold.**

---

* When any type of the gold clause is used, curency dollars are always loaned. When a gold value clause is used, currency dollars are also used in repayment. In *Olwine* and *Aztec Properties,* currency dollars were loaned and repaid.

** The gold can be in bullion or bullion coin form, so long as its weight and fineness are specified and objectively ascertainable.

This approach has several benefits. First, since the transaction is bullion-for-bullion, repayment of the loan is "in kind"—ironically, exactly what the *Olwine* and *Aztec Properties* courts required when they insisted on dollar-for-dollar repayment—thus creating no problem of increased value through indexing of a loan denominated in currency dollars. The transaction, at least as to principal,* has no relation to "money". Indeed, further proof that the transaction is unrelated to money can be found in the government's long-standing claim that gold has nothing to do with money.

Another important benefit is the ease with which the inflation protection provision of the loan can be drafted. In the conventional gold bullion and gold coin clause, care must be taken to provide specifically for the exact type of bullion or coin to be repaid. If repayment is to be in coin, special attention must be given to eliminating all numismatic considerations, assuring that the coin has only bullion value. If the gold value clause is used, the drafting problems become more acute. Since the indexing yardstick is, loosely speaking, "the price of gold," extreme care must be taken to mark exactly the dates of calculation, the gold market whose price will be the benchmark, whether the price will be an average one or something else. In contrast, protecting principal from inflation in a bullion-for-bullion transaction basically requires only a simple provision, stating that a given number of ounces of gold (either bullion or coins) of a certain fineness is being loaned and that exactly the same weight and fineness will be repaid.**

At this point the reader may wonder whether the inflation protection device just discussed, can actually be so easy to effectuate. How, one might ask, do the creditor and debtor move around all that bullion? When one's broker purchases, say, a utility bond, bank transfers are used, not armored cars loaded with gold.

A creditor might want to know what assurances there could be

---

* Obviously, there will also be interest to pay. However, protecting the interest from inflation is not nearly as serious a matter as protecting the principal. For one thing, the interest is rarely more than fifteen percent of the principal. For another, the interest can be calculated on the averaged-out value (in any currency, including dollars) of the principal during the duration of the loan, and be payable in currency dollars, so long as the statutory usury ceiling is not exceeded.

** As to how to handle the interest aspect of the transaction, see the footnote above.

that, when repayment time came, the debtor would even have the necessary gold. What if, during the period of the loan, the price of gold skyrocketed?

And, of course, there is always the ultimate doomsday question: what if we have a new New Deal? What if private gold ownership is illegalized, or another Joint Resolution is enacted stating that "every provision contained in or made with respect to any obligation which purports to give the obligee a right to require payment in gold or a particular kind of coin or currency, or in any amount in money of the United States measured thereby, is declared to be against public policy...?

First, as to the question of transporting the bullion: with gold anywhere over $300 per ounce, physical delivery weighs in at about $5,000 per pound—hardly difficult, let alone impossible, for a debtor or creditor of average strength in a modest loan situation. But when the sums are substantial, making physical delivery impossible, the solution is to use a warehouse receipt. Today, they are readily available for virtually any quantity of gold.

Next, as to the problem of the debtor having sufficient bullion to repay the debt: the creditor can easily assure this by requiring as a condition of the loan that the debtor purchase an adequate futures contract.* Just as mortgagees require evidence of fire insurance running to their benefit in mortgage loans on one family houses, for example, creditors can obtain exactly the same kind of protection from their debtors by means of gold futures.

Lastly, the doomsday problem: Even if history repeats itself with a new New Deal, the creditor can still outwit the government by falling back on a *silver* bullion contingency clause. The clause would be automatically activated by illegalization of private gold ownership, or nullfication of gold payment clauses.

The outline of an appropriate clause protecting the creditor's principal from inflation, combining the bullion-for-bullion provision and the silver bullion contingency, might go something like this:

> Debtor hereby borrows from creditor 100 ounces of gold bullion, of 999 fineness, and agrees to repay same to creditor on or before

---

* The idea of hedging the gold clause obligation has been discussed by Howard Ruff, in *The Ruff Times* issues of December 1 and December 15, 1977.

December 31, 1987.

If, for any reason, it shall become illegal or otherwise legally impossible for debtor to repay the aforesaid gold, the event causing such illegality or impossibility shall automatically convert debtor's obligation to one requiring the repayment of an amount of silver bullion which shall be equal to what the value of gold would have been at the time of repayment, all values to be established by the Zürich fixing.

In conclusion, it should be noted that the bullion-for-bullion alternative has been proposed only out of an excess of caution. It will be of interest only to the creditor who is a bit skittish about the traditional gold clause, who wishes to eliminate every possibility of a usury allegation.

For all other creditors, the traditional gold clause—relegalized by the federal government—should be of considerable interest. Despite *Olwine* and *Aztec Properties*, and despite the traditional gold clause being uncomfortably denominated in currency dollars, no serious challenge has been made to it since 1933. As of now, the gold clause is alive and well—and it ought to be used.

Footnotes

ONE

[1]For comparative discussions, see Midas, *Die Goldklausel in Waehrungsverfall* (1924); 3 Neumeyer, *Internationales Verwaltungsrecht*, part 2 III (1930) 337; Nussbaum, *Vertraglicher Schutz gegen Schwankungen des Geldwertes* (1928); Henry Ussing, *"Guldklausuler"*, *Ugeskrift for Retsvaesen* (Copenhagen) 1933 B 264; Nussbaum, *"La Clause-Or dans les contrats internationaux"* in (1934) Académie de Droit International de la Haye, 43 *Recueil des Cours* 559; Domke, *La Clause "Dollar-or"* (2d ed., 1935, Paris); Domke, *La clause valeur-or-dans la jurisprudence récente"*, Nouvelle Revue de Droit Int. Privé 1935, 29; Libourel, *Het Vraagstuk der Goud-Clausule in Nederland* (1932); John Gabriels, *Goud-Clausules* (Rotterdam, 1936); Wortley, *"The Gold Clause"*, (1936) *British Yearbook of Int. Law* 112; Ulrich, *Die Geldklausel* (Switzerland, year not indicated). Special literature on the national gold clause laws is referred to *infra*, p. 361, n. 25 (American); p. 335, n. 1 (French); p. 329, n. 12 (German); p. 349, n. 73 (Italian); p. 361, n. 19 (Swiss). The international aspects of the gold clause are dealt with *infra*, sec. 30. The *Bull,I.I.I.* and *Z.A.I.P.* contain regular reports on gold clause cases and writings.

[2]*Supra*, p. 10.

[3]Helfferich, *"Die geschichtliche Entwickelung der Münzsysteme"* in (1895) 64 *Jahrbücher für Nationaloekonomie und Statistik* 801, 808, points out that in Northern Germany, in the middle of the 18th century, pure and simple debts were still "something new". This is probably true for long-time debts. An English protective clause of the latter half of the fifteenth century is presented in Y.B. 9 Edward IV, 49 [Hill. T. pl. 61] (1470). A loan was given in 2 Ed. IV (1462/3) of 40 pound sterling in groates and nobles, nobles being a gold coin. The debtor obligated himself to pay back the said £40 in the same metal at the value they had when received. Uncommon, though significant, is a case decided in 1300 by the Fair Court of St. Ives. (1 Selden Society, *Select Cases in the Law Merchant* 80). The buyer paid the purchase price in crockards and pollards, inferior coin. When the seller objected, the buyer promised to exchange the coin for good ones if the seller should have difficulties in disposing of the former. Shortly afterward the coins were lowered in value. (*Statutum de falso moñeta*, 27 Edw. I (1299)). The buyer was held

173

liable for full compensation. See also as to "blanc-money" clauses, Hale, *The History of the Pleas of the Crown* (1736) 207.

[4]In "Molinaeus' *Geldschuldlehre*" (1928) 48.

[5]French: "*ecu au soleil*", the most important French gold coin. [The names *scutum* and *scutus* were used interchangeably.]

[6]On the *libra*, see *supra*, p. 10

[7]A protective clause resembling the ancient type appears in the lease of 1791 adjudicated in *Butler v. Horwitz*, 7 Wall. (74 U.S.) 258 (1868). The stipulation was for an "annual rent of fifteen pounds current money of Maryland, payable in English golden guineas weighing five penny-weights and six grains, at thirty-five shillings each—and other gold and silver at their present weights and rates established by Act of Assembly".

As a matter of fact the protective clauses of the "pre-system" period frequently became even more involved in trying not only to protect the creditor against the disadvantageous effects of debasements and other deterioration of coin, but also against disadvantageous "tariffing". The multitude of objectives easily led to obscure and even inconsistent stipulations. A considerable part of the activities of ancient jurists was devoted to the drafting and interpretation of monetary clauses and to the remedying of the mistakes and frauds connected with them. Some instances of controversial clauses are mentioned in Taeuber, *Geld und Kredit im Mittelalter* (1933) 296 n. 864.

with *Supplementa* and *Emendationes* 1785, 1788), one finds *sub. tit.* "*moneta*", "*monetae mutatio*", etc. scores of monographs more or less devoted to the interpretation of monetary stipulations. *E.g.*, Budelius, *De Monetis et Re Nummaria* (Cologne, 1591), for centuries the most famous treatise on money matters, is largely concerned with interpretative problems of the type mentioned.

[8]In *Holyoke Water Power Co.* v. *American Writing Paper Co., Inc.*, 68 F.(2d) 261 (C.C.A. 1st, 1933), the contract which had been drafted in 1859, provided for a yearly rent of 260 ounces troy weight of silver of the 1859 standard of American coinage or its equivalent in gold, the quantity of gold thus being made dependent on a silver value. The Court remarked that, owing to the discovery and mining of gold in 1849 and in the '50's silver was the more stable metal and that contracts frequently were written in terms of silver. See also silver clauses passed on in *Mather* v. *Kinike*, 51 Pa. 425 (1866), ground rent of 1773, and *Christ Church Hospital* v. *Fuechsel*, 54 Pa. 71 (1867), ground rent of 1794. Touching the validity of the clauses under the Joint Resolution of

1933, see *infra*, p. 359, n. 9.

The most important silver clause case was decided by the Austrian Supreme Court in the matter of the 1873 and 1874 bonds of the Austrian State Railways Corporation *(Staats-Eisenbahn-Gesellschaft;* abbreviated *Steg)*. The creditors were entitled to receive Austrian crowns or French francs at their then parity, crowns to be payable in "real silver coin". In 1930 the clause was held good, giving the creditors a yield higher than the stipulated franc amount, because of the depreciation of the franc. Judgment of Dec. 17, 1930, *Die Rechtsprechung* 1931, 1. Silver clauses were also dealt with by the Italian Court of Cassation, April 18, 1932, *Foro Italiano* 1933 I 193. They seem to appear more frequently in Dutch mortgage deeds, Libourel, *Het Vraagstuk der Goud-Clausule in Nederland* (1932) 37.

[9]*D.P.* 1872 II 51, note.

[10]See *Trebilcock* v. *Wilson*, 12 Wall. (79 U.S.) 687 (1871), and particularly *In re Missouri Pac. R. Co.*, 7 F. Supp. 1, at 3 (D.C.E.D. MO., 1934), where a short history of the clause is given. *Hartley* v. *McAnulty*, 4 Yeates (Pa.) 95 (1804), states that "specie" means gold and silver coin.

[11]The clause is expressly mentioned in the Austrian Civil Code 986. See also Appellate Court of Venice, July 15, 1937, *Foro delle Venezie*, 1937, 763.

[12]The same concept underlies the definitions of gold clauses set out in the Dutch, Canadian, and Manitoba Gold Clause Acts and the American Joint Resolution of June 5, 1933 which, however, does not employ the term "gold clause". See *infra*, sec. 29 I. The statutes differ somewhat in drawing the boundary line.

[13]In France, too, sometimes in long-time rural lease contracts, see *Riviere Revue de Droit International Privè*, 1932, 1. For an instance, see French *Cour de Cassation*, Nov. 27, 1933, *D.H.* 1933, 585. The same seems to be true in Holland and Belgium, the Gold Clause Acts of which (see *infra*, sec. 29, n. 5) expressly provide for abrogation of gold clauses contained in leases. And during the English parliamentary debates in 1811 on the report of the Bullion Committee, it was mentioned that in Ireland there were clauses in many of the leases for payment of gold. 19 Hansard, *Parliamentary Debates* 977 (speech of Mr. Huskisson). As to the Irish currency, see 2 Palgrave, *Dictionary of Political Economy* (1917) 457.

[14]Before the World War there was frequent use of "gold francs" in the Balkans and in the Near East, and of "gold lire" in foreign trade with Italy. Midas, *Die Goldklausel im Währungsverfall (1924) 18*. After the

war the employment of gold units became common in Germany and other inflation-striken countries, *infra,* p. 312. Bills of exchange and checks were allowed to be articulated in terms of gold marks by a German decree of Feb. 6, 1924, *R.G.Bl.* 1924 I 50. This decree was repealed in 1933, see *infra,* sec. 27, n. 21.

[15]In *Woodruff* v. *Mississippi,* 162 U.S. 291 (1895), the levee board of Mississippi had in 1872 issued bonds payable "in gold coin of the United States", the coupons, however, being payable "in currency of the United States". The explanation lies probably in the fact that the board anticipated the rise of the dollar to parity before the bonds would have matured. In the *Rosario* and *San Paolo* cases, *infra,* sec. 26, n. 1 and 4, a gold clause was promised probably solely for interest, although the Court extended it to principal. The Swiss Federal Tribunal, Feb. 11, 1931, *Amtliche Sammlung,* 57 II 69, *J.D.Int.* 1931, 510 at 518, is mistaken in declaring that a gold clause limited to interest constitutes an "anomaly and an absurdity".

The Court of Appeal in *British and French Trust Corp., Ltd.* v. *New Brunswick Ry. Co.,* [1937] 4 All. E.R. 516 at 537 (C.A., 1937), extends the gold clause of a bond to coupons which did not in terms contain the clause. This view would seem acceptable.

[16]*N.Y. Herald-Tribune,* April 13, 1933, section 2, at 8 col. 1 gives these approximate figures of gold obligations in the United States: 27 billion dollars, U.S.A. Security Bonds; 16 billion dollars, state and municipal bonds; 12 billion dollars, foreign dollar bonds; more than 50 million dollars, corporation bonds and real estate mortgages. The statistics were compiled, the writer understands, by the Institute of International Finance, New York. Another estimate totals $123,869,023.89, Hanna, "Currency Control and Private Property", (1933) 33 *Col. L.R.* 617, at 633, n. 20. In *Norman* v. *Baltimore and Ohio R.R.,* 294 U.S. 240 at 313 (1935), a gold clause case, the court figured the total of gold obligations at 75 billion dollars or more.

[17]The Federal District Court of Missouri, *In Re Missouri Pac. R. Co.,* 7 F. Supp. 1 at 3 (1934), characterizes the customary American gold clause as "a sonorous and mouth-filling phrase" which "adds a dignity and a glamour of richness to all bonds, particularly to those which the maker had not and never had the remotest intention of ever paying in anything".

[18]*Infra,* p. 312.

[19]Decree of March 15, 1848, repealed by law of August 6, 1850, *D.P.* 1848 IV 49, 50 and 1850 IV 183.

[20]Gold Clauses are also customary in Denmark and they are widespread in other Scandinavian countries. Ussing in *Z.A.I.P.* 1933, 958. On the Swedish "gold-crown" clause, *infra*, p. 321, n. 33.

[21]See *supra*, p. 261 (Resolution Vansittart).

[22]Treaty of Versailles, art. 262, Treaty of St. Germain, art. 214. Consequently, among the nine parts of the German Government International Loan of 1930 ("Young Loan") the English part is the only one which does not contain a gold clause. Another remarkable fact is that in South Africa before the World War protective clauses ordinarily called for payment of "good current British money" or of "British Sterling money", with no mention of gold. *Loxton* v. *McCrae*, 1 *South African L.T.* 56 (1932). When the pound sterling depreciated, the "sterling" clause was set aside in *Fisher, Simmons & Rodney (Pty.), Ltd.* v. *Munesari*, 53 Natal L.R. 77 (Durban Local Div., 1932).

[23]Namely in *Feist* v. *Société Intercommunale Belge d'Electricité*, [1934] 161 (H. of L., 1933) (*infra*, sec. 28, n. 64). The situation in the English dominions is different. Thus in mortgage transactions gold clauses are apparently used in the formerly German sections of New Guinea, *Jolley* v. *Mainka*, 49 C.L.R. 242 at 243 (High Court of Australia, 1933). This is attributable to German tradition. Canada, here as elsewhere, seems to lean towards the American model rather than toward the English; *infra*, n. 37.

[24]See Engelberts-Vissering-Libourel, *Inflatie en Goud-Clausule in Nederland* (1922) and Libourel, *Het Vraagstuk der Goud-Clausule in Nederland* (1932), *passim*. Both of these were valuable contributions to their subject matter and dissuaded from the introduction of gold clauses into Dutch practice. A special situation seems to have existed as to leases, *supra*, n. 13.

[25]The Swiss National Bank, in 1929, expressly objected to using the gold clause in domestic Swiss transactions. And such use seems not to have existed previously. See Henggeler, *"Die Abwertung des Schweizerfrankens"*, *Zeitschrift für Recht 1937*, 158a at 197a.

[26]Thus by Hubrecht, *Stabilization du Franc et Valorization des Creances* (1928) 447, 449.

[27]The German-Swiss Gold-Mortgage Treaty of 1920, *R.G.Bl.*, 1920, 2023 lists the following formulas: *in Gold; in deutschem Gold; in deutschem Reichsgoldgelde; in deutschem Reichsgoldmünzen; in deutschem Gold münzen; in teutscher Goldwährung; in Reichsgoldwährung; in klingender Müze; in klingendem Gelde.* (As to the two last mentioned

phrases, see *supra*, n. 11). Besides these, in *Reichsgericht* March 24, 1922, R.G.Z. 104, 218 the formula *in jetziger Reichsgoldmünze* is mentioned.

[28]However, "there is in law no such thing as a gold franc", Sup. Court of Ontario in *Derva* v. *Rio de Janeiro Tramway, Light & Power Co.*, [1928] 4 D.L.R. 542 at 552 (1928). See also as to gold marks, *infra*, p. 312, and as to gold peso, gold leva, etc., *infra*, pp. 320, 321.

[29]It appears, *e.g.*, in *Feist* v. *Societe Intercommunale Belge d'Electricite* [1934] A.C. 161 (H. of L., 1933); in *Reichsgericht*, April 27, 1936, 35 *Bank Archiv* 442; and in Swedish Appellate Court, April 16,1935, *re Skandia Insurance Cie, Ltd.* v. *Swedish National Debt Office*, 2 Plesch, *The Gold Clause* (1936) 66. Some Swiss examples are cited by Henggeler, "*Abwertung des Schweizerfrankens*" in *Zeitschrift für Schweizerisches Recht* 1937, at 216a;, n. 19

[30]The only American instance on record seems to be *Levy* v. *Asbestos, Inc.*, 153 Misc. 125, 273 N.Y. Supp. 911 (1934) [promise by a mortgagor to "pay the difference between the proper value of the mortgage or increase the mortgage to its value in gold measured in paper dollars." This is an example of very poor draftsmanship.] A promise by the mortgagor to pay, in silver or notes, an amount "on the rate of gold coin" sometimes appears in Dutch deeds. Libourel, *Het Vraagstuk der Goud-Clausule in Nederland* (1932) 36.

[31]Reese v. Stearns, 29 Cal. 273 (1865); *Mitchell* v. *Henderson*, 63 N.C. 643 (1869); *Killough* v. *Alford*, 32 Tex. 458 (1870); *Dunn* v. Barnes, 73 N.C. 273 (1875). Similarly *Jolley* v. *Mainka*, 49 C.L.R. 242 (High Court of Australia, 1933) ["payable in gold or in currency equivalent thereto"]. See also Act of March 18, 1869, 16 Stat. 1, 31 U.S.C. 731, providing for payment in "coin or its equivalent."

[32]*Lane* v. *Gluckauf*, 28 Cal. 289 (1865).

[33]*Brown* v. *Welch*, 26 Ind. 116 (1866).

[34]*Infra*, sec. 28 IV.

[35]Nussbaum, Das Geld (1925) 164; Gēny, "*La validité juridique de la clause 'payable en or'*", *Revue Trimestrielle de Droit Civil* 1926, 557 at 564; Ascarelli, *La Moneta* (1928) 160; Ussing in *Ugeskrift for Retsvaesen* (Copenhagen) 1933 B 264.

[36]*Norman* v. *Baltimore and Ohio R. R.*, 294 (1935). See Nussbaum, "Comparative and international aspects of American gold clause abrogation," (1934) 44 Yale L.J. 55.

[37]48 Stat. 112, 31 U.S.C. 463. The Canadian Gold Clause Act of 1937

adheres closely to the American model. *Bull. I.I.I.* 37, 109.

[38]The main problem is whether a gold value clause is implied in a gold coin clause, *infra*, sec. 28 IV.

[39]*Supra*, p. 179.

[40]Lord Romer, of the English Court of Appeal felt the words "or equal to" to be "mere surplusage", [1933] 1 Ch. 684 at 708.

[41]300 U.S. 324 (1937). Comment in (1937) 15 *North Carolina L.R.* 196.

[42]300 U.S. 324 at 336.

[43]As done in *Dewing* v. *Sears*, 11 Wall. (78 U.S.) 379 (1871), reversing 96 Mass. 413 (1867), and in *Emery Bird Thayer Dry Goods et al.* v. *Williams et al.*, 15 F. Supp. 938 (D.C.W.D. Mo., 1936). In the first case the contract called for a payment in four installments of a yearly rent of 4 ounces, 2 pennyweights and 12 grains of pure gold, in coined money. The court ordered the judgment to be rendered in terms of coined dollars, under the theory of *Bronson* v. *Rodes*, *infra*, sec. 27, n. 5. In the *Emery Bird* case the contract was for a yearly rental of 557,280 grains of pure unalloyed gold, with an option in the lessors to demand a quarterly payment of $6000 in lawful money. The monetary implications of such ostensible bullion-clauses are obvious, but were held irrelevant by the Court. Nevertheless, and despite the Holyoke decision, this theory of the *Emery Bird* case was subsequently sustained, 98 F.(2d) 166 (C.C.A. 85h, 1938), by means of a conceptualistic interpretation of the Joint Resolution as well as of the gold clause in question. Judge Woodrough dissenting in a striking opinion.

[44]*R.G.Bl.* 1923 I 407.

[45]Decree of April 17, 1924, R.G.Bl. 1924 I 414.

[46]*Supra*, p. 253, n. 17.

[47]Italian Civil Code 1823; Spanish Civil Code 1754(2); Dutch Civil Code 1795.

TWO

[1]*See* Barry, *Gold*, 20 Va. L. Rev. 263, 269-70 (1934).

[2]*Eder I, supra* note 22, at 380 n.57. Indeed, in 1843, the Secretary of the Treasury, pursuant to a law enacted in 1837, 5 Stat. 201, issued notes effectively redeemable on demand at par and bearing interest at a rate not exceeding six percent. A resolution of the House of Representatives promptly declared these notes unconstitutional bills of credit, beyond the power of the Federal Government to issue. H.R. Rep. No. 379, 28th Cong., 1st Sess. 516, 651, 655 (1844).

[3]Act of March 3, 1863, ch. 75, 12 Stat. 731.

[4]The act of August 5, 1861, ch. 45, 12 Stat. 292, 309-311. This Act, taxing incomes over $800, was repealed by an Act taxing incomes over $600. Act of July 1, 1862, ch. 119, § 89, 12 Stat. 432, 473-75. The latter act was re-enacted to impose three different tax rates. *See* Act of June 30, 1864, 13 Stat. 218, which was held constitutional in the face of contentions that it was a forbidden direct tax, in *Springer v. United States*, 102 U.S. 586 (1880).

[5]Ironically, even in the Confederacy, poorer than the Union and fighting for the "right" to force some men to be other men's slaves, the Confederate Congress had never promulgated legal tender laws to force men to accept government IOU's. However, a few of the rebel States had made their own paper money legal tender for limited purposes. And several cases of the use of "unofficial" duress on confederate citizens who were loath to accept paper money surfaced after the War. *See* Dawson & Coultrap, *The Effect of Inflation on Private Contracts: United States, 1861-1879*, 33 Mich. L. Rev. 706, 714 n.26 (1935)

[6]Fairman, *supra* note 65 at 678.

[7]*Id.* at 683.

[8]All of the legal tender measures were universally viewed as temporary expedients. The Attorney General himself, in oral argument in *Hepburn v. Griswold*, 75 U.S. (12 Wall.) 603 (1870), called them "necessary for emergencies, pernicious as a constant resource." 19 L. Ed.at 516 (1870). Justice Bradley, concurring separately in the *Legal Tender Cases,*

stated: "No one supposes that these government certificates are never to be paid [in gold]–that the day of specie payments is never to return...." 79 U.S. (12 Wall.) 457, 561 (1871). The Act of January 14, 1875, ch. 15, 18 Stat. 296, directed resumption of specie payments on January 1, 1879. *But see* the Act of May 31, 1878, ch. 146, 20 Stat. 87, halting withdrawal of the greenbacks. Significantly, however.

> Upon the earlier issues there had been impressed the privilege of converting at face value into 5-20 6 percent gold bonds. At Chase's urging, this was omitted from the third issue, and as to the earlier greenbacks the right was cut off at July 1, 1863. The Secretary wanted to borrow at less than 6 percent. "This ill-fated action as to 'conversion,' prevented the currency from purifying itself by a natural process at the close of the war"—so wrote Professor Barrett in his monograph on *The Greenbacks and Resumption of Specie Payments*—for the reason that "with the rise of government bonds above par, greenbacks would have flowed profitably into the funded debt and disappeared permanently from circulation." Spaulding, writing in 1875, called it "the great mistake—greater than all other mistakes in the management of the war." ...And John Sherman, in retrospect, said that "the most essential legal attribute of the note was taken away ....[F]or my part in acquiescing in and voting for it I have felt more regret than for any [other] act of my official life."

Fairman, *supra* note 65, at 689 (footnotes omitted).

[9]*Id.* at 683-84, *quoting* CONG. GLOBE, 37th Cong., 2d Sess. at 525 (1862). The opinion was given unofficially because Attorney General Bates could officially answer only requests that came directly from the executive branch.

[10]*Id.*

[11]*Id.* at 684.

[12]The House passed the bill on February 6, 1862. CONG. GLOBE, 37th Cong., 2d Sess. at 695 (1862). Senate passage followed on February 12. *Id.* at 804. Ironically, "it took so long to effect the printing of the greenbacks that they did not become available until April; it was by other means that the Treasury survived the crisis of February." FAIRMAN, *supra* note 65, at 688.

[13]*Id.* at 685.

[14]The legal tender clause in the original act reads as follows:

[A]nd such notes herein authorized shall be receivable in payment of all taxes, internal duties, excises, debts, and demands of every kind due to the United States, except duties on imports, and of all claims and demands against the United States of every kind whatsoever, except for interest upon bonds and notes, which shall be paid in coin, and shall also be lawful money and a *legal tender in payment of all debts, public and private,* with the United States, *except* duties on imports and interest as aforesaid.

Act of Feb. 25, 1862, ch. 33, 12 Stat. 345 (emphasis added). The successor acts were: Act of Mar. 17, 1862, ch. 45, 12 Stat. 370; Act of July 11, 1862, ch. 142, 12 Stat. 532; Act of Mar. 3, 1863, ch. 73, 12 Stat. 709; Act of Jan. 17, 1864, Res. 9, 12 Stat. 822.

[15]*See* statutes cited note 82 *supra. See also* FAIRMAN, *supra* note 65, at 686, 689-91.

[16]For a table of greenback values in gold for the years 1862-78, see 77 CONG. REC. 1034 (1933).

[17]*See, e.g.,* Thompson v. Riggs. 72 U.S. (5 Wall.) 663 (1867); Bank v. Supervisors, 74 U.S. (7 Wall.) 26 (1869); Lane County v. Oregon, 74 U.S. (7 Wall.) 71 (1869); Bronson v. Rodes, 74 U.S. (7 Wall.) 229 (1869); Butler v. Horwitz, 74 U.S. (7 Wall.) 258 (1869); Willard v. Tayloe, 75 U.S. (8 Wall.) 557 (1870); Hepburn v. Griswold, 75 U.S. (8 Wall.) 603 (1870); Broderick's Ex'r v. Magraw, 75 U.S. (8 Wall.) 639 (1870); Dewing v. Sears, 78 U.S. (11 Wall.) 379 (1871); Legal Tender Cases, 79 U.S. (12 Wall.) 457 (1871). One case had been brought in New York to test the constitutionality of the Legal Tender Acts before the close of the Civil War. FAIRMAN, *supra* note 65, at 693; that case, too, reached the Supreme Court prior to the war's end, but the Court dismissed the case for want of jurisdiction. Roosevelt v. Meyer, 68 U.S. (11 Wall.) 512 (1864). Curiously, the Court had erred in dismissing the case, as it later admitted in Trebilcock v. Wilson, 79 U.S. (12 Wall.) 687 (1872).

[18]There exist numerous accounts of this controversy. For contemporaneous commentary, see, *e.g.,* E. SPAULDING, HISTORY OF THE LEGAL TENDER PAPER MONEY ISSUED DURING THE THE GREAT REBELLION (2d ed. 1875) (a somewhat partisan account authored by the "father of the greenbacks"); Anon., *The Legal Tender Acts;,* 2 AM. L. REV. 403 (1867); Chamberlain, *The "Legal Tender" Decision of 1881, 18 AM L. REV. 618*

(1884). See also Fairman, *supra* note 65, ch XIV; D. Barrett, The Greenbacks and Resumption of Specie Payments, 1862-79 (1931); Dunne, *supra* note 38, ch. III; W. Mitchell, History of the Greenbacks (1903).

[19]Thompson v. Riggs, 72 U.S. (5 Wall.) 663 (1867): Bank v. Supervisors, 74 U.S. (7 Wall.) 26 (1869); Lane County v. Oregon, 74 U.S. (7 Wall.) 71 (1869); Bronson v. Rodes, 74 U.S. (7 Wall.) 229 (1869); Butler v. Horwitz, 74 U.S. (7 Wall.) 258 (1869); Willard v. Tayloe, 75 U.S. (8 Wall.) 557 (1870).

[20]74 U.S. (7 Wall.) 229 (1869).

[21]*Id.* at 245.

[22]*Id.*

[23]*Id.* at 246.

[24]*Id.* at 250.

[25]*Id.*Only Justice Miller dissented from this exemption of gold clause contracts from the operation of the Legal Tender Acts. *Id.* at 255-58.

[26]The "bullion" or "commodity" analogy is read as the basis for *Bronson* in Gregory v. Morris, 96 U.S. 619 (1878) and in United States v. Erie Railway, 106 U.S. 327 (1862), *reh. denied*, 107 U.S. 1 (1883).

[27]Support for the "dual money" theory may be gleaned from: Hepburn v. Griswold, 75 U.S. (8 Wall.) 603, 609 (1870) (reading the *ratio decidendi* of *Bronson* to have been independent of "the law of contracts for the delivery of specified articles"); Trebilcock v. Wilson, 79 U.S. (12 Wall.) 687, 695-96 (1871) (expanding upon the "dual money" theory while paying slight heed to the "commodity" or "bullion" theory); Thompson v. Butler, 95 U.S. 694, 696-97 (1877); Norman v. Baltimore & O.R.R., 294 U.S. 240, 300-02 (1935). *See also* Nebolsine, *The Gold Clause in Private Contracts*, 42 Yale L.J. 1051, 1065-68 (1933).

[28]After deciding *Bronson*, the Court next had occasion to rule on the effect of the Acts upon a quasi-bullion contract that had been drawn in 1791. In Butler v. Horwitz, 74 U.S. (7 Wall.) 258 (1869), an obligation for rent was specified to be the amount of "fifteen pounds current money of Maryland, payable in English golden guineas" (of the standard of 1791); these guineas has been stipulated at nisi prius to be worth forty dollars in gold and silver, where it also had been stipulated that, on the date that the rent had come due, gold dollars were worth 140 percent of what paper dollars were worth. Of course, a tender of forty dollars in green-

backs had been refused by the obligee. At trial, judgment had been entered (for $59.71 plus costs) in greenbacks. The Supreme Court sustained the judgment for the larger sum in accordance with *Bronson,* but reversed and remanded with instructions that the judgment be entered in coin rather than in paper money because the parties had contracted in gold coin. 74 U.S. (7 Wall.) at 261. However, the *Butler* Court uttered dictum as to the effect the absence of a contractual stipulation for payment in gold would have:

> [T]he absence of any express stipulation..., in contracts for payment in money, generally warrants the opposite inference of an understanding between the parties that such contracts may be satisfied, before or after judgment, by the tender of any lawful money.

Id. at 261. Subsequent cases are in accord. *See* Legal Tender Cases; 79 U.S. (12 Wall.) 457, 548 (1871); Maryland v. Railroad Co., 89 U.S. (22 Wall.) 105 111-112 (1874); Juilliard v. Greenman, 110 U.S. 421, 449 (1884); Woodruff v. Mississippi, 162 U.S. 291 (1896). *See also* Trebilcock v. Wilson, 79 U.S. (12 Wall.) 699 (1872) (a note "[p]ayable in specie" was held, unsurprisingly, to call for payment in dollars made of specie, i.e., gold or silver); Dewing v. Sears, 78 U.S. (11 Wall.) 379 (1871) (a lease for a "yearly rent of four ounces, two pennyweights and twelve grains of pure gold in coined money" called for judgment in coin).

[29]75 U.S. (8 Wall.) 603 (1870).

[30]*Id.* at 606.

[31]*Id.* at 607.

[32]U.S. CONST. art. I, § 8, cl. 18.

[33]17 U.S. (4 Wheat.) 316 (1819).

[34]75 U.S. (8 Wall.) at 627 (Miller, J., dissenting).

[35]Only the States were constitutionally prohibited, *in haec verba,* from passing any "Law impairing the Obligation of Contracts...." U.S. CONST. art I, § 10. Therefore, although congressional enactment of a law impairing the obligation of contracts violated the spirit of the Constitution, it would not violate its letter. The *Hepburn* Court invoked the Northwest Ordinance of July 13, 1787, in support of its thesis that federal impairment of the obligation of contracts violated fundamental principles of civil liberty that were part of the spirit of the Constitution. 75 U.S. (8 Wall.) at 622-23. The Court observed that article II of the Ordinance

had stated that

> in the just preservation of rights and property it is understood
> and declared; that no law ought ever to be made [by Congress]
> ...that shall in any manner whatever interfere with or affect
> private contracts or engagements bona fide and without fraud
> previously formed.

32 JOURNALS OF THE CONTINENTAL CONGRESS 334, 340 (1936). Additionally, the Court indicated its view that the Act was an unjust deprivation of private property, in violation of the Due Process Clause of the fifth amendment insofar as it compelled obligees to be satisfied with payment of less value than that for which value than that for which they had contracted. *Id.* at 623-25.

[36]*Id.* at 626. The *Hepburn* Court took pains to state the precise issue to be decided five times and the exact scope of its holding twice. *Id.* at 606, 610, 613, 615, 619, 625, 626.

[37]The record in *Hepburn* was filed on December 30, 1865. FAIRMAN, *supra* note 65, at 700. Yet, *Hepburn* was not decided until February 7, 1870. *Id.*

[38]On "the same day and at about the same hour that *Hepburn* was announced, President Grant nominated William Strong...and Joseph P. Bradley to be Justices."*Id.* at 677. The votes of these two new appointees, coupled with the resignation of Justice Grier, was instrumental in bringing about *Hepburn's reversal. Id.*

[39]Knox v. Lee and Parker v. Davis, 79 U.S. (12 Wall.) 457 (1871). *Parker* raised the question whether the Legal Tender Acts were constitutional as applied to contracts made before their passage, a question that had been decided in the negative in *Hepburn.* 57, Parker had agreed to sell Davis certain realty for a down payment and the balance to follow. Davis' subsequent tender of the balance in greenbacks had been refused. In 1867, the Supreme Judicial Court of Massachusetts decreed specific performance and Davis paid the greenbacks into court; Parker persisted in demanding gold. The Supreme Judicial Court then decreed that either form of money constituted lawful payment. Parker v. Davis, 96 Mass. (14 Allen) 94 (1867). *Knox* raised the question whether the acts were constitutional as applied to post-Act contracts. The manner in which the Legal Tender Acts were involved in *Knox* is somewhat obscure. Knox had purchased a flock of sheep, which had been confiscated from Mrs. Lee in 1863 under the Confederacy's Sequestration Act. In a subsequent suit for conversion, the court had instructed the jury that the judgment could be

paid in greenbacks rather than in gold. Curiously, opposing counsel in *Knox* agreed that the Legal Tender Acts were constitutional, while counsel in *Parker* submitted their causes solely on briefs that evaded the constitutional question. FAIRMAN, *supra* note 65, at 755. Yet in both cases, a majority of the Court discussed only the constitutional questions at issue, without once referring to the facts of either case.

[40]79 U.S. (12 Wall.) at 529.

[41]*Id.* at 531, *quoting* Commonwealth v. Smith, 4 Binn. 117, 123 (Pa. 1811).

[42]*Id.* at 532.

[43]*Id.* at 535.

[44]*See generally id.* at 532-35.

[45]*Id.* at 535-36.

[46]*Id.*at 542.

[47]75 U.S. (8 Wall.) at 637-38.

[48]17 U.S. (4 Wheat.) 316 (1819).

[49]*Id.* at 407 (emphasis in original).

[50]*Id. (passim). Cf.* Marbury v. Madison, 5 U.S. (1 Cranch) 137 (1803).

[51]Legal Tender Cases, 79 U.S. (12 Wall.) at 549 (emphasis added).

[52]*Id.* at 551 (emphasis added).

[53]*Id.* at 560.

[54]*Id.* at 560-61.

[55]*Id.* at 563.

[56]Address of President Lincoln, Gettysburg, Pa., Nov. 19, 1863.

THREE

[1]The standard form of gold clause now in use in this country reads as follows: "The corporation ... promises to pay ... to the holder hereof ... $1,000, in gold coin of the United States of America of the standard of weight and fineness existing June 1, 1932, ..." The date specified is, of course, the date of the creation of the obligation.

There are, however, many variations of this standard form. Some clauses, instead of specifying a date, merely say "of the present standard of weight and fineness". Another common variation is to insert the words "or equal to" before the words "the standard of weight and fineness". A variation that may change the meaning of the clause is to add at the end the words "or the equivalent thereof". Gold bonds or notes containing this form of the clause have been denied listing on the New York Stock Exchange, under the recent practice and rulings of the Committee on Stock List. The effect of the addition of these words is discussed at p. 1241, *infra*. A form which we understand is rather common in individual notes in some localities reads " in United States gold coin of the present standard of weight and fineness, at the option of the holder". The gold clause commonly used in obligations of the United States government substitutes the words 'of the present standard of value" in place of the words "of the [present] standard of weight and fineness".

[2]It has been estimated that more than $100,000,000,000 of funded indebtedness contains a gold clause. This figure is made up, in part, of about $22,000,000,000 of United States Government obligations, about $16,000,000,000 of state and municipal obligations, and about $12,000,000,000 of foreign dollar obligations. The amount of long-term commercial contracts, individual obligations, and urban and farm mortgages, which contain gold clauses, cannot be accurately estimated. See Wanders, N. Y. Herald Tribune, April 23, 1933, §§ II-IV, at 8.

[3]No special consideration has been given herein to the obligations of the United States declared to be payable in gold. See, on this point, Savage v. United States, 92 U.S. 382 (1875); Sinking Fund Cases, 99 U.S. 700, 718-19 (1878); United States v. Northern Pac. Ry., 256 U.S. 51 (1921).

[4]In the 72d Congress, Second Session, and the 73rd Congress, First Session, the gold clause has been discussed at various times. See, *e.g.*,

CONG. REC., Jan. 24, 1933, at 2506 *et seq.; id.* April 18, 1933, at 1894-96 *et seq., id.* April 22, 1933, at 2173-74, 2216-17; *id.* April 24, 1933, at 2245; *id.* April 25, 1933, at 2354-55; *id.* April 26, 1933, at 2405 *et seq., id.* April 28, 1933, at 2568 *et seq.* A Bill to nullify gold clauses was introduced by Representative Campbell of Iowa on February 8, 1933. "Be it enacted, … that, notwithstanding any provision in any contract to the contrary, any contract obligation to pay money may be paid in such currency of the United States as, under the laws of the United States, is legal tender, and any such payment shall constitute a discharge of the obligation." H. R. 14604, 72d Cong., 2d Sess. There are similar provisions in bills introduced in the 73d Congress, First Session; see, *e.g., H. R. 5073, H. R. 5160, H R. 5172.*

[5]It has been impossible to include a discussion of the law on this question in countries other than the United States and England. For a treatment of the gold clause in international debts, see Hudson, *The Eighth Year of the Permanent Court of International Justice* (1930) 24 AM. J. OF INT. L. 20, 21, 26.

[6]Public No. 10, 73d Cong. tit. III, §§ 43-46. An amendment proposed by Senator Bulkeley to abrogate gold clauses was rejected. CONG. REC., April 28, 1933, at 2576-79.

[7]On the power of Congress to delegate its functions to the executive, see Hampton & Co. v. United States, 276 U.S. 394 (1928); Springer v. Philippine Islands, 277 U.S. 189 (1928); Wisconsin v. Illinois, 278 U.S. 367 (1929).

[8]Senator Thomas, sponsoring the amendment, said, "It may transfer from one class to another class in these United States value to the extent of almost $200,000,000,000". 77 CONG. REC. 2229 (April 24, 1933).

[9]See President Roosevelt's speech of May 7, 1933, N. Y. Times, May 8, 1933, at i. See also note 78, *infra.*

[10]See the discussion of the affirmative powers, at page 1243, *et seq., infra,* and also notes 100, 101, *infra.* No decision of the Supreme Court has yet considered if Congress may use the coinage and borrowing power for the purpose of relieving debtors or promoting commerce. The only appreciable currency inflation which the country has had—the Legal Tender period, 1862-1878—was assumed by the courts to have had as its objective the raising of money by the government. See DEWEY, FINANCIAL HISTORY OF THE UNITED STATES (1915) 284-90, 360-62, 370-72; Johnson, *Constitutional Limitations and the Gold Standard* (1933) 67 U.S. L. REV. 187.

[11]7 Wall. 229 (U.S.) 1868).

[12]Rodes v. Bronson, 34 N. Y. 649 (1866). Bronson, the mortgagee, argued that Rodes should pay him the market value of gold in legal tender notes, *i.e.*, $3,390.75, *since $2.25 in legal tender notes was then worth one dollar in gold.* The court rejected this argument as a fallacy, since it would treat the gold coins both as currency and as a commodity.

[13]"... such notes ... shall ... be lawful money and a legal tender in payment of all debts, public and private, ..." See 12 STAT. 345 (1862).

[14]Mr. Justice Miller dissented on the grounds that the intent of the parties was merely to exclude payment in state bank notes, and also that the Legal Tender Act was intended to embrace such contracts within the words "private debts", regardless of the intent of the parties.

[15]See 7 Wall. at 250. See also *Id.* at 245, 246. The decision is criticized in HUNT, LAW OF TENDER (1903) 111-16. In Butler v. Horwitz, 7 Wall. 258, 260 (U.S. 1868), the Court said that "the obvious intent" of such a con tract is "to provide against fluctuations in the medium of payment".

The decision overruled a large group of state cases, which had almost unanimously followed the rule laid down in Rodes v. Bronson, 34 N. Y. 649 (1866). See, *e.g.*,Whetstone v. Colley, 36 Ill. 328 (1865); Brown v. Welch, 26 Ind. 116 (1866); Riley's Ex'r v. Sharp, 1 Bush 348 (Ky. 1866) (a contrary rule was followed in equity. Hord v. Miller, 2 Duval 103 (Ky. 1865)); Galliano v. Leon Pierre & Co., 18 La. Ann. 10 (1866); Howe v. Nickerson, 14 Allen 400 (Mass. 1867); Buchegger v. Shultz, 13 Mich. 420 (1865); Legal Tender Cases, 52 Pa. 9 (1866). But see Dutton v. Palairet, 52 Pa. 109 (1806), *aff'd,* 154 U.S. 563 (1869). The cases are collected in (1896) 29 L. R. A. 512. Apparently the only square decision the other way during this period was Myers & Marcus v. Kauffman, 37 Ga. 600 (1868).

About the same time, "Specific Contract" acts were passed, in almost identical language, in California, Idaho, and Nevada, providing that "In an action on a contract or obligation in writing, for the direct payment of money, made payable in a specified kind of money or currency, judgment for the plaintiff ... may ... be made payable in the kind of money or currency specified therein...." See CAL. CODE CIV. PROC. (Deering, 1931) § 667; IDAHO CODE (1932) §7-1104; NEV. COMP. LAWS (Hillyer, 1929) § 8825. The cases construing these statutes show much confusion. Hathaway v. Brady, 26 Cal. 581 (1864; Vilhac v. Biven, 28 Cal. 409 (1865); Reese v. Stearns, 29 Cal. 273 (1865); Hazard v. Cole, 1 Idaho 276, 287-89 (1869); Wells, Fargo & Co. v. Van Sickle, 6 Nev. 45 (1870).

[16]Butler v. Horwitz, 7 Wall. 258 (U.S. 1868); Dewing v. Sears, 11 Wall. 379 (U.S. 1870); Trebilcock v. Wilson, 12 Wall. 687 (U.S. 1871);

The Vaughan and Telegraph, 14 Wall. 258 (U.S. 1871); The Emily Souder, 17 Wall. 666 (U.S. 1873); Thompson v. Butler, 95 U.S. 694 (1877); Gregory v. Morris, 96 U.S. 619 (1877);*cf.* Thompson v. Riggs, 5 Wall. 663 (U.S. 1866); Maryland v. Railroad Co., 22 Wall. 105 (U.S. 1874); Woodruff v. Mississippi, 162 U.S. 291 (1896).

[17] The Court reviewed, at some length, the currency statutes since 1792, and concluded that gold dollars and paper dollars were not actual equivalents, "nor was there anything in the currency acts purporting to make them such". See 7 Wall. at 251-52. Particular emphasis was laid on the fact that §§ 1 and 5 of the Act of Feb. 25, 1862, (12 Stat. 345, 346), required that duties on imports and interest on the public debt be paid in coin. *Cf.* Trebilcock v. Wilson, 12 Wall. 687, 695-97 (U.S. 1871); Sears v. Dewing, 14 Allen 413(Mass. 1867), *rev'd*, 11 Wall. 379 (U.S. 1870).

[18] See Trebilcock v. Wilson, 12 Wall. 687, 695, 696 (U.S. 1871); *cf.* Bronson v. Rodes, 7 Wall. 229, 251-52 (U.S. 1868). The contrary idea, that all legal tender is the same in the eyes of the law, and that parties cannot be allowed to stipulate one kind of legal tender to the exclusion of all others, was expressed in most of the state cases cited in note 15, *supra.* See HUNT, LAW OF TENDER § § 96.

[19] 26 STAT. 289 § 2 (1890);, 31 U.S. C. §§ 410, 453 (1926), provided that the Treasury notes issued thereunder should be a legal tender for all debts, public and private, "except where otherwise expressly stipulated in the contract, ..." The same exception was made in the case of silver dollars. 20 STAT. 25 (1878), 31 U.S. C. § 458 (1926). Obligations of the United States have, for many years, contained the gold clause. See, *e.g.,* 16 STAT. 1 (1869), 31 U.S. C. § 731 (1926); 39 STAT. 1000, 1003 (1917); 40 STAT. 35, 288, 503 (1918) (Liberty Bond Acts). But *cf.* 46 STAT. 19 (1929).

The government, in the capacity both of a debtor and a creditor of foreign governments, has inserted gold clauses in its contracts. In the convention with Panama proclaimed February 26, 1904, the United States, in Art XIV, agreed to pay the Republic of Panama, as compensation for the privileges granted, $10,000,000 "in gold coin of the United States", and $250,000 annually "in like gold coin". 33 STAT. Pt. II, 429 (1904); 2 MALLOY's TREATIES 1349 (1910). In the debt-funding agreements with other countries, the government required, in every instance, that the dollar obligations to be used by the debtor country should contain a gold clause in the usual form.

It has been suggested that a new policy was written into the statutes by § 1 of the Parity Act (31 STAT. 45 (1900), 314 (1926)), which makes the dollar, consisting of 25.8 grains of gold nine-tenths fine, the standard unit of value, and provides that "all forms of money issued or coined by the

United States shall be maintained at a parity of value with this standard."
Thorpe, *Contracts Payable in Gold* (1933) SEN. DOC. No. 43, 73d Cong.
1st Sess. It seems clear that any policy intended to be expressed in this
section is not strong enough to support the conclusion that Bronson v.
Rodes would be decided differently today, particularly in view of the
statutes and treaties later than 1900, cited above. The Thomas amendment, *supra* note 6, does not expressly introduce any such policy, in spite
of some of the purposes, including the reduction of fixed debts,
expressed by the sponsors.

[20]The gold eagle ($10) first contained 277 grains of "standard" gold,
which was about eleven-twelfths fine. 1 STAT. 699. And in 1837 the last
change in content was made, the fineness being reduced to nine-tenths. 5
STAT. 136. 137, 138.

[21]In Knox v. Lee, 12 Wall. 457, 552 (U.S. 1870);, the Court implied
that the constitutional problems raised by the reduction of the gold content of the dollar in 1834, *supra* note 20, were the same as those raised by
the depreciation of the paper dollar.

[22]A change in the gold content might raise minor difficulties if the
amount of the gold in the old coins contracted for could not be exactly
matched in new gold coins, but this does not seem a serious difficulty.
See note 52, *infra*.

[23]The decision of Mr. Justice Farwell in the Chancery Division was
handed down on October 27, 1932, and is reported in shortened form in
49 T.L.R. 8. This decision was unanimously affirmed by the Court of
Appeal, March 17, 1933; the decision being reported, also in shortened
form, in 49 T.L.R. 344. The page references to the opinions in both courts
are, in each case, to the typewritten transcripts of the Shorthand Notes of
the Reporter.

[24]See notes 1, 22, *supra*.

[25]P. 11.

[26]"No doubt the parties to this contract contemplated and, it may be,
desired to obtain payment in one particular way, but the contract, in my
judgment, is a simple contract to secure payment of a sum of money, and
if the defendants tendered the sum of money in question in whatever
might happen to be legal tender at the date the payment was due, they
have discharged their obligation, ... In my judgment, to attempt to
impose upon the debtor an obligation to pay in a particular form and not
anything which is legal tender, is an attempt to do something which can
be enforced if the contract is a mere contract for the payment of money."
P. 12.

[27]I feel the difficulty of adopting the view which I have adopted, because I agree with Mr. Cohen that I am, if I adopt that meaning, very largely or perhaps wholly giving no effect to the words 'in gold coin of the United Kingdom of or equal to the standard of weight and fineness existing on the 1st day of September 1928'". P. 10.

[28]Mr. Justice Farwell rejected the construction that the obligor had the option whether to pay the specified number of gold coins or their market value in currency, since this would make the amount of the obligation indeterminate till maturity, and the figures $100 were impressed all over the bond. He also decided that "... this ... cannot be construed as a contract for the delivery of bullion." P. 11.

[29]"Every contract, sale, payment, bill, note, instrument, and security for money, and every transaction, dealing, matter, and thing whatever relating to money, or involving the payment of or the liability to pay any money, which is made, executed, or entered into, done or had, shall be made, executed, entered into, done and had according to the coins which are current and legal tender in pursuance of this Act, and not otherwise, unless the same be made, executed, entered into, done or had according to the currency of some British possession or some foreign state." 33 & 34 VICT. c. 10, § 6 (1870).

[30]A contract that a debt shall be discharged by payment of gold coins (being one form of legal tender) cannot abrogate the enactment by the legislature that the debt may be discharged by payment in bank notes (being another form of legal tender)." P. 11.

[31]"This seems to render illegal a contract to exclude the provisions of the Act as to legal tender. It would be strange if it were not so, for these provisions are an essential feature of our currency law, and great confusion and public inconvenience and loss might be occasioned if they were to be disregarded." P. 17.

[32]The question in the case, as Lord Justice Romer expressed it, was "whether effect can be given in law to an agreement to pay a sum of money in one only of the forms of legal tender to the exclusion of all others", P. 15.

[33]See Note (1896) 10 HARV L. REV 178, where the writer concluded, "The holders of obligations payable in money of a specified kind may rely with tolerable certainty upon the protection of the United States Constitution, whatever may be the will of Congress."
Two states have legislated against clauses in money contracts limiting the medium of payment. A Kansas statute provides that all obligations of debt, stated in terms of dollars," if not dischargeable in United States

legal-tender notes, shall be payable in either the standard silver or gold coins authorized by the congress of the United States, all stipulations in the contract to the contrary notwithstanding." KAN. REV. STAT. ANN, (1923) c. 16-111. A South Dakota statute is similar. S.D. COMP. LAWS (1929) § 777. Apparently neither of these sections has ever been passed on by any court. A somewhat similar statute was held unconstitutional in Dennis v. Moses, 18 Wash. 537, 52 Pac. 333 (1898).

[34]Bronson v. Rodes did not fall with the overruling of Hepburn v. Griswold, 8 Wall. 603 (U.S. 1869), in Knox v. Lee, 12 Wall. 457 (U.S. 1870); it was followed thereafter in Trebilcock v. Wilson, 12 Wall. 687 (U.S. 1871); The Emily Souder, 17 Wall. 666 (U.S. 1873); Thompson v. Butler, 95 U.S. 694 (U.S. 1877).

If the obligation of the gold clause is exclusively to deliver gold coins, questions of impossibility and purposelessness of performance are presented. These points are briefly referred to at pp. 1233-39, *infra*. See Nebolsine, *The Gold Clause in Private Contracts* (May, 1933) 42 YALE L.J.

[35]On its face, the Feist case may seem to assume that there can be no such thing as an alternative contract in favor of the obligee. This does not seem to be a correct reading of that case: The judges all felt compelled to choose between alternatives for the reason that they thought the possible alternatives were so inconsistent with each other as to make the contract senseless—just as if the promise had been to pay, on January 1, $100 on July 1.

[36]Wall. 229, 250 (U.S. 1868). But the case was decided "upon the assumption ... that engagements to pay coined dollars may be regarded as ordinary contracts to pay money rather than as contracts to deliver certain weights of standard gold...." *Id.* at 251.

[37]See 12 Wall. 687, 695 (U.S. 1871); *cf.* Gregory v. Morris, 96 U.S. 619, 625 (1877).

[38]95 U.S. 694 (1877).

[39]*Id.* at 697

[40]See 31 STAT. 45 (1900), 31 U.S.C. § 314 (1926).

[41]An interesting example of an early attempt (1828) to make a money contract appear to be a commodity contract was presented in Dewing v. Sears, 11 Wall. 379 (U.S. 1870). The amount of rent specified in a lease was "'four ounces, two pennyweights, and twelve grains of pure gold, in coined money.'" The Supreme Judicial Court of Massachusetts had decided that it was a commodity contract, rather than a money contract, and had given judgment for the market value of the

gold in greenbacks. 14 Allen 413 (Mass. 1867). The Supreme Court treated it as a money contract, and, applying the rule laid down in Bronson v. Rodes, concluded that the judgment should have been "for coined dollars and parts of dollars".

[42]See NEGOTIABLE INSTRUMENTS LAW § 1(2).

[43]It is on this precise point that the American rule and the English rule are most clearly at issue. The two most persuasive opinions in the Feist case—those of Mr. Justice Farewell and Lord Justice Romer—adopted this construction as reflecting the intention of the parties, but both these judges concluded that nevertheless, either because the Coinage Act of 1870 expressly prohibited it, or because the policy of that Act showed a public policy against it, the contract was solvable in legal tender generally.

[44]This rule is not rested on any doctrine of specific performance in equity, nor even on the analogous doctrine of specific performance at law, but rather on the ground that federal courts are authorized to give judgment in any form of lawful money, and that when a contract calls for payment in a certain kind of lawful money, the courts can give judgment in the same kind of money. *Cf.* 1 STAT. 246, 250-51 (1791), 31 U.S.C. § 371 (1926); see Bronson v. Rodes, 7 Wall. 229, 254 (U.S. 1868).

Limitation of space makes it impossible to discuss this rule at any length. Although the final result of the cases is somewhat doubtful, it seems clear that if the action is directly on the gold obligation, the creditor is entitled to judgment in gold coins, if he wishes it. Bronson v. Rodes, 7 Wall. 229, 254-55 (U.S. 1868); Trebilcock v. Wilson, 12 Wall. 687 (U.S. 1871); The Emily Souder, 17 Wall. 666 (U.S. 1873). In Butler v. Horwitz, 7 Wall. 258 (U.S. 1868), the creditor sued for, and recovered, the value of the gold in currency; yet, on the debtor's appeal, the Supreme Court reversed solely because the judgment was not for gold coins. A possible explanation of this decision may be that the debtor, on appeal, insisted on the gold judgment, since greenbacks were somewhat higher, in terms of gold, in 1868, when the decision of the Supreme Court was given, than they were in 1866 when the obligation matured. See the table of the value of greenbacks in gold, 1862-1878, CONG. REC. March 30, 1933, at 1034. The same hypothesis may explain Dewing v. Sears, 11 Wall. 379, 380 (1870). See also The Vaughan and Telegraph, 14 Wall. 258 (U.S. 1871); Gregory v. Morris, 96 U.S. 619 (1877); Cheang-Kee v. United States, 3 Wall. 320 (U.S. 1865); United States v. Erie Ry., 107 U.S. 1 (1882); Phillips v. Dugan, 21 Ohio 466 (1871); Chrysler v. Renois, 43 N.Y. 209 (1870); Atkinson & Clark v.Lanier, 69 Ga. 460 (1882); Churchman v. Martin, 54 Ind. 380 (1876).

⁴⁵Wall. 687 (U.S. 1871).

⁴⁶Much of the confusion in this line of cases arises from the fact that the Supreme Court, at that time, seems to have had no clear rule as to the date as of which an amount due in anything other than legal tender generally was to be converted into legal tender for the purposes of judgment. See HUNT, LAW OR TENDER § 100, n.4. Generally, the judges seem to have assumed that the correct date was the date of the accrual of the cause of action. *Cf.* The Vaughan and Telegraph, 14 Wall. 258 (U.S. 1871); Gregory v. Morris, 96 U.S. 619 (1877);Dewing v. Sears,11 Wall. 379 (U.S. 1870); see Trebilcock v. Wilson, 12 Wall. 687, 698 (U.S. 1871). The result was that, in those cases where gold had appreciated between the date of accrual and the date of judgment it was the creditor who demanded a judgment in gold coins; whereas, in those cases where gold had depreciated during that period, it was the debtor who insisted on such a judgment. For modern cases enunciating the federal judgment day rule, see Hicks v. Guinness, 269 U.S. 71 (1925); Deutsche Bank Filiale Nurnberg v. Humphrey, 272 U.S. 517 (1926). For the New York accrual day rule, see Hoppe v. Russo-Asiatic Bank, 235 N.Y.37, 138 N.E. 497 (1923).

⁴⁷12 STAT. 345, 346 (1862).

⁴⁸See 12 Wall. at 696 (italics inserted).

⁴⁹See 7 Wall. 258, 260-61(U.S. 1868) (italics inserted).

⁵⁰The construction that the obligation simply calls for the delivery of gold coins would probably not raise any peculiar difficulty regarding the binding effect of a payment of paper money in the face amount. The rule is well established that unless the creditor objects to a tender of money which is not legal tender, expressly on that ground, the tender is a good one. Juilliard v. Greenman, 110 U.S. 421, 445 (1884); May v. Findley, 189 Ala. 196, 66 So. 463 (1914); Edmunds Electrical Const. Co. v. Mariotte, 162 Inc. 329, 69 N.E. 396 (1904); Neal v. Finley, 136 Ky. 346, 124 S.W. 348 (1910); 3 WILLISTON, CONTRACTS § 1819. *Cf.* Cheney v. Libby, 134 U.S. 68 (1890). The same rule has been applied in a case where the obligation was payable in gold coin, paper dollars at the time being redeemable in gold. Hidden v. German Savings & Loan Soc., 48 Wash. 384, 93 Pac. 668 (1908); H.E. Wright & Ceo. v. Douglas, 26 Wyo. 305, 183 Pac. 786 (1919). The rule has also been applied in the case of a gold obligation, even when paper dollars were at a discount. Lefferman v. Renshaw, 45 Md. 119 (1876); and this, too, although the creditor accepted the tender with a reservation of rights. Gilman v. County of Douglas, 6 Nev. 27 (1870). See also Bickle v. Beseke, 23 Ind. 18 (1864);

Savage v. United States, 92 U.S. 382 (1875). Whether the acceptance of a tender of bank notes or bank bills, in the face amount of the obligation, at a time when the issuing bank is not redeeming its bills or notes in specie, is a good discharge, the authorities do not agree. See Ward v. Smith, 7 Wall. 447 (U.S. 1868); Ontario Bank v. Lightbody, 13 Wend. 101 (N.Y. 1834); *cf.* Manry v. Phoenix Mutual Life Ins. Co., 42 Ga. App. 24, 155 S.E. 43 (1930). Some of the cases on this point are collected in (1929) 48 C.J. 601, § 30.

Generally, in the case of an unliquidated or disputed claim the acceptance by the creditor without express objection on that ground, of a less amount than he claims is a complete discharge. Jenks v. Burr, 56 Ill. 450 (1870); Hill v. Carter, 101 Mich. 158, 59 N.W. 413 (1894); Bundy v. Wills, 88 Neb. 554, 130 N.W. 273 (1911). But if the amount is liquidated, and there is no dispute, the acceptance of a tender of a less amount operates only as a payment *pro tanto*. St. Joseph School Board v. Hull, 72 Mo. App. 403 (1897); Grapes v. Rocque, 97, Vt. 531, 124 Atl. 596 (1924); HUNT, LAW OF TENDER §§ 195, 408.
HUNT, LAW OF TENDER §§ 195, 408.

On the effect of an acceptance of a tender of a less amount of dollars than the exchange value of an amount due in foreign money, as an accord and satisfaction, see San Juan v. St. John's Gas Co. Ltd., 195 U.S. 510 (1904); Saunders v. Whitcomb, 177 Mass. 457, 59 N.W. 192 (1901); Mundler v. Palmer, 162 N.Y. Supp. 605 (Sup. Ct. 1917); Pennsylvania R.R. v. Cameron, 280 Pa. 458, 124 Atl. 638 (1924); *cf.* St. Louis, B.&M. Ry. v. United States, 268 U.S. 175-76 (1925).

[51]In the Case of Brazillian Loans, Publications of the Permanent Court of International Justice, Ser. A. No. 20 (1929) the court said, at page 120: "The economic dislocation caused by the Great War has not, in legal principle, released the Brazilian Government from its obligations. As for gold payments, there is no impossibility because of inability to obtain gold coins, if the promise be regarded as one for the payment of gold value. The equivalent in gold value is obtainable."

[52]All the judges who passed on the Feist case made the point that the half-yearly interest of £2.15:0 could not be paid in any existing gold coins. Shorthand Notes, Chancery Division, p. 11; Shorthand Notes, Court of Appeal, pp. 7, 9, 15.

The existing gold coins of the United States are the half-eagle ($5), the eagle ($10), and the double-eagle ($20). 26 STAT. 485 (1890), 46 STAT. 154 (1930), 31 U.S.C. § 315 (1926), *id*, SUPP. VI § 315a (1932). Perhaps, as to any balance over the highest amount determinable in multiples of existing gold coins, the doctrine *de minimis* might be applied.

[53]Under this construction the value of paper dollars in gold would be a question of fact, just as the value of Confederate dollars in United States dollars was a question of fact. Thorington v. Smith, 8 Wall. 1 (U.S. 1868). There was apparently a free market in gold and gold coins throughout the Legal Tender period. Whether or not the value of the dollar in gold, on a world market, would be accepted as evidence does not seem to have been passed on. *Cf.* Richard v. National City Bank, 231 App. Div. 559, 248 N.Y. Supp. 113 (1921); Richard v. American Union Bank. 241 N.Y. 163, 149 N.E. 338 (1925); s.c. 253 N.Y. 166, 170 N.E. 532 (1930).

[54]See note 15, *supra. Cf.* Paup v. Drew, 10 How. 218, 223 (U.S. 1850).

[55]In the Case of Serbian Loans, Publications of the Permanent Court of International Justice, Ser. A. No. 21 (1929), the court said, at page 33: "These were to be gold payments, but there were no gold coins for such amounts. It is manifest that the Parties, in providing for gold payments, were referring, not to payment in gold coins, but to gold as standard of value. It would be in this way, naturally, that they would seek to avoid, as was admittedly their intention, the consequences of a fluctuation of the Serbian dinar."

[56]See note 44, *supra.* But in Dutton v. Palairet, 154 U.S. 563 (1869), the Supreme Court affirmed a judgment for the currency value of the gold.

[57]The main difficulty is to determine the date as of which the values are to be taken. If the date of breach is taken, and judgment is given in dollars, the creditor gets a windfall if dollars appreciate between that date and the date of judgment. *Cf.* The Vaughan and Telegraph, 14 Wall. 258 (U.S. 1871). But this difficulty is inherent in the problem of converting one kind of money into another for purposes of judgment. See note 46, *supra.*

[58]96 U.S. 619 (1877). The question arose over the method of assessing the damages suffered by Morris, who had sold cattle to Gregory for prices stipulated in gold and had reserved a lien on the cattle for the price, as the result of an unsuccessful replevin action by Gregory. The jury had given a verdict for the currency value of the gold prices which Morris would have gotten if he had been able to exercise his lien. The Supreme Court, in affirming this, said: "While we have decided that a judgment upon a contract payable in gold may be for payment in coined

dollars, we have never held that in all cases it must be so.... Certainly, if Morris had in good faith sold the cattle under his power of sale for currency, and received payment in that kind of money, *he would have been entitled to convert the currency into gold before crediting it upon his debt.* So here, if, with the approbation of the court, he takes a judgment that may be discharged in currency of the specified amount of coin as bullion." *Id.* at 625-26 (italics inserted).

[59]The state cases which Bronson v. Rodes overruled were unanimous in holding that courts could not enter judgments specifically for gold coin. See note 15, *supra.* The gold judgment rule enunciated in Bronson v. Rodes was an innovation. This was an incidental reason, in most of those cases, for refusing to enforce the gold clause. The Supreme Court, however, did not seem to consider the rule essential to the enforceability of the gold clause; rather, it considered the right to a gold judgment as an additional advantage to the creditor, over and above his right to have the gold clause enforced.

After Bronson v. Rodes, the state courts generally gave gold judgments. See note 44, *supra.* But there are a few such cases containing decisions or dicta that a judgment for the currency value of the gold is proper, if the creditor does not object. *Cf.* Hittson v. Davenport, 4 Colo. 169 (1878); Walkup v. Houston, 65 N.C. 501 (1871); Tyers' Case, 5 Ct. Cl. 509 (1869); Bedford v. Woodward, 158 Ill. 122, 41 N.E. 1097 (1895); see also Morrell's Case, 7 Ct. Cl. 421 (1871).

[60]See. *e.;g.,* Henderson v. McPike, 35 Mo. 255, 259 (1864), where the court, reversing such a judgment and holding the creditor entitled only to the nominal amount of the debt in greenbacks, said "The theory has a fair look, but is without any legal support".

[61]This is probably the construction required by that form of the gold clause which reads "in gold coin of the United States of America of the standard of weight and fineness existing January 1, 1933, *or the equivalent thereof*". See note 1, *supra. Contra;* Killaugh v. Alford, 32 Tex. 457 (1870).

[62]Myers & Marcus v. Kauffman, 37 Ga. 600 (1868)), and Bond v. Greenwald & Co., 4 Heisk. 453, 469 (Tenn. 1871), indicated that the option is in the obligor; Lane v. Gluckauf, 28 Cal. 288 (1865), suggests that it is in the obligee.

[63]Section 6(5). "The validity and negotiable character of an instrument are not affected by the fact that [it]: ... (5) Designates a particular kind of current money in which payment is to be made". *Cf.* Eastman v. Sunset Park Land Co., 35 Cal. App. 628, 170 Pac. 642 (1917). For a dis-

cussion of cases discussing instruments payable "in currency" or "in current funds", see Brannan's Negotiable Instruments Law (5th ed. 1932) 160-61. Before the passage of the Uniform Act, it was held that a draft for "gold dollars" was negotiable. Chrysler v. Renois, 43 N.Y. 209 (1870).

[64]Dinsmore v. Duncan, 57 N.Y. 573 (1974); see also Chafee, *Acceleration Provisions in Time Paper* (1919) 32 Harv. L. Rev 747.

[65]See 12 Wall. 457, 567 (U.S. 1870).

[66]See note 15, *supra*.

[67]The difficulty in preserving the distinction is illustrated in Adair v. United States, 208 U.S. 161, 180 (1908): ". . . the provision . . . must be held to be repugnant to the Fifth Amendment as not embraced by nor within the power of Congress to regulate interstate commerce. . . ." See 3 Willoughby, The Constitutional Law of the United States (2d ed. 1929) 1866; Burdick, The Law of the American Constitution (1922) 407. Burdick, The Law of the American Constitution (1922) 407.

[68]Possibly both aspects could be treated as a single question, but they are separated here for purposes of clarity. The affirmative aspect is treated in subdivision A and the due process limitation in subdivision G.

[69]Of course the Constitution is not confined to a literal construction. See M'Culloch v. Maryland, 4 Wheat. 316, 407 (U.S. 1819); Gibbons v. Ogden, 9 Wheat. 1, 187-89 (U.S. 1824). Furthermore, legislation has the presumption of validity. Knox v. Lee, 12 Wall. 457, 531 (U.S. 1870); Adkins v. Children's Hospital, 261 U.S. 525, 544 (1923).

[70]8 Wall. 603 (U.S. 1869).

[71]Knox v. Lee, 12 Wall. 457, 534 (U.S. 1870). See also *id.* at 532-34; United States v. Gettysburg Electric Ry., 160 U.S. 668, 683 (1896).

[72]See 1 Willoughby, *op. cit. supra* note 67, §§ 49, 54, 58. In Kansas v. Colorado, 206 U.S. 46 (1907), the doctrine of inherent sovereignty, ardently advocated by Theodore Roosevelt in his speech of August 31, 1910, was repudiated. See Cushman *The National Police Power Under the Commerce Clause of the Constitution* (1919) 3 Minn. L. Rev. 289. It cannot be gainsaid, however, that the Federal Government has sovereign powers, that the Constitution confers sovereignty within the delegated sphere, except as other provisions limit such sovereignty. See M'Culloch v. Maryland, 4 Wheat. 316, 410 (U.S. 1819); Ruppert v. Caffey, 251 U.S. 264, 301 (1920); *In re* Debs, 158 U.S. 564, 578 (1895).

[73]See, *e.g.*, the quotation from Juilliard v. Greenman, 110 U.S. 421 (1884), at p. 1248, *infra*.

[74]In Ruppert v. Caffey, 251 U. 264, 301 (1920), the Court said: "Some confusion of thought might perhaps have been avoided, if, instead of distinguishing between powers by the terms express and implied, the terms specific and general had been used. For the power conferred by clause 18 of § 8 'to make all laws which shall be necessary and proper for carrying into execution' powers specifically enumerated is also an express power."

[75]See the cases in note 101, *infra*.

[76]4 Wheat. 316 421 (U.S. 1819). See also *id.* at 405, 407-08, 411-12, 415. An excellent illustration of the implied power to carry out the purposes of the power to borrow money and the power to coin money is Juilliard v. Greenman, 110 U.S. 421, 449-50 (1884). It is interesting to note how closely this exposition of the implied powers, resting on the 18th clause of Section 8 of Article 1, resembles the present-day interpretation of due process.

For the liberal construction applied to the words "necessary and proper", see M'Culloch v. Maryland, *supra*, at 413; United States v. Fisher, 2 Cranch 358, 396 (U.S. 1805).

[77]12 Wall. 457 (U.S. 1870).

[78]The other express powers set forth at the outset of the discussion of the affirmative powers seem foreign to the problem but merit some comment. The general welfare provision included in the taxing power has been interpreted as a limitation to taxation for public purposes, rather than as an original grant of power superseding the other express powers. Loan Ass'n v. Topeka, 20 Wall. 655 (U.S. 1874); BURDICK, *op. cit. supra* note 67, at 533. It is the source of the power of appropriation of federal moneys. See STORY, COMMENTARIES ON THE CONSTITUTION (5th ed. 1891) §§ 958-92, 1273-78; 1 WILLOUGHBY, *op. cit. supra* note 67, §§ 61-66. Conceivably the commerce power might be relevant if the gold clause affects or interferes with interstate commerce, but this would seem to be dependent on the gold clause interfering with the objectives of the money powers. It is therefore subordinate. For a full discussion, see Wyatt, *Constitutionality of Legislation Providing a Unified Commercial Banking System for the United States* (March, 1933) FED. RES. BULL. 166, 179. See also *Ames, Legal Tender* (1887) 1 HARV. L. REV. 73. 92-93. The bankruptcy power has never been interpreted, so far as we know, as a power to scale debts as an adjudication of partial bankruptcy. See note 116, *infra*.

[79]8 Wall. 533 (U.S. 1869). For an excellent discussion of the power to provide a national currency, see Wyatt *supra* note 78, at 175, in which the general counsel for the Federal Reserve Board concludes that congress has power to establish a single banking system.

[80]See *Veazie Bank* v. *Fenno,* 8 Wall. 533, 548 (U.S. 1869).

[81]Id. at 548-49.

[82]*Knox v. Lee,* 12 Wall. 457, 545-46 (U.S. 1870). See also *id* at 545-47, and Justice Bradley's concurring opinion at 562.

[83]110 U.S. 421, 448 (1884); see also *id.* at 447-50.

[84]"No person shall be deprived of life, liberty or property without due process of law; nor shall private property be taken for public use, without just compensation."

[85]See 3 WILLOUGHBY, *op. cit. supra* note 67, at 1862.

[86]148 U.S. 312 (1893). See also United States v. Cress, 243 U.S. 316 (1917)

[87]261 U.S. 502 (1923). See also Scranton v. Wheeler, 179 U.S. 141 (1900).

[88]148 U.S. 312, 336. "It should be noticed that here there is unquestionably a taking of the property, and not a mere destruction. It is not a case in which the government required the removal of an obstruction." *id.* at 337.

[89]261 U.S. 502, 513. The essential distinction is more broadly set forth at 508-09; "But destruction of, or injury to, property is frequently accomplished without a 'taking' in the constitutional sense. To prevent the spreading of a fire, property may be destroyed without compensation to the owner, ... There are many laws and governmental operations which injuriously affect the value of or destroy property—for example, restrictions upon the height or character of buildings, destruction of diseased cattle, trees, etc. to prevent contagion—but for which no remedy is afforded. Contracts in this respect do not differ from other kinds of property." See also the clear exposition in Knox v. Lee, 12 Wall. 457, 551 (U.S. 1870).

[90]23 Wall. 457 (U.S. 1870).

[91]See 12 Wall. 457, 549-50 (U.S. 1870). The court, however, stated that there was no impairment. See note 114, *infra.* See also Juilliard v. Greenman, 110 U.S. 421, 448 (1884).

[92]218 U.S. 302 (1910)

[93]*Id.* at 310.

[94]*Id.* at 311. For the applicability of the constitutional limitations to the Philippine Islands, see Kepner v. United States, 195 U.S. 100 (1904); Dorr v. United States, 195 U.S. 138 (1904); Downes v. Bidwell, 182 U.S. 244, 283 (1901); BURDICK, *op cit. supra* note 67, at 295-305. The due process requirement is specifically incorporated into the statute under which the islands are administered. 32 STAT. 691, 692, § 5 (1902). The Act is set forth, in part, and construed in Kepner v. United States, *supra.*

[95]Under the power to establish a system of bankruptcies, contract rights may be impaired. This most closely approximates a *power* to impair contracts. See Hanover Nat. Bank v. Moyses, 186 U.S. 181, 188 (1902).

[96]219 U.S. 467 (1911).

[97]Id. at 482. This same power over contracts with public service companies is allowed to the states. It is not an impairment of the obligation of contracts within the meaning of the constitutional provision in state cases, where the power is dependent upon the public service character. Union Dry Goods Co. v. Georgia Public Service Corp., 248 U.S. 372 (1919); Note (1919) 33 HARV. L. REV. 97, 98; (1919) 3 MINN. L. REV. 199, 202. This is analogous to cases holding that a state cannot contract away its police power. See Fertilizing Co. v. Hyde Park, 97 U.S. 659 (1877).

[98]See cases cited in note 101, *infra.* In Addyston Pipe & Steel Co. v. United States, 175 U.S. 211, 230 (1899), the Court affirmed a decree enjoining the continuance of a combination entered into in restraint of trade, saying: "Commerce is the important subject of consideration, and anything which directly obstructs and thus regulates that commerce which is carried on among the States whether it is state legislation or private contracts between individuals or corporations, should be subject to the power of Congress in the regulation of that commerce."

[99]See Hanover Nat. Bank v. Moyses, 186 U.S. 181, 192 (1902). For a complete discussion of the due process clause, see BURDICK, *op cit. supra* note 67, §§ 148-58, 230-74; 3 WILLOUGHBY, *op cit supra* note 67, §§1108-1266. See also Hough, *Due Process of Law—Today* (1919) 32 HARV. L. REV. 218.

[100]Note the combination of the two interpretations of due process in Adair v. United States, 208 U.S. 161, 179-80 (1908). See Highland v. Russell Car & Snow Plow Co., 279 U.S. 253, 261 (1929); Wilson v. New, 243 U.S. 332, 346 (1917); Hammer v. Dagenhart, 247 U.S. 251 (1918); Champion v. Ames, 188 U.S. 321 (1903); Chicago, R.I. & Pac. Ry. v. United

States, 284 U.S. 582 (1931). In Adair v. United States, *supra,* and Adkins v. Children's Hospital, 261 U.S. 525 (1923), involving questions of the liberty of contract, legislation was held unconstitutional under the due process clause on the ground that it was not reasonably adapted to a lawful objective.

On the plenary character of the powers and the effect of the due process limitation, see Billings v. United States, 232 U.S. 261, 282 (1914); McCray v. United States, 195 U.S. 27 (1904). But see Atlantic Coast Line R.R. v. Riverside Mills, 219 U.S. 186, 202 (1911); Nichols v. Coolidge, 274 U.S. 531, 542 (1927); Heiner v. Donnan, 285 U.S. 312 (1932); all indicating that the powers cannot be exercised unreasonably or arbitrarily.

[101]Knox v. Lee, 12 Wall. 457 (U.S. 1870); Addyston Pipe & Steel Co. v. United States, 175 U.S. 211 (1899); Atlantic Coast Line R.R. v. Riverside Mills, 219 U.S. 186 (1911) Lousiville & Nashville R.R. v. Mottley, 219 U.S. 467 (1911). See also M'Culloch v. Maryland, 4 Wheat. 316, 427 (U.S. 1819); Northern Securities Co. v. United States, 193 U.S. 197, 335-37, 341-42 (1904); Chicago, B. & Q. R.R. v. McGuire, 219 U.S. 549, 567 (1911); Philadelphia B. & W. R.R. v. Schubert, 224 U.S. 603, 609 (1912); Houston, East & West Texas Ry v. United States, 234 U.S. 342, 355 (1913); United States v. Ferger, 250 U.S. 199, 203 (1919); Wisconsin R.R. Comm. v. Chicago, B & Q. R.R., 257 U.S. 563, 586 (1921);New York v. United States, 257 U.S. 591 601 (1921); Stafford v. Wallace, 258 U.S. 495, 521 (1922); Hill v. Wallace, 259 U.S. 44, 69 (1922); United Mine Workers v. Coronado Co. 259 U.S. 344, 408 (1922).

[102]See cases collected in note 101, *supra.*

[103]3 WILLOUGHBY, *op. cit. supra* note 67, at 1857. See comment on the Thomas Amendment at page 1227. *supra.*

[104]Chicago, Milwaukee & St. Paul Ry. v. Minnesota, 134 U.S. 418, 456-57 (1890).

[105]Wilson v. New, 243 U.S. 332, 348 (1917); Block v. Hirsch, 256 U.S. 135, 157 (1920); The Chastleton Corp. v. Sinclair, 264 U.S. 543, 547-48 (1924). *Cf.* Adkins v. Children's Hospital, 261 U.S. 525, 551-52 (1923). The Supreme Court has indicated that Congress is the judge of the existence of such an emergency. Knox v. Lee, 12 Wall. 457, 542 (U.S. 1870); Juilliard v. Greenman, 110 U.S. 421, 450 (1884). If the gold clause constitutes an interference with a lawful objective in recurring crises, it should be considered a permanent obstruction. Stafford v. Wallace, 258 U.S. 495, 521 (1922).

[106]See cases cited in note 101, *supra.*

[107]262 U.S. 1 (1923).

[108]*Id.* at 37-38. See also Stafford v. Wallace, 258 U.S. 495, 521 (1922); Hill v. Wallace, 259 U.S. 44, 69 (1922); Biklé, *Judicial Determination of Questions of Fact Affecting the Constitutional Validity of Legislative Action* (1924) 38 HARV. L. REV. 6; 3 WILLOUGHBY, *op. cit. supra* note 67, § 1172.

[109]Compare the analogous situation in Veazie Bank v. Fenno, 8 Wall. 533 (U.S. 1869). See also Wyatt, *supra* note 78, at 166.

[110]In this connection it should be noted that the choice of the means to accomplish a lawful purpose, so long as the means are fairly related to the end, is a matter for Congress. United States v. Fisher, 2 Cranch 358 (U.S. 1805); Martin v. Hunter's Lessee, 1 Wheat. 304, 326-27 (U.S. 1819); Gibbons v. Ogden, 9 Wheat. 1, 196-97 (U.S. 1824); Farmers' & Mechanics' National Bank v. Dearing, 91 U.S. 29, 33 (1875).

[111]The first of the acts was passed Feb. 25, 1862. 12 STAT. 345.

[112]Bronson v. Rodes, 7 Wall. 229 (U.S. 1868).

[113]See note 91, *supra.*

[114]See 12 Wall. 457, 549 (U.S. 1870). Of course contracts for the payment of money generally, based on the presumed intent of the parties, are dischargeable in whatever constitutes legal tender at maturity. Knox v. Lee, 12 Wall. 457, 548 (U.S. 1870); Juillard v. Greenman, 110 U.S. 421, 449 (1884). See also Butler v. Horwitz, 7 Wall. 258, 261 (U.S. 1868). This raises the question whether the court, in stating there was no impairment, had reference to this rule or to the scope of the money power. It appeared to have reference to the latter.

[115]See Johnson, *supra* note 10, at 187.

[116]It is important to recognize the distinction between the scope of the money power *per se* and the question of an interference with a lawful objective of the delegated powers, whether such objective be derived from a single power or a composite of powers, since a statute purporting to nullify gold clauses would not necessarily be a coinage and currency statute.

FOUR

[1]48 STAT. L. 112.

[2]Daily Cong. Rec. (April 24, 1933) 2229.

[3]H.R. 169 73d Cong., 1st Sess. In placing a construction upon a statute great weight is given to the reports of committees in charge of the bill in its passage through Congress. This has been extended to statements made on the floor of the Senate or House by the Chairman or other member of the committee in charge of the bill. Duplex Company v. Deering, 254 U.S. 443, 474, 475, 41 Sup. Ct. 172, 65 L. Ed. 349 (1921).

[4]H.R. 169, 73d Cong. 1st Sess.

[5]Still more violent was the dissension among the Supreme Court Justices themselves, both in open court and in the conference chamber. The account of these dissensions is found in the "Miscellaneous Writings" of Honorable Joseph P. Bradley, Associate Justice of the Supreme Court of the United States, (1902), in the article entitled, "The Legal Tender Cases in 1970," pages 45 to 74. It is there distinctly shown that the first legal tender decision against the constitutionality of the acts was rendered by a bare majority of the court composed of less than the normal number of judges and by the vote of one judge as to whom it was not very clear that he voted understanding what he was voting on. Opinions continue to differ as to which decision of the Supreme Court is right. There can be no doubt of the propriety of the court rehearing the question before a full bench.

[6]Legal Tender Cases, 12 Wall. 457, 20 L. Ed. 287 (U.S. 1870).

[7]Legal Tender Case, 110 U.S. 421, 4 Sup. Ct. 122, 28 L. Ed. 204 (1884).

[8]Id. 110 U.S. 421, 449.

[9]Bronson v. Rodes, 7 Wall. 229, 19 L. Ed. 141 (U.S. 1869).

[10]12 Wall. 687, 697, 20 L. Ed. 460 (U.S. 1871).

[11]Supra 9.

[12]Butler v. Horowitz, 7 Wall. 258, 19 L. Ed. 149 (U.S. 1869).

[13]Gregory v. Morris, 96 U.S. 619, 625, 24 L. Ed. 740 (1878).

[14]*Supra* note 6 at 548.

[15]148 U.S. 312, 13 Sup. Ct. 623, 73 L. Ed. 463 (1893).

[16]*Id.* at 324.

[17]208 U.S. 161, 28 Sup. Ct. 277, 52 L. Ed. 436 (1908).

[18]*Id.* at 180.

[19]261 U.S. 525, 43 Sup. Ct. 394, 67 L. Ed 785 (1923).

[20]*Id.* at 545, 546, 561.

[21]165 U.S. 578, 17 Sup. Ct. 427, 41 L. Ed. 832 (1897).

[22]*Id.* at 591.

[23]236 U.S. 1, 35 Sup. Ct. 240, 59 L. Ed. 441 (1915).

[24]*Id.* at 11.

[25]244 U.S. 590, 37 Sup. Ct. 662, 61 L. Ed. 1336 (1917).

[26]*Id.* at 597.

[27]262 U.S. 522, 43 Sup. Ct. 630, 67 L. Ed. 1103 (1923).

[28]*Id.* at 534.

[29]273 U.S. 418, 47 Sup. Ct. 426, 71 L. Ed. 718 (1927).

[30]*Id.* at 429.

[31]Daily Cong. Rec. (April 26. 1933) Senate 2417, 2418. See for full text of House of Lords decision, 1 U.S. Law Week 397 (1934).

[32](1933) 1 Chancery Div. 373.

[33]8 Wall. 1, 19 L. Ed. 361 (U.S. 1869).

[34]Hamilton's Works, vol. 3, p. 518.

[35]96 U.S. 432, 445, 449, 24 L. Ed. 760 (1878).

[36]15 Pet. 391, 392 (U.S. 1842).

[37]96 U.S. 30, 36, 24 L. Ed. 647 (1878).

[38]10 Ct. Cl. 494, 502 (1875).

[39]91 U.S. 321, 23 L. Ed. 397 (1876).

[40]233 U.S. 165, 171, 172, 34 Sup. Ct. 553, 58 L. Ed. 898 (1914).

[41]268 U.S. 186, 188, 45 Sup. Ct. 469, 69 L. Ed. 907 (1925).

[42]33 STAT. L., part 2, p. 2238 (1903).

[43]4 Wall. 21, 120, 121 (U.S. 1867).

[44]243 U.S. 332, 37 Sup. Ct. 298, 61 L. Ed. 755 (1917).

[45]*Id. at 348.*

[46]Block v. Hirsh, 256 U.S. 135, 41 Sup. Ct. 458, 65 L. Ed. 865 (1921).

[47]Chastleton Corp. v. Sinclair, 264 U.S. 543, 44 Sup. Ct. 405, 68 L. Ed. 841 (1942).

[48]Marcus Brown Holding Co. v. Feldman, 256 U.S. 170, 41 Sup. Ct. 465, 65 L. Ed. 877 (1921).

[49]258 U.S. 242, 42 Sup. Ct. 289, 66 L. Ed. 595 (1922).

FIVE

Outline of the Gold Clause Cases

† Mr. MacLean supervised the preparation of the Government's briefs in all of the Gold Clause Cases. The principal argument in the Missouri Pacific Case was made by Attorney General Homer Cummings, with Mr. Stanley Reed assisting for the Reconstruction Finance Corporation. The Perry and Nortz cases were argued by Mr. MacLean. He also argued the Government's intervention in the Missouri Pacific Case at St. Louis, and prepared the petition to have the case brought directly to the Supreme Court. He was at that time Assistant Solicitor General of the United States.

[1]Norman v. Baltimore & Ohio Ry., U.S. v. Banker's Trust Co., 294 U.S. 240, 55 Sup. Ct. 407, 79 L. Ed. 885 (1935).

[2]Perry v. U.S. 294 U.S. 330, 55 Sup. Ct. 432, 79 L. Ed. 912 (1935).

[3]Nortz v. U.S. 294 U.S. 317, 55 Sup. Ct. 428, 79 L. Ed. 907 (1935).

[4]48 Stat. 113 (1933), 31 U.S.C.A. §§462, 463 (1936).

[5]7 Wall. 229, 19 L. Ed. 141 (1868).

[6]8 Wall. 603, 19 L. Ed. 513 (1870).

[7]Legal Tender Cases, 12 Wall. 457, 20 L. Ed. 287 (1872) Juilliard v. Greenman, 110 U.S. 421, 4 Sup. Ct. 122, 28 L. Ed. 204 (1884).

[8]12 Wall. 545, 20 L. Ed. 310.

[9]Feist v. Société Intercommunale Belge d'Electricité [1934] A.C. 161.

[10]Serbian and Brazilian Bond Cases, P.C.I.J., series A., Nos. 20/21 (1929).

Analysis of the Gold Clause Cases.

[1]48 Stat. 112 (U.S.C.A. tit. 31, Supp., secs. 462, 463). Section 2 of the joint resolution is an amendment to the Agricultural Relief Act of May 12, 1933, and provides that "All coins and currencies of the United States (including Federal Reserve notes and circulating notes of Federal

211

Reserve banks and national banking associations) heretofore or hereafter coined or issued, shall be legal tender for all debts, public and private.   .   .   ."

[2](U.S. 1935) 55 Sup. Ct. 428, Justices McReynolds, Van Devanter, Sutherland, and Butler dissenting.

[3](U.S. 1935) 55 Sup. Ct. 432, Justices McReynolds, Van Devanter, Sutherland, and Butler dissenting.

[4]The opinion of Mr. Justice McReynolds says (55 Sup. Ct. 407 at 423): "The authority exercised by the President and the Treasury in demanding all gold coin, bullion, and certificates is not now challenged; neither is the right of the former to prescribe weight for the standard dollar. These things we have not considered."

In another place Mr. Justice McReynolds clearly indicates his opinion that the owners of gold coin or gold bullion are entitled to compensation for its value in the event that its appropriation is authorized for governmental purposes. *Ibid.*, pp. 425-426.

[5]The withdrawal of gold coin from circulation had commenced on March 6, 1933, the day on which the bank holiday was declared. The Secretary of the Treasury then issued instructions that payments in gold in any form were to be made by the Treasury only on special license of the Secretary. Proclamation No 2040, U.S.C.A. tit. 12, Supp., p. 44 (1933).

By the Emergency Banking Relief Act of March 9, 1933 (48 Stat. 1) this action of the Secretary of the Treasury was confirmed and the President was also authorized during periods of national emergency to "investigate, regulate, or prohibit .   .   . export, hoarding, melting, or earmarking of gold or silver coin or bullion or currency, by any person within the United States or any place subject to the jurisdiction thereof. .   .   ." By the same act the Secretary of the Treasury was authorized to require all persons to deliver to the Treasurer of the United States "any or all gold coin, gold bullion, and gold certificates" owned by them, for which they were to receive "an equivalent amount of any other form of coin or currency coined or issued under the laws of the United States." Under the authority thus conferred the following orders were issued:

(1) By executive order No. 6102, signed by the President on April 5, 1933 (U.S.C.A. tit. 12, Supp., p. 68), all persons were required to deliver to a Federal Reserve Bank or to a member bank of the Federal Reserve system all gold coin, gold bullion, or gold certificates owned by them. Exceptions recognized were "Such amount of gold as may be required for legitimate and customary use in industry, profession or art within a reasonable time", gold coin and certificates up to the amount of $100 and

gold coins "having a recognized special value to collectors of rare and unusual coins"; gold coin and bullion earmarked or held in trust for recognized foreign governments or foreign central banks; and gold coin or bullion licensed for other proper transactions. Fines up to $10,000 and imprisonment up to 10 years were authorized for violation of the order.

(2) By a Presidential order of April 20, 1933, the earmarking of gold coin, gold bullion, or gold certificates for foreign account and their export to foreign countries was prohibited except on license from the Secretary of the Treasury. Executive Order No. 6111 (U.S.C.A. tit. 12, Supp., p. 46).

(3) By regulations of the Secretary of the Treasury on April 29, 1933, the export of gold coin, gold bullion, and gold certificates except on license of the Secretary was again prohibited, and the grant of licenses for domestic use was provided for in detail. (Quoted in brief for the Government, App., pp. 22-34)

(4) By Presidential order (Executive Order No. 6260) of August 28, 1933 (U.S.C.A. tit. 12, Supp., p. 46), the earlier orders of April 5 and April 20 were revoked, but the substance of their provisions was re-enacted and detailed provisions were added for investigation into domestic ownership of gold and for report by owners and custodians of gold to local collectors of internal revenue.

Other executive orders and regulations, repeating in substance the provisions above outlined, were issued on September 12, 1934, December 28, 1934, January 15, 1934 and January 30 and January 31, 1934.

[6](U.S. 1935) 55 Sup. Ct. 428 at 431. One of the three questions certified to the Supreme Court by the Court of Claims had purported to raise this question of constitutionality. The Court of Claims asked whether the provisions of the Emergency Banking Act and the regulations of the Secretary of the Treasury issued thereunder amounted to a taking of property within the meaning of the Fifth Amendment, in so far as they required the plaintiff to surrender the gold certificates in his possession. The Court said that this question was "academic," in view of the fact that the surrender had already occurred and in view further of its holding that no damages were shown by the plaintiff through failure to secure gold coin.

[7]United States v. Campbell, (D.C.   S.D.   N.Y. 1933) 5 F. Supp. 156, a criminal prosecution for failing to report ownership of gold bullion and for retaining ownership and possession without license. [Lower court decision discussed 32 MICH. L. REV. 405 (1934).] The opinion of Judge Woolsey declared (p. 169) that gold "is a commodity affected with a public interest as a potential source of currency and credit," sustained the power of Congress to investigate throughout the nation the location and

ownership of gold coin or bullion, and asserted the right of the Government to prevent gold-hoarding. But the second count of the indictment, based on defendant's continued *possession* of gold bullion, was held insufficient on demurrer, on the ground that the power conferred on the Secretary of the Treasury to enforce the surrender of outstanding gold coin or bullion, could not be validly exercised by the President. It was also suggested (pp. 170-172) that the requisitioning of gold coin or gold bullion was an exercise of the power of eminent domain and that the Government would become liable on "implied contract" for the fair value of the gold appropriated. The appeal form Judge Woolsey's decision was dismissed by the Supreme Court in 291 U.S. 686, 54 Sup. Ct. 455 (1934), and a motion to reinstate the appeal was denied in 291 U.S. 648, 54 Sup. Ct. 459 (1934). The case is discussed in 47 HARV. L. REV. 479 (1934).

[8]Ling Su Fan v. United States, 218 U.S. 302, 31 Sup. Ct. 21, 30 L.R.A. (N.S.) 1176 (1910), a prosecution for violating a law of the Philippine Legislature, prohibiting the export of silver coin or bullion. In the particular case the defendant had attempted to export silver *coin*, but the power of the Legislature to maintain the parity of silver with other monetary media was asserted in broad language. After pointing out that Congress had delegated to the Philippine Legislature the power to create a local currency, the Court said (at pp. 310-311):

it is said, that if the particular measure resorted to be one which operates to deprive the owner of silver pesos, of the difference between their bullion and coin value, he has had his property taken from him without compensation, and, in its wider sense, without that due process of law guaranteed by the fundamental act of July, 1902

Conceding the title of the owner of such coins, yet there is attached to such ownership those limitations which public policy may require by reason of their quality as a legal tender and as a medium of exchange. These limitations are due to the fact that public law gives to such coinage a value which does not attach as a mere consequence of intrinsic value. Their quality as a legal tender is an attribute of law aside from their bullion value. They bear, therefore, the impress of sovereign power which fixes value and authorizes their use in exchange. As an incident, the Government may punish defacement and mutilation and constitute any such act, when fraudulently done, a misdemeanor. Rev. Stat. §§ 5459, 5189.

"However unwise a law may be, aimed at the exportation of such coins, in the face of the axioms against obstructing the free flow of commerce, there can be no serious doubt but that the power of coin money includes the power to prevent its outflow from the country of its origin. To justify the exercise of such a power it is only necessary that it shall appear that the means are reasonably adapted to conserve the general public interest and are not an arbitrary interference with private rights of contract or property. The law here in question is plainly within the limits of the police power, and not an arbitrary or unreasonable interference with private rights. If a local coinage was demanded by the general interest of the Philippine Islands, legislation reasonably adequate to maintain such a coinage at home as a medium of exchange is not a violation of private right forbidden by organic law.

[9]This had been held in Marion & Rye Valley Ry. v. United States, 270 U.S. 280, 46 Sup. Ct. 253 (1926), an action for compensation for the value of the use and possession of a railroad taken over by the Director-General during the war. In Nortz v. United States another reason suggested by the majority for denying recovery was the fact that on January 17, 1934, the gold content of the dollar had not been legally altered. (U.S. 1935) 55 Sup. Ct. 428 at 431. It was not until January 31, 1934, that the President, acting under the authority conferred by the Gold Reserve Act of 1934, by proclamation reduced the gold content to 15 5/21 grains of gold nine-tenths fine, U.S. C.A. tit. 31, sec. 821, note.

[10]Authority was conferred on the Secretary of the Treasury to purchase gold bullion newly mined in the United States by Executive Order No. 6261, issued August 29, 1933 (quoted in brief for the Government, App., pp. 49-50). This authority was confirmed by Executive Order No. 6359, Oct. 25, 1933 (U.S.C.A. tit. 12, Supp., p. 69); and Regulations of Jan. 31, 1934, Art. 6 (quoted in brief for the Government, App., pp. 137-141). By sec. 8 of the Gold Reserve Act of Jan. 30, 1934 (48 Stat. 337) The Secretary of the Treasury was authorized, with the approval of the President, to "purchase gold in any amounts, at home or abroad" with coin or currency of the United States; on terms and conditions fixed by him.

It will be recalled that it was through purchases of newly-mined gold bullion and foreign gold coin and gold bullion that the currency dollar was steadily pushed down by the Administration to the value now fixed by Presidential Proclamation. It could be urged, in support of Mr. Justice McReynolds' contention, that a gold value thus officially fixed by the Treasury was the best possible index of value for the gold coin claimed by the plaintiff in Perry v. United States. Indeed, for the classes of gold which the Government purchased freely from all comers, it would seem that the Government should not be allowed to contradict its own official price.

[11]GIERKE, JOHANNES ALTHUSIUS 76-122 (1913); I GIERKE, NATURAL LAW AND THE THEORY OF SOCIETY, 1500 TO 1800 (translated by Barker) 107-111 (1934).

[12]Dicta in the Sinking-Fund Cases, 99 U.S. 700 at 719, 25 L. Ed. 496 (1878); United States v. Smith, 94 U.S. 214 (1876); United States v. Central Pacific R.R., 118 U.S. 235 (1886); Garrison v. United States, 7 Wall. (74 U.S.) 688 (1868); Hollerbach v. United States, 233 U.S. 165, 34 Sup. Ct. 553 (1914); United States v. Northern Pacific Ry., 256 U.S. 51, 41 Sup. Ct. 439 (1921); Reading Steel Casting Co. v. United States, 268 U.S. 186, 45 Sup. Ct. 469 (1925); Grismore, "Contracts with the United States," 22 MICH. L. REV. 749 (1924).

[13]292 U.S. 571, 54 Sup. Ct. 840 (1934). There the Court had said, speaking through Mr. Justice Brandeis (at p. 579); "That the contracts of war risk insurance were valid when made is not questioned. As Congress had the power to authorize the Bureau of War Risk Insurance to issue them, the due process clause prohibits the United States from annulling them, *unless, indeed, the action taken falls within the federal police power or some other paramount power*." (Italics ours.)

[14]The remarks of Chief Justice Hughes must be described as dicta, inasmuch as they do not affect the decision of Perry v. United States. Nevertheless, it should be pointed out that they were concurred in by three other justices and the four dissenting Justices were even more emphatic in stating their view that the solemn obligation of the Government could not be repudiated or qualified by this attempted exercise of the currency power.

[15]It is uncertain how far the Chief Justice and his associates mean to carry the argument that the power to pledge the credit of the United States can be used to restrain the exercise of an independent governmental power. It might be suggested that in this case the gold clause in Government obligations is at most an indirect interference with the currency powers of Congress. It seems clear that the devaluation policy of Congress can be carried out without repudiation of the *secondary* obligation to pay the paper-money value of the coin promised. In other words, the gold clause need not be construed as a contract *not* to devalue the dollar, but rather as a contract to pay an increased sum in paper money *if* the dollar is devalued. This suggestion is not supported by any language in the opinion of the Chief Justice, but it may assist in

reconciling the position taken with the decisions in a number of other cases.

It has been repeatedly held, for example, that certain phases of the police power of states and other governmental units cannot be bargained away. Stone v. Mississippi, 101 U.S. 814, 25 L. Ed. 1079 (1880), grant by state of right to operate a lottery for 25 years; Boston Beer Co. v. Massachusetts, 97 U.S. 25, 24 L. Ed. 989 (1877), franchise granted to private corporation to sell beer; Butchers' Union Slaughter-House Co. v. Crescent City Live-Stock Landing Co., 111 U.S. 746, 4 Sup. Ct. 652 (1884), act of state legislature conferring a monopoly of the slaughter-house business in New Orleans; Newton v. Commissioners, 100 U.S. 548, 25 L. Ed. 710 (1880), statute providing that county seat should be located at a particular place and "permanently established" there; Northern Pac. Ry. v. Minnesota, 208 U.S. 583, 28 Sup. Ct. 341 (1908), contract alleged to have effect of relieving railroad of duty to make repairs or improvements in its right of way; Denver and Rio Grande R.R. v. Denver, 250 U.S. 241, 39 Sup. Ct. 450 (1919), city ordinance authorizing establishment of railroad tracks in congested district of city. For a recent assertion of the same doctrine see Home Building & Loan Ass'n v. Blaisdell, 290 U.S. 398 at 436, 54 Sup. Ct. 231 (1934). There would seem to be no doubt that it applies as well to contracts of the federal Government restraining the exercise of certain classes of governmental powers. North American Commercial Co. v. United States, 171 U.S. 110, 18 Sup. Ct. 817 (1897); United Shoe Machinery Corp. v. United States, 258 U.S. 451, 42 Sup. Ct. 363 (1922); Straus v. American Publishers' Ass'n, 231 U.S. 571, 616, 54 Sup. Ct. 641, 840 (1934), declaring the government bound by its contrtacts "unless the action taken falls within the police power or some other paramount power."

But it appears from other decisions that certain other phases of the police power can be restrained to a greater or less degree by express contract. For example, it was held in New Orleans Gas-Light Co. v. Louisiana Light Co., 115 U.S. 650, 6 Sup. Ct. 252 (1885), that an exclusive franchise for the sale of gas in New Orleans could not be revoked or impaired through subsequent adoption in the state constitution of a policy against monopoly of such services. See also the regulation of rates of a public utility involved in Minneapolis v. Minneapolis Street Ry., 215 U.S. 417, 30 Sup. Ct. 118 (1910), and the tax exemptions involved in Piqua Branch of State Bank of Ohio v. Knoop, 16 How. (57 U.S.) 369, 14 L. Ed. 977 (1853); Farrington v. Tennessee, 95 U.S. 679, 24 L. Ed. 558 (1878); Humphrey v. Pegues, 16 Wall. (83 U.S.) 244, 21 L. Ed. 326 (1873); St. Anna's Asylum v. New Orleans, 105 U.S. 362, 26 L. Ed. 1128 (1882), and numerous other cases. Compare also Baltimore v.

Baltimore Trust Co., 166 U.S. 673, 17 Sup. Ct. 696 (1897), with Grand Trunk Western R.R. v. South Bend, 227 U.S. 544, 33 Sup. Ct. 3032 (1912). In Lynch v. United States, *supra,* the interest of the Government in securing a general reduction of governmental expenses was held an insufficient justification for modification of war-risk insurance policies.

It would appear, then, that in prior decisions a shadowy line of distinction has been marked out between different phases of the police power and that the Government has been conceded the power to bargain away the immediate right to exercise some of them. As it is sometimes said, these phases of the police power *can be exercised* by the act of entering into contracts. It is notable that these phases are for the most part concerned with economic regulation, as distinguished from the more vital matters of public health, public safety, etc.

The language of the Chief Justice in Perry v. United States is sweeping. But one hesitates to ascribe to him the notion that the NIRA administration could be authorized by Congress to draft a code of fair competition in such a form as to restrict the powers of Congress in regulating interstate commerce. Could a contract by the Government for the sale and delivery of goods to a private party preclude a subsequent embargo or restriction on interstate or foreign commerce? It would appear from Horowitz v. United States, 267 U.S. 458, 45 Sup. Ct. 344 (1925), that even an express agreement by the Government not to exercise this or some other paramount power would be ineffective. Compare the patent and copyright cases of United Shoe Machinery Corp. v. United States, 258 U.S. 451, 42 Sup. Ct. 363 (1922), and Straus v. American Publishers' Ass'n, 231 U.S. 222, 34 Sup. Ct. 84 (1913).

[16](U.S. 1935) 55 Sup. Ct. 438-439: "I do not understand the government to contend that it is any the less bound by the obligation than a private individual would be, or that it is free to disregard it except in the exercise of the constitutional power 'to coin money' and 'regulate the value thereof.' In any case, there is before us no question of default apart from the regulation by Congress of the use of gold as currency.

"While the government's refusal to make the stipulated payment is a measure taken in the exercise of that power, this does not disguise the fact that its action is to that extent a repudiation of its undertaking. As much as I deplore this refusal to fulfill the solemn promise of bonds of the United States, I cannot escape the conclusion, announced for the

Court, that in the situation now presented, the government, through the exercise of its sovereign power to regulate the value of money, has rendered itself immune from liability for its action.   .   .   .

"Moreover, if the gold clause be viewed as a gold value contract, as it is in Norman v. Baltimore & Ohio R. Co., supra, it is to be noted that the government has not prohibited the free use by the bondholder of the paper money equivalent of the gold clause obligation; it is the prohibition, by the Joint Resolution of Congress, of payment of the increased number of depreciated dollars required to make up the full equivalent, which alone bars recovery. In that case it would seem to be implicit in our decision that the prohibition, at least in the present situation, is itself a constitutional exercise of the power to regulate the value of money.

"I therefore do not join in so much of the opinion as may be taken to suggest that the exercise of the sovereign power to borrow money on credit, which does not override the sovereign immunity from suit, may nevertheless preclude or impede the exercise of another sovereign power, to regulate the currency which we now hold to be superior to the obligation of the bonds."

[17]It is not entirely clear whether the holders of gold certificates and the owners of gold coin, gold bullion, or gold certificates who have surrendered them under pressure to the Treasury would also be entitled to sue in this contingency. The plaintiff in Nortz v. United States proposed two distinct theories of recovery—express contract to pay coin on which the Government had consented to be sued, and "implied" contract to pay the value of property appropriated for a public use. The majority opinion left open the question whether either theory could be used for recovery on the gold certificates, and disposed of the case on the ground no substantial damages were shown. There is a suggestion, however, that holders of gold certificates must be satisfied with gold coin of the new standard. 55 Sup. Ct. 428 at 430.

In the case of gold coin, gold bullion, or gold certificates *already surrendered* to the Treasury, the eminent domain theory would clearly be the only one available. The case of United States v. Campbell (cited above, note 7) indicates that a contract to pay the value of gold bullion can be implied *in fact* (quasi-contract claims not being included in the jurisdiction conferred on the Court of Claims by the Tucker Act). The decisions of the United States Supreme Court on this question do not permit any clear lines to be drawn, but apparently the tests for "implied contract" are met in the instant case. See 43 YALE L.J. 497 (1934), and 43 YALE L.J. 674 (1934).

In any case, whether the theory be express contract or implied contract for the value of property taken on eminent domain, presumably the damages would be measured as of the date of the breach or appropriation. A subsequent removal of restrictions on the private sale or export of gold would not, on that analysis, entitle the claimant to substantial damages.

[18]The volume of outstanding gold-clause obligations is sufficiently large to require serious attention to this possibility. By February 18, 1935, the total of bonds and treasury notes containing the gold clause had been reduced from their peak of over $20,000,000,000 to $14,565,727,180. New York Times, issue of Feb. 19, 1935, p. 13. Partly for the saving of interest charges and partly, no doubt, to escape prospective liability on the gold clause, the Treasury has undertaken extensive conversion operations. Between now and October 15, 1935, the Treasury will be in a position to redeem treasury notes and bonds (particularly the large issues of the First and Fourth Liberty Loan) to a total of over $6,000,000,000. These issues have already been called for redemption in most instances. This would leave somewhat more than $8,000,000,000, however, a large percentage of which will not be callable before 1940.

[19]In the able brief for the Government in Perry v. United States it was argued (pp. 80-83) that the Joint Resolution of June 5, 1933, by implication withdrew the consent of the Government to be sued on gold clause obligations. This contention was apparently rejected by the Supreme Court. Whether Congress will resort to an express restriction of the jurisdiction of the Court of Claims in this class of cases is a question of morality and political expediency on which no predictions are possible. It is to be hoped that this desperate expedient will not be necessary, if only for the reason that the position of a great creditor country would be thus irretrievably jeopardized in the international sphere.

The position of foreign holders of government gold-clause obligations deserves additional comment. Aliens can sue in the Court of Claims if their governments extend a similar privilege to citizens of the United States. 36 Stat. 1139, U.S.C.A. tit. 28, sec. 261. Both this class of aliens and United States citizens resident abroad could therefore bring suit against the United States Government under the present Judiciary Act. Nevertheless, since the bonds are payable at the Treasury, such persons would be in the same position as domestic holders and would suffer no substantial damage so long as the present restrictions on sale and export of gold are maintained. Although the moral claims of foreign private bondholders are strong, it is unlikely that the Supreme Court will discriminate in their favor. As a practical matter, to admit such discrimination would make it possible for domestic holders to sell Government bonds abroad and thus evade the policy of Congress.

[20](U.S. 1935) 55 Sup. Ct. 432 at 438.

[21]See the Bureau of Labor Statistics Index of wholesale prices published in the SURVEY OF CURRENT BUSINESS, SUPPLEMENT, for March 21, 1935. On a basis of 1926 as 100, an average of prices for 784 commodities for the week of March 11, 1933, gave an index number of 60.2. After a considerable jump during the spring and early summer of 1933, prices rose more slowly through 1934. For the week of March 9, 1935, the index number had reached 79.6.

There is still some distance to go before the general level of 1926 prices, the declared objective of the Administration, will be restored; and wholesale prices are still approximately half their war and postwar peak. See the Index Numbers of Wholesale Prices published by the United States Deparetment of Labor in 40 MONTHLY LABOR REV., No. 1, p. 239 (Jan. 1935).

[22]265 N.Y. 37, 191 N.E. 726, 92 A.L.R. 1523 (1934).

[23](D.C.E.D. Mo. 1934) 7 F. Supp. 1. This suit involved two cases. The original proceeding was a reorganization of the Missouri Pacific Railroad under the 1933 amendment to the Bankruptcy Act. The Bankers' Trust Co. and another intervened, the United States and the Reconstruction Finance Corp. intervened jointly in opposition to its claim, and the two causes were consolidated below for hearing.

[24](U.S. 1935) 55 Sup. Ct. 407, Justices McReynolds, Van Devanter. Sutherland, and Butler dissenting.

[25]The English House of Lords and the Permanent Court of International Justice had likewise held that gold-coin clauses were secondarily gold-value clauses, so that the obligee was entitled to the paper-money equivalent of the coin promised when a discrepancy appeared between them. Feist v. Société, [1934] A.C. 161; Cases of Serbian and Brazilian loans, Publications of the Permanent Court of International Justice, Series A. Nos. 20/21. See also the decisions of other foreign courts cited by Nussbaum, "Comparative and International Aspects of American Gold Clause Abrogation," 44 YALE L.J. 53 at 57 (1934).

The contrary decisions of the German Reichsgericht are severely criticized by Professor Nussbaum, *ibid.*, at p. 56, and in his book DAS

GELD 84-89, 179-183 (1925), and the JURISTISCHE WOCHENSCHRIFT, 1925, p. 1483. These decisions rested in part on art. 245 of the German Civil Code, providing that clauses specifying a particular kind of coin should be ignored when the specified kind of coin disappeared from circulation. They also depended in the case of mortgage obligations on the requirement of the land registry laws that mortgages, in order to be registered, must be for a fixed sum of money. DECISIONS OF THE REICHSGERICHT IN CIVIL MATTERS, vol. 101, p. 141 (Dec. 18, 1920); vol. 103, p. 384 (Jan. 11, 1922); vol. 121, p. 110 (Apr. 26, 1928); JURISTISCHE WOCHENSCHRIFT, 1925, p. 1483 (Dec. 3, 1924).

[26]If there were any purpose now in making such a contention, it could be argued that the obligations in suit were, at the time they were made, for a "fixed sum of money" (i.e., a fixed sum in gold coin) and that the subsequent devaluation of the dollar does not deprive them of the quality of negotiability then acquired. Even in contracts made after the devaluation had occurred, it would still be true that they expressed a fixed sum in lawful money, even though gold coin by executive order is withdrawn from circulation. This question has now become academic. The problem of negotiability is more serious and is still active in connection with promises to pay a sum of money computed on a commodity price base. See the next article, entitled " Contracting by Reference to Price Indices," infra. p. 685.

[27]Bronson v. Rodes, 7 Wall. (74 U.S.) 229, 19 L. Ed. 141 (1868); Butler v. Horwitz, 7 Wall. (74 U.S.) 258, 19 L. Ed. 149 (1868).

[28]Trebilcock v. Wilson, 12 Wall. (79 U.S.) 687, 20 L. Ed. 460 (1871); Thompson v. Butler, 95 U.S. 694, 24 L. Ed. 540 (1877).

[29]Knox v. Lee, 12 Wall. (79 U.S.) 457, 20 L. Ed. 287 (1871).

[30]8 Wall. (75 U.S.) 533, 19 L. Ed. 482 (1869).

[31]Juilliard v. Greenman, 110 U.S. 4211, 4 Sup. Ct. 122 (1884).

[32]Ling Su Fan v. United States, 218 U.S. 302, 31 Sup Ct. 21, 30 L.R.A. (N.S.) 1176 (1910), quoted above, note 8.

[33]Addyston Pipe & Steel Co. v. United States, 175 U.S. 211, 20 Sup. Ct. 96 (1899); Louisville and Nashville R.R. v. Mottley, 219 U.S. 467, 31 Sup. Ct. 265, 34 L.R.A. (N.S.) 671 (1911); Second Employers' Liability Cases, 223 U.S. 1, 32 Sup. Ct 169, 38 L.R.A. (N.S.) 44 (1912), among many others.

[34]Sup. Ct. 407 at 418.

[35]Sup. Ct. 407 at 419.

[36]The arguments of the dissenting opinion against this result attracted public attention on account of the fervor and eloquence with which they were stated. Mr. Justice McReynolds argued that promises to pay in gold coin had been lawful when made, that the withdrawal of gold coin from circulation left untouched the secondary obligation to pay its present value in paper money, and that the destruction by Congress of this obligation was a taking of "property" forbidden by the Fifth Amendment. He declared that the legislation aimed ostensibly at regulation of currency values, but that its real purpose was the destruction of private obligations, so that its end was not "legitimate." In support of this statement he resorted to evidence that seems wholly inadmissible for the purpose—a statement in the Senate by Senator Thomas, in sponsoring the Thomas Amendment to the Agricultural Adjustment Act. Senator Thomas had said that the purpose of the proposed amendment was to cheapen the dollar so as to raise agricultural prices and that its *effect* would be to transfer wealth within the United States to the extent of almost $200,000,000,000. Even if this statement, made in support of another bill than the one in question, could be taken into account at all, the motives that induced Congress to devalue the dollar seem in this instance to lie outside the scope of judicial review. The argument of Mr. Justice McReynolds, which seems to imply the contrary, can scarcely be accepted at its face value. After devaluation had been decided upon, it became simply a question of fact whether outstanding gold-clause obligations interfered with the exercise of a constitutional power. It is on this last question that there is room for difference of opinion.

[37]All these commodities and various others were adopted as official currencies by the legislatures of the colonial period, and at times the legal tender quality was attached. BULLOCK, THE MONETARY HISTORY OF THE UNITED STATES, Part II, c. 2 (1900); HEPBURN, A HISTORY OF CURRENCY IN THE UNITED STATES 1-4 (1924); WHITE, MONEY AND BANKING 2-6 (1914). There is nothing, however, in the legal tender cases after the Civil War to indicate that these unorthodox monetary media could themselves be made legal tender, unless it be broad language used in sustaining the legal tender quality of paper money.

[38]The dissenting opinion of Mr. Justice McReynolds in the gold-clause cases appears to include in its sweeping denunciation the whole devaluation policy of Congress. If it appeared that the *sole* purpose in changing the content of the dollar was to destroy lawfully acquired rights, it is true the action of Congress, even under an acknowledged constitutional power, would be subject to judicial nullification. The decision of the majority, then, must construed as a decision that a change

in the monetary standard lies within the currency power of Congress and that in this case other motives appeared than the one attributed to Congress by the dissenting opinion.

[39]This occurred in 1834, when the gold content of the dollar was reduced by 6 per cent to compensate for the fall in the value of silver and to restore parity between gold and silver coins. Mr. Justice McReynolds, in discussing this incident, was able to distinguish it from the devaluation of 1933-1934 on the ground that "The purpose was to restore the use of gold as currency—not to force up prices or destroy obligations. There was no apparent profit on the books of the Treasury. No injury was done to creditors; none was intended." Norman v. Baltimore and Ohio R.R., (U.S. 1935) 55 Sup. Ct. 407 at 423.

[40]The "commodity dollar" proposed by Professor Irving Fisher would not, of course, require the adoption of price indices as the legislative standard of value for the dollar. Gold would be retained as the standard, but the gold content would be periodically altered to adjust the purchasing power of the dollar to the movements of prices. See FISHER, STABILIZING THE DOLLAR, c. 4 (1920).

[41]This occurred, as is well known, through the issues of greenbacks during the Civil War. The economic and legal effects of the Northern greenback inflation will be more fully discussed in the April issue of this REVIEW.

[42]The various devices by which the value of money can be controlled through governmental agencies, particularly by the regulation of bank credit, have been the subject of a voluminous modern literature. It will be enough here to cite 2 KEYNES, A TREATISE OF MONEY (1930), and CURRIE, THE SUPPLY AND CONTROL OF MONEY IN THE UNITED STATES, Part II (1934).

[43]During the extreme inflation of the French Revolution, legislative control of prices has been thought by as modern writer to have had some effect in checking the general rise. HARRIS, THE ASSIGNATS, c. 6 (1930). During the inflation in Germany after the Great War governmental control prices likewise had some effect on certain groups of commodities, though it merely postponed the inevitable disaster. GRAHAM, EXCHANGE, PRICES, AND PRODUCTION IN HYPER-INFLATION: GERMANY, 1920-1923, pp. 78-79 (1930).

[44]See Nebbia v. New York, 291 U.S. 502, 54 Sup. Ct. 505 (1934), discussed in 32 MICH. L. REV. 832 (1934).

For a recent article in which similar views are expressed as to the limits of the power to "regulate the value" of money, see Eder, "Legal Theories of Money." 20 CORN. L.Q. 52 at 66-68 (1934).

The control of prices as an incident to the regulation of interstate commerce has, of course, been undertaken on a large scale under the NIRA. How far the Supreme Court will sustain the legislation in this respect is as yet uncertain. The current of decisions in the lower federal courts has, until very recently, been quite uniformly in favor of the power to regulate prices for this purpose. See 44 YALE L.J. 90 at 95-96 (1934).

[45]This appears from the text of the resolution itself. The "obligations" in which gold clauses are invalidated are defined in sec. 1 (b) of the resolution as "obligations payable in money of the United States." Obligations for the delivery of a specified *weight* in gold bullion (or even in gold coin?) would appear to be contracts for a commodity and not "money" obligations. It is submitted that in this respect we are now in the situation where state courts found themselves after the Civil War, during the period when gold clauses were held to be invalidated merely by implication drawn from the legal tender legislation (state cases reaching this result are cited below, note 54). It came then to be recognized that contracts for the delivery of a specified *quantity* of coin or bullion were valid. Essex Co. v. Pacific Mills, 14 Allen (96 Mass.) 389 (1867); Sears v. Dewing, 14 Allen (96 Mass.) 413 (1867); Mather v. Kinike, 51 Pa. St. 425 (1866); Christ Church Hospital v. Fuechsel, 54 Pa. St. 71 (1867). In their construction of the language of particular contracts, however, these cases can scarcely be considered good authority at the present time. See, for example, Butler v. Horwitz, 7 Wall.(74 U.S.) 258, 19 L. Ed. 149 (1868); Dewing v. Sears, 11 Wall. (78 U.S.) 379, 20 L. Ed. 189 (1870).

It follows from the text of the joint resolution that *money* obligations in which gold is used as a standard of value are invalid. This would appear true whether gold coin or gold *bullion* be used as a standard.

[46]12 Stat. 345. 532, 709.

[47]The remarks on this point by Mr. Justice Strong, speaking for the majority, were suggested by the argument that "the unit of money value must possess intrinsic value." In disposing of this contention, Justice Strong said:

"The legal tender acts do not attempt to make paper a standard of value. We do not rest their validity upon the assertion that their emission is coinage, or any regulation of the value of money; nor do we assert that Congress may make anything which has no value money. What we do assert is, that Congress has power to enact that the government's promises to pay money shall be, for the time being, equivalent in value to the representative of value determined by the coinage acts, or to multiples thereof. It is hardly correct to speak of a standard of value. The Constitution does not speak of it. It contemplates a standard for that which has gravity or extension; but value is an ideal thing. . . . It is, then, a mistake to regard the legal tender acts as either fixing a standard of value or regulating money values, or making money that which has no intrinsic value." Knox v. Lee, 12 Wall. (79 U.S.) 457 at 553 (1870).

[48]Juilliard v. Greenman, 110 U.S. 421, 4 Sup. Ct. 122 (1884).

[49]In Nortz v. United States, (U.S. 1935) 55 Sup. Ct. 428 at 430, the Chief Justice says that the Court can lay aside the question whether gold certificates constitute express contracts on which the United States has consented to be sued. The opinion declares that on this theory the plaintiff has shown no substantial damages and cannot sue in the Court of Claims. But before announcing this conclusion the Court says, " Compare Horowitz v. United States, 267 U.S. 458, 461, 45 S. Ct. 344, 69 L. Ed. 736," and proceeds to quote in the margin from United States v. State Nat. Bank, 96 U.S. 30, 24 L. Ed. 647 (1877).

The Horowitz case, decided in 1925, was an action to recover damages for breach of contract for the sale of silk to the plaintiff, made by the Ordnance Department in December 1919. Shipment of the silk to plaintiff in New York was delayed by an embargo placed on freight shipments by the United States Railroad Administration. When the silk finally arrived, the price of silk had declined greatly on the New York market. In holding that the petition was properly dismissed on demurrer, the Supreme Court quoted with approval from a decision of the Court of Claims as follows (p. 461): "The two characters which the government possesses as a contractor and as a sovereign cannot be thus fused; nor can the United States while sued in the one character be made liable in damages for their acts done in the other. . . . Though their sovereign acts performed for the general good may work injury to some private contractors, such parties gain nothing by having the United States as their defendants."

In citing United States v. State Nat. Bank, supra, the Chief Justice is concerned only with showing that the power of the Government to modify or abrogate its contracts was not there involved. Money or property which had been received by the Government "by means of a fraud to which its agent was a party" was there held to be recoverable on "implied contract." The Chief Justice quotes language from the case to the effect that in such a case the sovereignty of the United States was "in no wise involved."

[50]Quoted above, note 16.

[51]If it were conceivable that any single commodity or small group of commodities (other than gold or silver) could be adopted very widely as a standard of value for money obligations, it is possible that the currency power could be extended to include the regulation of their value, as it has been in the case of gold. It is believed, however, that a real interference with Congressional policy would have to be made out before such extension would be justified. The commodity or commodities in question would have to perform the function of a general standard of value to something like the extent that this function is performed by gold. In the not distant future this position may be resumed by silver. It seems unlikely that any others will appear.

One other possibility should be suggested. Can Congress altogether prohibit the resort to particular commodities or to price-indices as standards of value? A recent writer has argued that such a prohibition would be an unconstitutional invasion of freedom of contract. Elder, "Legal Theories of Money," 20 CORN. L. Q. 52 at 67-68 (1934). At least it seems clear that the interference of such contracts with Congressional control over the currency would have to be established before a blanket prohibition could be justified. Even though the standard of value chosen was in fact unstable, or the methods of computing the sums due were complex, it would hardly seem that the currency power could be used to prohibit them entirely.

[52]Norman v. Baltimore and Ohio R.R., (U.S. 1935) 55 Sup. Ct. 407 at 414: "The Constitution 'was designed to provide the same currency, having a uniform legal value in all the States.' It was for that reason that the power to regulate the value of money was conferred upon the federal government, while the same power, as well as the power to emit bills of credit, was withdrawn from the states . . . . The authority to impose requirements of uniformity and parity is an essential feature of this control of the currency." In another passage, at p. 418, referring to the fact that at the time of the Joint Resolution devaluation was in prospect and "a uniform currency was intended." Again, at p. 419: "the Congress has undertaken to establish a uniform currency, and parity between kinds of currency, and to make that currency, dollar for dollar, legal tender for the payment of debts."

[53]See the references in Nussbaum, "Comparative and International

Aspects of American Gold Clause Abrogation," 44 YALE L. J. 53 at 60-61 (1934).

In France, without express legislation, gold clauses were held invalid by the courts, except in transactions of an international character. The confused and unsatisfactory results of this judicial legislation are described by Nussbaum, *ibid.*; 44 YALE L.J. 53 at 61-62, and more fully by the same author in his book VERTRAGLICHER SCHUTZ GEGEN SCHWANKUNGEN DES GELDWERTES 11-25 (1928). Some French tribunals even went so far as to invalidate money obligations defined in terms of commodity prices. See decisions cited by Nussbaum, VERTRAGLICHER SCHUTZ GEGEN SCHWANKUNGEN DES GELDWERTES 14-15 (1928).

[54]Wood v. Bullens, 6 Allen (88 Mass.) 516 (1863); Howe v. Nickerson, 14, Allen (96 Mass.) 400 (1867); Tufts v. Plymouth Gold Mining Co., 14 Allen (96 Mass.) 407 (1867); Thayer v. Hedges, 23 Ind. 141 (1864); Frothingham v. Moni, 45 N.H. 545 (1864); Henderson v. McPike, 35 Mo. 255 (1864); Appel v. Woltmann, 38 Mo. 194 (1866); Whetstone v. Colley, 36 Ill. 328 (1865); Buchegger v. Schultz, 13 Mich. 420 (1865); Warnibold v. Schlichting, 16 Iowa 243 (1864); Wilson v. Trebilcock, 23 Iowa 331 (1867); Rodes v. Bronson, 34 NY 649 (1866); Schollenberger v. Brinton, 52 Pa. St. 10 at 100 (1866); Brown v. Welch, 26 Ind. 110 (1866); Galliano v. Pierre & Co., 18 La. Ann. 10, 89 Am. Dec. 643 (1866); Olanyer v. Blanchard, 18 La Ann. 616 (1866); Shaw v. Trunsler, 30 Tex. 390 (1867). In some states the refusal to give effect to gold clauses was due chiefly to the supposed inability of courts to specify the kind of currency in which the judgment would be payable. Gist v. Alexander, 15 Rich. Law (S.C.) 50 (1867); Spear v. Alexander, 42 Ala. 572 (1868). In Nevada and Idaho it was even held that the legal tender acts by implication invalidated express state legislation, authorizing judgments for coin on written contracts calling expressly for coin. Milliken v. Sloat, 1 Nev. 573 (1865); Hastings & Co. v. Burning Moscow Co., 2 Nev. 93 (1866); Betts v. Butler, 1 Idaho 185 (1868). In California, however, similar legislation was held constitutional. Carpentier v. Atherton, 25 Cal. 564 (1864).

In Brown v. Welch, 26 Ind. 116 (1866), and Jones v. Smith, 48 Barb. (N.Y. Sup. Ct.) 552 (1867), it was likewise held that contracts calling expressly for gold coin or for its "equivalent" in paper money could be discharged in the same sum in legal tender notes.

To be set against this formidable array of authorities were the decisions in Myers & Marcus v. Kauffman, 37 Ga. 600 (1868); Chesapeake Blank v. Swain, 29 Md. 485 (1868); some dubious decisions in North Carolina [Gibson v. Groner, 63 N.C. 10 (1868), and Mitchell v. Henderson, 63 N.C. 643 (1869)]; and some cases in Kentucky enforcing gold clauses in equitable actions [Hord v. Miller, 2 Duvall (63 Ky.) 103 (1865), and Hall v. Hiles, 2 Bush (65 Ky.) 532 (1866)].

[55]The Supreme Court decisions were rendered in the well-known cases of Bronson v. Rodes, 7 Wall. (74 U.S.) 229, 19 L. Ed. 149 (1869), and Butler v. HOROWITZ, 7 Wall. (74 U.S.) 258, 19 L. Ed (1869). It will be recalled that Mr. Justice Miller dissented in both these cases and that Mr. Justice Bradley joined in his dissent in the later case of Trebilcock v. Wilson, 12 Wall. (79 U.S.) 687 (1871). These decisions were in general treated as binding authorities and were followed in state courts. Independent Ins. Co. v. Thomas, 104 Mass. 192 (1870); McCalla v. Ely, 64 Pa. St. 254 (1870); Chrysler v. Renois, 43 N.Y. 209 (1870); and numerous other cases cited in 84 A.L.R. 1510-1511 (1933). Sporadic decisions still appeared holding gold clauses unenforceable. Killough v. Alford, 32 Tex. 457 (1870); Van Alstyne v. Sorley, 32 Tex. 518 (1870); Brassell v. McLemore, 50 Ala. 476 (1874). But see Smith v. Wood, 37 Tex. 616 (1872), and Holt v. Given & Co., 43 Ala. 612 (1869).

[56]It is clear that credit inflation can produce a considerable rise in commodity prices (and a corresponding decrease in the value of gold), while the country is still officially on the gold standard. The doubling of prices in the United States during and after the Great War is a sufficient illustration. It might be argued that creditors in gold-clause obligations have at least a moral claim to the increased value of gold during periods of falling commodity prices, if they are thus subjected to the risk of a depreciation in its value. But creditors have already secured a considerable increase in the purchasing power of money owed or paid to them, as a result of the drop in prices during the world depression. It was precisely for the purpose of correcting the resultant maladjustments in the economic system that the present concerted effort to raise prices was undertaken.

[57]That the gold-clause resolution would be sustained by the Supreme Court was predicted in all the published discussions of the subject. Nussbaum, "Comparative and International Aspects of American Gold Clause Abrogation," 44 YALE L.J. 53 (1954); Collier, "Gold Contracts and Legislative Power," 2 GEO. WASH. L. REV. 303 (1934); Johnson, "Constitutional Limitations and the Gold Standard," 67 U.S.L. REV. 187, 239 (1933); EDER THE LAW AS TO THE GOLD CLAUSE IN INTERNATIONAL CONTRACTS (1933); and comments in 31 MICH. L. REV. 953 (1933); 9 WIS L. REV. 295 (1934); 2 UNIV. CHI. L. REV. 138 (1934); 83 UNIV. PA L. REV. 88 (1934). A less confident prediction was made by Post and Willard, "The

Power of Congress to Nullify Gold Clauses," 46 HARV. L. REV. 1225 (1933), and Payne "The Gold Clause in Corporate Mortgages," 20 A.B.A.J. 370 (June 1934).

[58]See above, note 45.

[59]One ounce of gold would purchase 38.22 ounces of silver in 1910, 15.31 ounces in 1920, and 53.38 ounces in 1930. 1 LAUGHLIN, A NEW EXPOSITION OF MONEY, CREDIT AND PRICES 95-96 (1931); WARREN AND PEARSON, PRICES 139 at 144 (1933). See also Smith, "Silver—Its Status and Outlook," 13 HARV. BUS. REV. 44 (1934).

[60]The gold-clause resolution, sec. 1 (b), defines the "obligations" within its scope as obligations "payable in money of the United States"; and defines the "coin or currency" in which such obligations are payable or by which such obligations are measured, as "coin or currency of the United States."

[61]See above, note 37.

[62]The standard was calculated on the prices of beef, corn, wool, and leather. See FISHER, STABLE MONEY 12 (1934); Fisher, "The Tabular Standard in Massachusetts History," 27 QUAR. J. OF ECON. 417 at 437 (1913).

[63]Professor Fisher refers to a 1000-year lease executed in Boston on September 8, 1817, with a yearly rental of 10 tons of first quality iron which was in fact paid in the currency value of such iron. FISHER, THE MONEY ILLUSION 116 (1928).

The legal effect of such an agreement was considered in Faulcon v. Harriss, 2 Hen. & Munf. (12 Va.) 550 (1808), where plaintiff, an administrator, sued on a bond for the purchase price of land sold by his intestate on May 3, 1782. The bond provided that defendant would pay "1000 l. specie, or such further sum as shall be equal to the said 1000 l. in the year 1774, that is to say, to purchase as much land and negroes, as it might have done in ready money, at the aforesaid time." It was further provided that if the parties could not agree on the sum to be paid, three arbitrators should determine it. The plaintiff sued in an action of debt, alleging nonpayment of the sum due but not alleging the exact amount to which plaintiff was entitled. The case finally went off on the ground that this declaration entitled plaintiff to only £1000 recovery. Evidence introduced by plaintiff to show that £2000 would purchase only half as much land and half as many slaves between 1782 and 1786 as it would in 1774 was held inadmissible under these pleadings. One judge, however, said (at p. 554): "Smarting, *possibly*, under the effects of the then recent depreciation of paper money, and wishing, in any event, to receive the value of his land; the intestate of the appellant, stipulated for an eventual resort to a standard more stable than money, which is liable to be diminished in its value by casual and fortuitous circumstances, and even by a natural and progressive depreciation. A resort to this standard is no more unlawful and usurious, than a reference to *corn* or any other article of the first necessity."

[64]See, for example, the proposal of the Secretary of the Treasury of the Confederate States in 1864, for a "multiple standard of value, founded on the agricultural staples of cotton, corn, and wheat," to be used by the Treasury in its fiscal operations. SMITH, "History of the Confederate Treasury," 5 PUBLICATIONS OF THE SOUTHERN HISTORICAL ASSOCIATION 188 at 196 (1901).

[65]GRAHAM, EXCHANGE, PRICES, AND PRODUCTION IN HYPER-INFLATION: GERMANY, 1920-1923, p. 72 (1930); Suskind in the JURISTICHE WOCHENSCHRIFT, 1923, p. 107.

[66]Gesetz uber wertbestandige Hypotheken (June 23, 1923), REICHSGESETZBLATT, 1923, I, 407, and complementary legislation of June 29, 1923 (REICHSGESETZ-BLATT, 1923, I, 482), and Oct. 5, 1923 (REICHSGESETZBLATT, 1923, I, 933). This legislation allowed reference only to the "officially published" prices of these commodities. It was especially necessary in the field of land mortgages because of the requirement in the land registry laws that mortgages, for public registry, must be expressed in fixed sums of money.

[67]Gesetz uber die Ausgabe wertbestandiger Schuldverschreibungen auf den Inhaber (June 23, 1923). REICHSGESEIZBLATT, 1923 I, 407.

[68]Professor Nussbaum quotes an estimate of the mortgages of this type still outstanding in 1927 at a total of over 19 million hundredweight of "rye value." VERTRAGLICHER SCHUTZ GEGEN SCHWANKUNGEN DES GELDWERTES 76 (1928).

[69]This was clearly shown in the litigation involving the Roggenrentenbank, reported in DECISIONS OF THE REICHSGERICHT IN CIVIL MATTERS, vol. 109, p. 174 (Nov. 13, 1924). An action was there

brought for the value of an installment of interest, due January 1, 1924, on a bond issued by the mortgage bank, whose assets consisted of "rye mortgages" given by borrowers from the bank. The bond held by the plaintiff provided expressly that interest payments should be measured by the official price of rye six weeks before the installment was due. This provision was made necessary by the financial operations involved in collecting from the mortgagors the sums in paper marks which would eventually be paid out as interest to bondholders. Because of the possibility that the price of rye on a particular day might be influenced by artificial factors, an *average* was used for the month prior to the date fixed. Thus the installment due January 1, 1924, was calculated on the basis of average prices for rye from October 15 to November 14, 1923. In an admirable discussion of the whole economic problem the Reichsgericht came to the conclusion that the risk of currency depreciation in this interval must fall on the holder of the bond, and that it would "correspond neither with the purpose nor the organization" of the mortgage bank for it to assume this risk, since it was merely an "intermediary" between the investing creditor and the borrowing landowner.

It should be pointed out, however, that the loss through money depreciation which was thus assumed as well as the loss through fluctuations in the value of rye could not be compared with the loss which creditors in simple money obligations suffered through the accelerating decline of the mark.

[70]NUSSBAUM, VERTRAGLICHER SCHUTZ GEGEN SCHWANKUNGEN DES GELDWERTES 75-76, 79 (1928).

[71]FISHER, THE MAKING OF INDEX NUMBERS 340 (1923). Other students of monetary problems would undoubtedly disagree with the choice of any particular number of commodities for this purpose. As will be pointed out in the next article, some current price-indices are based on less than this number and some are based on considerably more. Professor Fisher's own series is based on 120 commodities.

[72]The problem of weighting will be referred to in the next article entitled "Contracting by Reference to Price Indices," infra, p. 685. The practical difficulties in collecting quotations for particular commodities are described by Mitchell, "The Making and Using of Index Numbers," BULLETIN No. 284 OF THE UNITED STATES BUREAU OF LABOR STATISTICS 7 at 25-31 (1921). As Professor Mitchell there points out (at p. 25):

We commonly speak of *the* wholesale price of articles like pig iron, cotton, or beef as if there were only one unambiguous price for any one thing on a given day, however this price may vary from one day to another. In fact there are many different prices for every great staple on every day it is dealt in, and most of these differences are of the sort that tend to maintain themselves even when markets are highly organized and competition is keen.

Among the factors suggested as producing variations in price quotations are differences in grade and quality, differences in prices for large and small quantities, differences in prices paid by manufacturer, jobber and local buyer, variations from place to place, cash discounts, premiums, and rebates. In the field of retail prices and wages all these complicating factors are, it may be assumed, enormously multiplied.

[73]FISHER, THE MONEY ILLUSION 19 (1928).

[74]The information summarized in this paragraph is derived from Mitchell, "The Making and Using of Index Numbers," BULLETIN No. 284 OF THE UNITED STATES BUREAU OF LABOR STATISTICS 7-10 (1921); and the briefer account in FISHER, THE MAKING OF INDEX NUMBERS, App. IV (1923).

[75]It is assumed that the due process clause of the Fifth Amendment operates as a limit on Congressional action, even within the sphere of admitted constitutional power. Effort has been chiefly directed in this article to suggesting the limits of Congressional power over the currency, either through the express grant of power "To coin money, [and] regulate the Value thereof" or through related powers that may be used for similar purposes. At the outer limits of Congressional action, the question as to the existence of power and the question of due process converge. Unless legislation invalidating price-index provisions had some reasonable relation to the purposes which Congress was authorized to achieve, it would appear that Congress had exceeded its power and that the due process clause would also be violated.

[76]Chief Justice Hughes in Norman v. Baltimore and Ohio R.R., (U.S. 1935) 55 Sup. Ct. 407 at 414. It was on this ground that the Washington Supreme Court held invalid an act of the state legislature which, like the gold-clause resolution of 1933, abrogated any provision in contracts which attempted to distinguish between classes of lawful money of the United States. Dennis v. Moses, 18 Wash. 537, 52 Pac. 333, 40 L.R.A. 302 (1898).

[77]Bronson v. Rodes, 7 Wall. (74 U.S.) 229, 19 L Ed. 141 (1869); Butler v. Horwitz, 7 Wall. (74 U.S.) 258, 19 L. Ed. 149 (1869).

[78]Butler v. Horwitz, 7 Wall. (74 U.S.) 258, 19 L. Ed. 149 (1869): Dewing v. Sears, 11 Wall. (78 U.S.) 379, 20 L. Ed. 189 (1871); Woodruff v. Mississippi. 162 U.S. 291, 16 Sup. Ct. 820 (1896). The last case, in particular, is instructive.

[79]Ames v. Quimby, 96 U.S. 324, 24 L. Ed. 635 (1878), where the standard of value referred to was gold.

[80]See the next article entitled "Contracting by Reference to Price Indices," *infra*, p. 685.

[81]See the suggestion to the same effect by Terpenning, "Standardizing Values Instead of Trying to Nail Down the Restless Dollar," FORUM 56-61 (1932).

SIX

Gold Clauses: Dead or Well?

[1]48 Stat. 113 (1933; 31 U.S.C. § 463.

[2]See Friedman & Schwartz, *Monetary History of the United States 1867-1960* 468 (1963).

[3]Pub. L. No. 93-110 (1973), and Pub. L. No. 93-373 (1974).

[4]See e.g., Treasury Statement on Gold Clause Resolution (Dec. 9, 1974); Administrator of National Banks, Banking Circ. (Dec. 9, 1974); FDIC Release No. 72-74 (Dec. 9, 1974); N.Y. Banking Dep't Letter, Dec. 20, 1974; Mo. Comm. of Finance, Prop. Rul. No. 32; Pa. Dep't of Banking, Release (Dec. 3, 1974).

[5]When the reason for the law abates, so does the law itself.

[6]Williams v. Standard Oil Co., 278 U.S. 235 (1929).

[7]See Ellis v. Dyer, 73-130 (1975); Socialist Labor Party v. Atorney General, 419 U.S. 1314 (1974); and Dombroski v. Pfester, 380 U.S. 479 (1965).

[8]See note 3 *supra*.

[9]294 U.S. at 361 (1935).

[10]Reynolds v. United States, U.S. at 164 (1879).

Gold Clause Prohibitions—Alive and Well

[1]See "Gold Clauses: Dead or Well?" 92 Banking L.J. 927 (1975).

[2]Olwine v. Torrens, "Banking Decisions," *infra*, this issue.

[3]Aztec Properties Inc. v. Union Planters Nat'l Bank, 44 U.S.L.W. 2209 (U.S., Nov. 11, 1975) "Banking Decisions," *infra*, this issue.

[4]307 U.S. 247 (1939).

[5]*Id.* While the Court did not do so, it might well have cited Dr. Milton Friedman's "Using Escalators to Fight Inflation,"

Fortune 94 (July 1974), a tour de force, eviscerated by the rationale of the *Aztec* decision.

[6]Guaranty Trust v. Henwood, note 4 *supra*, at 252.

Decisions

The Equitable Life Assurance Society of the United States
v.
Charles Niles Grosvenor III

[1]In the instant case the disparity of conditions would require the plaintiff to pay rent for the month of January 1975 in the amount of $13,469.63 after receiving $1500 in currency from its charges and prices.

Anne T. Henderson and Helen T. Wilkes
v.
Mann Theaters Corporation

[1]Subdivision (c) of section 3 of the 1973 Act provides as previously stated, that the provisions of this section shall take effect when the President finds and reports to Congress that "international monetary reform shall have proceeded to the point where elimination of regulations on private ownership of gold will not adversely affect the United States' international monetary position."

[2]For example, the Department of the Treasury issued a news release on December 9, 1974, in response to inquiries whether repeal of the restrictions on private ownership of gold affected "continuing validity" of the Joint Resolution of 1933. The news release stated in part:

Under the Resolution a contract clause providing for payment in gold, or in United States dollars equivalent to a certain amount of gold, is not enforceable if the subject of the contract is something other than gold, so that gold as a commodity has no relationship to the business being transacted. In such a case, gold would be used solely for the purpose of establishing the value of the obligation. This view is based on judicial decisions which held unenforceable a lease providing for payment in gold bullion as one method of rent settlement, since the intention of the parties by using gold in the contract was solely to stabilize the dollar value of the rent. *Holyoke Water Power Co. v. American Writing Paper Co.*, 300 U.S. 324 [57 S. Ct. 485, 81 L. Ed. 678] (1937); *Emery Bird Thayer* Dry *Goods Co. v. Williams*, 107 F. 2d 965 [8th Cir.] 1939) Similarly, loans of certificates of deposit repayable in gold, or in an amount of dollars measured in terms of gold, would be unenforceable.... The United States law making gold clauses unenforceable has been in effect solely during the period in which private ownership of gold by United States citizens was prohibited. Nonetheless, there is nothing inconsistent between private ownership of gold and the Gold Clause Joint Resolution. Also, the Federal Reserve Board issued guidelines as follows: "... obligations payable in gold are still unenforceable under the law making it illegal for banks to enter into deposit contracts giving customers an option of taking payment in cash or gold."(*Government Issues Warnings on Gold Dealings,* Comm. & Finan.Chr. 219:2, Dec. 16, 1974).

[3]According to respondent, appellants originally contended that payment should be in gold coin of the weight and fineness as it existed on October 8, 1929; and that appellants "shifted their position on appeal, "acknowledging the impossibility and illegality of paying in gold coin." They now contend that payment should be in gold bullion.

Ralph Feldman and Mark Loren
v.
Great Northern Railway Company

[1]Act of September 21, 1973, Pub.L. 93-110, 87 Stat. 352, Tit. I; Act of August 14, 1974, Pub.L. 93-373, 88 Stat. 445.

[2]Joint Resolution of June 5, 1933, 31 U.S.C. § 463.

[3]Burlington Northern Inc. became successor obligor of the bonds with the merger of Great Northern Railway Company into Burlington Northern on March 2, 1970. Citibank, N.A., corporate successor to the First National Bank of the City of New York and First National City Bank, is the successor trustee under the 1921 indenture.

[4]See 31 U.S.C. §§ 315b, 408a.

[5]Joint Resolution of June 5, 1933, 31 U.S.C. § 463, provides:

Joint Resolution
To assure uniform value to the coins and currencies of the United States.

Whereas the holding of or dealing in gold affect the public interest, and are therefore subject to proper regulation and restriction: and

Whereas the existing emergency has disclosed that provisions of obligations which purport to give the obligee a right to require payment in gold or a particular kind of coin or currency of the United States, or in an amount in money of the United States measured thereby, obstruct the power of the Congress to regulate the value of the money of the United States, and are inconsistent with the declared policy of the Congress to maintain at all times the equal power of every dollar, coined or issued by the United States, in the markets and in the payment of debts. Now, therefore, be it

Resolved by the Senate and House of Representatives of the United States of America in Congress assembled, That (a) every provision contained in or made with respect to any obligation which purports to give the obligee a right to require payment in gold or a particular kind of coin or currency, or in an amount in money of the United States measured thereby, is declared to be against public policy; and no such provision shall be contained in or made with respect to any obligation hereafter incurred. Every obligation, heretofore or hereafter incurred, whether or not any such provision is contained therein or made with respect thereto, shall be discharged upon payment, dollar for dollar, in any coin or currency which at the time of payment is legal tender for public and private debts. Any such provision contained in any law authorizing obligations to be issued by or under authority of the United States, is hereby repealed, but the repeal of any such provision shall not invalidate any other provision or authority contained in such law.

(b) As used in this resolution, the term 'obligation' means an obligation (including every obligation of and to the United States, excepting currency) payable in money of the United States; and the term 'coin or currency' means coin or currency of the United States including Federal Reserve notes and circulating notes of Federal reserve banks and national banking associations.

SEC. 2. The last sentence of paragraph (1) of subsection (b) of section 43 of the Act entitled 'An Act to relieve the existing national economic emergency by increasing agricultural purchasing power, to raise revenue for extraordinary expenses incurred by reason of such emergency, to provide emergency relief with respect to agricultural indebtedness, to provide for the orderly liquidation of joint-stock land banks, and for other purposes', approved May 12, 1933, is amended to read as follows:

'All coins and currencies of the United States (including Federal Reserve notes and circulating notes of Federal Reserve banks and national banking associations) heretofore or hereafter coined or issued, shall be legal tender for all debts, public and private, public charges, taxes, duties, and dues, except that gold coins, when below the standard weight and limit of tolerance provided by law for the single piece, shall be legal tender only at valuation in proportion to their actual weight.'

[6]*Norman v. Baltimore & O. R. R.*, 294 U.S. 240, 293, 55 S.Ct. 407, 79 L.Ed. 885 (1935).

[7]*Id.* at 295-97. 55 S.Ct. 407.

[8]Ch. 6, 48 Stat. 337-44 (codified in scattered sections of 31 U.S.C.).

[9]Note 1, *supra.*

[10]Act of September 21. 1973, Pub.L. 93-110, 87 Stat. 352, Tit. I, provides:

"Sec. 3. (a) Sections 3 and 4 of the Gold Reserve Act of 1934 (31 U.S.C. 442 and 443) are repealed.

(b) No provision of any law in effect on the date of enactment of this Act, and no rule, regulation or order under authority of any such law, may be construed to prohibit any person from purchasing, holding, selling, or otherwise dealing in gold.

(c) The provisions of this section, pertaining to gold, shall take effect when the President finds and reports to the Congress that international monetary reform shall have proceeded to the point where elimination of regulations on private ownership of gold will not adversely affect the United States' international monetary position."

[11]Act of August 14, 1974, Pub.L. 93-373, 88 Stat. 445, provides:

"Sec. 2. Subsections 3(b) and (c) of Public Law 93-110 (87 Stat. 352) are repealed and in lieu thereof add the following:

'(b) No provision of any law in effect on the date of enactment of this Act, and no rule, regulation, or order in effect on the date subsections (a) and (b) become effective may be construed to prohibit any person from purchasing, holding, selling, or otherwise dealing with gold in the United States or abroad.

'(c) The provisions of subsections (a) and (b) of this section shall take effect either on December 31, 1974, or at any time prior to such date that the President finds and reports to Congress that international monetary reform shall have proceeded to the point where elimination of regulations on private ownership of gold will not adversely affect the United States' International monetary position.'"

[12]*Id.*

[13] Hearings on Private Ownership of Gold Before a Subcomm. of the

Senate Comm. on Banking, Housing and Urban Affairs, 93d Cong., 1st Sess. (1973).

[14]*Id.* at 54.

[15]*Id.* at 55-56.

[16]Hearings on H.R. 17475 Before the Subcomm. on International Finance of the House Comm. on Banking and Currency, 93rd Cong., 2d Sess. 7 (1974) (emphasis added).

In addition, several federal agencies with responsibility for monetary and currency affairs, including the Comptroller of the Currency, Federal Deposit Insurance Corporation, Federal Home Loan Bank Board, and the Federal Reserve Bank, have all opined in similar fashion. See 4 CCH Fed.Banking L.Rep. ¶ 56,368 at 35,222-26 (1974).

[17]Wholly apart from the propriety of *prospectively* permitting use of gold clauses, we note that there were gold clause obligations representing an estimated $300,000,000 in principal amounts already outstanding at the time the Gold Ownership Amendments became effective. See Business Week, Jan. 12, 1976, at 68. If all of these bonds are to be payable in multiples approximating the instant case (*i. e.*, more than six and one-half times the principal amount), the obligors may be required to pay an aggregate of some $1.95 billion (depending, of course, on the market price of gold at the various maturity dates), or some *$1.65 billion more than the face amounts.*

[18]For example, the House Committee on Banking and Currency recommended passage of H.R. 6912, the bill that was to become Pub.L. 93-110, with language plainly indicating that the Treasury regulations, and not the Gold Clause Resolution, were the targets of the legislation:

> "The Committee view is that while there is nothing wrong in principle with removing the *Treasury gold regulations,* this should not be done at some arbitrary date. . . In short, the President under this amendment has authority to eliminate the *gold regulations* when he finds that action will be in the best interests of the United States." H.R. Rep. No. 203, reprinted in 2 U.S. Code Cong. & Admin. News 1973, 93d Cong., 1st Sess. pp. 2050, 2062 (emphasis added).

The other committee reports and debates reflect a similar focus. See, *e.g.*, S. Rep. No. 58, 93d Cong., 2d Sess. (1973); S. Rep. No. 78, 93d Cong., 1st Sess. (1973); H.R. Rep. No. 203, 93d Cong., 1st Sess. (1973); H.R. Rep. No. 78, 93d Cong. 1st Sess. (1973); H.R. Conf. Rep. No. 424, 93d Cong., 1st Sess. (1973); H.R. Rep. No. 1142, 93d Cong. 2d Sess. (1974); Hearings on S. 929 Before a Subcomm. of the Senate Comm. on

Banking, Housing and Urban Affairs, 93d Cong., 1st Sess. (1973); Hearings on H.R. 13120 Before the House Comm. on Banking and Currency, 92d Cong., 2d Sess. (1972); Hearings on S. 3160, S. 2709, S. 2879, S. 3162 and S. Con. Res. 43 Before the Senate Comm. on Banking, Housing and Urban Affairs, 92d Cong. 2d Sess. (1972). See also 119 Cong. Rec. 11073-80, 1694-695 (1973) (passim); 120 Cong. Rec. 22006 et seq. (passim).

Southern Capital Corporation

v.

Southern Pacific Company

[1]The Honorable G. Thomas Eisele, United States District Judge for the Eastern District of Arkansas.

[2]The Supreme Court upheld the Joint Resolution's constitutionality as to governmental obligations in *Nortz v. United States*, 294 U.S. 317, 55 S.Ct. 428, 79 L.Ed. 907 (1935), and *Perry v. United States*, 294 U.S. 330, 55 S.Ct. 432, 79 L.Ed. 912 (1935).

[3]In *Feldman v. Great Northern Ry.*, 428 F. Supp. 979, 985-86 (S.D.N.Y. 1977), the following was stated concerning the legislative history of the enactments of 1973 and 1974:

> On May 1, 1973, in the Senate hearings considering private ownership of gold, the following brief colloquy took place between Senator Johnston, Chairman of the subcommittee, and Jack F. Bennett, Deputy Under Secretary of the Treasury:
>
> "Senator JOHNSTON. * * * If we permitted the possession of gold, would it make any further difference if we permitted its use for payment of contracts, as legal tender?
>
> Mr. BENNETT. Well, there could be technical difficulties once we permitted private ownership and allowed private trading in gold, and futures trading and so sorth [sic]; there might be technical difficulties in continuing restrictions on the freedom of individuals to contract in gold as they can contract in pork bellies. I think that the question, however, ought to be looked at carefully as to whether some restrictions on indexing dollar contracts in gold should be retained."

Pursuant to Senator Johnston's suggestion, Bennett did consider the question further and wrote to Senator Johnston on May 16, 1973, saying in part:

> "Any decision to repeal the Gold Clause Resolution would have to be based on consideration of its effect on our economy from both a domestic and international viewpoint. Repeal

would also have to be reviewed in the light of its effect on the ability of Congress to regulate the value of money of the United States—the original reason for the adoption of the Resolution.

✳ ✳ ✳ ✳ ✳ ✳

Consequently based on these preliminary concerns, repeal of the Gold Clause Resolution should not be undertaken by the Congress without a thorough consideration of all the issues and consequences involved. Since neither the hearings before your Subcommittee nor the debates on other gold legislation pending in the Senate have focused on the gold clause issue, we believe that it would be inadvisable to include the Joint Resolution among the gold laws which are proposed to be repealed by Congress.

✳ ✳ ✳ ✳ ✳ ✳

As we interpret them, the bills now before Congress on private gold ownership, although broadly phrased, are limited to holding and dealing in gold and do not affect the Gold Clause Joint Resolution. It would be helpful if the report of your Subcommittee explaining the objectives of these bills made this interpretation explicit through a statement to the effect that the proposed gold legislation would in no way affect the continuing validity of the Joint Resolution of June 5, 1933."

While the committee did not respond to the suggestion that the report explicitly reaffirm the continuing validity of the Gold Clause Resolution, there was no indication anywhere else in the hearings or committee reports that Bennett's interpretation was rejected or even questioned. The matter was not explicitly addressed either way.

Over a year and a half later, on December 4, 1974, Secretary of the Treasury Simon testified before a House subcommittee considering delaying the effective date of the Gold Ownership Amendments:

"Contracts payable alternatively in gold or in an amount of money measured thereby are both against public policy and unenforceable in our courts under the provisions of the Congressional Gold Clause Joint Resolution of 1933. *This clause continues to apply after the lifting of restrictions on bullion ownership.*"

Here again, there is no indication of congressional rejection of the Secretary's interpretation, or even any discussion of it. [Footnotes omitted.]

EIGHT

Olwine v. Torrens

[1]The Act of May 28, 1858, P.L. 622, § 3. The Act was subsequently amended in 1968, 1970, 1972, and 1973, but these amendments are inapplicable here.

"Aztec Properties" Discussed

[1]TENN. CONST. art. 11, § 7; TENN. CODE ANN. § 47-14-104 (Supp. 1975).

[2]The text of the indexing clause read:

> Amount of principal due shall equal the amount of original principal multiplied by the consumer price index adjustment factor. This adjustment factor shall be computed by dividing the consumer price index at maturity by the consumer price index on date of borrowing. Said consumer price index numbers shall be for the most recent month available preceding borrowing and maturity dates. This consumer price index shall be the index not seasonably adjusted for all items as reported by the United States Department of Labor.

Aztec Properties, Inc. v. Union Planters Nat'l Bank, 530 S.W. 2d 756, 757 (Tenn.)

[3]*Id.* at 760-61.

[4]2 RESTATEMENT OF CONTRACTS § 526 (1932), *as quoted in* Aztec Properties, Inc. v. Union Planters Nat'l Bank, 530 S.W. 2d 756, 757 (Tenn. 1975) (emphasis added by court).

[5]530 S.W. 2d at 759.

[6]Providence A.M.E. Church v. Sauer, 45 Tenn. App. 287, 323 S.W. 2d 756, 760 (Tenn. 1975).

[7]*See* Shanks, *Practical Problems in the Application of Archaic Usury Statutes*, 53 VA. L. REV. 327, 346 *et seq.* (1967), *cited in* Aztec Properties, Inc. v. Union Planters Nat'l Bank, 530 S.W. 2d 756, 760 (Tenn. 1975).

[8]TENN. CODE ANN. § 48-402(g) (Supp. 1975).

[9]Tenn. CONST. art 11, § 7; McKinney v. Memphis Overton Hotel

Co., 59 Tenn. 104 (1873), *cited in* Aztec Properties, Inc. v. Union Planters Nat'l Bank, 530 S.W. 2d 756, 760 (Tenn. 1975).

[10]530 S.W. 2d at 761.

[11]H.R.J. Res. 192, ch. 48, 48 Stat. 112 (1933). *See* 31 U.S.C. § 463 (1970).

[12]31 U.S.C. § 463(a) (1970), *quoted in* Aztec Properties, Inc. v. Union Planters Nat'l Bank, 530 S.W. 2d 756, 760 (Tenn. 1975).

[13]307 U.S. 247 (1938).

[14]530 S.W. 2d at 760, *quoting from* Guaranty Trust Co. v. Henwood, 307 U.S. 247, 252-53 (1938).

[15]*See* F. RYAN, USURY AND USURY LAWS 8-20 (1924); Benfield, *Money, Mortgages and Migraine—The Usury Headache,* 19 CASE W.
RES. L. REV. 819, 831-33 (1968); Shanks, *Practical Problems in the Application of Archaic Usury Statutes,* 53 VA. L. REV. 327, 328-29 (1967); Note, *Usury—an Analysis of Usury Legislation and the Mississippi Corporate Exception Statute,* 38 MISS. L.J. 347, 351-52 (1967).

[16]Shanks, *Practical Problems in the Application of Archaic Usury Statutes,* 53 VA. L. REV. 327, 328 (1967). Shanks traces the religious history of the American usury statutes: "They were based on the assumption that there was a fair and just price for the use of money and on the belief that this price could be fixed once and for all time—essentially a theological task." *Id.* at 328.

[17]*See* note 15 *supra.*

[18]F. RYAN, USURY AND USURY LAWS (1924).

[19]*Id.* at 10.

[20]*Id.* at 8.

[21]Loiseaux, *Some Usury Problems in Commercial Lending,* 49 TEX. L. REV. 419, 443 (1971).

[22]*See* Shanks, *Practical Problems in the Application of Archaic Usury Statutes,* 53 VA. L. REV. 327, 348-49 (1967).

[23]TENN. CONST. art. 11, § 7; McKinney v. Memphis Overton Hotel Co., 59 Tenn. 104 (1873); Hazen v. Union Bank, 33 Tenn. 115 (1853).

[24]Dennis v. Sears, Roebuck & Co. 223 Tenn. 415, 446 S.W. 2d 260 (Tenn. 1969). This exception applies to the time-price differential, applicable to sales but not to consumer loans.

[25]Alabama, Georgia, Kentucky, Mississippi, Missouri and North

Carolina all offer a higher rate to corporate lenders than does Tennessee and all either prohibit the corporate usury defense or make it subject to the corporate rate. 1 CCH Consumer Credit Guide ¶ 510 (1976).

[26]*See* Shanks, *Practical Problems in the Application of Archaic Usury Statutes,* 53 Va. L. Rev. 327, 329 (1967).

[27]*See generally* Benfield, *Money, Mortgages and Migraine—The Usury Headache,* 19 Case W. Res. L. Rev 819 (1968);Loiseaux, *Some Usury Problems in Commercial Lending,* 49 Tex. L. Rev. 419 (1971); Shanks, *Practical Problems in the Application of Archaic Usury Statutes,* 53 Va. L. Rev. 327 (1967).

[28]Alternative use costs compensate the lender for the profit he could make investing his funds elsewhere. *See generally* McManus, *Variable Mortgage Note: Route to Increased Housing,* 55 A.B.A.J. 557 (1969).

[29]Shanks, *Practical Problems in the Application of Archaic Usury Statutes,* 53 Va. L. Rev. 327, 330 (1967).

[30]F. Ryan, Usury and Usury Laws, Append. D (1924).

[31]Act of Oct. 29, 1974, Pub. L. No. 93-501, 88 Stat. 1557, *as cited in* 1 U.S. Code Cong. & Ad. News 1793 (1974).

[32]3 U.S. Code Cong. & Ad. News 6259, 6261-62 (1974).

[33]*Id.* at 6261.

[34]Okla. Const. art. 14, § 2 provides for classification of loans and lenders and gives the legislature the authority to fix maximum rates of interest by specific legislation, but in the absence of specific legislation 10 percent is the maximum contract rate.

[35]1 CCH Consumer Credit Guide ¶ 510 (1976). The states, including Puerto Rico and the District of Columbia are Delaware, Georgia, Hawaii, Illinois, Iowa, Kansas, Kentucky, Louisiana, Maryland, Michigan, Minnesota, Missouri, New Jersey, New Mexico, New York, Ohio, Oklahoma, Pennsylvania, South Carolina, South Dakota, Virginia, Washington, West Virginia and Wisconsin.

[36]1 CCH Consumer Credit Guide ¶ 510 (1976). Maryland, Michigan, Missouri, North Dakota and Vermont embrace "businesses" as well as corporations within the exception.

[37]1 CCH Consumer Credit Guide ¶ 510 (1976). Alabama, Arizona, Connecticut, Florida, Idaho, Mississippi North Carolina, Oregon and Texas use this variation.

[38]Note, *Stemming Abuses of Corporate Exemptions from the Usury Laws: A Legislative and Judicial Analysis*, 59 Iowa L. Rev. 91, 93 (1973).

[39]*See* Benfield, *Money, Mortgages and Migraine—The Usury Headache*, 19 Case W. Res. L. Rev. 819 (1968).

[40]*Id.*

[41]Stricklin v. Investors Syndicate Life Ins. & Annuity Co., 391 F. Supp. 246 (W.D. Okla. 1975).

[42]There is no corporate rate ceiling in Oklahoma but the defense of usury is not available to a corporation. Okla. Stat. tit 18 § 1.26 (1971);4 CCH Consumer Credit Guide (Okla.) ¶ 4178 (1976).

[43]Moneylenders Act of 1927, 17 & Geo. 5, c. 21.

[44]*See* Note, *An Ounce of Discretion for a Pound of Flesh: A Suggested Reform for Usury Laws*, 65 Yale L.J. 105 (1955).

[45]*Id.* at 110.

[46] Meth, A Contemporary Crisis: The Problem of Usury in the United States, 44 A.B.A.J. 637, 638-40 (1958).

[47]*Id.* at 639-40.

[48]*Id.* at 640.

[49]*See* Loiseaux, *Some Usury Problems in Commercial Lending*, 49 Tex. L. Rev. 419, 443 (1971). Professor Loiseaux recommended a statute similar to Pa. Stat. Ann. tit. 41 § 3 (Supp. 1975-76): "[S]uch interest rate . . . shall include the total amortized cost of such loan, including any points, premiums, finders fees or other charges levied directly or indirectly against the person obtaining the loan . . . ."

[50]Comment, *The Variable Interest Note: An Answer to Uncertainty in a Fluctuating Money Market*, 1971 Law & Social Order 600; Comment, *The Variable Interest Rate Clause and Its Use in California Real Estate Transactions.* 19 U.C.L.A.L. Rev. 468 (1972): Comment, *Adjustable Interest Rates in Home Mortgages: A Reconsideration*, 1975 Wis. L. Rev. 742.

[51]*See* Comment, *Adjustable Interest Rates in Home Mortgages: A Reconsideration*, 1975 Wis. L. Rev. 742, 747.

[52]Uniform Commercial Code § 3-104(1)(b) requires a promise or order to pay a *sum certain* in money (emphasis added).

[53]15 U.S.C. §§ 1601-81t (1970), *as amended*, (Supp. IV, 1974), *cited*

in Comment, *The Variable Interest Note: An Answer to Uncertainty in a Fluctuating Money Market,* 1971 Law & Social Order 600, 608 (1971). The purpose of the Act is to require lender disclosure, which notice is difficult to give with a varying interest rate.

[54]*e.g.,* Comment, *The Variable Interest Note: An Answer to Uncertainty in a Fluctuating Money Market,* 1971 Law & Social Order 600.

[55]Gold Clause Resolution of 1933, H.R.J. Res. 192, ch. 49, 49 Stat. 112. *See* 31 U.S.C. § 463 (1970).

[56]H.R.J. Res. 192, 73rd Cong. 1st Sess., 77 Cong. Rec. 4889, 4890 (1933).

[57]*Id.* at 4900.

[58]Norman v. B. & O. R.R., 294 U.S. 240, 315-16 (1935).

[59]*Id.* at 312.

[60]H.R.J. Res. 192, 73rd Cong. 1st Sess. 77 Cong. Rec. 4889, 4908 (1933). $6½ billion of bonded indebtedness of the United States, payable alternately in gold, was about to become due and there were only $4 billion in the treasury to meet these debts.

[61]307 U.S. at 252 (emphasis added). "Particular kind of currency" included Federal Reserve notes and circulating notes of Federal Reserve banks and national banking associations except gold coins below the standard of weight provided by law. H.R.J. Res. 192, ch. 48, § 2, 48 Stat. 113 (1933).

[62]307 U.S. at 252.

[63]See Hirschberg, *Index Value Clauses,* 88 Banking L.J. 867, 871 (1971); McManus, *Variable Mortgage Note: Route to Increased Housing, 55 A.B.A.J. 557, 560 (1969).*

[64]*See* Dawson, *The Gold Clause Decisions,* 33 Mich. L. Rev. 647, 683-84 (1935).

[65]Dawson, *The Gold Clause Decisions,* 33 Mich. L. Rev. 647, 683 (1935); Hirschberg, *Index Value Clauses,* 88 Banking L.J. 867, 871 (1971).

[66]Hirschberg, *Index Value Clauses,* 88 Banking L.J. 867, 871 (1971).

[67]Nebolsine, *The Gold Clause in Private Contracts,* 42 Yale L.J. 1051, 1095 (1933).

[68]*See* notes 25-29 *supra* and accompanying text.

NINE

[1]See *The New York Times*, February 4, 1970, p. 48, Col. 5.

[2]Even the Supreme Court of Tennessee once recognizd the economic facts of life. In *Dennis* v. *Sears, Roebuck & Co.*, 223 Tenn. 415, 446 S.W. 2d 260 (1969), the court approved an eighteen percent charge by bank credit cards for deferred payment. Evidently, a time-price differential for a retail credit sale of merchandise was not usurious interest.

There are other examples of states recognizing that anti-usury laws are counterproductive. One is legislation exempting government borrowers (e.g., school districts) from interest ceilings. Another is the exemption for corporate borrowers. In some jurisdictions, the "contingency" exception avoids usury problems if the loan is not absolutely repayable, but only contingently so. Elsewhere, the transaction is scrutinized for "usurious intent."

The following Supreme Court gold clause cases are reprinted here by the offset process because it was thought that the interested reader would benefit by having them in their original, authoritative format.

NORMAN *v.* BALTIMORE & OHIO RAILROAD CO.*

CERTIORARI TO THE SUPREME COURT OF NEW YORK.

UNITED STATES ET AL. *v.* BANKERS TRUST CO. ET AL., TRUSTEES.

CERTIORARI TO THE CIRCUIT COURT OF APPEALS FOR THE EIGHTH CIRCUIT.

Nos. 270, 471 and 472.   Argued January 8, 9, 10, 1935.—Decided February 18, 1935.

1. A bond for the future payment of a stated number of dollars in gold coin of the United States "of or equivalent to the standard of weight and fineness existing" on the date of the bond, or for payment in gold coin of the United States "of the standard of weight and fineness prevailing" on the date of the bond, is not a contract for payment in gold coin as a commodity, or in bullion (cf. *Bronson* v. *Rodes*, 7 Wall. at p. 250), but is a contract for payment in money. Pp. 298–302.

2. Such "gold clauses" are intended to afford a definite standard or measure of value, and thus to protect against depreciation of the currency and discharge of the obligations by payment of a lesser value than that prescribed. P. 302.

3. In determining whether the Joint Resolution of June 5, 1933, exceeded the power of Congress by undertaking to nullify such "gold clause" stipulations in preëxisting money contract obligations, and by providing that such obligations shall be discharged, dollar for dollar, in any coin or currency which at the time of payment is legal tender for public and private debts, the Resolution must be considered in its legislative setting, with other measures *in pari materia* (p. 297), and in the light of the following principles, which have heretofore been laid down by this Court, viz:

    (a) The broad and comprehensive national authority over the subjects of revenue, finance and currency is derived from the ag-

---

* No. 270, *Norman* v. *Baltimore & Ohio R. Co.;* Nos. 471 and 472, *United States* v. *Bankers Trust Co.;* No. 531, *Nortz* v. *United States, post,* p. 317; and No. 532, *Perry* v. *United States, post,* p. 330, popularly called the "Gold Clause Cases," were disposed of in three opinions (*post,* pp. 291, 323, and 346). Mr. Justice Stone filed a concurring opinion in the *Perry* case, *post,* p. 358. The dissenting opinion, *post,* p. 361, applies to all of the cases.

gregate of the powers granted to the Congress, embracing the powers to lay and collect taxes, to borrow money, to regulate commerce with foreign nations and among the several States, to coin money, regulate the value thereof, and of foreign coin, and fix the standards of weights and measures, and the added express power " to make all laws which shall be necessary and proper for carrying into execution " the other enumerated powers. P. 303.

(b) The Constitution means to provide the same currency of uniform value in all the States; and therefore the power to regulate the value of money was withdrawn from the States and vested in Congress, exclusively. P. 302.

(c) Congress has power to enact that paper currency shall be equal in value to the representative of value determined by the coinage acts, and impress upon it such qualities as currency for purchases and for payment of debts as accord with the usage of sovereign governments. P. 304.

(d) The authority to impose requirements of uniformity and parity is an essential feature of the control of the currency; and Congress is authorized to provide a sound and uniform currency for the country and secure the benefit of it to the people by appropriate legislation. P. 304.

(e) The ownership of gold and silver coin is subject to those limitations which public policy may require by reason of their quality as legal tender and as a medium of exchange. Hence, the power to coin money includes the power to forbid mutilation, melting and exportation of gold and silver coin. P. 304.

(f) Private contracts must be understood as having been made subject to the possible exercise of the rightful authority of the Government; and their impairment, resulting from such exercise, is not a taking of private property for public use without compensation, or a deprivation of it without due process of law. Pp. 304–305.

4. In the exercise of the constitutional authority of Congress to regulate the currency and establish the monetary system of the country, existing contracts of private parties, States or municipalities, previously made, and valid when made, but which interfere with the policy constitutionally adopted by Congress, may be set aside, not only through the indirect effect of the legislation, but directly, by express provision. Pp. 306–309.

5. Whether the gold clauses of the contracts here in question may be deemed to interfere with the monetary policy of Congress, depends upon an appraisement of economic conditions and upon determi-

nations of questions of fact, as to which Congress is entitled to use its own judgment. P. 311.

6. The Court may inquire whether the action of Congress, invalidating such clauses, was arbitrary or capricious; but if that action has reasonable relation, as an appropriate means, to a legitimate end, the decision of Congress as to the degree of necessity for its adoption is final. P. 311.

7. Congress was entitled to consider the great volume of obligations with gold clauses, because of its obvious bearing upon the question whether their existence constituted a substantial obstruction to the congressional policy. P. 313.

8. Taken literally, as calling for actual payment in gold coin, these promises were calculated to increase the demand for gold, to encourage hoarding, and to stimulate attempts at exportation of gold coin, in direct opposition to the policy of Congress. P. 313.

9. Congress has power, in its control of the monetary system, to endeavor to conserve the gold resources of the Treasury, to insure its command of gold in order to protect and increase its reserves, and to prohibit the exportation of gold coin or its use for any purpose inconsistent with the needs of the Treasury. P. 313.

10. Treated as " gold value " clauses, such stipulations are still hostile to the policy of Congress, and subject to prohibition, for the following reasons:

(a) Although, at the date of the Joint Resolution, the dollar had not yet been devalued, devaluation (reduction of the weight of the gold dollar as the standard of value, which occurred later) was then in prospect and a uniform currency was intended. P. 314.

(b) Congress could constitutionally act upon the gold clauses in anticipation of this devaluation, if the clauses interfered with its policy. P. 315.

(c) It may be judicially noticed that the bonds issued by States, municipalities, railroads, other public utilities and many industrial corporations contain such gold clauses. P. 315.

(d) If States, municipalities, railroads, public utilities, industrial corporations, etc., receiving all their income in the devalued currency were obliged to pay their gold clause obligations in amounts of currency determined on the basis of the former gold standard, it is easy to see that this disparity of conditions would cause a dislocation of the domestic economy. P. 315.

265 N. Y. 37; 191 N. E. 726, affirmed.

Dist. Ct. U. S. (unreported), affirmed.

WRITS OF CERTIORARI were granted (293 U. S. 546, 548) to review two decisions sustaining the power of Congress to invalidate " gold clauses " in private money contracts.

In the first case, an action on a coupon from a railroad bond, the Court of Appeals of New York sustained the trial court in limiting the recovery to the face of the coupon, dollar for dollar, in currency.

In the second case, a proceeding under § 77 of the Bankruptcy Act, a federal District Court made a like ruling with respect to certain other railroad bonds. In this case two appeals were taken to the Circuit Court of Appeals, one allowed by that court and the other by the District Judge. While they were pending, this Court granted writs of certiorari on the petition of the United States and the Reconstruction Finance Corporation, which had both intervened in the District Court.

Mr. Emanuel Redfield for Norman, petitioner. *Mr. Dalton Dwyer* was with him on the brief, from which the following summary is extracted:

The gold clause implies payment in equivalent of gold if payment in gold becomes impossible. Its purpose is to guard against a depreciated currency.

Congress has power to coin money and regulate the value thereof. To coin money is to give the impression a governmental authority. " To regulate the value thereof " would mean to state the character of that coin in terms of its exchange value and to give it a content of a nominal amount. To regulate the value of money does not imply that every obligation payable in money is susceptible of regulation by Congress. In *Fox* v. *Ohio,* 5 How. 410, the Court indicated this difference and denied that the money powers of Congress included the right to control private transactions within the States.

There is no power in Congress directly to enlarge or diminish an obligation. Such powers belong to the States, if they exist at all. Congress desiring to tamper with the content of the gold unit, finds the outstanding gold-clause obligations inconvenient, because they are so many. Therefore, to suit its convenience, they are abolished. If only one million dollars of such obligations had existed, the inconvenience would not have been deemed substantial, and they would have been allowed to exist.

These gold obligations were no part of the monetary system. They were economic transactions in a price system. The money unit and medium were mere incidents of the transaction.

The proposition that contracts payable in gold or its equivalent would control the value of the currency, i. e., prevent a raising or lowering of the content, is refuted by the fact that the object of the parties is to fix a more accurate measure of the value of their exchange.

The use of any standard as the measure of the intent of the parties does not, by " prophetic discernment," hinder the monetary functions of the Government. Surely, if the value of wheat were used as the standard, the power to regulate money would not be affected. If parties receive an equivalent of any measure in paper money or credits, whether that measure be gold or wheat, the currency is not affected. The bargain is merely performed according to their intent.

The *Legal Tender Cases* are distinguishable. This Court there held that the paper had the characteristics of money and that acceptance of it could be compelled as payment of an obligation. The compulsion was directed at the mode of payment, not the extent of the obligation.

The obligation of the gold clause is not the nominal face amount, but the equivalent of the gold coin in legal tender. Thus understood, the integrity of the obligation and the power of legal tender to discharge it in dollars, are preserved. See *Trebilcock* v. *Wilson,* 12 Wall. 687; *Gregory* v. *Morris,* 96 U. S. 619. The *Legal Tender Cases* did not decide that the power to compel acceptance of paper currency in discharge of an obligation implied a power to

NORMAN *v.* B. & O. R. CO. 245

diminish an obligation that was measured in a special way. This Court repeatedly implied the contrary.

This Court has before passed upon legislation masquerading as an aid to an express constitutional power. *Mugler* v. *Kansas,* 123 U. S. 623, 661; *McCullough* v. *Maryland,* 4 Wheat. 316, 423; *Hammer* v. *Dagenhart,* 245 U. S. 251; *Kidd* v. *Pearson,* 128 U. S. 1; *United States* v. *Chicago, M., St. P. & P. R. Co.,* 282 U. S. 311; *First Employers' Liability Cases,* 207 U. S. 463; *United States* v. *DeWitt,* 9 Wall. 41; *Paul* v. *Virginia,* 8 Wall. 168; *Ducat* v. *Chicago,* 10 Wall. 410; *Hill* v. *Wallace,* 259 U. S. 44; *Blumenstock Bros.* v. *Curtis,* 252 U. S. 436; *Trade Mark Cases,* 100 U. S. 82; *United States* v. *Fox,* 95 U. S. 670; Kent's Commentaries, 12th ed., vol. 1, p. 254, Mr. Justice Holmes; Field, J. dissent, *Legal Tender Cases,* 12 Wall. 651; *Bailey* v. *Drexel Furniture Co.,* 259 U. S. 20; *McCray* v. *United States,* 195 U. S. 27, 63, 64; McReynolds, J., dissent, *Rupert* v. *Caffey,* 251 U. S. 264, 304; *Lambert* v. *Yellowley,* 272 U. S. 581, 597.

The use of gold as a measure of value is not an evil. Any object could be used as such a measure. Yet no one can insist that a contract calling for a payment measured by the value of any commodity is subject to action by Congress. This, we submit, is of greater moment when one considers that under the " Gold Reserve Act of 1934," the coining of gold has been withdrawn and gold as a circulating medium of exchange has been abolished. Now, it is only a base for values. It is now the same as the standard weights and measures kept in seclusion in Washington. Could any one assert that Congress could pass a law under its power to regulate weights and measures, stating that a contract for the delivery of a bushel of wheat could be discharged by the delivery of only half a bushel?

Bankruptcy laws are express laws that impair the obligations of contracts. That power is specific for that purpose, and includes the power to regulate the relation of debtor and creditor by the process of composition. If this specific power exists for those purposes, it can hardly be said that the power over money includes an implied power to compose and regulate the obligations between creditor and debtor.

Assuming an emergency exists, an emergency cannot grant a power. *Home Bldg. & Loan Assn.* v. *Blaisdell,* 290 U. S. 398.

If this legislation purports to be based upon an emergency, it is defective because there is no time limit set in the law as the duration of the emergency. *Chastleton Corp.* v. *Sinclair,* 264 U. S. 543; *Worthen* v. *Thomas,* 292 U. S. 426.

Should it be argued that the power is derived from the power of Congress to borrow money, petitioner submits in reply the very arguments set forth above regarding the alleged money power. Furthermore, repudiation can not be an aid to borrowing credit. *Lynch* v. *United States,* 292 U. S. 571, 580.

Should it be held that the gold clause legislation is sustained by the money powers of Congress, a new field of unlimited centralized control will be opened. The same power might apply to any form of financial transactions,—to wages of child labor, suspension of mortgage payments, etc. This would wipe out the dual form of our indestructible union consisting of indestructible States. *Texas* v. *White,* 7 Wall. 700.

The Joint Resolution deprives petitioner of his property without due process of law and without just compensation. The Fifth Amendment is a limitation upon the powers of Congress. *McCray* v. *United States,* 195 U. S. 27; *Flint* v. *Stone Tracy Co.,* 220 U. S. 107, 154; *Adair* v. *United States,* 208 U. S. 161, 172; *Monongahela Navigation Co.* v. *United States,* 148 U. S. 312, 336; *Adkins* v.

Children's Hospital, 261 U. S. 525, 545, 546, 561; *Fairbanks* v. *United States,* 181 U. S. 283, 289; Day, J., dissent, *Wilson* v. *New,* 243 U. S. 332, 366; *United States* v. *Chicago, M., St. P. & P. R. Co.,* 282 U. S. 311, 327; *Milliken* v. *United States,* 283 U. S. 15; *Heiner* v. *Donnan,* 285 U. S. 312, 326; *Nichols* v. *Coolidge,* 274 U. S. 531; *Untermyer* v. *Anderson,* 276 U. S. 440; *Sturges* v. *Crowninshield,* 4 Wheat. 122.

The Federal Government is one of enumerated delegated powers. If no power to impair contracts is granted, it is difficult to see how the power can be derived. The only power specifically mentioned in the Constitution to impair contracts, is the provision for bankruptcy laws. This fact alone indicates that if the power to impair contracts were intended for the Federal Government, specific mention would have been made of it. The prohibition against state action, however, was specifically made because the omission in the Constitution to prohibit the States might have been deemed a permission for such legislation under the sovereign powers of the States which are inherent. See *Calder* v. *Bull,* 3 Dall. 386, 388; The Federalist, No. 44; Cooley, Story on the Constitution, 4th ed., vol. 2, § 1399, p. 261.

The due process clause covers Acts of Congress impairing the obligation of contracts. *Sinking Fund Cases,* 99 U. S. 700, 718. See also *United States* v. *Northern Pacific Co.,* 256 U. S. 51, 64; *Choate* v. *Trapp,* 224 U. S. 665, 674.

Impairment of contracts, incident to the exercise of a power of Congress, may be unobjectionable, if the exercise be found reasonable. *Marcus Brown Co.* v. *Feldman,* 256 U. S. 170; *Home Bldg. & Loan Assn.* v. *Blaisdell,* 290 U. S. 398; *New York* v. *United States,* 257 U. S. 591, 601. Aliter, if unreasonable: *Blodgett* v. *Holden,* 275 U. S. 142, 147. Distinguishing: *Louisville & N. R. Co.* v. *Mottley,*

219 U. S. 467; *Philadelphia, B. & W. R. Co.* v. *Schubert,* 224 U. S. 603. Cf. *New York Central R. Co.* v. *Gray,* 239 U. S. 583.

If Congress exercised the power to cancel the obligation of gold clauses, because it deemed it necessary for a better regulation of the monetary system, the property of petitioner was taken for a public use, and adequate and just provision should have been made to compensate him for his loss in being required to take, dollar for dollar, in depreciated currency. *Monongahela Navigation Co.* v. *United States,* 148 U. S. 312; *Ochoa* v. *Hernandez,* 230 U. S. 139.

Merely to state that a thing obstructs the exercise of a power does not take it out of the class of cases where compensation must be paid. Here actually is no obstruction. There was merely a condition of inconvenience that rendered dollar devaluation inopportune. Therefore, the nullification of the obligation was not a regulation but an out and out taking for an alleged public need. See *Osborn* v. *Nicholson,* 13 Wall. 654.

Petitioner was deprived of the equal protection of the laws. The purpose and effect were to transfer property from the class called creditors to those termed debtors.

Mr. Frederick H. Wood for the Baltimore & Ohio R. Co. From the brief:

The gold clause is a " gold coin," not a " gold value " clause, but is equally within the Resolution whether interpreted as the one or the other.

An instrument so framed or interpreted is not one for the payment of a sum certain, but one for the payment of an indeterminate sum ascertainable only at date of payment, and is not negotiable. Negotiable Instruments Law of New York, Art. 3, § 20 (2); Laws of Maryland, 1898, c. 119, § 20 (2); Uniform Negotiable Instruments Law,

Art. I, § 1 (2). It is dischargeable only in the coin specified and not in that amount of other money which at the time of payment will buy such coin. *Bronson* v. *Rodes,* 7 Wall. 229; *Trebilcock* v. *Wilson,* 12 Wall. 687; *The Emily Souder,* 17 Wall. 666; *Butler* v. *Horwitz,* 7 Wall. 258; *Dewing* v. *Sears,* 11 Wall. 379. Distinguishing: *Gregory* v. *Morris,* 96 U. S. 619; *Feist* v. *Société Intercommunale Belge d'Electricité,* L. R. (1934) A. C. 161; *The Brazilian Loans,* P. C. I. J., Series A, No. 20.

The Congress has an authority with respect to the national monetary system and the currency not confined by the limitations of any one specific grant in the Constitution. The exertion of this authority may be supported by the "resulting" or "composite" powers arising through the combination or aggregation of any or all of the specific grants of power. *The Legal Tender Cases,* 12 Wall. 457; *Juilliard* v. *Greenman,* 110 U. S. 421; *McCulloch* v. *Maryland,* 4 Wheat. 316, 407–12. See *Fong Yue Ting* v. *United States,* 149 U. S. 698, 711–712; *The Insular Cases,* 182 U. S. 244, 288, 300; 195 U. S. 138, 140, 143, 149; 258 U. S. 298, 305; *United States* v. *Gettysburg Electric Ry.,* 160 U. S. 668; *Mackenzie* v. *Hare,* 239 U. S. 299, 311; *Selective Draft Cases,* 245 U. S. 366, 377; *McGrain* v. *Daugherty,* 273 U. S. 135, 161.

The sovereign character of the National Government must be given weight in determining the scope of the powers granted to it over the monetary system and the currency. In construing the great clauses of the Constitution the Court has frequently been guided by the fact that the primary purpose was to create a sovereign nation as distinguished from a mere federation of States.

Congress is empowered to provide the people with a national monetary system and a national currency suitable to their needs, and to secure to them the full and unimpaired benefits thereof through the adoption of any measures appropriate either to the accomplishment of such purpose or for the removal of obstructions thereto.

Congress is empowered to declare of what the currency shall consist, to give to every unit and description thereof the character and qualities of money having a legally defined value, to regulate the value of such money and to make every unit legal tender at its face value for the discharge of all money obligations, whether previously existing or subsequently incurred.

An unqualified grant of power " to regulate the value " of money necessarily comprehends the regulation of its value when used for the performance of any of its functions as money, and hence includes the power to control the use of money as a standard of value. The word " regulate " means " to control " or " to govern." *Second Employers' Liability Cases*, 223 U. S. 1, 47, 48. The word "value" connotes equivalency according to a standard.

The express power to regulate the value of foreign coin is obviously a power to regulate its use in this country as a standard of value.

The power includes the power to determine and regulate the value of the several units of the currency in terms of each other and to prohibit the attempted use of one kind of money as a commodity for the purpose of realizing in another kind of money a value greater than the stated value of the first. Cf. *Ling Su Fan* v. *United States,* 218 U. S. 302.

The comprehensiveness of this power is evidenced by the previous decisions of this Court arising under the power of Congress over the monetary system and currency; also by the decisions of this Court in respect of the related power to create national banks; also by the decisions arising under the commerce clause, one of the clauses upon which the power of Congress over the monetary system and currency is based.

Private individuals may not " by prophetic discernment," through contracts previously entered into, any more than by contracts subsequently made, withdraw from the control of Congress any part of its legislative field or limit or obstruct the exercise of its powers therein.

Gold clause obligations, at all times a latent threat to the stability of the monetary system and currency, had, at the time of the adoption of the Resolution, become a plain obstacle to the maintenance of a stable monetary system and currency, which it was within the power of the Congress to remove both to meet the then existing emergency and to prevent its recurrence.

Gold clause obligations constituted an obstruction to the adjustment of the value of the dollar in the interest of our foreign commerce.

In the last analysis, those who challenge the validity of the Resolution would deny to Congress the choice of means by which to effect such change in the monetary system as was believed by it to be required by the needs of the people and their commerce, both foreign and domestic.

As related to the subsequent devaluation of the dollar, the Resolution was a valid exercise of all of the powers of the Congress over the monetary system and the currency.

Attorney General Cummings, orally, on behalf of the United States in these and the two following cases: * . . .

Underlying these four cases are certain fundamental constitutional considerations which I think are determinative of the entire matter. . . .

Although it may seem trite to do so, I draw attention to what, for want of a better term, may be called the " presumption of constitutionality."

This doctrine has been laid down in innumerable cases, some of which are cited in our briefs, but nowhere, I think,

---

* Mr. Cummings' address, stenographically reported, has been printed in full by the Government Printing Office. Omissions from the present report are marked by dots. He also closed the argument in all of the cases.

is it more effectively stated than in the *Legal Tender
Cases,* in which this Court said:

"A decent respect for a coördinate branch of the Government demands that the judiciary should presume, until
the contrary is clearly shown, that there has been no transgression of power by Congress, all the members of which
act under the obligation of an oath of fidelity to the Constitution. Such has always been the rule."

But this doctrine, I apprehend, goes still further, and
carries with it the proposition that this Court will accord
great weight to the findings and reasons set forth by the
Congress for enacting the legislation which it has passed.

The next cardinal principle is that, in selecting the
means to carry out the purpose of the Congress, the Congress has wide discretion. Unless it is shown that the
exercise of that discretion has been clearly arbitrary or
capricious or unreasonable, this Court will not interfere
with it.

I have adverted to these considerations not because they
are not recognized, but because they are so well recognized
that they are taken as a matter of course. We are in-
clined, I fear, to pay them a sort of lip service and then
pass on to the consideration of matters of a more controversial character. Therefore, we are apt to find ourselves in the position of ignoring certain fundamental
matters which are so obvious that they are, at times, forgotten or overlooked. These doctrines to which I have
referred are not only necessary and vital doctrines, essential to our form of Government, but they surcharge the
whole atmosphere of constitutional discussion. . . . In
these pending cases we have before us not only the resolu-
tions of the Congress and its declarations and findings,
but we have also the instructions, the declarations, and
the findings of the President of the United States, as well
as his public statements, his message to the Economic
Conference of July 3, 1933, and, in addition to that, we

have the findings, declarations, and instructions of the Secretary of the Treasury.

The matters to which I have referred, it seems to me, under the peculiar circumstances which are presented here, carry an authority and a persuasiveness which our friends upon the other side have nowhere successfully met. I think their briefs may be searched in vain for any well-considered and sustained argument showing that the course pursued was unreasonable or arbitrary, or that adequately meets the allegations, findings, and declarations to which I have just referred.

Therefore, I think that it is fair to assert that these considerations assume, in the pending cases, an unusual and an almost unprecedented importance.

Now, of course, if the Court please, the conditions which existed on the sixth day of March, 1933, are so fresh in our memories and have been so completely covered in the elaborate briefs which have been presented, that it seems quite unnecessary to refer to them again or at length.

The fact remains, however, and it is enough to say, that an emergency of the highest importance confronted the Nation. Banks. sound and unsound, were failing or closing upon every hand; gold coin, gold certificates, and, indeed, all other forms of currency, were being hoarded by millions of dollars, and, perhaps, by millions of people. Gold was taking flight either into foreign currencies or into foreign lands; and foreign trade had been brought to a standstill. International finance was completely disorganized. The whole situation was one of extreme peril. Price levels were falling. Industries were closing. Millions of people were out of work. Failures and bankruptcies were reaching enormous and, indeed, unparalleled proportions; and, with constant acceleration, our people, confessedly, were slipping toward a lower level of civilization. I undertake to say that no man of imagination could have witnessed that distressing spectacle of painful retrogression without acute apprehension and profound sorrow.

Now, in addition to that, we had the experiences of other nations; we had their example. There was not a nation on the face of the earth that was not in distress.

At that time—and the time I refer to was the 6th day of March 1933—the Swiss franc, the Dutch guilder, and the United States dollar were the only coins that had not been devalued or depreciated. Country after country was going off the gold standard, and thirty countries had passed drastic legislation with regard to finance, foreign commerce, and the regulation of money. Embargoes, trade restrictions, and quotas were characteristic of the day and of the time.

So, as I say, we were confronted by an industrial and monetary and financial crisis of the most terrifying character. Amongst the various measures which were adopted to meet the situation were those which are in the group within which falls the Joint Resolution of the 5th of June 1933, which is so seriously under attack here today.

At the risk of being a little bit wearisome, permit me briefly to refer to these measures. [Here the Attorney General explained the various Acts of Congress enacted and Executive Orders and Orders of the Secretary of the Treasury promulgated between March 6, 1933, and January 31, 1934.] . . .

Thus, it is apparent that the Congress acted in this matter four times during the period to which I have referred—on March 9, 1933, the Emergency Banking Act; May 12, the Agricultural Adjustment Act; June 5, the Joint Resolution; and January 30, 1934, the Gold Reserve Act.

During this period the President of the United States acted upon five important occasions (and upon sundry other occasions of not such major significance); on March

6, the bank holiday; on March 9, the extension of the bank holiday; on April 5, the gold hoarding order; on August 28, additional gold hoarding orders; and on the 31st of January, the devaluation of the dollar.

Thus, in a hectic period of eleven months, a sweeping change was effected in the financial and monetary structure of our country. Our system was completely reorganized. Gold and gold bullion were swept into the Treasury of the United States; gold certificates were placed where they were readily within the control of the Government of the United States; foreign exchange was regulated; banks were being reopened; gold hoarding was brought under control; parity was maintained; and a complete transition was effected from the old gold-coin standard to the gold-bullion standard, with the weight of the dollar fixed at an endurable amount.

Now, I undertake to suggest that no one can consider this series of acts without sensing their continuity and realizing their consistent purpose.

Moreover, these measures must be read as a whole, and read against the background of utter national need. I think they tell the story of a nation finding its way out of financial chaos into a safer and sounder position.

Moreover, it must be remembered that in these matters two great branches of our Government, the legislative and the executive, were acting in perfect harmony and for a common end. It was a sweeping change, adopted by an overwhelming majority of the Congress, and promptly approved by the President of the United States; and appealing to both as essential to the happiness and prosperity and welfare of our country.

I contend, and later shall undertake to show, that to admit the validity of the claims of those who are appearing here in behalf of the holders of gold certificates, and in behalf of the gold-bond obligations, would mean the

break-down and the wreckage of the structure thus carefully erected.

Moreover, it would create a preferred class who, because
of a contract of a special character, are able to take themselves outside, as it were, of the financial structure of their
own country.

To admit such claims to the extent of $100,000,000,000,
an unthinkable sum, would be to write up the public debts
and the private debts of our country by $69,000,000,000
and, overnight, reduce the balance of the Treasury of the
United States by more than $2,500,000,000.   It would add
$10,000,000,000 to the public debt.   The increased interest
charges alone would amount to over $2,500,000,000 per
annum, and that sum is twice the value of the combined
wheat and the cotton crops of this country in the year
1930.   The stupendous catastrophe envisaged by this conservative statement is such as to stagger the imagination
It would not be a case of " back to the Constitution."   It
would be a case of " back to chaos." . . .

The primary difficulty, as I see it, with the argument
in behalf of the gold obligations, and one which vitiates
it entirely, is that the question is approached without
reference to this background, and is based merely upon
the supposed sanctity and inviolability of contractual obligations.   That our Government is endowed with the
power of self-preservation I make no doubt, and that a
written understanding must yield to the public welfare
has been so often reiterated that it is not necessary to
dwell upon it any further.

There were some priceless words used by Mr. Justice
Butler in *Highland* v. *Russell Car & Snow Plow Co.*, 279
U. S. 253, 261, when he said:

" It is also well established by the decisions of this
Court that such liberty [meaning liberty of contract] is
not absolute or universal, and that Congress may regu-

late the making and performance of such contracts whenever reasonably necessary to effect any of the great purposes for which the national Government was created."

But that is not exactly the case here. Those who insist upon the strict letter of the bond are insisting upon it in a matter dealing with gold, and gold lies at the basis of our financial structure. Gold is the subject of national legislation. Gold is the subject of international concern. Gold is not an ordinary commodity. It is a thing apart, and upon it rests, under our form of civilization, the whole structure of our finance and the welfare of our people. Gold is affected with a public interest. These gold contracts, therefore, deal with the very essence of sovereignty, for they require that the Government must surrender a portion of that sovereignty. To put it another way, these gold contracts have invaded the federal field. It is not a case of federal activity reaching out into a private area. So obsessed are our opponents by the idea of the sanctity of contracts that they are even prepared to assert their validity when they preëmpt the federal field. To me this seems a monstrous doctrine. These claimants are upon federal territory. They are squatters in the public domain, and when the Government needs the territory they must move on.

And so say the authorities. In dealing with currency and its metallic basis, the Government is exercising a prerogative of sovereignty and is dealing with a subject matter affected with a public interest. . . .

The contention that the Joint Resolution constitutes a taking of property without just compensation is clearly without foundation. The provision of the Fifth Amendment which bears upon that proposition relates to the taking of private property by the Government for a public use; and the Resolution, as applied to gold clauses in private contracts, is not a taking of property in a constitu-

tional sense, but merely frustrates a purpose contained in
a private obligation found to be incompatible with the
exercise of national power.

Frustration, it is said in one of the leading decisons,
if I recall correctly—" frustration and appropriation are
essentially different things."

Now, this doctrine is supported by so many authorities
that it is a work of supererogation to refer to them—The
Legal Tender Cases, Louisville & Nashville R. Co. v.
Mottley [219 U. S. 467], and hosts of others, which appear in our various briefs.

This leaves for consideration only the question whether
that portion of the Fifth Amendment is affected or is involved in this controversy which deals with the deprivation
of property without due process of law.

I think it is clear, and I think I shall make it even more
apparent as I proceed, that the Joint Resolution was enacted pursuant to the exercise of functions derived from
the Constitution.   Now, it has been held that under certain circumstances the United States may—I am now using
the language of the books—consistently with the Fifth
Amendment, impose restrictions upon private property
for all permitted purposes which result in a depreciation
of its value.   That language, I think, is found in *Calhoun*
v. *Massie*, 253 U. S. 170.

Again, it is said that this may be done for a legitimate
governmental purpose, *Sinking Fund Cases* (99 U. S. 700),
since preëxisting contracts do not limit the sovereign right
of the Government.   *Calhoun* v. *Massie; Louisville &
Nashville R.* v. *Mottley; Union Dry Goods Co.* v. *Georgia
Public Service Corp.*, 248 U. S. 372.

This principle has been expressed in varying language.
I think that it is absolutely accurate to say that the sound
conclusion is that private contracts may not fetter governmental action within the powers entrusted to it by the
Constitution.   That is the doctrine of the *Schubert* case,

224 U. S. 603, *Sproles* v. *Binford,* 286 U. S. 374, *Veazie Bank* v. *Fenno,* and many others. It is in the first two of these cases that there appears that happy and suggestive phrase, "prophetic discernment."

The guarantee of due process in the Fifth Amendment demands no more than that the means selected by the Congress, as this Court has said, be for the attainment of ends within its power, and have a real and substantial relation to the attainment of such ends. And so, as seems inevitable in so many constitutional arguments, we go back to the case of *McCulloch* v. *Maryland.* And later we come to the *Ling Su Fan* case; and, if we want a more recent authority, we turn our hopeful eyes toward the decision in the *Nebbia* case, 291 U. S. 502.

The Joint Resolution was a bona fide exercise of constitutional power. It was not a mere arbitrary interference with private rights or with contract rights under the cloak of the currency power.

Now, that being true, any supposed collateral purposes or motives of the Congress, to which reference was made in argument here, and repeatedly in the briefs, are, to use the language of the Court, " matters beyond the scope of judicial inquiry." I think the quotation is from the *Magnano* case. See also the statements made in the *McCray* case, 195 U. S. 27, and also in the *Kentucky Distilleries* case, in an opinion written, I believe, by Mr. Justice Brandeis.

In view of the foregoing, it is not necessary to discuss the irrelevant and unsubstantial allegation that the purpose of the legislation was to transfer wealth from one class of our citizens to another. . . .

Now, of course, the primary power upon which the Joint Resolution rests is that portion of article I, § 8, of the Constitution, which grants to the Congress the power " to coin money, regulate the value thereof and of foreign coin, and fix the standard of weights and measures."

The power also rests upon the constitutional authority " to regulate commerce with foreign nations and among the several States," and " to borrow money on the credit of the United States," and upon that " composite power " which has been referred to in that language, or in similar language, in many of our cases. . . .

I have never been impressed, and I am not now impressed, by the significance of *Bronson* v. *Rodes*, 7 Wall. 229, in connection with this controversy. And yet, by some peculiar form of common consent, it seems to stand at the threshold of the monetary discussion. It did not pass upon any constitutional question whatsoever. It explicitly, in its own language, set forth that it did not pass upon any constitutional question. It recognized the existence of the dual monetary system. It recognized the fact that greenbacks were not payable for all forms of public obligations. It recognized that these two forms of currency were circulating simultaneously and fluctuating violently, as measured in terms of each other. And, therefore, the Court found that the debts referred to in the Legal Tender act did not apply to the kinds of debts specified in the case of *Bronson* v. *Rodes*.

Then came, of course, one year later, in 1869, I believe, the well-known case of *Hepburn* v. *Griswold*, 8 Wall. 603. I think *Hepburn* v. *Griswold* is far more interesting than *Bronson* v. *Rodes,* because *Hepburn* v. *Griswold* did deal with questions that are pertinent here, and dealt with them in such a fashion that the Court later set aside that decision in the *Legal Tender Cases*, 12 Wall. 457.

Following *Bronson* v. *Rodes,* are a group of cases—*Butler* v. *Horwitz, Dewing* v. *Sears, The Emily Souder, Gregory* v. *Morris,* and *Trebilcock* v. *Wilson*—all aside, as I see it, from the essentials involved here. . . .

But in the *Legal Tender Cases,* following the *Hepburn* v. *Griswold* case, there are some observations which are exceedingly interesting. There is a wealth of learning to be found not only in the opinions, but in the elaborate briefs of counsel who appeared in those historic cases.

Now, in the *Legal Tender Cases* if there is anything clear it is that the Court passed on two questions: first, whether the Congress had power to make paper money a legal tender for any debt; and, second, if it had this power, was such power limited to debts created after the passage of the Legal Tender statute? . . .

Here, then, was a decision making it perfectly apparent that, in exercising its Constitutional power in the matter of making paper money legal tender, the Congress had as much power to deal with existing debts as it had to deal with debts created after the passage of the act. This, as I see it, if the Court please, is the most important contribution made to our present-day discussion by any of the cases of that era.

Now, let me pursue that matter just a bit further. In reaching its conclusion, the majority opinion contends that the only obligation was to pay money which the law recognizes as money when payment is made. But Mr. Justice Strong, who wrote the opinion of the Court, disposed of many of the arguments made in the present case. Where an attempt is made to identify money contracts with other types of contracts the Court speaks of these comparisons as " a false analogy "; and, on page 549, says:

" There is a wide distinction between a tender of quantities or of specific articles and a tender of legal values. Contracts for the delivery of specific articles belong exclusively to the domain of state legislation, while contracts for the payment of money are subject to the authority of Congress, at least so far as relates to the means of payment. They are engagements to pay with lawful money of the United States, and Congress is empowered to regulate that money. It cannot, therefore, be maintained that the Legal Tender acts impaired the obligation of contracts."

Moreover, in considering the argument that the contract to pay simply in dollars was a contract to pay in the sort of dollars that had been established by law at the time the contract was made, the Court disposed of that suggestion on pages 549 and 550, saying:

" Nor can it be truly asserted that Congress may not by its action indirectly impair the obligation of contracts, if by the expression be meant rendering contracts fruitless or partially fruitless." . . .

Now, of course, the next important case is *Juilliard* v. *Greenman,* 110 U. S. 421, where the power of the Congress was more fully developed and confirmed with reference to the matter of currency, and where it was declared that this power existed in time of peace as well as in time of war.

And then we have the *Ling Su Fan* case, to which I have referred before, which is of controlling significance.

I think it is clear that when the Supreme Court, in the *Legal Tender Cases,* extended the power over contracts to those which existed prior to the passage of the Legal Tender Acts as well as those that arose subsequently, it established a principle which, carried to its logical conclusion, sustains the power of the Congress as exercised in the Joint Resolution of June 5, 1933.

In fact, we seriously urge upon this Court the suggestion that to sustain the contention of those who appear here in opposition to the validity of the Joint Resolution would constitute an unfortunate recurrence to the mistaken principles of *Hepburn* v. *Griswold.* It would turn back the pages of history more than sixty years.

In the *Mottley case,* decided in 1911, this Court took strong ground on the fundamental proposition of the right to brush aside interference with the exercise of a constitutional power.

In the *Blaisdell case* [290 U. S. 398], the Chief Justice said:

" Not only are existing laws read into contracts in order
to fix obligations as between the parties, but the reservation of essential attributes of sovereign power is also read
into contracts as a postulate of the legal order."

I stand upon that language, and upon the language laid
down in the other cases to which I have referred. I stand
not only upon these cases and upon the *Nebbia* case, but
upon the fundamental proposition that the Congress has
plenary power, in a whole range of subjects, no matter
what private parties may endeavor to do, and no matter
how completely they may attempt to thwart the exercise
of constitutional authority.

We have found it entirely possible to prohibit lotteries,
no matter what contractual obligations may have been set
up with reference to them.

The cases which deal with intoxicating liquors reached
the same result. The same observation may be made with
reference to zoning laws; the maintenance of nuisances;
and the regulation of the rates and services of utilities—
all along the line there is a recognition of this essential
power of the Government.

So I contend, both upon authority and upon reason,
that the Joint Resolution of June 5, 1933, was a valid exercise of constitutional power, not limited by the Fifth
Amendment or by any other clause of restriction in the
Constitution. . . .

It is my belief that the word " regulate " as used in the
Constitution has never been completely and carefully
analyzed in all of its implications. How far does the term
" regulate " carry us? Manifestly it reaches to the regulation of value, and value, itself, is a relative thing. Value
appears only in relation to the value of other things.

And, moreover, the word " regulate " implies a continuing power, and is the same term that is used with reference
to commerce, and connotes the power of adjustment. It
implies the power of making the condition accord more
fully with reality and with justice.

But when you come to the power " to fix the standard of weights and measures," the Constitution abandons the word " regulate " and uses the word " fix."

All these things, philosophically or semiphilosophically considered, have some relationship to these sudden and violent fluctuations in commodity prices which so completely disarrange important equities; and to the proposition that, as a matter of essential justice, the dollar we borrow should be, in purchasing power, substantially the dollar we are expected to repay. What that relationship is I do not assume to suggest, what the future may develop with regard to this aspect of the constitutional question I do not know. These things will follow in due course.

But I am moved to mention these matters, because on the 14th page of the appendix to the plaintiff's brief in the *Perry* case, there is a chart, which is designed to show the terrible losses suffered by the claimant in that case. So far as I recall, that is the only proof he has submitted to indicate that he has suffered any loss whatsoever.

This table is made up in peculiar fashion. It is constructed by charting commodity prices in the United States of America; and then the price of the gold dollar is calculated in the discount thereof in terms of foreign coinage—in terms of the gold coinage of France, Belgium, Holland, and Switzerland. Having found the rate of discount at which the gold dollar is depressed below these standards, the results are reduced to percentages, and these percentages are then subtracted from the range of commodity prices in this country in order to show the loss sustained.

In other words, it is a synthetic chart, having no relation to any known problem whatsoever. It attempts to trace the history of a dollar that has ceased to exist. . . .

The gold clause attempts to override the legal tender and parity provisions established by law. If valid, it further would have the effect of making certain that, whatever may be the policy of the Congress, the coins and currency of the United States shall *not* have equal value in the discharge of all classes of debts.

The gold clause is a serious obstacle to the maintenance of parity. The conventional method of maintaining parity is by the redemption of currency in gold coin.

The startling withdrawals of gold coin for hoarding and the flight into foreign currencies and into foreign countries which took place in February and during the first few days of March 1933 made it impossible to continue such redemption. The Government's stock was being rapidly depleted. During the period to which I have just referred $476,100,000 in gold had been withdrawn from the Federal Reserve banks and the United States Treasury, of which $311,000,000 was for export, or to be earmarked for foreign accounts. Simultaneously there was a great demand for money of all kinds for domestic hoarding.

At that time the outstanding gold obligations amounted to $100,000,000,000, and the available gold supply of this country was only $4,000,000,000, and in the entire world only $11,000,000,000.

Moreover, there were conditions of equity that had to be borne in mind. To have permitted, after the 9th of March, the conversion of gold certificates and United States notes into gold would have been to prefer the demand claims of the gold creditors, foreign and domestic, so long as the supply should last.

And to have prohibited the conversion of such demand obligations and yet to have continued the conversion of time obligations—calling for gold in each instance—would have been to prefer time obligations, both public and private. Either alternative would have been to deny equal treatment to creditors with equal claims to consideration.

All of the foregoing suggestions bear on the question of maintaining parity after the suspension of gold redemption. Why, parity could not have been maintained under the previously existing system, if outstanding gold certificates and United States notes had been redeemed in anything except gold coin. To have redeemed them in currency at the higher rate demanded by these claimants would have immediately brought back the double standard of currency which had wrought such havoc in times gone by.

It is, therefore, apparent that to maintain parity under the existing conditions, gold certificates and United States notes had to be treated upon an absolute equality with other forms of currency, and by that same token it was necessary to abrogate the gold clause in gold obligations.

There is another reason why the gold clause is an obstruction to the power to regulate the value of money. One method of regulating the value of money is by lessening the gold content of the dollar. I do not understand that any responsible person seriously disputes the right upon the part of the Government to lessen the gold content of the dollar. Nevertheless, that power could not have been actually used if it had entailed the redemption or payment of $100,000,000,000 of obligations at the rate of $169,000,000,000. . . .

Let me pause for a moment to emphasize the proposition that the only alternative open to the Congress was a reduction in the gold content of the dollar, accompanied by a denunciation of gold clauses. In choosing this alternative, the Government acted in the public interest, and it cannot fairly be contended that it acted arbitrarily, capriciously, or unfairly or unjustly, or for any improper purpose.

There can be no doubt that the gold clause was a hindrance to the borrowing power. Such obligations, if permitted to exist, would have preëmpted or, at least, measurably restricted, the sources from which borrowed money is obtained. There is no doubt that the gold clause likewise interfered with international obligations and negotiations; and with foreign exchange and foreign commerce. If it had been impossible to break the prewar tie to the gold dollar we would have been denied the privilege, open to all other civilized governments, of dealing effectively with our own currency.

No adequate reason has been advanced why the holders of interest-bearing time obligations should be preferred over holders of demand obligations, as, clearly, these forms of understandings are of equal solemnity. The holders of $20,000,000,000 of federal gold obligations, with an annual interest charge of $700,000,000, could, in a relatively short time, have drained all of the available gold out of the Treasury. This would have been tantamount—and I say it deliberately—to delivering the destiny of our gold reserves into private hands, and by that same token delivering the destiny of America into private hands.

Oh, I have found in the briefs of learned counsel upon the other side many suggestions indicative of the proposition that our Government acted hastily, and even in bad faith. But The Hague Court, in the opinion in the *Royal Dutch Shell* case, rendered on the 15th day of February 1934, had no such misgivings as seem to afflict counsel in this case. In that court it was said:

" There cannot be any question about violation of public order, as the measure " (that is the Joint Resolution they are talking about) " according to its purpose set forth in the preamble has been enacted as required by urgent necessity and public interest " (meaning American public interest) " and not at all in order to injure the creditor."

Apparently the contentions of our opponents in this matter deal with questions of ethics and economics and morals and good faith. But who shall say that all of these considerations plead for the claimants? I hesitate to venture upon the high ground of ethics and morality so completely occupied by those who argue for the sanctity of the written word, and who assert that it should be maintained at all hazards. That field has been pretty thoroughly occupied by counsel for the bondholders. Such arguments make me feel a stranger in this preëmpted territory.

But, after all, is the morality all on one side? Are there not certain essentials of justice which the written word may defeat and which it is the higher purpose of the law to preserve? . . .

Should the claims of the owners of these gold obligations be approved, it would create a privileged class which, in character, in immunity, and in power, has hitherto been unparalleled in the history of the human race. I feel the walls of this courtroom expand; I see, waiting upon this decision, the hopes, the fears, and the welfare of millions of our fellow citizens.

These measures which are under attack were thoroughly considered and carefully worked out. They represent the overwhelming sentiment of the Congress. They represent the considered judgment of the President. What is attacked here is the joint work of the legislative branch of the Government and the executive branch of the Government, operating in complete and wholesome accord. Those who contest the wisdom of these results, their propriety, their legality, their necessity, or their essential justice have a heavy burden to carry.

The validity of our contention in this case rests, however, upon wider and even more compelling considerations. The authority to coin money and regulate the value thereof is an attribute of sovereignty which cannot be restrained by private contract nor subordinated to the tenor of individual obligations.

That the United States of America is a sovereign nation and possesses the essentials of sovereignty has been repeatedly declared by this Court. This of necessity must be so. When the Constitution, by § 8 of Article I, confided the power over the currency to the Congress, it did so in representative terms, similar to those used in the same article setting forth the other essential attributes of sovereignty.

I like that old expression which will be found in the Legal Essays of Thayer, on page 75 in the edition of 1908. There is meat in this rather homely expression:

" The Constitution, in giving to Congress the power to coin money, is not, just then, concerned with the technicalities of law or political economy; it is disposing of one of the ' *jura majestatis* ' in brief and general terms, in phrases which are the language of statesmen."

In the case of *Juilliard* v. *Greenman* the Court speaks of this power as one which accords " with the usage of sovereign governments."

Any lingering doubt upon this subject is dispelled by reading § 10 of Article I of the Constitution, which takes from the States all power over the currency. The state governments were emptied of such power. All the scattered sovereignties of the different States went over *en bloc* to the Government of the United States, and they were not lost in transit.

I think it may safely be said—at least, it may reasonably be argued—that the state governments succeeded to the powers of the Crown, the King, and Parliament in the control over currency, and exercised this power sometimes wisely and sometimes recklessly. Those who framed the Constitution of the United States realized this situation, and, knowing what had happened in the colonies, took pains to see that this power, just like the power of the sword, this great attribute of sovereignty, should reside in one single authority. Hence the Constitution not only affirmatively grants this power to the Congress of the United States, but forbids its exercise by the various States.

In sweeping terms the Federal Government was given the power to collect taxes to provide for the common defense and the general welfare; to coin money; to declare war; to maintain armies; to provide a Navy; and, in general, to deal in these sovereign matters on an equality with the other members of the family of nations.

These enumerated grants in § 8 of Article I of the Constitution are set forth in representative terms, which, taken together, imply all the essentials of a comprehensive federal power over the whole subject of the medium of exchange, standards of measure and value, coinage of money, and the control of credit.

Of course, I am not arguing here for any inherent sovereign power. But I am maintaining that, in certain matters, in which currency is included, the Government of the United States has the same type of sovereign power which was accorded to the Crown in the *Mixed Money Case,* and which has not, so far as I am aware, been successfully controverted in any court in any country since that time.

The history of money is fascinating. It has been tied up with the progress of the human race. There has never been an important era in which the destinies of men were at hazard, where the problem of currency was not involved. Every drama in the international field involves some aspect of the money question.

In the earliest days, of course, the currency was crude in form. It developed as civilization went on. Finally we come to the period referred to in the *Mixed Money Case,* where its characteristics were beginning to be understood. We then come to the early colonial days, with their chaos and their disorder, and their conflict in matters of currency. And, following this, these sovereign powers of the States, which had in so many instances been unwisely used, were turned over to the Federal Government, and, for the first time on this continent, the control of currency was confided to a central authority.

It was then a little-understood subject—and, I must say, it is a little-understood subject now. We have passed through many vicissitudes—the Greenback Era; the period of the *Legal Tender Cases*; the experience with the double currency standard; until we reached a more or less settled status, which many people fatuously believed was the final status. The gold standard, as it was then known, survived the panic of the Cleveland administration, but it did not survive the vicissitudes of the World War. The problem moved out into international areas. Governments began to send representatives to conferences to discuss this mutually vexing problem of gold.

It would be idle to deny that things are still in a formative stage. Indeed, great things are afoot. The London Economic Conference of 1933 did not achieve its objective, but it had for one of its purposes the problem of the stabilization of the currencies of the world.

On the third of July, 1933, the President of the United States cabled to the Economic Conference dealing with this subject and, in the course of his message, confirmed the proposition that our broad purpose is permanent stabilization of every national currency.

Oh, we have not seen the last of international economic and monetary conferences. Already these events may be dimly seen on the horizon. I do not know when it will be. That is written in the inscrutable bosom of time. But the day will come when the United States of America will be conferring with the other nations of the earth, with a view to the stabilization of currencies, the fixing of standards, and making those arrangements which are essential amongst civilized nations if we are to dwell together in any reasonable degree of harmony and prosperity.

Let nothing be said here that makes our Nation enter such a conference on crutches, a cripple amongst the nations of the earth.

Mr. Justice Holmes once very wisely said—I think it was in the *Holland* case—

" It is not lightly to be assumed that, in matters requiring national action, ' a power which must belong to and somewhere reside in every civilized government ' is not to be found."

If the Court please, other nations, impelled by the requirements of necessity and acting for the public welfare, have devalued their currencies, abandoned the gold standard, and abrogated gold contracts by specific laws enacted for that purpose. Without challenge and without question they have done precisely what the Congress of the United States has done. Belgium, France, Germany, Rumania, Mexico, Norway, and Sweden have enacted such laws. It is an essential attribute of sovereignty.

I ask this Court to lay down in unequivocal language the proposition that, in matters of currency, the courses of action open to other governments are not denied to this country, and that, in employing these sovereign powers, we act upon an equality with all the other nations of the earth.

Mr. Stanley Reed made the oral arguments for the Reconstruction Finance Corporation.

Summary of the brief for the United States and the Reconstruction Finance Corporation, on which were the *Attorney General, Mr. Stanley Reed, Solicitor General Biggs,* and *Assistant Solicitor General MacLean:*

An act of the legislature is presumed to be constitutional. [Citing many cases.]

In choosing the means to carry out its powers the Congress has an extremely wide discretion and its judgment will not be overturned unless clearly arbitrary and capricious. *McCulloch* v. *Maryland,* 4 Wheat. 316, 418; *United States* v. *Fisher,* 2 Cranch 358; *Legal Tender Cases,* 12 Wall. 457; *Farmers' and Mechanics' National Bank* v.

Dearing, 91 U. S. 29, 33; *Juilliard* v. *Greenman,* 110 U. S. 421; *Ex parte Curtis,* 106 U. S. 371; *Northern Securities Co. v. United States,* 193 U. S. 197; *Ling Su Fan* v. *United States,* 218 U. S. 302; and *Board of Trustees of University of Illinois* v. *United States,* 289 U. S. 48.

The importance of the gold clause is due to the overwhelming amount of obligations calling for payment in gold coin issued and outstanding on June 5, 1933, the best estimates placing the amount at approximately $100,000,-000,000.

Congress was justified in declaring that gold clauses are contrary to public policy and inconsistent with our present monetary system. The gold clause had its origin in a period when there was in existence a dual monetary system;—that is, two kinds of money, United States coins and circulating notes, were permitted to circulate, fluctuating in value one against the other. *Bronson* v. *Rodes,* 7 Wall. 229, was decided during this period. The dual monetary system went out of existence after the resumption of specie payments in 1879.

The recent monetary and financial crisis called for the exercise of Congressional power over coinage and currency. In 1933 the dollar, the Swiss franc and the Dutch guilder were the only monetary units of commercially important countries which were not devalued or depreciated substantially below prewar parities. A number of countries have placed restrictions upon the export of gold and suspended the redemption of currency in gold coin. Between 1929 and 1933 the wholesale commodity price index of the United States Department of Labor declined by nearly 40% and our national income had shrunk about 50%. During February and until March 6, 1933, when the banking holiday was proclaimed, $476,100,000 in gold was withdrawn from the Federal Reserve Banks and the Treasury.

Monetary legislation enacted by Congress in this situation included the Emergency Banking Act of 1933, authorizing the regulation and prohibition of the withdrawal, export, and hoarding of gold; the Act of May 12, 1933, making all forms of money legal tender for all debts and authorizing a reduction in the gold content of the dollar; and the Gold Reserve Act of 1934, amending the Act of May 12, 1933, directing the Secretary of the Treasury to melt down all gold coins, and authorizing redemption of currency only in gold bullion and only for the settlement of international balances and the maintenance of the parity of all forms of money. The President and the Secretary of the Treasury issued Orders pursuant to the Emergency Banking Act of 1933; and on January 31, 1934, the President issued a Proclamation reducing the gold content of the dollar to 15 5/21 grains nine-tenths fine.

Gold clauses, if enforceable, would have obstructed the exercise of the monetary and other powers of the Federal Government, whether such clauses are construed to call for payment in gold coin itself or in an asserted equivalent in currency. The gold clause would nullify the power of the Congress to make all forms of coins and currency of the United States legal tender for all payments. It is an obstruction to the power of the Congress to regulate the value of money by changing the gold content of the dollar. The effect of the clause, if interpreted to call for an asserted equivalent in currency, is to increase gold-clause debts in direct and invariable proportion to the change in the statutory value of gold. In the present situation the increase would be 69.32%. The increase in interest payments on outstanding private gold-clause obligations would be about $2,600,000,000 annually. This potential increase in the debt burden is particularly significant in the light of the already existing burden of long term debt service, which had grown from 9.2% of the national income in 1929 to 21.1% in 1932. In the case of carriers, utilities and industries whose income is and must be in dollars, the added burden of an enforceable gold clause would bring widespread bankruptcy. Non-enforcement of gold clauses results in no real loss to creditors. Because of the drastic decline in the price level, a coupon holder who now received $16.93 on a $10 coupon could purchase twice as much as could have been purchased with the $10 during 1921–1929.

The gold clause, construed as calling for payment in gold coin, is incompatible with legislation to protect the currency reserves and to provide for more effective use of gold. The gold reserves of this country have been subject to sudden, violent and unpredictable withdrawals. Such withdrawals, coupled with increased demands for currency for hoarding and export, caused the reserve ratio of the Federal Reserve System to fall from 65.6% on February 1, 1933, to 45.1% on March 4, 1933. The Gold Reserve Act of 1934, providing for withdrawal and melting down of gold coin, conformed to the postwar practice of foreign countries and the recommendations of economists and bankers.

Gold clauses are an obstruction to the power of Congress to borrow money; for pending a change in the gold content of the dollar, bonds would be issued which might incur for the taxpayers a debt greatly in excess of the amount received for the bonds. It would be impractical to eliminate the gold clause from future issues only, since investors would prefer the old issues, public or private, to such an extent as to require prohibitive rates on the new.

Gold clauses, by interfering with a change in the gold content of the dollar, obstruct the power of Congress to regulate foreign exchange and foreign commerce.

The Joint Resolution is within the delegated powers of Congress. The power over the currency includes the power to reduce the gold content of the dollar, as was done in 1834, and so to subject creditors to a corresponding loss. *Legal Tender Cases,* 12 Wall. 457, 551–2. Congress may require creditors to accept irredeemable paper money in discharge of debts contracted when only gold and silver coin were legal tender. *Legal Tender Cases, supra; Juilliard* v. *Greenman,* 110 U. S. 421. Congress may legislate to assure uniformity in the value of all forms of money. *Veazie Bank* v. *Fenno,* 8 Wall. 533; *National Bank* v. *United States,* 101 U. S. 1; *Ling Su Fan* v. *United States,* 218 U. S. 302. The power to borrow money affords broad scope for legislation. *McCulloch* v. *Maryland,* 4 Wheat. 316; *Smith* v. *Kansas City Title & Trust Co.,* 255 U. S. 180; *Weston* v. *Charleston,* 2 Pet. 449; *Missouri Insurance Co.* v. *Gehner,* 281 U. S. 313; *United States* v. *Fisher,* 2 Cranch 358. Congress may protect our foreign trade against the adverse effect of depreciated foreign currencies. *Hampton & Co.* v. *United States,* 276 U. S. 394. In its international relations the Federal Government possesses the full attributes of sovereignty. *Burnet* v. *Brooks,* 288 U. S. 378, 396; *Legal Tender Cases, supra,* p. 555; *Fong Yue Ting* v. *United States,* 149 U. S. 698, 711.

Congress is empowered to declare unenforceable private agreements whose purpose and effect are to usurp, frustrate or obstruct the exercise of its powers. The Fifth Amendment does not forbid such legislation. *Addyston Pipe & Steel Co.* v. *United States,* 175 U. S. 211, 229; *Home Building & Loan Assn.* v. *Blaisdell,* 290 U. S. 398, 435; *Louisville & Nashville R. Co.* v. *Mottley,* 219 U. S. 467; *Philadelphia, B. & W. R. Co.* v. *Schubert,* 224 U. S. 603; *Calhoun* v. *Massie,* 253 U. S. 170; *New York* v. *United States,* 257 U. S. 591; *Sproles* v. *Binford,* 286 U. S. 374; *Chicago, B. & Q. R. Co.* v. *McGuire,* 219 U. S. 549, 567; *Atlantic Coast Line R. Co.* v. *Riverside Mills,* 219 U. S. 186, 201; *Highland* v. *Russell Car & Snow Plow Co.,* 279 U. S. 253.

The gold hoarding orders, independently of the Joint Resolution of June 5, 1933, require that the claim on the bonds be limited to the face amount thereof. A free domestic gold market did not exist, in consequence of these

NORMAN *v.* B. & O. R. CO.

orders, from the time of the banking holiday in March, 1933, to the present. The gold clause should be interpreted as calling simply for payment in gold coin. *Bronson* v. *Rodes,* 7 Wall. 229; *Trebilcock* v. *Wilson,* 12 Wall. 687; *The Emily Souder,* 17 Wall. 666; *Butler* v. *Horwitz,* 7 Wall. 258; *Dewing* v. *Sears,* 11 Wall. 379. The following cases are distinguishable: *The Vaughan and Telegraph,* 14 Wall. 258; *United States* v. *Erie Ry. Co.,* 107 U. S. 1; *Gregory* v. *Morris,* 96 U. S. 619; *Feist* v. *Société Intercommunale Belge d'Electricité,* [1934] A. C. 161; Cases of *Serbian and Brazilian Bonds,* P. C. I. J., Series A, Nos. 20–21. Payment in gold coin is impossible and illegal because of the gold hoarding orders, and should be excused. *The Tornado,* 108 U. S. 342; *Western Hardware & Manufacturing Co.* v. *Bancroft Charnley Steel Co.,* 116 Fed. 176 (C. C. A. 7th); *Browne* v. *United States,* 30 Ct. Cl. 124; *International Paper Co.* v. *Rockefeller,* 161 App. Div. 180. *Moore & Tierney, Inc.* v. *Roxford Knitting Co.,* 250 Fed. 278 (N. D. N. Y.). *Metropolitan Water Board* v. *Dick Kerr & Co.,* [1918] A. C. 119; *Shipton, Anderson & Co.* v. *Harrison,* 3 K. B. 676 (1915). *Manigault* v. *Springs,* 199 U. S. 473; *Louisville & Nashville R. Co.* v. *Mottley,* 219 U. S. 467; *Omnia Commercial Co.* v. *United States,* 261 U. S. 502, 511; *Board of Commissioners* v. *Young,* 59 Fed. 96 (C. C. A. 6th); *Northern Pac. Ry. Co.* v. *St. P. & Tacoma Lumber Co.,* 4 F. (2d) 359 (C. C. A. 9th); *Operators' Oil Co.* v. *Barbre,* 65 F. (2d) 857 (C. C. A. 10th); Restatement of the Law of Contracts, § 458 of c. 14; Williston on Contracts, § 1938. Recovery is properly limited to the face amount of the bonds. Since if gold coin were paid to the creditors it would be worth to them only its face amount, payment of a greater sum would be a windfall, not indemnity for loss. *Wicker* v. *Hoppock,* 6 Wall. 94; *United States* v. *Behan,* 110 U. S. 338.

If the gold clause is interpreted to call for an equivalent in currency, the equivalent is the amount of currency which would purchase the stipulated gold coin. *The Vaughan and Telegraph, supra; Gregory v. Morris, supra.* In the existing restricted gold market, equivalence is on a dollar-for-dollar basis. Even if the statutory price of gold, unreflected in a free domestic market, is the proper measure of equivalence, it is inapplicable here, for the bonds matured on May 1, 1933, when the gold dollar was at its old parity. *Hicks* v. *Guinness,* 269 U. S. 71; *Effinger* v. *Kenney,* 115 U. S. 566, 575; *Feist* v. *Société Intercommunale Belge d'Electricité, supra.*

Power over coinage and currency is an attribute of sovereignty. *Cohens* v. *Virginia,* 6 Wheat. 264, 380; *Juilliard* v. *Greenman, supra; Mackenzie* v. *Hare,* 239 U. S. 299, 311; *Burnet* v. *Brooks,* 288 U. S. 378; *Tiaco* v. *Forbes,* 228 U. S. 549, 556; *Georgia* v. *Chattanooga,* 264 U. S. 472, 480; *Ling Su Fan* v. *United States,* 218 U. S. 302, 310; Story on the Constitution (5th ed.), Vol. 2, p. 59; *Mixed Money Case,* Sir John Davies' Report 48, 51, 55; Thayer, Legal Essays, p. 75; *Martin* v. *Hunter,* 1 Wheat. 326. Whatever power there is over the currency is vested in Congress. If the power to declare what is money is not in Congress, it is annihilated. *Legal Tender Cases, supra.*

Mr. Edward J. White for the Trustees of the Missouri Pacific R. Co., petitioners. Points from brief:

The Joint Resolution was valid under § 8, Art. I, of the Constitution; also under the general welfare clause. *Massachusetts* v. *Mellon,* 262 U. S. 448; Alexander Hamilton, Report on Manufacturers, 1791; Story, Constitution, 5th ed., §§ 975, 978, 992. See *Heisler* v. *Colliery Co.,* 260 U. S. 245.

Emergency is the occasion for the exercise of the power.

Under the general welfare clause, Congress has a large discretion as to the means to be employed in the exercise of any power granted it. *Northern Securities Co.* v. *United States,* 193 U. S. 343; *Fairbank* v. *United States,* 181 U. S. 287; *Logan* v. *United States,* 144 U. S. 282; *Legal Tender Cases,* 12 Wall. 538.

The declared object in the Preamble to " promote the general welfare," and the broad grant of power in Art. I, § 8, should be held to include all means adopted by Congress to attain the ends in view which are not expressly prohibited by the Constitution.

In this bankruptcy proceeding the court possessed the power to impair the existing obligations of contracts.

The inhibition against the impairment of contract obligations applies only to the States and is not a limitation upon the power of Congress.

Whether *malum in se* or *malum prohibitum,* no illegal contract can furnish the basis for a legal remedy.

Messrs. James H. McIntosh and *Edward W. Bourne,* with whom *Messrs. Clifton P. Williamson* and *Thomas W. White* were on the brief, for Bankers Trust Co. et al., respondents. The following summary is from the brief:

By promising to pay a specified sum " in gold coin of the present standard of weight and fineness " the obligor undertakes to pay a specified amount of money in coin having a specified bullion content, or, if that is not available, to pay the equivalent in current money. The opinion of the lower court that the agreement constituted a promise to pay in gold " as a mere commodity " was clearly wrong. *Thompson* v. *Butler,* 95 U. S. 694; *Bronson* v. *Rodes,* 7 Wall. 229, 252. The parties intended to fix a standard or measure of value, if the debt should not be paid in the exact coin agreed upon. They contemplated that, when the time came to pay, there might be gold dollars of a new standard. They must have known that, if such were introduced, " gold coin of the present standard " would pass from circulation. They intended that, in any such contingency, the Railway Company could discharge its debt by paying the equivalent in gold value of the May 1, 1903, dollar—and, correlatively, that it must pay the equivalent so long as the equivalent could be measured in terms of current money. In other words, if the new standard gold dollar of 15 5/21 grains had been coined, a tender of 1,000 new standard gold dollars in coin would not have paid a bond. The new dollars now circulating are the equivalent of a new coin dollar of 15 5/21 grains, both by statute and in market value. How, then, can 1,000 of the new dollars now circulating pay a debt which they could not satisfy if they were in gold coin of the present so-called standard?

The gold clause or its equivalent has been in use time out of mind and has been used not merely in money contracts between private persons, but in money contracts of this Government.

This use has not been confined to this country. Some of the cases next to be cited illustrate its use abroad, and the language of the Treaty of Versailles, Art. 262, is identical with the clause involved in this case, except that the Treaty uses the date and these bonds used the word " present," to fix the time.

This Court has repeatedly enforced gold clause contracts according to their true intent; and other courts of the highest distinction have construed and enforced them as a measure of value. *Gregory* v. *Morris,* 96 U. S. 619; *Serbian Loan Case,* and *Brazilian Loan Case,* Publications de la Cour Permanente de Justice Internationale, Series A, Nos. 20, 21, pp. 5–89, 91–155. The effect of the two decisions last cited was to require each of the two Governments to pay about five times as many French paper francs, or new French gold francs, as they would have been required to pay if the court had not held that the gold clause meant a "gold standard of value." To the like effect, *Feist* v. *Société Intercommunale Belge d'Elec-*

tricité, L. R. (1934) A. C. 161, which involved bonds of a Belgian corporation promising to pay in gold coin of the United Kingdom of or equal to the standard of weight and fineness existing on September 1st, 1928. The conclusions reached by the Permanent Court and by the House of Lords represent the accepted view everywhere except in Germany, whose courts profess to see a difference between a "gold coin" clause and a "gold value" clause. See 44 Yale L. J., pp. 56–57.

The Joint Resolution of June 5, 1933, contains an implied admission that the gold clause prescribes a measure of recovery.

These contracts were lawful when made, and were made for a proper purpose, in terms which this Court for nearly half a century before the issue of these bonds had recognized as legal and repeatedly approved as binding. *Bronson* v. *Rodes,* 7 Wall. 229; *Gregory* v. *Morris,* 96 U. S. 619; *Butler* v. *Horwitz,* 7 Wall. 258; *Bronson* v. *Kimpton,* 8 Wall. 444; *Dewing* v. *Sears,* 11 Wall. 379; *Trebilcock* v. *Wilson,* 12 Wall. 687; *United States* v. *Erie R. Co.,* 106 U. S. 327; 107 U. S. 1; *The Telegraph* v. *Gordon,* 14 Wall. 258; *The Emily B. Souder* v. *Pritchard,* 17 Wall. 666; *Thompson* v. *Butler,* 95 U. S. 694.

In every one of the cases involving a promise to pay in gold coin, this Court insisted upon the entry of judgment either for gold coin or for its equivalent in currency.

The *Legal Tender Cases* did not overrule *Bronson* v. *Rodes* nor weaken its authority on this question, because those cases referred only to contracts payable in money, simply. *Knox* v. *Lee,* 12 Wall. 457, 459; *Juilliard* v. *Greenman,* 110 U. S. 421, 449; *Trebilcock* v. *Wilson,* 12 Wall. 687.

Preliminary to a discussion of the Joint Resolution of June 5, 1933, and its validity, we remind the Court " that a legislative declaration of facts that are material only as to the ground for enacting a rule of law . . . may not be held conclusive by the courts." *Block* v. *Hirsh,* 256 U. S. 135, 154; that provisions of Bills of Right are limitations upon all the powers of Government, *Hurtado* v. *California,* 110 U. S. 516, 531–532; that " It is the duty of courts to be watchful for the constitutional rights of the citizen, and against any stealthy encroachments thereon," *Mononga-hela Navigation Co.* v. *United States,* 148 U. S. 312, 325; that " The good of society as a whole cannot be better served than by the preservation against arbitrary restraint of the liberties of its constituent members." *Adkins* v. *Children's Hospital,* 261 U. S. 525, 561.

The Joint Resolution directly involves two constitutional grants of power,—(1) the power to " coin money, regulate the value thereof," and (2) the power to " borrow money on the credit of the United States "; and one limitation of power, namely, the limitation imposed by the Fifth Amendment. It also directly involves an encroachment by the Federal Government on the sovereign power of the States.

No one constitutional power can be construed to override another. The power to borrow money is as important as the power to coin money and regulate the value thereof. Hence what Congress has done in the exercise of the one power it cannot undo in the exercise of the other power. When, during the war and at other times, Congress borrowed money on the credit of the United States and promised to pay it back in dollars " of the present standard of value," it was exercising a power which the Constitution gave it; therefore how could Congress afterwards say the contracts it then made in the exercise of its power to borrow money are now contrary to public policy?

If it were true that such contracts, so made under the borrowing power, really interfered with the power of Congress to coin money and regulate the value thereof—that the two powers conflicted and that the coinage power limited the borrowing power—this would mean that no Congress ever had, or could have, the power to issue bonds containing a promise to repay the money borrowed in coin or dollars of any agreed standard of value. If this were true, then the Congress of 1863 and 1864 had no power to finance the last campaigns of the Civil War by issuing bonds payable " in gold coin of the present standard of value "; and every Congress which has issued bonds since February 4, 1910, has made a promise it had no power to make (c. 25, 36 Stat. 192; 31 U. S. C., § 768), and neither the present Congress nor any future Congress can ever issue bonds containing a binding obligation to repay the debt measured by the standard of value which prevailed when the debt was contracted.

Thus the wholly unwarranted scope which the Congress gives to the power to " coin money, regulate the value thereof," would, if it were the true scope of that power, make the borrowing power of Congress, which is at least equally important, an ineffective thing.

Similarly, the power to regulate the value of money cannot be used in direct violation of the limitations imposed upon Congress by the Fifth Amendment. If by this Resolution Congress were really exercising the power to regulate the value of money, and the legitimate exercise of that power indirectly or incidentally impaired the obligations of gold clause contracts, a different question would be presented. But the Resolution is not, and does not purport to be, a regulation of the value of money, nor is its effect on these contracts indirect or incidental. On the contrary, its sole purpose and its effect are, not to regulate the value of money, but directly and immediately, not indirectly nor incidentally, to change these contracts by destroying their most valued obligation. Thus the Resolution not only undertakes to restrict the expressed and vastly important power of Congress to borrow money on the credit of the United States, but it directly violates the limitation of power imposed by the Fifth Amendment.

Moreover, by this Resolution the Federal Government directly encroaches upon the sovereign power of the States by interfering with their power to borrow money on whatever terms they choose to make; by changing the terms of the contracts which they have made in borrowing money; by impairing their credit; and by interfering with and hindering their future financing. States, and municipalities under the authority of the States, have made gold clause contracts in vast sums. They have done this in the exercise of their sovereign power to borrow money for state and municipal purposes on whatever terms they chose to make. The Federal Government has no authority to interfere with them in this exercise of their sovereign power. *Pollock* v. *Farmers Loan & Trust Co.*, 157 U. S. 429, 585.

This Resolution is not, and does not purport to be, an emergency measure. Besides, if this were an emergency measure, it would end with the emergency, and then the Railway Company would have to pay these bondholders what it agreed to pay. But it purports to be legislation for all time.

This Resolution says these gold clause contracts " obstruct the power of Congress to regulate the value of money." Gold clause contracts have been in common use since before the adoption of the Constitution. During all this time Congress has regulated the value of money.

It is obvious that the act of regulating the value of money is not obstructed by the existence of gold clause contracts. A medium of exchange can be abandoned and a new medium substituted, irrespective of the existence or amount of outstanding gold clause contracts. The substitution of a new medium may change the number of units payable on the contracts, but that is merely one effect of the change in medium, not an obstruction to the change. There has been merely a nominal increase in the units of currency payable,—an increase in the number of units but not an increase in the value to be paid when measured by the standard agreed upon in the bonds. See *Brazilian Loans Case, supra,* p. 117.

When Congress authorized the devaluation of the dollar in 1933, its declared purpose was to increase nominal prices, which was the same thing as reducing the real value of currency and of fixed obligations to pay a fixed number of dollars, simply. The devaluation was expected to increase the nominal prices of wheat, cotton, and other farm products, and, we assume, also of silver, land, and other forms of property. And it was certain to have the automatic effect of increasing the nominal value of gold exactly in proportion to the devaluation.

Congress, proceeding on the theory that a devaluation of the dollar would increase prices correspondingly, saw that the nominal value of gold clause contracts would rise in proportion to the devaluation, thus preserving the real value of those obligations. What Congress wanted to do was to devalue the dollar for the purpose of correspondingly raising prices and reducing the real value of all debts. The gold clause in contracts prevented Congress from reducing the real value of those obligations. The gold clause did not obstruct the power of Congress to devalue the dollar; it merely limited the effect as to contracts which contained the gold clause.

Congress has no power to regulate the nominal, or even the real, effects of an exercise of one of its powers, either before or after. It may consider before it exercises a power what the results of its exercise of power may be, but it cannot change the situation before it acts, in order to prevent results of its action which it considers undesirable. If it could do this, it could change or regulate everything, including both debts and prices.

Nor are gold clause contracts "inconsistent with the declared policy of Congress to maintain at all times the equal power of every dollar, coined or issued by the United States, in the markets and in the payment of debts."

This policy is the policy of having every dollar which is authorized by law, and is in circulation, on a parity with every other dollar that is authorized by law and is in circulation at the same time. Parity in the payment of debts is established by legal tender laws. Parity in the markets is maintained by redemption, convertibility, and acceptance of the circulating money by the Government in payment of duties and imposts. But parity means equality between dollars circulating at the same time.

Since the establishment of the new gold dollar, Congress has maintained all circulating dollars on a parity with the new gold dollar. Gold clause contracts have not obstructed this in any way. All the dollars now circulating have an equal power to pay gold clause contracts. The same number of new dollars is required to pay a gold bond today, no matter what kind of new dollars may be used. A law which provides for paying a bond with a less number of the new dollars than the bond itself requires, simply impairs the obligation of the bond.

The policy of maintaining the equal power of every dollar in the markets and in the payment of debts does not mean that the policy of Congress is to control the " purchasing power of the dollar "; the policy involves only the relation of circulating dollars to each other. Whatever the dollar, its purchasing power varies, and must vary. If Congress had authority to regulate the purchasing power of money, it could fix all prices and all wages without limit.

The making of agreements to pay in gold coin of the standard established by the United States, or its equivalent in value, could not have been against public policy when these contracts were made; nor was the existence of those contracts against public policy on June 5, 1933, when the Joint Resolution was passed. No change in conditions, no emergency, could make existing contracts, which use the standard of value provided by law as their basis, against public policy.

No conditions could ever arise which would make it public policy for a great nation to deny the binding force of its own obligations, lawfully issued under a paramount power and validly outstanding. Conditions might arise which would compel an honorable nation to admit, after every possible effort to meet its obligations, that it could not do so. But what conditions could justify an announcement by a sovereign nation that its promise to pay back the equivalent of what it had borrowed was a promise it would not keep and that it would not do what it had agreed to do?

Under our dual system of government, no conditions could ever arise which would make it federal public policy to change the contracts, impair the credit and restrict the borrowing power of the States.

Nor can conditions ever arise which will make it a matter of public policy to impair a whole class of valid private money obligations, by whomsoever owed.

All these inconsistencies in the Joint Resolution are due to distorting the scope of the " power to coin money, regulate the value thereof." The true scope of that power is to establish a " suitable medium of exchange " and a " sound and uniform currency," which neither requires nor permits the impairment of a particular class of contracts.

Although Congress does have the power to issue paper money as well and to make it legal tender, it does not derive that authority from the coinage power. *Juilliard v. Greenman*, 110 U. S. 421, 448. " Regulate " means to " fix " and change from time to time. " Value " means " monetary value," not purchasing power in a particular transaction or power to discharge a particular class of debts. *Fox* v. *Ohio*, 5 How. 410, 433.

The full scope of the so-called money power was stated in *Veazie Bank* v. *Fenno,* 8 Wall. 533, 549, in which Chief Justice Chase said that the Congress could "satisfy the wants of the community in respect of a circulating medium" and "secure a sound and uniform currency."

The power to issue paper money and to make it legal tender is primarily an incident of the borrowing power. *Knox* v. *Lee,* 12 Wall. 457; *Juilliard* v. *Greenman,* 110 U. S. 421.

The impairment of the real value of money contracts does not have any tendency whatever to provide such a "sound and uniform currency."

The power to "coin money, regulate the value thereof" is a very different thing from a power to regulate money contracts. Money is a medium of exchange, a mere instrument for use in commerce. Money contracts are property created through the use of the medium. The devaluation of the dollar is authorized because Congress has control over the medium itself. One result of a devaluation is that it impairs all outstanding contracts made in a fixed number of dollars, simply. But that does not mean that all contracts must be made in a fixed number of dollars, simply; nor does it mean that Congress has the power to eliminate from money contracts any clause providing a standard of value. The scope of the power is over the medium of exchange, not over contracts made in the medium.

If the Joint Resolution is sustained, it means, and must mean, that no one, neither the Government itself, States, municipalities, nor private persons, can make a money contract according to any fixed standard of value, even if established by law, and lawfully provide therein that the contract shall be performed in the same fixed standard of value in which it was made; it means, and must mean, that Congress has power at all times to impair or destroy at will all money contracts.

This is not only contrary to this Court's decisions in *Bronson* v. *Rodes, supra,* and in the long line of gold clause cases that followed it, but it is inconsistent with the whole idea of any fixed standard at all. It is an appropriate function of government to provide a standard of value as an aid to commerce; for a standard of value is indispensable to business prosperity and to the maintenance of regular and profitable trade and commerce. *United States* v. *Marigold,* 9 How. 559, 566.

Obviously, the object, purpose and effect of this Joint Resolution are not to coin money or regulate the value thereof, nor to do anything which the Constitution authorizes Congress to do. On the contrary, it is a plain, unqualified and direct attempt to violate the obligations of contracts which the Government itself made with authority of Congress in the exercise of its borrowing power; to encroach upon the sovereign power of the States by interfering with their power to borrow money on whatever terms they choose to make, by changing the terms of the contracts which they have made in borrowing money, by impairing their credit, and by interfering with and hindering their future financing; and to take the property of one class of persons and give it to another class without compensation and without due process of law. It is not a case where legislation passed by Congress within its constitutional powers incidentally affects private rights. It is a case where Congress undertakes directly and solely to legislate about contracts, to change their terms and impair their value. See *Osborn* v. *Nicholson,* 13 Wall. 654, 662.

To provide that these bonds can be discharged upon payment of the nominal amount in any kind of dollars, whatever their gold value, is to take the property of one private person and give it to another private person.

The Fifth Amendment protects the integrity of every contract, "whether the obligor be a private individual, a municipality, a State, or the United States." *Lynch* v. *United States,* 292 U. S. 571, 579.

We have said nothing about Congress having no powers except the powers the people expressly gave it in the Constitution and the powers implied from the powers expressly granted.　We have said little or nothing about the reluctance of the people, because of their jealousy for their personal liberty and their apprehensions for the security of their private property, to grant to Congress the limited powers they finally did grant, and then only upon conditions which brought about the prompt adoption of the first ten Amendments.　These and other kindred facts, such as the Tenth Amendment, which are fundamental and are at the threshold of every discussion relating to constitutional power, are so familiar to this Court that we do not know of anything we could say on any one of them that might help a decision of this case.

The security of private property is one of the chief concerns of the Constitution.　No person shall be deprived of his property without due process of law, nor shall private property be taken for public use without just compensation.　And yet our opponents here ask the Court to sustain the validity of a Resolution of Congress, the sole object, purpose and direct effect of which is to deprive persons of their property without due process of law and to take private property for private, not public, use without any compensation.　Surely this cannot be done if the Government is a government of limited powers and the language of the Constitution means what it so plainly says.

Mr. Edwin S. S. Sunderland filed a brief on behalf of the Guaranty Trust Co. et al., Trustees under the First and Refunding Mortgage of Missouri Pacific R. Co., interveners.

By leave of Court, briefs of *amici curiae* were filed by *Messrs. H. W. O'Melveny, Walter K. Tuller,* and *Louis W. Myers,* and by *Mr. Paul Bakewell, Jr.,* in support of the proposition that the Joint Resolution of June 5, 1933, is unconstitutional and void.

NORMAN *v.* B. & O. R. CO.   291

MR. CHIEF JUSTICE HUGHES delivered the opinion of the Court.

These cases present the question of the validity of the Joint Resolution of the Congress, of June 5, 1933, with respect to the " gold clauses " of private contracts for the payment of money. 48 Stat. 112.

This Resolution, the text of which is set forth in the margin,[1] declares that " every provision contained in or

---

[1] " JOINT RESOLUTION.

" To assure uniform value to the coins and currencies of the United States.

" Whereas the holding of or dealing in gold affect the public interest, and are therefore subject to proper regulation and restriction; and

" Whereas the existing emergency has disclosed that provisions of obligations which purport to give the obligee a right to require payment in gold or a particular kind of coin or currency of the United States, or in an amount in money of the United States measured thereby, obstruct the power of the Congress to regulate the value of the money of the United States, and are inconsistent with the declared policy of the Congress to maintain at all times the equal power of every dollar, coined or issued by the United States, in the markets and in the payment of debts.   Now, therefore, be it

" *Resolved by the Senate and House of Representatives of the United States of America in Congress assembled,* That (a) every provision contained in or made with respect to any obligation which purports to give the obligee a right to require payment in gold or a particular kind of coin or currency, or in an amount in money of the United States measured thereby, is declared to be against public policy; and no such provision shall be contained in or made with respect to any obligation hereafter incurred.   Every obligation, heretofore or hereafter incurred, whether or not any such provision is contained therein or made with respect thereto, shall be discharged upon payment, dollar for dollar, in any coin or currency which at the time of payment is legal tender for public and private debts.   Any such provision contained in any law authorizing obligations to be issued by or under authority of the United States, is hereby repealed, but the repeal of any such provision shall not invalidate any other provision or authority contained in such law.

made with respect to any obligation which purports to give the obligee a right to require payment in gold or a particular kind of coin or currency, or in an amount in money of the United States measured thereby" is "against public policy." Such provisions in obligations thereafter incurred are prohibited. The Resolution provides that "Every obligation, heretofore or hereafter incurred, whether or not any such provision is contained therein or made with respect thereto, shall be discharged upon payment, dollar for dollar, in any coin or currency which at the time of payment is legal tender for public and private debts."

In No. 270, the suit was brought upon a coupon of a bond made by the Baltimore and Ohio Railroad Company under date of February 1, 1930, for the payment of $1,000 on February 1, 1960, and interest from date at the rate

---

"(b) As used in this resolution, the term 'obligation' means an obligation (including every obligation of and to the United States, excepting currency) payable in money of the United States; and the term 'coin or currency' means coin or currency of the United States, including Federal Reserve notes and circulating notes of Federal Reserve banks and national banking associations.

"Sec. 2. The last sentence of paragraph (1) of subsection (b) of section 43 of the Act entitled 'An Act to relieve the existing national economic emergency by increasing agricultural purchasing power, to raise revenue for extraordinary expenses incurred by reason of such emergency, to provide emergency relief with respect to agricultural indebtedness, to provide for the orderly liquidation of joint-stock land banks, and for other purposes,' approved May 12, 1933, is amended to read as follows:

"'All coins and currencies of the United States (including Federal Reserve notes and circulating notes of Federal Reserve banks and national banking associations) heretofore or hereafter coined or issued, shall be legal tender for all debts, public and private, public charges, taxes, duties, and dues, except that gold coins, when below the standard weight and limit of tolerance provided by law for the single piece, shall be legal tender only at valuation in proportion to their actual weight.'

"Approved, June 5, 1933, 4:40 p. m."

of 4½ per cent. per annum, payable semi-annually. The bond provided that the payment of principal and interest "will be made . . . in gold coin of the United States of America of or equal to the standard of weight and fineness existing on February 1, 1930." The coupon in suit, for $22.50 was payable on February 1, 1934. The complaint alleged that on February 1, 1930, the standard weight and fineness of a gold dollar of the United States as a unit of value "was fixed to consist of twenty-five and eight-tenths grains of gold, nine-tenths fine," pursuant to the Act of Congress of March 14, 1900 (31 Stat. 45); and that by the Act of Congress known as the "Gold Reserve Act of 1934" (January 30, 1934, 48 Stat. 337), and by the order of the President under that Act, the standard unit of value of a gold dollar of the United States " was fixed to consist of fifteen and five-twenty-firsts grains of gold, nine-tenths fine," from and after January 31, 1934. On presentation of the coupon, defendant refused to pay the amount in gold, or the equivalent of gold in legal tender of the United States which was alleged to be, on February 1, 1934, according to the standard of weight and fineness existing on February 1, 1930, the sum of $38.10, and plaintiff demanded judgment for that amount.

Defendant answered that by Acts of Congress, and, in particular, by the Joint Resolution of June 5, 1933, defendant had been prevented from making payment in gold coin "or otherwise than dollar for dollar, in coin or currency of the United States (other than gold coin and gold certificates)" which at the time of payment constituted legal tender. Plaintiff, challenging the validity of the Joint Resolution under the Fifth and Tenth Amendments, and Article I, § 1, of the Constitution of the United States, moved to strike the defense. The motion was denied. Judgment was entered for plaintiff for $22.50, the face of the coupon, and was affirmed upon appeal. The Court of Appeals of the State considered the federal question and

decided that the Joint Resolution was valid. 265 N. Y.
37; 191 N. E. 726. This Court granted a writ of certiorari, October 8, 1934.

In Nos. 471 and 472, the question arose with respect to
an issue of bonds, dated May 1, 1903, of the St. Louis,
Iron Mountain & Southern Railway Company, payable
May 1, 1933. The bonds severally provided for the payment of " One Thousand Dollars gold coin of the United
States of the present standard of weight and fineness,"
with interest from date at the rate of four per cent. per
annum, payable " in like gold coin semi-annually." In
1917, Missouri Pacific Railroad Company acquired the
property of the obligor subject to the mortgage securing
the bonds. In March, 1933, the United States District
Court, Eastern District of Missouri, approved a petition
filed by the latter company under § 77 of the Bankruptcy
Act. In the following December, the trustees under the
mortgage asked leave to intervene, seeking to have the
income of the property applied against the mortgage debt
and alleging that the debt was payable " in gold coin of
the United States of the standard of weight and fineness
prevailing on May 1, 1903." Later, the Reconstruction
Finance Corporation and the United States, as creditors
of the debtor, filed a joint petition for leave to intervene,
in which they denied the validity of the gold clause contained in the mortgage and bonds. Leave to intervene
specially was granted to each applicant on April 5, 1934,
and answers were filed. On the hearing, the District
Court decided that the Joint Resolution of June 5, 1933,
was constitutional and that the trustees were entitled, in
payment of the principal of each bond, to $1,000 in money
constituting legal tender. Decree was entered accordingly and the trustees (respondents here) took two appeals to the United States Circuit Court of Appeals.[2]

---

[2] One appeal was allowed by the District Judge and the other by
the Circuit Court of Appeals.

NORMAN *v.* B. & O. R. CO. 295

While these appeals were pending, this Court granted writs of certiorari, November 5, 1934.

The Joint Resolution of June 5, 1933, was one of a series of measures relating to the currency. These measures disclose not only the purposes of the Congress but also the situations which existed at the time the Joint Resolution was adopted and when the payments under the " gold clauses " were sought. On March 6, 1933, the President, stating that there had been " heavy and unwarranted withdrawals of gold and currency from our banking institutions for the purpose of hoarding" and " extensive speculative activity abroad in foreign exchange " which had resulted " in severe drains on the Nation's stocks of gold," and reciting the authority conferred by § 5 (b) of the Act of October 6, 1917 (40 Stat. 411), declared " a bank holiday " until March 9, 1933. On the same date, the Secretary of the Treasury, with the President's approval, issued instructions to the Treasurer of the United States to make payments in gold in any form only under license issued by the Secretary.

On March 9, 1933, the Congress passed the Emergency Banking Act. 48 Stat. 1. All orders issued by the President or the Secretary of the Treasury since March 4, 1933, under the authority conferred by § 5 (b) of the Act of October 6, 1917, were confirmed. That section was amended so as to provide that during any period of national emergency declared by the President, he might " investigate, regulate or prohibit," by means of licenses or otherwise, " any transactions in foreign exchange, transfers of credit between or payments by banking institutions as defined by the President, and export, hoarding, melting, or earmarking of gold or silver coin or bullion or currency, by any person within the United States or any place subject to the jurisdiction thereof." The Act also amended § 11 of the Federal Reserve Act (39 Stat. 752) so as to authorize the Secretary of the Treasury to require all persons to deliver to the Treasurer of the United States " any or all gold coin, gold bullion, and gold certificates " owned by them, and that the Secretary should pay therefor " an equivalent amount of any other form of coin or currency coined or issued under the laws of the United States." By Executive Order of March 10, 1933, the President authorized banks to be reopened, as stated, but prohibited the removal from the United States, or any place subject to its jurisdiction, of " any gold coin, gold bullion, or gold certificates, except in accordance with regulations prescribed by or under license issued by the Secretary of the Treasury." By further Executive Order of April 5, 1933, forbidding hoarding, all persons were required to deliver, on or before May 1, 1933, to stated banks " all gold coin, gold bullion and gold certificates," with certain exceptions, the holder to receive " an equivalent amount of any other form of coin or currency coined or issued under the laws of the United States." Another Order of April 20, 1933, contained further requirements with respect to the acquisition and export of gold and to transactions in foreign exchange.

By § 43 of the Agricultural Adjustment Act of May 12, 1933 (48 Stat. 51), it was provided that the President should have authority, upon the making of prescribed findings and in the circumstances stated, "to fix the weight of the gold dollar in grains nine tenths fine and also to fix the weight of the silver dollar in grains nine tenths fine at a definite fixed ratio in relation to the gold dollar at such amounts as he finds necessary from his investigation to stabilize domestic prices or to protect the foreign commerce against the adverse effect of depreciated foreign currencies," and it was further provided that the "gold dollar, the weight of which is so fixed, shall be the standard unit of value," and that "all forms of money shall be maintained at a parity with this standard," but that "in no event shall the weight of the gold dollar be fixed so as to reduce its present weight by more than 50 per centum."

Then followed the Joint Resolution of June 5, 1933. There were further Executive Orders of August 28 and 29, 1933, October 25, 1933, and January 12 and 15, 1934, relating to the hoarding and export of gold coin, gold bullion and gold certificates, to the sale and export of gold recovered from natural deposits, and to transactions in foreign exchange, and orders of the Secretary of the Treasury, approved by the President, on December 28, 1933, and January 15, 1934, for the delivery of gold coin, gold bullion and gold certificates to the United States Treasury.

On January 30, 1934, the Congress passed the "Gold Reserve Act of 1934" (48 Stat. 337) which, by § 13, ratified and confirmed all the actions, regulations and orders taken or made by the President and the Secretary of the Treasury under the Act of March 9, 1933, or under § 43 of the Act of May 12, 1933, and, by § 12, with respect to the authority of the President to fix the weight of the gold dollar, provided that it should not be fixed "in any event at more than 60 per centum of its present weight." On January 31, 1934, the President issued his proclamation declaring that he fixed " the weight of the gold dollar to be 15 5/21 grains nine tenths fine," from and after that date.

We have not attempted to summarize all the provisions of these measures. We are not concerned with their wisdom. The question before the Court is one of power, not of policy. And that question touches the validity of these measures at but a single point, that is, in relation to the Joint Resolution denying effect to "gold clauses" in existing contracts. The Resolution must, however, be considered in its legislative setting and in the light of other measures *in pari materia.*

First. The interpretation of the gold clauses in suit. In the case of the *Baltimore and Ohio Railroad Company,* the obligor considers the obligation to be one " for the payment of money and not for the delivery of a specified number of grains or ounces of gold"; that it is an obligation payable in money of the United States and not less so because payment is to be made " in a particular kind of money "; that it is not a " commodity contract " which could be discharged by " tender of bullion." At the same time, the obligor contends that, while the Joint Resolution is constitutional in either event, the clause is a " gold coin " and not a " gold value " clause; that is, it does not imply " a payment in the ' equivalent ' of gold in case performance by payment in gold coin is impossible." The parties, runs the argument, intended that the instrument should be negotiable and hence it should not be regarded as one " for the payment of an indeterminate sum ascertainable only at date of payment." And in the reference to the standard of weight and fineness, the words " equal to " are said to be synonymous with " of."

In the case of the bonds of the *St. Louis, Iron Mountain & Southern Railway Company,* the Government urges that by providing for payment in gold coin the parties showed an intention " to protect against depreciation of one kind of money as compared with another, as for example, paper money compared with gold, or silver compared with gold "; and, by providing that the gold coin should be of a particular standard, they attempted " to assure against payment in coin of lesser gold content." The clause, it is said, " does not reveal an intention to protect against a situation where gold coin no longer circulates and all forms of money are maintained in the United States at a parity with each other"; apparently, " the parties did not anticipate the existence of conditions making it impossible and illegal to procure gold coin with which to meet the obligations." In view of that impossibility, asserted to exist both in fact and in law, the

Government contends that " the present debtor would be excused, in an action on the bonds, from the obligation to pay in gold coin," but, " as only one term of the promise in the gold clause is impossible to perform and illegal," the remainder of the obligation should stand and thus the obligation " becomes one to pay the stated number of dollars."

The bondholder in the first case, and the trustees of the mortgage in the second case, oppose such an interpretation of the gold clauses as inadequate and unreasonable. Against the contention that the agreement was to pay in gold coin if that were possible, and not otherwise, they insist that it is beyond dispute that the gold clauses were used for the very purpose of guarding against a depreciated currency. It is pointed out that the words " gold coin of the *present* standard " show that the parties contemplated that when the time came to pay there might be gold dollars of a new standard, and, if so, that " gold coin of the present standard " would pass from circulation; and it is taken to be admitted, by the Government's argument, that if gold coins of a lesser standard were tendered, they would not have to be accepted unless they were tendered in sufficient amount to make up the " gold value " for which, it is said, the contract called. It is insisted that the words of the gold clause clearly show an intent " to establish a measure or standard of value of the money to be paid if the particular kind of money specified in the clause should not be in circulation at the time of payment." To deny the right of the bondholders to the equivalent of the gold coin promised is said to be not a construction of the gold clause but its nullification.[3]

---

[3] As illustrating the use of such clauses as affording a standard or measure of value, counsel refer to Article 262 of the Treaty of Versailles with respect to the monetary obligations of Germany, which were made payable in gold coins of several countries, with the stated

The decisions of this Court relating to clauses for payment in gold did not deal with situations corresponding to those now presented. *Bronson* v. *Rodes,* 7 Wall. 229; *Butler* v. *Horwitz,* 7 Wall. 258; *Dewing* v. *Sears,* 11 Wall. 379; *Trebilcock* v. *Wilson,* 12 Wall. 687; *Thompson* v. *Butler,* 95 U. S. 694; *Gregory* v. *Morris,* 96 U. S. 619. See, also, *The Vaughan and Telegraph,* 14 Wall. 258; *The Emily Souder,* 17 Wall. 666. The rulings, upholding gold clauses and determining their effect, were made when gold was still in circulation and no act of the Congress prohibiting the enforcement of such clauses had been passed. In *Bronson* v. *Rodes, supra,* p. 251, the Court held that the legal tender acts of 1862 and 1863, apart from any question of their constitutionality, had not repealed or modified the laws for the coinage of gold and silver or the statutory provisions which made those coins a legal tender in all payments. It followed, said the Court, that " there were two descriptions of money in use at the time the tender under consideration was made, both authorized by law, and both made legal tender in payments. The statute denomination of both descriptions was dollars; but they were essentially unlike in nature." Accordingly, the contract of the parties for payment in one sort of dollars, which was still in lawful circulation, was sustained. The case of *Trebilcock* v. *Wilson, supra,* was decided shortly after the legal tender acts had been held valid. The Court again concluded (pp. 695, 696) that those acts applied only to debts which were payable

---

purpose that the gold coins mentioned " shall be defined as being of the weight and fineness of gold as enacted by law on January 1, 1914." Reference is also made to the construction of the gold clause in the bonds before the House of Lords in *Feist, appellant, and Société Intercommunale Belge d'Electricité, respondents,* L. R. (1934) A. C. 161, 173, and to the decisions of the Permanent Court of International Justice in the cases of the Serbian and Brazilian loans (Publications of the Permanent Court of International Justice, Series A, Nos. 20/21) where the bonds provided for payment in gold francs.

in money generally, and that there were " according to that decision, two kinds of money, essentially different in their nature, but equally lawful." In that view, said the Court, " contracts payable in either, or for the possession of either, must be equally lawful, and, if lawful, must be equally capable of enforcement."

With respect to the interpretation of the clauses then under consideration, the Court observed, in *Bronson* v. *Rodes, supra,* p. 250, that a contract to pay a certain number of dollars in gold or silver coins was, in legal import, nothing else than an agreement to deliver a certain weight of standard gold, to be ascertained by a count of coins, each of which is certified to contain a definite proportion of that weight." The Court thought that it was not distinguishable, in principle, " from a contract to deliver an equal weight of bullion of equal fineness." That observation was not necessary to the final conclusion. The decision went upon the assumption " that engagements to pay coined dollars may be regarded as ordinary contracts to pay money rather than as contracts to deliver certain weights of standard gold." *Id.* p. 251.

In *Trebilcock* v. *Wilson, supra,* where a note was payable " *in specie,*" the Court said (pp. 694, 695) that the provision did not " assimilate the note to an instrument in which the amount stated is payable in chattels; as, for example, to a contract to pay a specified sum in lumber, or in fruit, or in grain "; that the words " *in specie* " were " merely descriptive of the kind of dollars in which the note is payable, there being different kinds in circulation, recognized by law "; that they meant " that the designated number of dollars in the note shall be paid in so many gold or silver dollars of the coinage of the United States." And in *Thompson* v. *Butler, supra,* pp. 696, 697, the Court adverted to the statement made in *Bronson* v. *Rodes,* and concluded that " notwithstanding this, it is a contract to pay money, and none the less so because it designates for payment one of the two kinds of money which the law has made a legal tender in discharge of money obligations." Compare *Gregory* v. *Morris, supra.*

We are of the opinion that the gold clauses now before us were not contracts for payment in gold coin as a commodity, or in bullion, but were contracts for the payment of money. The bonds were severally for the payment of one thousand dollars. We also think that, fairly construed, these clauses were intended to afford a definite standard or measure of value, and thus to protect against a depreciation of the currency and against the discharge of the obligation by a payment of lesser value than that prescribed. When these contracts were made they were not repugnant to any action of the Congress. In order to determine whether effect may now be given to the intention of the parties in the face of the action taken by the Congress, or the contracts may be satisfied by the payment dollar for dollar, in legal tender, as the Congress has now prescribed, it is necessary to consider (1) the power of the Congress to establish a monetary system and the necessary implications of that power; (2) the power of the Congress to invalidate the provisions of existing contracts which interfere with the exercise of its constitutional authority; and (3) whether the clauses in question do constitute such an interference as to bring them within the range of that power.

Second. The power of the Congress to establish a monetary system. It is unnecessary to review the historic controversy as to the extent of this power, or again to go over the ground traversed by the Court in reaching the conclusion that the Congress may make treasury notes legal tender in payment of debts previously contracted, as well as of those subsequently contracted, whether that authority be exercised in course of war or in time of peace. *Knox* v. *Lee,* 12 Wall. 457; *Juilliard* v. *Greenman,* 110 U. S. 421. We need only consider certain postulates upon which that conclusion rested.

The Constitution grants to the Congress power " To coin money, regulate the value thereof, and of foreign coin." Art. I, § 8, par. 5. But the Court in the legal tender cases did not derive from that express grant alone the full authority of the Congress in relation to the currency. The Court found the source of that authority in all the related powers conferred upon the Congress and appropriate to achieve " the great objects for which the government was framed,"—" a national government, with sovereign powers." *McCulloch* v. *Maryland,* 4 Wheat. 316, 404–407; *Knox* v. *Lee, supra,* pp. 532, 536; *Juilliard* v. *Greenman, supra,* p. 438. The broad and comprehensive national authority over the subjects of revenue, finance and currency is derived from the aggregate of the powers granted to the Congress, embracing the powers to lay and collect taxes, to borrow money, to regulate commerce with foreign nations and among the several States, to coin money, regulate the value thereof, and of foreign coin, and fix the standards of weights and measures, and the added express power " to make all laws which shall be necessary and proper for carrying into execution " the other enumerated powers. *Juilliard* v. *Greenman, supra,* pp. 439, 440.

The Constitution " was designed to provide the same currency, having a uniform legal value in all the States." It was for that reason that the power to regulate the value of money was conferred upon the Federal government, while the same power, as well as the power to emit bills of credit, was withdrawn from the States. The States cannot declare what shall be money, or regulate its value. Whatever power there is over the currency is vested in the Congress. *Knox* v. *Lee, supra,* p. 545. Another postulate of the decision in that case is that the Congress has

power " to enact that the government's promises to pay
money shall be, for the time being, equivalent in value
to the representative of value determined by the coinage
acts, or to multiples thereof." *Id.,* p. 553. Or, as was
stated in the *Juilliard* case, *supra,* p. 447, the Congress is
empowered " to issue the obligations of the United States
in such form, and to impress upon them such qualities as
currency for the purchase of merchandise and the payment of debts, as accord with the usage of sovereign governments." The authority to impose requirements of
uniformity and parity is an essential feature of this control of the currency. The Congress is authorized to provide " a sound and uniform currency for the country,"
and to " secure the benefit of it to the people by appropriate legislation." *Veazie Bank* v. *Fenno,* 8 Wall. 533,
549.

Moreover, by virtue of this national power, there attach to the ownership of gold and silver those limitations which public policy may require by reason of their
quality as legal tender and as a medium of exchange.
Ling Su Fan v. *United States,* 218 U. S. 302, 310. Those
limitations arise from the fact that the law " gives to such
coinage a value which does not attach as a mere consequence of intrinsic value." Their quality as legal tender
is attributed by the law, aside from their bullion value.
Hence the power to coin money includes the power to forbid mutilation, melting and exportation of gold and silver
coin,—" to prevent its outflow from the country of its
origin." *Id.,* p. 311.

Dealing with the specific question as to the effect of the
legal tender acts upon contracts made before their passage, that is, those for the payment of money generally,
the Court, in the legal tender cases, recognized the possible consequences of such enactments in frustrating the
expected performance of contracts,—in rendering them
" fruitless or partially fruitless." The Court pointed out

that the exercise of the powers of Congress may affect
" apparent obligations " of contracts in many ways. The
Congress may pass bankruptcy acts. The Congress may
declare war, or, even in peace, pass non-intercourse acts,
or direct an embargo, which may operate seriously upon
existing contracts. And the Court reasoned that if the
legal tender acts " were justly chargeable with impairing
contract obligations, they would not, for that reason, be
forbidden, unless a different rule is to be applied to them
from that which has hitherto prevailed in the construction of other powers granted by the fundamental law."
The conclusion was that contracts must be understood as
having been made in reference to the possible exercise of
the rightful authority of the Government, and that no
obligation of a contract " can extend to the defeat " of
that authority. *Knox* v. *Lee, supra,* pp. 549–551.

On similar grounds, the Court dismissed the contention
under the Fifth Amendment forbidding the taking of
private property for public use without just compensation
or the deprivation of it without due process of law. That
provision, said the Court, referred only to a direct appropriation. A new tariff, an embargo, or a war, might
bring upon individuals great losses; might, indeed, render
valuable property almost valueless,—might destroy the
worth of contracts. "But whoever supposed" asked the
Court, "that, because of this, a tariff could not be changed
or a non-intercourse act, or embargo be enacted, or a war
be declared." The Court referred to the Act of June 28,
1834, by which a new regulation of the weight and value
of gold coin was adopted, and about six per cent. was taken
from the weight of each dollar. The effect of the measure
was that all creditors were subjected to a corresponding
loss, as the debts then due "became solvable with six per
cent. less gold than was required to pay them before."
But it had never been imagined that there was a taking
of private property without compensation or without due

process of law. The harshness of such legislation, or the
hardship it may cause, afforded no reason for considering
it to be unconstitutional. *Id.*, pp. 551, 552.

The question of the validity of the Joint Resolution of
June 5, 1933, must be determined in the light of these
settled principles.

*Third. The power of the Congress to invalidate the pro-
visions of existing contracts which interfere with the exercise of its constitutional authority.* The instant cases
involve contracts between private parties, but the question
necessarily relates as well to the contracts or obligations of
States and municipalities, or of their political subdivisions,
that is, to such engagements as are within the reach of the
applicable national power. The Government's own contracts—the obligations of the United States—are in a distinct category and demand separate consideration. See
Perry v. *United States,* decided this day, *post,* p. 330.

The contention is that the power of the Congress,
broadly sustained by the decisions we have cited in relation to private contracts for the payment of money generally, does not extend to the striking down of express
contracts for gold payments. The acts before the Court
in the legal tender cases, as we have seen, were not
deemed to go so far. Those acts left in circulation two
kinds of money, both lawful and available, and contracts
for payments in gold, one of these kinds, were not dis-
turbed. The Court did not decide that the Congress
did not have the constitutional power to invalidate existing contracts of that sort, if they stood in the way of the
execution of the policy of the Congress in relation to the
currency. Mr. Justice Bradley, in his concurring opinion,
expressed the view that the Congress had that power and
had exercised it. *Knox* v. *Lee, supra,* pp. 566, 567. And,
upon that ground, he dissented from the opinion of the
Court in *Trebilcock* v. *Wilson, supra,* p. 699, as to the

validity of contracts for payment *"in specie."*[4] It is significant that Mr. Justice Bradley, referring to this difference of opinion in the legal tender cases, remarked (in his concurring opinion) that " of course " the difference arose " from the different construction given to the legal tender acts." " I do not understand," he said, " the majority of the court to decide that an act so drawn as to embrace, in terms, contracts payable in specie, would not be constitutional. Such a decision would completely nullify the power claimed for the government. For it would be very easy, by the use of one or two additional words, to make all contracts payable in specie."

Here, the Congress has enacted an express interdiction. The argument against it does not rest upon the mere fact that the legislation may cause hardship or loss. Creditors who have not stipulated for gold payments may suffer equal hardship or loss with creditors who have so stipulated. The former, admittedly, have no constitutional grievance. And, while the latter may not suffer more, the point is pressed that their express stipulations for gold payments constitute property, and that creditors who have not such stipulations are without that property right. And the contestants urge that the Congress is seeking not to regulate the currency, but to regulate contracts, and thus has stepped beyond the power conferred.

This argument is in the teeth of another established principle. Contracts, however express, cannot fetter the constitutional authority of the Congress. Contracts may create rights of property, but when contracts deal with a subject matter which lies within the control of the Con-

---

[4] Mr. Justice Miller also dissented in *Trebilcock* v. *Wilson*, 12 Wall., pp. 699, 700, upon the ground " that a contract for gold dollars, in terms, was in no respect different, in legal effect, from a contract for dollars without the qualifying words, specie, or gold, and that the legal tender statutes had, therefore, the same effect in both cases."

gress, they have a congenital infirmity. Parties cannot remove their transactions from the reach of dominant constitutional power by making contracts about them. See *Hudson Water Co.* v. *McCarter,* 209 U. S. 349, 357.

This principle has familiar illustration in the exercise of the power to regulate commerce. If shippers and carriers stipulate for specified rates, although the rates may be lawful when the contracts are made, if Congress through the Interstate Commerce Commission exercises its authority and prescribes different rates, the latter control and override inconsistent stipulations in contracts previously made. This is so, even if the contract be a charter granted by a State and limiting rates, or a contract between municipalities and carriers. *New York* v. *United States,* 257 U. S. 591, 600, 601; *United States* v. *Village of Hubbard,* 266 U. S. 474, 477, *note.* See, also, *Armour Packing Co.* v. *United States,* 209 U. S. 56, 80–82; *Union Dry Goods Co.* v. *Georgia Public Service Corp.,* 248 U. S. 372, 375.

In *Addyston Pipe & Steel Co.* v. *United States,* 175 U. S. 211, 229, 230, the Court raised the pertinent question,— if certain kinds of private contracts directly limit or restrain, and hence regulate, interstate commerce, why should not the power of Congress reach such contracts equally with legislation of a State to the same effect? "What sound reason," said the Court, "can be given why Congress should have the power to interfere in the case of the State, and yet have none in the case of the individual? Commerce is the important subject of consideration, and anything which directly obstructs and thus regulates that commerce which is carried on among the States, whether it is state legislation or private contracts between individuals or corporations, should be subject to the power of Congress in the regulation of that commerce."

Applying that principle, the Court held that a contract, valid when made (in 1871) for the giving of a free pass by an interstate carrier, in consideration of a release of a claim for damages, could not be enforced after the Congress had passed the Act of June 29, 1906, 34 Stat. 584. *Louisville & Nashville R. Co.* v. *Mottley,* 219 U. S. 467.[5] Quoting the statement of the general principle in the legal tender cases, the Court decided that the agreement must necessarily be regarded as having been made subject to the possibility that, at some future time, the Congress " might so exert its whole constitutional power in regulating interstate commerce as to render that agreement unenforceable or to impair its value." The Court considered it inconceivable that the exercise of such power " may be hampered or restricted to any extent by contracts previously made between individuals or corporations." " The framers of the Constitution never intended any such state of things to exist." *Id.,* p. 482. Accordingly, it has been " authoritatively settled " by decisions of this Court that no previous contracts or combinations can prevent the application of the Anti-Trust Acts to compel the discontinuance of combinations declared to be illegal. *Addyston Pipe & Steel Co.* v. *United States, supra; United States* v. *Southern Pacific Co.,* 259 U. S. 214, 234, 235. See, also, *Calhoun* v. *Massie,* 253 U. S. 170, 176; *Omnia Commercial Co.* v. *United States,* 261 U. S. 502, 509; *Stephenson* v. *Binford,* 287 U. S. 251, 276.

The principle is not limited to the incidental effect of the exercise by the Congress of its constitutional authority. There is no constitutional ground for denying to the Congress the power expressly to prohibit and invalidate contracts although previously made, and valid when made,

---

[5] Compare *New York Central & Hudson R. R. Co.* v. *Gray,* 239 U. S. 583; *Calhoun* v. *Massie,* 253 U. S. 170, 176.

when they interfere with the carrying out of the policy it
is free to adopt. The exercise of this power is illustrated
by the provision of § 5 of the Employers' Liability Act
of 1908 (35 Stat. 65, 66) relating to any contract the
purpose of which was to enable a common carrier to exempt itself from the liability which the Act created. Such
a stipulation the Act explicitly declared to be void. In
the *Second Employers' Liability Cases,* 223 U. S. 1, 52, the
Court decided that as the Congress possessed the power
to impose the liability, it also possessed the power "to
insure its efficacy by prohibiting any contract, rule, regulation or device in evasion of it." And this prohibition
the Court has held to be applicable to contracts made before the Act was passed. *Philadelphia, B. & W. R. Co.* v.
Schubert, 224 U. S. 603. In that case, the employee,
suing under the Act, was a member of the "Relief Fund"
of the railroad company under a contract of membership,
made in 1905, for the purpose of securing certain benefits.
The contract provided that an acceptance of those benefits
should operate as a release of claims, and the company
pleaded that acceptance as a bar to the action. The Court
held that the Employers' Liability Act supplied the gov-
erning rule and that the defense could not be sustained.
The power of the Congress in regulating interstate commerce was not fettered by the necessity of maintaining
existing arrangements and stipulations which would conflict with the execution of its policy. The reason is manifest. To subordinate the exercise of the Federal authority
to the continuing operation of previous contracts would
be to place to this extent the regulation of interstate commerce in the hands of private individuals and to withdraw
from the control of the Congress so much of the field as
they might choose by " prophetic discernment " to bring
within the range of their agreements. The Constitution
recognizes no such limitation. *Id.,* pp. 613, 614. See,

also, *United States* v. *Southern Pacific Co., supra; Sproles* v. *Binford,* 286 U. S. 374, 390, 391; *Radio Commission* v. *Nelson Brothers Co.* 289 U. S. 266, 282.

The same reasoning applies to the constitutional authority of the Congress to regulate the currency and to establish the monetary system of the country. If the gold clauses now before us interfere with the policy of the Congress in the exercise of that authority they cannot stand.

Fourth. The effect of the gold clauses in suit in relation to the monetary policy adopted by the Congress. Despite the wide range of the discussion at the bar and the earnestness with which the arguments against the validity of the Joint Resolution have been pressed, these contentions necessarily are brought, under the dominant principles to which we have referred, to a single and narrow point. That point is whether the gold clauses do constitute an actual interference with the monetary policy of the Congress in the light of its broad power to determine that policy. Whether they may be deemed to be such an interference depends upon an appraisement of economic conditions and upon determinations of questions of fact. With respect to those conditions and determinations, the Congress is entitled to its own judgment. We may inquire whether its action is arbitrary or capricious, that is, whether it has reasonable relation to a legitimate end. If it is an appropriate means to such an end, the decisions of the Congress as to the degree of the necessity for the adoption of that means, is final. *McCulloch* v. *Maryland, supra,* pp. 421, 423; *Juilliard* v. *Greenman, supra,* p. 450; *Stafford* v. *Wallace,* 258 U. S. 495, 521; *Everard's Breweries* v. *Day,* 265 U. S. 545, 559, 562.

The Committee on Banking and Currency of the House of Representatives stated in its report recommending favorable action upon the Joint Resolution (H. R. Rep. No. 169, 73d Cong., 1st Sess.) :

" The occasion for the declaration in the resolution that the gold clauses are contrary to public policy arises out of the experiences of the present emergency. These gold clauses render ineffective the power of the Government to create a currency and determine the value thereof. If the gold clause applied to a very limited number of contracts and security issues, it would be a matter of no particular consequence, but in this country virtually all obligations, almost as a matter of routine, contain the gold clause. In the light of this situation two phenomena which have developed during the present emergency make the enforcement of the gold clauses incompatible with the public interest. The first is the tendency which has developed internally to hoard gold; the second is the tendency for capital to leave the country. Under these circumstances no currency system, whether based upon gold or upon any other foundation, can meet the requirements of a situation in which many billions of dollars of securities are expressed in a particular form of the circulating medium, particularly when it is the medium upon which the entire credit and currency structure rests."

And the Joint Resolution itself recites the determination of the Congress in these words: [6]

" Whereas the existing emergency has disclosed that provisions of obligations which purport to give the obligee a right to require payment in gold or a particular kind of coin or currency of the United States, or in an amount in money of the United States measured thereby, obstruct the power of the Congress to regulate the value of the money of the United States, and are inconsistent with the

---

[6] See Note 1.

declared policy of the Congress to maintain at all times the equal power of every dollar, coined or issued by the United States, in the markets and in the payment of debts."

Can we say that this determination is so destitute of basis that the interdiction of the gold clauses must be deemed to be without any reasonable relation to the monetary policy adopted by the Congress?

The Congress in the exercise of its discretion was entitled to consider the volume of obligations with gold clauses, as that fact, as the report of the House Committee observed, obviously had a bearing upon the question whether their existence constituted a substantial obstruction to the congressional policy. The estimates submitted at the bar indicate that when the Joint Resolution was adopted there were outstanding seventy-five billion dollars or more of such obligations, the annual interest charges on which probably amounted to between three and four billion dollars. It is apparent that if these promises were to be taken literally, as calling for actual payment in gold coin, they would be directly opposed to the policy of Congress, as they would be calculated to increase the demand for gold, to encourage hoarding, and to stimulate attempts at exportation of gold coin. If there were no outstanding obligations with gold clauses, we suppose that no one would question the power of the Congress, in its control of the monetary system, to endeavor to conserve the gold resources of the Treasury, to insure its command of gold in order to protect and increase its reserves, and to prohibit the exportation of gold coin or its use for any purpose inconsistent with the needs of the Treasury. See *Ling Su Fan* v. *United States, supra.* And if the Congress would have that power in the absence of gold clauses, principles beyond dispute compel the conclusion that private parties, or States or municipalities, by making such contracts could not prevent or embarrass its exercise. In that view of the import of the gold clauses, their obstructive character is clear.

But, if the clauses are treated as "gold value" clauses, that is, as intended to set up a measure or standard of value if gold coin is not available, we think they are still hostile to the policy of the Congress and hence subject to prohibition. It is true that when the Joint Resolution was adopted on June 5, 1933, while gold coin had largely been withdrawn from circulation and the Treasury had declared that "gold is not now paid, nor is it available for payment, upon public or private debts," [7] the dollar had not yet been devalued. But devaluation was in prospect and a uniform currency was intended.[8] Section 43 of the Act of May 12, 1933 (48 Stat. 51), provided that the President should have authority, on certain conditions, to fix the weight of the gold dollar as stated, and that its weight as so fixed should be "the standard unit of value" with which all forms of money should be maintained "at a parity." The weight of the gold dollar was not to be reduced by more than 50 per centum. The Gold Reserve Act of 1934 (January 30, 1934, 48 Stat. 337), provided that the President should not fix the weight of

---

[7] Treasury Statement of May 26, 1933.

[8] The Senate Committee on Banking and Currency, in its Report of May 27, 1933, stated: "By the Emergency Banking Act and the existing Executive Orders gold is not now paid, or obtainable for payment, on obligations public or private. By the Thomas amendment currency was intended to be made legal tender for all debts. However, due to the language used doubt has arisen whether it has been made legal tender for payments on gold clause obligations, public and private. This doubt should be removed. These gold clauses interfere with the power of Congress to regulate the value of the money of the United States and the enforcement of them would be inconsistent with existing legislative policy." Sen. Rep. No. 99, 73d Cong., 1st sess.

the gold dollar at more than 60 per cent. of its present weight. The order of the President of January 31, 1934, fixed the weight of the gold dollar at 15 5/21 grains nine-tenths fine as against the former standard of 25 8/10 grains nine-tenths fine. If the gold clauses interfered with the congressional policy and hence could be invalidated, there appears to be no constitutional objection to that action by the Congress in anticipation of the determination of the value of the currency. And the questions now before us must be determined in the light of that action.

The devaluation of the dollar placed the domestic economy upon a new basis. In the currency as thus provided, States and municipalities must receive their taxes; railroads, their rates and fares; public utilities, their charges for services. The income out of which they must meet their obligations is determined by the new standard. Yet, according to the contentions before us, while that income is thus controlled by law, their indebtedness on their " gold bonds " must be met by an amount of currency determined by the former gold standard. Their receipts, in this view, would be fixed on one basis; their interest charges, and the principal of their obligations, on another. It is common knowledge that the bonds issued by these obligors have generally contained gold clauses, and presumably they account for a large part of the outstanding obligations of that sort. It is also common knowledge that a similar situation exists with respect to numerous industrial corporations that have issued their " gold bonds " and must now receive payments for their products in the existing currency. It requires no acute analysis or profound economic inquiry to disclose the dislocation of the domestic economy which would be caused by such a disparity of conditions in which, it is insisted, those debtors under gold clauses should be required to pay one dollar and sixty-nine cents in currency while respectively receiving their taxes, rates, charges and prices on the basis of one dollar of that currency.

We are not concerned with consequences, in the sense that consequences, however serious, may excuse an invasion of constitutional right. We are concerned with the constitutional power of the Congress over the monetary system of the country and its attempted frustration. Exercising that power, the Congress has undertaken to establish a uniform currency, and parity between kinds of currency, and to make that currency, dollar for dollar, legal tender for the payment of debts. In the light of abundant experience, the Congress was entitled to choose such a uniform monetary system, and to reject a dual system, with respect to all obligations within the range of the exercise of its constitutional authority. The contention that these gold clauses are valid contracts and cannot be struck down proceeds upon the assumption that private parties, and States and municipalities, may make and enforce contracts which may limit that authority. Dismissing that untenable assumption, the facts must be faced. We think that it is clearly shown that these clauses interefere with the exertion of the power granted to the Congress and certainly it is not established that the Congress arbitrarily or capriciously decided that such an interference existed.

The judgment and decree, severally under review, are affirmed.

No. 270.　Judgment affirmed.

Nos. 471 and 472.　Decree affirmed.

MR. JUSTICE MCREYNOLDS, MR. JUSTICE VAN DEVANTER, MR. JUSTICE SUTHERLAND, and MR. JUSTICE BUTLER dissent. See *post,* p. 361.

NORTZ *v.* UNITED STATES.   **317**

NORTZ *v.* UNITED STATES.*

CERTIFICATE FROM THE COURT OF CLAIMS.

No. 531. Argued January 10, 1935.—Decided February 18, 1935.

1. A demurrer to a petition in the Court of Claims admits facts well pleaded, but not allegations amounting to conclusions of law. P. 324.

2. A gold certificate certifying that there have been deposited in the Treasury of the United States a stated number of dollars payable to the bearer on demand, and which is legal tender for public and private debts, is not a warehouse receipt or a contract for a certain amount of gold as a commodity, but is currency. P. 326.

3. *Quaere,* Whether the issue of a gold certificate creates an express contract upon which the United States may be sued in the Court of Claims under Jud. Code, § 145. P. 327.

4. The Court of Claims cannot entertain a claim for nominal damages. P. 327.

5. Congress has complete authority over the currency system, including authority to provide that all gold bullion, gold coin, and gold certificates outstanding shall be taken over by the Government. P. 328.

6. Assuming that the holder of a gold certificate, who, prior to the devaluation of the dollar, was required under the Emergency Banking Act and Treasury orders to deliver the certificate to the Treasury, was entitled by its terms to receive the amount of the certificate in gold coin of the then existing standard of weight and fineness, it cannot be said that, in being obliged to accept payment, dollar for dollar, in legal tender currency not redeemable in gold, he suffered any actual loss, since, if the gold coin had in fact been paid him, he could not have held it or dealt in it (having no license) but would have been compelled to surrender it to the Treasury for the same number of currency dollars. P. 328.

7. In a suit in the Court of Claims for damages claimed to have been caused by refusal of the Government, on January 17, 1933, to pay a gold certificate in gold coin, and substitution of other currency, dollar for dollar, an allegation that gold was of a value of $33.43 per ounce necessarily involves a conclusion of law; since under applicable legislative requirements there was not on that

---

* See note, p. 240.

date a free market for gold in the United States or any market for the gold coin claimed, or any right for persons unlicensed to dispose of it abroad. P. 329.

Question answered " No."

RESPONSE to questions propounded by the Court of Claims arising out of a claim based on gold certificates.

Mr. Otto C. Sommerich opened the argument for the plaintiff; *Mr. Angus MacLean,* the Assistant Solicitor General, followed for the United States; and *Mr. Raymond T. Heilpern* closed for the plaintiff.

Summary of argument from the brief of *Messrs. Otto C. Sommerich, Raymond T. Heilpern,* and *Maxwell C. Katz,* for the plaintiff.

The gold certificates were express contracts of the United States in its corporate or proprietary capacity, whereby the Government agreed, upon presentation of the certificates, to redeem them in gold in the amount specified.

Since, under § 314, Title 31, U. S. C., the dollar consisted of 25.8 grains of gold, nine-tenths fine, it is apparent that plaintiff was entitled to receive, for each dollar of gold certificates tendered, 25.8 grains of gold, nine-tenths fine. *Bank of Boston* v. *United States,* 10 Ct. Cls. 519; aff'd, 96 U. S. 30; *State Nat. Bank of Boston* v. *United States,* 24 Ct. Cls. 488. It must be borne in mind that, at the time of the presentation of the certificates by petitioner, the gold content of the dollar had not been deflated and that § 314 was still in effect.

That both the Legislative and Executive branches of the Government deemed gold certificates to be the equivalent of gold, is clearly shown by the Emergency Banking Act of March 9, 1933, and the orders issued thereunder. Gold bullion, gold coin, and gold certificates are all classed in one group, and residents of this country were required to surrender them all. If Congress and the Executive Department had not assumed that the owner of the gold certificate had the contract right to demand in exchange a specified amount of gold, why did the defendant think it necessary to compel the citizen to surrender this gold certificate?

Under Jud. Code, § 145, the Court of Claims has jurisdiction of all claims founded upon any contract, express or implied, with the Government.

Congress could not, even in the emergency prevailing during 1933, by virtue of its plenary power to regulate the currency system of the United States, deprive plaintiff of his contract right to have his gold certificate redeemed in gold, without providing just compensation. *Lynch* v. *United States,* 292 U. S. 571; *Sinking Fund Cases,* 99 U. S. 700.

The Fifth Amendment operates, even in the great emergency created by war, to protect a citizen of this country from confiscation of his contract rights without just compensation. *Brooks-Scanlon Corp.* v. *United States,* 265 U. S. 106.

We do not deny that Congress had authority to compel all residents of this country to deliver to the Government all gold bullion, gold coins, and gold certificates in their possession. But it was not within the province of Congress to determine what should be just compensation, that being a judicial question.

The courts have uniformly held that the taking of property by the Government gives rise to an implied promise to pay the fair value thereof, to be determined judicially. *United States* v. *Pacific R. Co.,* 120 U. S. 227; *United States* v. *Great Falls Mfg. Co.,* 112 U. S. 645; *Langford* v. *United States,* 101 U. S. 341; *United States* v. *Russell,* 13 Wall. 623; *United States* v. *Lynah,* 188 U. S. 445; *Olson* v. *United States,* 292 U. S. 246.

That a contract calling for the payment of a specified sum in gold cannot be satisfied by the delivery merely of currency of a similar face amount, even though such currency has been legally declared by Congress to be legal tender, has been frequently held. *Bronson* v. *Rodes,* 7 Wall. 229; *Butler* v. *Horwitz,* 7 Wall. 258; *Bronson* v. *Kimpton,* 8 Wall. 444; *Trebilcock* v. *Wilson,* 12 Wall. 687; *Gregory* v. *Morris,* 96 U. S. 619.

The United States Government is not responsible for a consequential injury flowing from its lawful acts; but, in the case at bar, the legislation involved a definite repudiation by the Government of its existing agreement.

The question of the economic necessity for the banking and currency legislation passed by the last Congress is not involved in this suit.

The petition herein alleged that, on January 17, 1934, the date of plaintiff's tender, and for some time prior and subsequently thereto, an ounce of gold was of the value of at least $33.43. A statement in a pleading as to the value of an article is a statement of fact. *Prendergast* v. *N. Y. Telephone Co.,* 262 U. S. 43, 47. Therefore, by demurring to the petition, the Government has conceded the value of gold so stated. The truth of the allegation is, moreover, sustained by published records and transactions.

In October 1933, pursuant to the announced policy of the President, the Government purchased gold, both here and abroad, its purchases here, however, being confined to gold newly mined in the United States. Such purchases, beginning on October 25th, were made by the Reconstruction Finance Corporation, and later by the New York Federal Reserve Bank, at prices ranging between $33.36 an ounce on October 25, 1933, and $34.45 an ounce on January 19, 1934. The price paid by the Government on January 17, 1934, the date of plaintiff's tender, was $34.45. These statements are based upon the reports contained in the " Financial Chronicle."

Gold has an intrinsic value and is bought and sold in the world markets. It is patently absurd to contend that though gold in London, or any other place outside of the United States, and newly mined gold, has a value in excess of $30.00 an ounce, the gold in this country held by its residents is worth no more than $20.67 an ounce. Neither Legislative nor Executive fiat can accomplish such a feat.

The attempt to disregard the actual market price of gold and to fix an arbitrary value much lower, is an attempt on the part of the Government to repudiate its agreement and condemn property without payment of just compensation.

During the Great War the Government commandeered the total output of many factories manufacturing products needed for war purposes. Could it have made out a right to fix the prices it would pay for the things commandeered, by asserting that those things could not lawfully be sold to any other buyer and that the price offered by the Government was the sole price obtainable? Cf. *New River Collieries Co.* v. *United States,* 262 U. S. 341; *Olson* v. *United States,* 292 U. S. 246.

Summary of the brief for the United States; which bore the names of *Attorney General Cummings, Solicitor General Biggs, Assistant Solicitor General MacLean, Assistant Attorney General Sweeney,* and *Messrs. Alexander Holtzoff* and *Harry LeRoy Jones.*

Gold certificates, even if regarded as contracts, are not warehouse receipts for a specified quantity of gold, but are monetary obligations (12 Stat. 709, 711; Cong. Globe, 37th Congress, 3rd Session, Part 1, p. 458).

On January 17, 1934, when the plaintiff tendered his certificates, contractual obligations to pay a specified number of dollars could be lawfully liquidated by payment of the amount in any legal tender currency, and hence the defendant's obligation to the plaintiff, if contractual, has been fully satisfied. The Joint Resolution of June 5, 1933, made all coins and currencies of the United States legal tender for all debts, public and private. *Legal Tender*

Cases, 12 Wall. 457. *Bronson* v. *Rodes,* 7 Wall. 229, and similar cases are distinguishable.

The plaintiff has sustained no damage, since even if he had received gold coin on January 17, 1934, he would have been compelled to surrender it, in view of the Act of March 9, 1933, and the Order of the Secretary of the Treasury of December 28, 1933.

The plaintiff may not claim just compensation for a taking of private property, since his petition sets forth a cause of action on an express contract. In any event, he has already received just compensation, since if he had been paid gold coin, he could not have disposed of it for any greater sum.

The Emergency Banking Act of March 9, 1933, is not rendered invalid by the fact that Congress provides what compensation shall be paid for gold certificates delivered pursuant to its terms. *Monongahela Navigation Co.* v. *United States,* 148 U. S. 312, is inapplicable. The compensation provided and paid was just. Moreover, where the thing taken and the compensation given was money, it would have been inappropriate for Congress, which is empowered to regulate the value of money, not to have determined the amount to be paid.

The Government was exercising its undoubted sovereign power to retire one form of currency and issue another in place thereof, both being legal tender for the same amount. Whatever power there is over the currency is vested in Congress. If the power to declare what is money is not in Congress, it is annihilated. *Legal Tender Cases, supra.*

Abrogation of contract rights is not a taking of private property for public use. To frustrate a contract is not to appropriate it. *Omnia Commercial Co.* v. *U. S.,* 261 U. S. 502, 508, 513.

The Court of Claims has no jurisdiction, as gold certificates are money, or a medium of exchange, and do not constitute contracts of the United States in its corporate or proprietary capacity. *Ling Su Fan* v. *U. S.*, 218 U. S. 302, 310; *Horowitz* v. *U. S.*, 267 U. S. 458.

MR. CHIEF JUSTICE HUGHES delivered the opinion of the Court.

The facts certified by the Court of Claims may be thus summarized: Plaintiff brought suit as owner of gold certificates of the Treasury of the United States of the nominal amount of $106,300. He alleged that defendant, by these gold certificates and under the applicable acts of Congress, had certified that there had been deposited in the Treasury of the United States $106,300 in gold coin which would be paid to the claimant, as holder, upon demand; that at the time of the issue of these certificates, and to and including January 17, 1934, a dollar in gold consisted of 25.8 grains of gold, .9 fine; that claimant was entitled to receive from defendant one ounce of gold for each $20.67 of the gold certificates; that on January 17, 1934, he duly presented the certificates and demanded their redemption by the payment of gold coin to the extent above mentioned; that on that date, and for some time prior and subsequent thereto, an ounce of gold was of the value of at least $33.43, and that claimant was accordingly entitled to receive in redemption 5104.22 ounces of gold of the value of $170,634.07; that the demand was refused; that in view of the penalties imposed under the order of the Secretary of the Treasury, approved by the President, on January 15, 1934, supplementing the order of December 28, 1933, and the laws and regulations under which those orders were issued, which the claimant alleged were unconstitutional as constituting a deprivation of property without due process of law, claimant delivered the gold certificates to defendant under protest and received in exchange currency of the United States in the sum of $106,300 which was not redeemable in gold; and that in consequence claimant was damaged in the sum of $64,334.07, for which, with interest, judgment was demanded.

Defendant demurred to the petition upon the ground that it did not state a cause of action against the United States.

The questions certified by the Court are as follows:

"1. Is an owner of gold certificates of the United States, Series of 1928, not holding a Federal license to acquire or hold gold coins or gold certificates, who, on January 17, 1934, had surrendered his certificates to the Secretary of the Treasury of the United States under protest and had received therefor legal tender currency of equivalent face amount, entitled to receive from the United States a further sum inasmuch as the weight of a gold dollar was 25.8 grains, nine-tenths fine, and the market price thereof on January 17, 1934, was in excess of the currency so received?

"2. Is a gold certificate, Series of 1928, under the facts stated in question 1 an express contract of the United States in its corporate or proprietary capacity which will enable its owner and holder to bring suit thereon in the Court of Claims?

"3. Do the provisions of the Emergency Banking Act of March 9, 1933, and the Order of the Secretary of the Treasury dated December 28, 1933, requiring the plaintiff as owner of gold certificates as stated in question 1 to deliver the same to the Treasury of the United States in exchange for currency of an equivalent amount, not redeemable in gold, amount to a taking of property within the meaning of the Fifth Amendment to the Constitution of the United States?"

Defendant's demurrer, which admitted the facts well pleaded in the petition, did not admit allegations which amounted to conclusions of law in relation to the nature of the gold certificates or the legal effect of the legislation under which they were issued, held, or to be redeemed. *Dillon* v. *Barnard*, 21 Wall. 430, 437; *United States* v. *Ames*, 99 U. S. 35, 45; *Interstate Land Co.* v. *Maxwell Land Co.*, 139 U. S. 569, 577, 578; *Equitable Life Assurance Society* v. *Brown*, 213 U. S. 25, 43.

Gold certificates were authorized by § 5 of the Act of March 3, 1863 (12 Stat. 709, 711), which provided that the Secretary of the Treasury might receive " deposits of gold coin and bullion " and issue certificates therefor " in denominations of not less than twenty dollars each, corresponding with the denominations of the United States notes." The coin and bullion so deposited were to be retained in the treasury for the payment of the certificates on demand. It was further provided that " certificates representing coin in the treasury may be issued in payment of interest on the public debt, which certificates, together with those issued for coin and bullion deposited, shall not at any time exceed twenty per centum beyond the amount of coin and bullion in the treasury." See R. S., § 254; 31 U. S. C. 428. Section 12 of the Act of July 12, 1882 (22 Stat. 165) contained a further provision authorizing the Secretary of the Treasury " to receive deposits of gold coin " and to issue certificates therefor, also in denominations of dollars as stated. The Act of March 14, 1900 (31 Stat. 45) prescribed that the dollar " consisting of twenty-five and eight-tenths grains of gold nine-tenths fine, . . . shall be the standard unit of value, and all forms of money issued or coined by the United States shall be maintained at a parity of value with this standard, and it shall be the duty of the Secretary of the Treasury to maintain such parity." Section 6 of that Act also authorized the Secretary of the Treasury to receive deposits of gold coin and to issue gold certificates therefor, and provided that the coin so deposited should be held by the treasury for the payment of such certificates on demand and should be " used for no other purpose." And the latter clause appears in the amending Acts of March 4, 1907 (34 Stat. 1289) and of March 2, 1911 (36 Stat. 965). See 31 U. S. C. 429.

The Act of December 24, 1919 (41 Stat. 370) made gold certificates, payable to bearer on demand, "legal tender in payment of all debts and dues, public and private." And § 2 of the Joint Resolution of June 5, 1933 (48 Stat. 113), amending the Act of May 12, 1933 (48 Stat. 52) provided that "all coins and currencies of the United States . . . heretofore or hereafter coined or issued, shall be legal tender for all debts, public and private, public charges, taxes, duties and dues."

Gold certificates under this legislation were required to be issued in denominations of dollars and called for the payment of dollars.[1] These gold certificates were currency. They were not less so because the specified number of dollars were payable in gold coin, of the coinage of the United States. Being currency, and constituting legal tender, it is entirely inadmissible to regard the gold certificates as warehouse receipts.[2] They were not contracts

---

[1] The form of the gold certificates here in question is stated to be as follows:

" This certifies that there have been deposited in the Treasury of

THE UNITED STATES OF AMERICA
ONE THOUSAND DOLLARS

in gold coin payable to the bearer on demand.

" This certificate is a legal tender in the amount thereof in payment of all debts and dues public and private."

On the reverse side appear the following words:

" THE UNITED STATES OF AMERICA
ONE THOUSAND DOLLARS."

[2] The description of gold certificates in the reports of the Secretary of the Treasury, to which allusion was made in the argument at bar, could in no way alter their true legal characteristics. Reports for 1926, p. 80; 1930, pp. 29, 604, 607; 1933, p. 375.

NORTZ *v.* UNITED STATES. 327

for a certain quantity of gold as a commodity. They called for dollars, not bullion.

We may lay on one side the question whether the issue of currency of this description created an express contract upon which the United States has consented to be sued under the provisions of § 145 of the Judicial Code, 28 U. S. C. 250. Compare *Horowitz* v. *United States,* 267 U. S. 458, 461.[3] We may assume that plaintiff's petition permits an alternative view. Plaintiff urges as the gist of his contention that, by the Acts of Congress, and the orders thereunder, requiring the delivery of his gold certificates to the Treasury in exchange for currency not redeemable in gold, he has been deprived of his property, and that he is entitled to maintain this action to recover the just compensation secured to him by the Fifth Amendment. But, even in that view, the Court of Claims has no authority to entertain the action, if the claim is at best one for nominal damages. The Court of Claims " was not instituted to try such a case." *Grant* v. *United States,* 7 Wall. 331, 338; *Marion & R. V. Ry. Co.* v. *United States,* 270 U. S. 280, 282. Accordingly, we inquire whether the case which the plaintiff presents is one which would justify the recovery of actual damages.

By § 3 of the Emergency Banking Act of March 9, 1933 (48 Stat. 2), amending § 11 of the Federal Reserve Act (39 Stat. 752), the Secretary of the Treasury was authorized, whenever in his judgment it was necessary

---

[3] The point was not determined in *United States* v. *State Bank*, 96 U. S. 30, upon which plaintiff relies. The Court there decided that " where the money or property of an innocent person has gone into the coffers of the nation by means of a fraud to which its agent was a party, such money or property cannot be held by the United States against the claim of the wronged and injured party." The Court said that the basis of the liability was " an implied contract " by which the United States might well become bound in virtue of its corporate character. Its sovereignty was " in no wise involved."

" to protect the currency system of the United States,"
to require all persons " to pay and deliver to the treasurer
of the United States any or all gold coin, gold bullion,
and gold certificates " owned by them. Upon such delivery, the Secretary was to pay therefor " an equivalent
amount of any other form of coin or currency coined or
issued under the laws of the United States." Under that
statute, orders requiring such delivery, except as otherwise expressly provided, were issued by the Secretary on
December 28, 1933, and January 15, 1934. By the latter,
gold coin, gold bullion, and gold certificates were required
to be delivered to the treasurer of the United States on
or before January 17, 1934. It was on that date that
plaintiff made his demand for gold coin in redemption of
his certificates and delivered the certificates under protest. That compulsory delivery, he insists, constituted
the " taking of the contract " for which he demands compensation.

Plaintiff explicitly states his concurrence in the Government's contention that the Congress has complete authority to regulate the currency system of the country. He
does not deny that, in exercising that authority, the Congress had power " to appropriate unto the Government
outstanding gold bullion, gold coin and gold certificates."
Nor does he deny that the Congress had authority " to
compel all residents of this country to deliver unto the
Government all gold bullion, gold coins and gold certificates in their possession." These powers could not be
successfully challenged. *Knox* v. *Lee,* 12 Wall. 457;
Juilliard v. *Greenman,* 110 U. S. 421; *Ling Su Fan* v.
United States, 218 U. S. 302; *Norman* v. *Baltimore &
Ohio R. Co.,* decided this day, *ante,* p. 240. The question
plaintiff presents is thus simply one of " just compensation."

The asserted basis of plaintiff's claim for actual damages is that, by the terms of the gold certificates, he was

entitled, on January 17, 1934, to receive gold coin. It is plain that he cannot claim any better position than that in which he would have been placed had the gold coin then been paid to him. But, in that event, he would have been required, under the applicable legislation and orders, forthwith to deliver the gold coin to the Treasury. Plaintiff does not bring himself within any of the stated exceptions. He did not allege in his petition that he held a federal license to hold gold coin; and the first question submitted to us by the Court of Claims negatives the assumption of such a license. Had plaintiff received gold coin for his certificates, he would not have been able, in view of the legislative inhibition, to export it or deal in it. Moreover, it is sufficient in the instant case to point out that on January 17, 1934, the dollar had not been devalued. Or, as plaintiff puts it, "at the time of the presentation of the certificates by petitioner, the gold content of the United States dollar had not been deflated" and the provision of the Act of March 14, 1900, *supra,* fixing that content at 25.8 grains, nine-tenths fine, as the standard unit of money with which "all forms of money issued or coined by the United States" were to be maintained at a parity, was "still in effect." The currency paid to the plaintiff for his gold certificates was then on a parity with that standard of value. It cannot be said that, in receiving the currency on that basis, he sustained any actual loss.

To support his claim, plaintiff says that on January 17, 1934, "an ounce of gold was of the value at least of $33.43." His petition so alleged and he contends that the allegation was admitted by the demurrer. But the assertion of that value of gold in relation to gold coin in this country, in view of the applicable legislative requirements, necessarily involved a conclusion of law. Under those requirements, there was not on January 17, 1934, a free market for gold in the United States, or any market available to the plaintiff for the gold coin to which he claims to have been entitled. Plaintiff insists that gold had an intrinsic value and was bought and sold in the world markets. But plaintiff had no right to resort to such markets. By reason of the quality of gold coin, " as a legal tender and as a medium of exchange," limitations attached to its ownership, and the Congress could prohibit its exportation and regulate its use. *Ling Su Fan* v. *United States, supra.*

The first question submitted by the Court of Claims is answered in the negative. It is unnecessary to answer the second question. And, in the circumstances shown, the third question is academic and also need not be answered.

Question No. 1 is answered " No."

MR. JUSTICE MCREYNOLDS, MR. JUSTICE VAN DEVANTER, MR. JUSTICE SUTHERLAND, and MR. JUSTICE BUTLER dissent. See *post*, p. 361.

PERRY *v.* UNITED STATES.*

CERTIFICATE FROM THE COURT OF CLAIMS.

No. 532. Argued January 10, 11, 1935.—Decided February 18, 1935.

1. A provision in a Government bond for payment of principal and interest " in United States gold coin of the present standard of value " must be fairly construed; and its reasonable import is an assurance by the Government that the bondholder will not suffer loss through depreciation of the medium of payment. P. 348.
2. The Joint Resolution of June 5, 1933, insofar as it undertakes to nullify such gold clauses in obligations of the United States and provides that such obligations shall be discharged by payment, dollar for dollar, in any coin or currency which at the time of payment is legal tender for public and private debts, is unconstitutional. P. 349.
3. Congress cannot use its power to regulate the value of money so as to invalidate the obligations which the Government has there-

---

* See note, p. 240.

PERRY *v.* UNITED STATES. 331

tofore issued in the exercise of the power to borrow money on the credit of the United States. Pp. 350 *et seq.*

4. There is a clear distinction between the power of Congress to control or interdict the contracts of private parties, when they interfere with the exercise of its constitutional authority, and a power in Congress to alter or repudiate the substance of its own engagements when it has borrowed money under its constitutional authority. P. 350.

5. By virtue of the power to borrow money " *on the credit of the United States,*" Congress is authorized to pledge that credit as assurance of payment as stipulated,—as the highest assurance the Government can give, its plighted faith. To say that Congress may withdraw or ignore that pledge, is to assume that the Constitution contemplates a vain promise, a pledge having no other sanction than the pleasure and convenience of the pledgor. P. 351.

6. When the United States, with constitutional authority, makes contracts, it has rights and incurs responsibilities similar to those of individuals who are parties to such instruments. P. 352.

7. The right to make binding obligations is a power of sovereignty. P. 353.

8. The sovereignty of the United States resides in the people; and Congress cannot invoke the sovereignty of the people to override their will as declared in the Constitution. P. 353.

9. The power given Congress to borrow money on the credit of the United States is unqualified and vital to the Government; and the binding quality of the promise of the United States is of the essence of the credit pledged. P. 353.

10. The fact that the United States may not be sued without its consent, is a matter of procedure which does not affect the legality and binding character of its contracts. P. 354.

11. Section 4 of the Fourteenth Amendment, declaring that " The validity of the public debt of the United States, authorized by law, . . . shall not be questioned," is confirmatory of a fundamental principle, applying as well to bonds issued after, as to those issued before, the adoption of the Amendment; and the expression " validity of the public debt " embraces whatever concerns the integrity of the public obligations. P. 354.

12. The holder of a Liberty Bond, which was issued when gold was in circulation and when the standard of value was the gold dollar of 25.8 grains, nine-tenths fine, and which promised payment in gold of that standard, claimed payment after the Government, pursuant to legislative authority, had withdrawn all gold coin

from circulation, had prohibited its export or its use in foreign exchange, except for limited purposes under license, and had reduced the weight of gold representing the standard dollar to 15-5/21 grains and placed all forms of money on a parity with that standard. The Joint Resolution of June 5, 1933, had enacted that such bonds should be discharged by payment, dollar for dollar, in any coin or currency which, at time of payment, was legal tender for public and private debts. The bondholder, having been refused payment in gold coin of the former standard or in an equal weight of gold, demanded currency in an amount exceeding the face of the bond in the same ratio as that borne by the number of grains in the former gold dollar to the number in the existing one,—or $1.69 of currency for every dollar of the bond. The Treasury declined to pay him more than the face of the bond in currency, and he sued in the Court of Claims. *Held:*

(a) The fact that the Government's repudiation of the gold clause of the bond is unconstitutional does not entitle the plaintiff to recover more than the loss he has actually suffered and of which he may rightfully complain. P. 354.

(b) The Court of Claims has no authority to entertain an action for nominal damages. P. 355.

(c) The question of actual loss cannot be determined without considering the economic condition at the time when the Government offered to pay the face of the bond in legal tender currency. P. 355.

(d) Congress, by virtue of its power to deal with gold coin, as a medium of exchange, was authorized to prohibit its export and limit its use in foreign exchange; and the restraint thus imposed upon holders of such coin was incident to their ownership of it and gave them no cause of action. P. 356.

(e) The Court cannot say that the exercise of this power was arbitrary or capricious. P. 356.

(f) The holder of a bond of the United States, payable in gold coin of the former standard, so far as concerns the restraint upon the right to export the gold coin or to engage in transactions of foreign exchange, is in no better case than the holder of gold coin itself. P. 356.

(g) In assessing plaintiff's damages, if any, the equivalent in currency of the gold coin promised can be no more than the amount of money which the gold coin would be worth to the plaintiff for the purposes for which it could legally be used. P. 357.

(h) Foreign dealing being forbidden, save under license, and the domestic market being, not free, but lawfully restricted by Congress, valuation of the gold coin would necessarily have regard to its use as legal tender and as a medium of exchange under a single monetary system with an established parity of all currency and coins; and this would involve a consideration of the purchasing power of the currency dollars. P. 357.

(i) Plaintiff has not attempted to show that, in relation to buying power, he has sustained any loss; on the contrary, in view of the adjustment of the internal economy to the single measure of value as established by the legislation of the Congress, and the universal availability and use throughout the country of the legal tender currency in meeting all engagements, the payment to the plaintiff of the amount which he demands, would appear to constitute not a recoupment of loss in any proper sense, but an unjustified enrichment. P. 357.

Question answered " No."

RESPONSE to questions certified by the Court of Claims in an action on a Liberty Loan Gold Bond.

Mr. John M. Perry, pro se. Mr. Hersey Egginton was with him on the brief.

The gold clause prescribes, not the method of payment but the measure of the obligation.

The Joint Resolution of June 5, 1933, is a direct violation of § 4 of the Fourteenth Amendment, expressly limiting the delegated powers of Congress, and making the public debt of the United States inviolable at the hands of Congress.

A legislative interpretation of this provision was adopted by the first Congress meeting after its ratification, in the Act of March 18, 1869 (16 Stat. 1). It has never been necessary to apply the prohibition of this portion of § 4, for the reason that, since its adoption and until recently, no attempt has ever been made by Congress to attack the validity of the public debt. The Joint Resolution of June 5, 1933, is a complete repudiation of the gold clause in some 18 billion dollars of outstanding bonds of the United States, and is necessarily a direct violation of § 4.

The history of this part of the Amendment shows that it was inserted for the specific purpose of protecting for all time the public debt, intended to be payable in gold coin or its equivalent, from being made payable, dollar for dollar, in legal tender currency. See, Phanor J. Elder, Cornell Law Quarterly, Dec. 1933, pp. 1–19; Thorpe, Const. Hist., U. S., vol. 3, p. 297; Cong. Globe, May 23, 1866, pp. 2768, 2769; May 29, 1866, p. 2869; June 4, 1866, pp. 2938, 2940, 2941; June 8, 1866, pp. 3040, 3042; June 13, 1866, pp. 3148, 3149; Kendrick, Journal of the Joint Committee of Fifteen on Reconstruction (1914), pp. 315, 316; Dunning, Political History of the U. S. During Reconstruction (1880), pp. 93, 99, 109.

Under the rule of *Shreveport* v. *Cole,* 129 U. S. 36, the Amendment must be construed to operate prospectively.

No provision of the Federal Constitution authorizes Congress to enact that portion of the Joint Resolution of June 5, 1933, which purports to abrogate the gold clause in the claimant's Liberty Bond.

Every federal power must be express, or implied from some power or group of powers; and any attempted exercise of power not delegated violates the Tenth Amendment. *Martin* v. *Hunter's Lessee,* 1 Wheat. 304, 326. The doctrine of inherent sovereignty does not apply to the Federal Government. *Kansas* v. *Colorado,* 206 U. S. 46. Nor does the Constitution specifically authorize the Federal Government to alleviate national emergencies. *Jacobson* v. *Massachusetts,* 197 U. S. 11; *Ward* v. *Maryland,* 12 Wall. 418; The Federalist, No. 41. While a general scaling down of public indebtedness by making "gold clauses" inoperative and allowing the United States to pay in inflated currency might be a means of relieving the financial burden of the Government, neither the appropriateness of, nor the necessity for, federal action can create a federal power. *Kansas* v. *Colorado,* 206 U. S. 46; *Jacobson* v. *Massachusetts,* 197 U. S. 11; *Ward* v. *Maryland,* 12 Wall.

418; *Keller* v. *United States,* 213 U. S. 138; *Linder* v. *United States,* 268 U. S. 5; *Lynch* v. *United States,* 292 U. S. 571. Furthermore, it is constitutional heresy to claim that an Act unconstitutional in normal times becomes constitutional because Congress deems that an emergency exists. The reverse of this doctrine has been firmly established ever since the Civil War. *Ex parte Milligan,* 4 Wall. 2; *Home Bldg. & Loan Assn.* v. *Blaisdell,* 290 U. S. 398; *Lynch* v. *United States,* 292 U. S. 571.

No provision in the Constitution authorizes Congress to provide for the general relief of debtors. The power to establish " uniform laws on the subject of bankruptcies " cannot be said to authorize all measures for the relief of debtors. That power is limited to laws " for the benefit and relief of creditors and their debtors, in cases in which the latter are unwilling or unable to pay their debts." Story, Const., § 1102 *et seq.; United States* v. *Fox,* 95 U. S. 670; *United States* v. *Pusey,* Fed. Cas. No. 16,098; *In re Reiman,* Fed. Cas. No. 11,673.

The attempted abrogation of the gold clause is not an exercise of the power " to borrow money on the credit of the United States." Here, if nowhere else, lies a fundamental distinction between the present statute and the Legal Tender Acts of 1862 and 1863. Those Acts were finally sustained as an exercise of the borrowing and currency powers on the theory that the Government was borrowing on the legal tender currency. At the same time a medium of exchange was provided. These powers were, therefore, used in direct support of each other. See, *Knox* v. *Lee,* 12 Wall. 457; *Juilliard* v. *Greenman,* 110 U. S. 421. If this Joint Resolution had only invalidated the gold clauses contained in the obligations of private persons, corporations, States, and municipalities, it might have been argued that Congress was exercising authority necessarily incident to the borrowing power in that it was destroying obligations which affected or interfered with that power.

See, *Veazie Bank* v. *Fenno,* 8 Wall. 533. Even this argument is necessarily refuted by the fact that Congress has included in the Joint Resolution " obligations of the United States."

The attempted abrogation does not come within the scope of the power " to coin money, regulate the value thereof, and of foreign coin, and fix the standard of weights and measures." The three cases which have in some measure defined the extent of the coinage power, hold in general that it authorizes the establishment of a sound and uniform national currency. *Veazie Bank* v. *Fenno,* 8 Wall. 533; *Knox* v. *Lee,* 12 Wall. 457; *Juilliard* v. *Greenman,* 110 U. S. 421. These cases, however, do not decide that Congress may control obligations which are not currency.

Nor has it ever been decided that Congress may control obligations not currency on the theory that such obligations affect the value of money. The power is limited to the issuance and the direct regulation of the kind, amount and value of currency. Congress has no general power to regulate and control the kind, quality, amount, production, or prices of all property. Contract obligations, including obligations to pay money, have always been recognized to be property within the meaning of this rule. It has never even been suggested that the currency power gives Congress authority to fix the value of any obligation that does not circulate as money, on the theory that the value of money is regulated thereby.

The fact that the currency power must be held to be limited to the direct regulation of the media of exchange becomes more apparent when § 10 of Art. I is considered. This clause has been held merely to prevent the States from issuing currency and not to prevent the issuance of " Bills of Credit " which do not circulate as media of exchange. Its purpose has uniformly been said to be that of making effective the affirmative power over currency granted to Congress. *Ogden* v. *Saunders,* 12 Wheat. 213;

Craig v. *Missouri,* 4 Pet. 410; *Briscoe* v. *Kentucky Bank,* 11 Pet. 257; *Darrington* v. *Alabama Bank,* 13 How. 12; *Poindexter* v. *Greenhow,* 114 U. S. 270; *Houston & T. C. R. Co.* v. *Texas,* 177 U. S. 66.

The abrogation would deprive the claimant of his property without due process of law. That part of the Resolution is unreasonable, arbitrary and capricious; it is not reasonably appropriate to any legitimate legislative end; the purpose of its enactment is not comprehended within the objectives of the powers delegated to Congress.

Congress itself has left no doubt that the enactment was intended as an exercise of the currency power. The preamble of the Joint Resolution must be considered as an official statement of the facts upon which the specific exercise of power is based and as a declaration of the objects sought to be attained thereby.

The purpose of the gold clause was to provide a measure of the obligation, and its only possible effect is to fix the amount of legal tender currency payable in satisfaction thereof. How such provisions " obstruct the power of the Congress to regulate the value of the money of the United States, and are inconsistent with the declared policy of the Congress to maintain at all times the equal power of every dollar," and how their abrogation will " assure a uniform value to the coins and currencies of the United States," is difficult to comprehend. There was not then, nor can there be under existing circumstances, any disparity between the value of the kinds of currency lawfully in circulation, and Congress was untrammeled in its power to issue other forms of currency, to increase or decrease the amount of money in circulation, to change the standard, to declare what is and what shall be legal tender, to prohibit the circulation of unauthorized forms of currency, or otherwise regulate the value of money.

Furthermore, the second paragraph of the preamble of the Joint Resolution is misleading. It is there inferred that this statute is a regulation of the " holding of or deal-

ing in gold," which, it is stated, "affect the public interest
and are therefore subject to proper regulation and restriction; . . ." We do not deny that the " holding of or dealing in gold " may " affect the public interest " and for
that reason be " subject to proper regulation and restriction." *Ling Su Fan* v. *United States*, 218 U. S. 302. But
the " holding of or dealing in gold " had already been prohibited. A further regulation, not abrogating or in some
measure altering the former prohibitions, could be of no
effect and could only have been intended to disguise the
real purpose of the Joint Resolution.

Insofar as it purports to abrogate the gold clause in
claimant's bond, the Joint Resolution cannot be considered
a regulation of the value of money. The ordinary means
by which the value of the currency may be, and has been,
regulated is by changing the base at which it had previously been stabilized, or by issuing more currency, thus
creating a greater supply. Congress has also issued a new
form of currency stabilized at a new base, different from
preëxisting standards. The present statute does not and
did not, at the time of its enactment, do any of these
things. Gold payments were then, and have since remained, suspended. The outstanding currencies, thus, if
stabilized at all at that time, must be considered to have
been stabilized in terms of one dollar obligations, and these
currencies were and are legal tender, dollar for dollar, in
the payment of dollar obligations. The Joint Resolution
stated, in effect, that both gold and gold-value obligations
were payable, dollar for dollar, in this same currency.
This Resolution, therefore, purported simultaneously to
standardize the unit of currency in terms of dollar, gold
dollar, and gold-value obligations. That this is unreasonable, arbitrary, and capricious and cannot be considered
to be a regulation of the value of currency may easily be
shown.

Claimant's bond by its tenor may be satisfied by the
payment of legal tender money in a sum equal to the

gold-value of its face amount. Ordinarily the gold-value in legal tender currency is no greater than the face amount of the instrument. When, however, gold payments have been suspended, gold-value obligations, although they may still be satisfied by payment in legal tender currency, remain at par with gold, but, ordinarily, are at a premium in terms of irredeemable currency. This was the situation when the Joint Resolution was enacted. See index of wholesale commodity prices on a gold basis, contained in The Annalist Weekly, Dec. 14, 1934, p. 817. If this statute were given effect, an ordinary one dollar obligation and a similar gold-value obligation could both be satisfied by the payment of the same unit of currency. This Joint Resolution was, therefore, an attempt simultaneously to stabilize the unit of currency at two obligations for the payment of money, which obligations were definitely different in value. Manifestly this cannot be considered to be a regulation of the value of money within the currency power. Gold-value contracts do not affect the value of money in any greater measure than do other money obligations or commodity contracts. Any regulation increasing or decreasing the amount that obligees may recover from the obligors of gold-value contracts, has no more effect on the value of the medium of exchange than would a regulation increasing or decreasing the rights of obligees of any other classes of contracts to pay money, or for that matter, the rights of promisees of agreements for the delivery of commodities. No one would contend that Congress has the power to lessen the obligation of all contracts on the theory that it is thereby regulating the value of money.

The only possible effect that gold-value contracts may have on the value of money is by affecting the demand for money. It is undoubtedly true that if the supply of currency and the rate of circulation were constant, then the value of money would fluctuate directly as the demand. The effect upon that demand of the payment in gold-value of federal obligations upon the retirement of such obligations, spread over the years of their respective maturities, would, however, be negligible.

In every contract to be performed in the future, one or the other of the parties thereto must bear the risk of loss due to fluctuation in value of the subject of the contract. In the ordinary contract for the payment of money, the risk of loss arising from an increase in the value of money rests upon the debtor; that resulting from its decrease upon the creditor. Yet it is not to be contended that Congress has power to shift these risks on the theory that it is regulating the value of money. The logical extension of this doctrine would be to hold that Congress could forbid persons from protecting themselves against risk of loss in any situation, an obvious impossibility; and further, since this risk must fall on someone, that Congress could, *ex post facto,* choose the person upon whom it should fall. The Federal Government, by its own insertion of the gold clause in claimant's Liberty Bond, has voluntarily assumed the risk ordinarily borne by the creditor. It now seeks to transfer to its creditor the loss caused by its own act of devaluation, the very contingency which it itself contemplated when it issued the bond.

Claimant further contends that the Joint Resolution, insofar as it purports to abrogate the gold clause in the Liberty Bond, will not accomplish, or have a reasonable relation to, any proper legislative object.

The purpose of the Joint Resolution, in this respect, was not to execute or make effective any of the powers granted to Congress, but, under the guise of an exercise of the currency power, to commit an act of repudiation. This practice was condemned in *McCulloch* v. *Maryland,* 4 Wheat. 316, 423; dissenting opinion, *Sinking-Fund Cases,* 99 U. S. 700, 739.

Even if that part of the Joint Resolution which purports to abrogate existing gold clause obligations might in any way be considered to be an exercise of the power "to coin money, regulate the value thereof," it must, to the extent that the gold clause in claimant's Liberty Bond is affected, deprive him of his property without due process of law and be a violation of the Fifth Amendment.

The claimant in any event is entitled to recover just compensation for the taking of his property for public use.

That part of the Resolution which attempts to fix the just compensation for such taking at "dollar for dollar" in legal tender would in any event be utterly void, as an attempted exercise of judicial power by the legislature. The judicial measure of that just compensation is the value of the property as of the date of taking.

The value of the property on the date of taking is the same as the damages claimed for the breach of the express contract, for the date of breach of contract and the date of taking is the same. In any case, neither the breach of the express contract nor the taking and appropriation by defendant of claimant's property were complete until the claimant's bond had been called for redemption and defendant had refused to pay according to the tenor of the bond. Both of these events happened on May 24, 1934, when the bond was presented to the Treasury Department for payment. The just compensation is, therefore, equal in amount to the relief asked for in the petition.

The Court of Claims has jurisdiction.

Mr. Angus MacLean, Assistant Solicitor General, opened the argument for the United States in this case. *Attorney General Cummings* made a closing argument for this and the two preceding cases. Those who were with them on the Government's brief were *Solicitor General Biggs, Assistant Attorney General Sweeney,* and *Messrs. Alexander Holtzoff* and *Harry LeRoy Jones.* The brief is here summarized:

Justification of the gold clause was removed when the dual monetary system was ended by the parity provisions. *Bronson* v. *Rodes,* 7 Wall. 229, 251–253.

The gold clause is an obstruction to the power of Congress to maintain the parity of all coins and currencies of the United States. Besides the holders of some $20,000,-000,000 of gold-clause, interest-bearing obligations of the Federal Government, there were holders of more than $5,000,000,000 of currency issued or guaranteed by the United States; gold clauses were contained in or made with respect to all of this currency. When the Government found it necessary to suspend redemption of currency in gold, one group of creditors would have been preferred to another if gold-clause creditors had been allowed to enforce the asserted obligation of their bonds.

The gold clause is an obstruction to the power of Congress to regulate the value of money. If the gold clause had not been abrogated in Government as well as private obligations, investments like those of the claimant would have reaped a harvest by the artificial demand created for Government bonds. If the gold clause in Government bonds were sustained and construed to entitle the holders to $1.69 on every dollar face amount of the bond, a ten-thousand-dollar gold-clause bond would in 1934 purchase 2.87 times as much as the $10,000 invested in such bond in 1918.

The gold clause is an obstruction to the power of Congress to borrow money. Bonds in which the gold clause was allowed to remain would adversely affect the market for other types of bonds and thereby impair the borrowing power of the Government.

The gold clause is an interference with the powers of the Federal Government over international relations, foreign exchange transactions, and foreign commerce.

There does not appear to be any serious doubt as to the power of Congress to prohibit gold clauses in future obligations. *Hepburn* v. *Griswold,* 8 Wall. 603, 615.

The Joint Resolution, in its application to outstanding Government bonds, does not violate the due process clause of the Fifth Amendment. On June 5, 1933, there was no disparity in value in the United States between the gold dollar and other coins and currency of the United States. That being true, the claimant's argument fails.

The Legal Tender Cases are conclusive that §§ 1 and 2 of the Joint Resolution do not violate the Fifth Amendment. The decision in those cases was understood by the Court, and has since been understood, to sustain the constitutionality of the Legal Tender Acts as applied to public as well as private debts. 12 Wall. 529, 530, 539, 540, 635; and *Savage's Case,* 8 Ct. Cl. 545, affirmed 92 U. S. 382.

Public as well as private obligations may be affected as a result of action taken within the Federal police power or some other paramount power. *Lynch* v. *U. S.,* 292 U. S. 571, 579; *Home Bldg. & Loan Assn.* v. *Blaisdell,* 290 U. S. 398, 435; and *Horowitz* v. *U. S.,* 267 U. S. 458. The cases which have upheld such action by the State Legislatures, as applied to state obligations, go far to establish the propriety of similar action by Congress. *Atlantic Coast Line R. Co.* v. *Goldsboro,* 232 U. S. 548; *Chicago, B. & Q. R. Co.* v. *Nebraska,* 170 U. S. 57; *Stone* v. *Mississippi,* 101 U. S. 814; *Butchers Union Co.* v. *Crescent City,* 111 U. S. 746; *C., B. & Q. R. Co.* v. *Drainage Commr's,* 200 U. S. 561, 592; and *Chicago & Alton R. Co.* v. *Tranbarger,* 238 U. S. 67. Legislative powers cannot be expressly contracted away. *Newton* v. *Commr's,* 100 U. S. 548; *Illinois Central Ry.* v. *Illinois,* 146 U. S. 387; *Home Building & Loan Assn.* v. *Blaisdell,* 290 U. S. 398, 436; *Denver & R. G. R. Co.* v. *Denver,* 250 U. S. 241; *Stone* v. *Mississippi,* 101 U. S. 814; *N. Y. & N. E. R. Co.* v. *Bristol,* 151 U. S. 556; *Boyd* v. *Alabama,* 94 U. S. 645; *Straus* v. *American Publishers' Assn.,* 231 U. S. 222, 243; *United Shoe Machinery Co.* v. *United States,* 258 U. S. 451, 463; *North American Co.* v. *United States,* 171 U. S.

110, 137; James Parker Hall, in American Law and Procedure, Volume XII, Constitutional Law, pages 242, 243.

One Congress can no more convey or contract away the legislative powers entrusted by the Constitution so as to restrict the exercise of those powers by a subsequent Congress than can a State Legislature. *Lynch* v. *United States,* 292 U. S. 571, 579; *North American Co.* v. *United States,* 171 U. S. 110, 137; *United Shoe Machinery Co.* v. *United States,* 258 U. S. 451, 463.

From the point of view of justice and equity, claimant is receiving for his bond all that he is entitled to receive from the Government. The purchasing power of the dollar on June 5, 1933, and on April 15, 1934, when claimant's bond was called, and at the present time, is far greater than the purchasing power of the dollar that the Government received when it issued the Liberty Bonds. The Annalist, Weekly Index of Wholesale Commodity Prices, December 14, 1934.

The Joint Resolution does not violate § 4 of the Fourteenth Amendment. The word " validity " in § 4 refers to the essential existence of the obligation, as is shown by the legislative history. Nowhere in the cases involving the Legal Tender Acts as applied to public or private obligations is any reference made to this section. The word " debt," as used in the section, is not to be construed as including every provision contained in, or made with respect to, an obligation of the United States. The gold clause is a provision aside from the basic " debt." *Bronson* v. *Rodes,* 7 Wall. 229; *Butler* v. *Horwitz,* 7 Wall. 258; *Dewing* v. *Sears,* 11 Wall. 379; and *Maryland* v. *Railroad Co.,* 22 Wall. 105, 108. Historians who have considered § 4 limit its concept of public debt to that public debt existing at the time of the adoption of the Amendment. Burdick, The Law of the American Constitution, § 228; Dunning, Essays on the Civil War and Reconstruction (1931), 118; Eriksson & Rowe, American Constitutional

History (1933), 301; Flack, The Adoption of the Fourteenth Amendment (1908), 133; Magruder, The Constitution (1933), 328; Story, Constitution, 5th ed., § 1965; Watson, The Constitution of the United States (1910), 1657; 2 Blaine, "Twenty Years of Congress," 190; Guthrie, The Fourteenth Amendment (1898), 17; 44 Yale L. J., 53, 85. In any event, it can scarcely be contended that the limitation placed upon Congress by § 4 of the Fourteenth Amendment is more stringent than the limitation placed upon the States in the impairment-of-contracts clause.

The Joint Resolution may not be attacked as a taking of private property without just compensation. The claimant confuses the due process and the just compensation clauses of the Fifth Amendment. To frustrate a contract is not to appropriate it. *Omnia Commercial Co.* v. *U. S.*, 261 U. S. 502, 508, 513. Even if there was a taking, it was accomplished by the Joint Resolution on June 5, 1933. There was no drop in the market price of the claimant's bond upon the passage of the Resolution. There is no allegation that the bond depreciated in value either on that date or thereafter. The Government has provided just compensation if any is due; the claimant is entitled to be put in as good a position pecuniarily as if his property had not been taken, but is not entitled to more. *Olson* v. *U. S.*, 292 U. S. 246, 255. The relative market value of gold-clause and non-gold-clause obligations was not affected by the Joint Resolution. Moreover, if the claimant had, on June 5, 1933, received gold coin for his bond, he would have been required by the Orders then in force to deliver the coin to the United States in exchange for other coin or the currency of an equivalent amount. The claimant was in no position to secure any asserted "world price" for any gold held or received by him in the United States, since the Executive Orders promulgated under the Act of March 9, 1933, prohibited the export of gold coin from the United States. Such prohibition is constitutional. *Ling Su Fan* v. *U. S.*, 218 U. S. 302. There is no basis for the contention that compensation must be made for the increased value of property accruing after the taking. *Olson* v. *U. S.*, 292 U. S. 246; *Brooks-Scanlon Corp.* v. *U. S.*, 265 U. S. 106, 123.

The United States, as a contractor, is not liable to respond in damages in the Court of Claims for any breach of its proprietary and corporate contracts due to its public and general acts as a sovereign. *United States* v. *State Bank*, 96 U. S. 30, 36; and *Horowitz* v. *U. S.*, 267 U. S. 458.

Section 1 of the Joint Resolution has the effect of withdrawing the consent of the United States to be sued on gold clauses. *Lynch* v. *U. S.*, 292 U. S. 571, 580.

Annulment of the gold clause in Government bonds is no more repudiation than in private obligations. In both it is regulation rather than repudiation, and as such is an attribute of sovereignty. Whatever power there is over the currency is vested in Congress. If the power to declare what is money is not in Congress, it is annihilated. *Legal Tender Cases, supra.*

By leave of Court, *Messrs. Edward E. Gann* and *George C. Johnson* filed a brief as *amici curiae* in support of the contentions of the United States.

MR. CHIEF JUSTICE HUGHES delivered the opinion of the Court.

The certificate from the Court of Claims shows the following facts:

Plaintiff brought suit as the owner of an obligation of the United States for $10,000, known as " Fourth Liberty Loan 4¼% Gold Bond of 1933–1938." This bond was issued pursuant to the Act of September 24, 1917 (40 Stat. 288), as amended, and Treasury Department circular No. 121, dated September 28, 1918. The bond provided: " The principal and interest hereof are payable in United States gold coin of the present standard of value."

Plaintiff alleged in his petition that at the time the bond was issued, and when he acquired it, a dollar in gold consisted of 25.8 grains of gold .9 fine "; that the bond was called for redemption on April 15, 1934, and, on May 24, 1934, was presented for payment; that plaintiff demanded its redemption " by the payment of 10,000 gold dollars each containing 25.8 grains of gold .9 fine "; that defendant refused to comply with that demand, and that plaintiff then demanded " 258,000 grains of gold .9 fine, or gold of equivalent value of any fineness, or 16,931.25 gold dollars each containing 15 5/21 grains of gold .9 fine, or 16,931.25 dollars in legal tender currency "; that defendant refused to redeem the bond " except by the payment of 10,000 dollars in legal tender currency "; that these refusals were based on the Joint Resolution of the Congress of June 5, 1933 (48 Stat. 113), but that this enactment was unconstitutional as it operated to deprive plaintiff of his property without due process of law; and that, by this action of defendant, he was damaged " in the sum of $16,931.25, the value of defendant's obligation," for which, with interest, plaintiff demanded judgment.

Defendant demurred upon the ground that the petition did not state a cause of action against the United States.

The Court of Claims has certified the following questions:

"1. Is the claimant, being the holder and owner of a Fourth Liberty Loan 4¼% bond of the United States, of the principal amount of $10,000, issued in 1918, which was payable on and after April 15, 1934, and which bond contained a clause that the principal is 'payable in United States gold coin of the present standard of value,' entitled to receive from the United States an amount in legal tender currency in excess of the face amount of the bond?

" 2. Is the United States, as obligor in a Fourth Liberty Loan 4¼% gold bond, Series of 1933–1938, as stated in Question One, liable to respond in damages in a suit in the Court of Claims on such bond as an express contract, by reason of the change in or impossibility of performance in accordance with the tenor thereof, due to the provisions of Public Resolution No. 10, 73rd Congress, abrogating the gold clause in all obligations? "

First. The import of the obligation. The bond in suit differs from an obligation of private parties, or of States or municipalities, whose contracts are necessarily made in subjection to the dominant power of the Congress. *Norman* v. *Baltimore & Ohio R. Co.,* decided this day, *ante,* p. 240. The bond now before us is an obligation of the United States. The terms of the bond are explicit. They were not only expressed in the bond itself, but they were definitely prescribed by the Congress. The Act of September 24, 1917, both in its original and amended form, authorized the moneys to be borrowed, and the bonds to be issued, "on the credit of the United States" in order to meet expenditures needed "for the national security and defense and other public purposes authorized by law." 40 Stat. 288, 503. The circular of the Treasury Department of September 28, 1918, to which the bond refers "for a statement of the further rights of the holders of bonds of said series," also provided that the principal and interest "are payable in United States gold coin of the present standard of value."

This obligation must be fairly construed. The *"present* standard of value" stood in contradistinction to a *lower* standard of value. The promise obviously was intended to afford protection against loss. That protection was sought to be secured by setting up a standard or measure of the Government's obligation. We think that the reasonable import of the promise is that it was intended to assure one who lent his money to the Government and took its bond that he would not suffer loss through depreciation in the medium of payment.

The Government states in its brief that the total unmatured interest-bearing obligations of the United States outstanding on May 31, 1933, (which it is understood contained a " gold clause " substantially the same as that of the bond in suit,) amounted to about twenty-one billions of dollars. From statements at the bar, it appears that this amount has been reduced to approximately twelve billions at the present time, and that during the intervening period the public debt of the United States has risen some seven billions (making a total of approximately twenty-eight billions five hundred millions) by the issue of some sixteen billions five hundred millions of dollars " of non-gold-clause obligations."

Second. The binding quality of the obligation. The question is necessarily presented whether the Joint Resolution of June 5, 1933 (48 Stat. 113) is a valid enactment so far as it applies to the obligations of the United States. The Resolution declared that provisions requiring " payment in gold or a particular kind of coin or currency " were " against public policy," and provided that " every obligation, heretofore or hereafter incurred, whether or not any such provision is contained therein," shall be discharged " upon payment, dollar for dollar, in any coin or currency which at the time of payment is legal tender for public and private debts." This enactment was expressly extended to obligations of the United States, and provisions for payment in gold, " contained in any law authorizing obligations to be issued by or under authority of the United States," were repealed.[1]

---

[1] And subdivision (b) of § 1 of the Joint Resolution of June 5, 1933, provided: "As used in this resolution, the term ' obligation ' means an obligation (including every obligation of and to the United States, excepting currency) payable in money of the United States;

There is no question as to the power of the Congress to regulate the value of money, that is, to establish a monetary system and thus to determine the currency of the country. The question is whether the Congress can use that power so as to invalidate the terms of the obligations which the Government has theretofore issued in the exercise of the power to borrow money on the credit of the United States. In attempted justification of the Joint Resolution in relation to the outstanding bonds of the United States, the Government argues that " earlier Congresses could not validly restrict the 73rd Congress from exercising its constitutional powers to regulate the value of money, borrow money, or regulate foreign and interstate commerce "; and, from this premise, the Government seems to deduce the proposition that when, with adequate authority, the Government borrows money and pledges the credit of the United States, it is free to ignore that pledge and alter the terms of its obligations in case a later Congress finds their fulfillment inconvenient. The Government's contention thus raises a question of far greater importance than the particular claim of the plaintiff. On that reasoning, if the terms of the Government's bond as to the standard of payment can be repudiated, it inevitably follows that the obligation as to the amount to be paid may also be repudiated. The contention necessarily imports that the Congress can disregard the obligations of the Government at its discretion and that, when the Government borrows money, the credit of the United States is an illusory pledge.

We do not so read the Constitution. There is a clear distinction between the power of the Congress to control or interdict the contracts of private parties when they interfere with the exercise of its constitutional authority,

---

and the term ' coin or currency ' means coin or currency of the United States, including Federal Reserve notes and circulating notes of Federal Reserve banks and national banking associations."

PERRY *v.* UNITED STATES.   351

and the power of the Congress to alter or repudiate the substance of its own engagements when it has borrowed money under the authority which the Constitution confers. In authorizing the Congress to borrow money, the Constitution empowers the Congress to fix the amount to be borrowed and the terms of payment. By virtue of the power to borrow money " *on the credit of the United States,*" the Congress is authorized to pledge that credit as an assurance of payment as stipulated,—as the highest assurance the Government can give, its plighted faith. To say that the Congress may withdraw or ignore that pledge, is to assume that the Constitution contemplates a vain promise, a pledge having no other sanction than the pleasure and convenience of the pledgor. This Court has given no sanction to such a conception of the obligations of our Government.

The binding quality of the obligations of the Government was considered in the *Sinking-Fund Cases,* 99 U. S. 700, 718, 719. The question before the Court in those cases was whether certain action was warranted by a reservation to the Congress of the right to amend the charter of a railroad company. While the particular action was sustained under this right of amendment, the Court took occasion to state emphatically the obligatory character of the contracts of the United States. The Court said: " The United States are as much bound by their contracts as are individuals. If they repudiate their obligations, it is as much repudiation, with all the wrong and reproach that term implies, as it would be if the repudiator had been a State or a municipality or a citizen." [2]

---

[2] Mr. Justice Strong, who had written the opinion of the majority of the Court in the legal tender cases (*Knox* v. *Lee,* 12 Wall. 457), dissented in the *Sinking-Fund Cases,* 99 U. S. p. 731, because he thought that the action of the Congress was not consistent with the Government's engagement and hence was a transgression of legislative

When the United States, with constitutional authority, makes contracts, it has rights and incurs responsibilities similar to those of individuals who are parties to such instruments. There is no difference, said the Court in *United States* v. *Bank of the Metropolis,* 15 Pet. 377, 392, except that the United States cannot be sued without its consent. See, also, *The Floyd Acceptances,* 7 Wall. 666, 675; *Cooke* v. *United States,* 91 U. S. 389, 396. In *Lynch* v. *United States,* 292 U. S. 571, 580, with respect to an attempted abrogation by the Act of March 20, 1933 (48 Stat. 8, 11) of certain outstanding war risk insurance policies, which were contracts of the United States, the Court quoted with approval the statement in the *Sinking-Fund Cases, supra,* and said: " Punctilious fulfillment of contractual obligations is essential to the maintenance of the credit of public as well as private debtors. No doubt there was in March, 1933, great need of economy. In the administration of all government business economy had become urgent because of lessened revenues and the heavy obligations to be issued in the hope of relieving widespread distress. Congress was free to reduce gratuities deemed excessive. But Congress was without power to reduce expenditures by abrogating contractual obligations of the United States. To abrogate contracts, in the attempt to lessen government expenditure, would

---

power. And with respect to the sanctity of the contracts of the Government, he quoted, with approval, the opinion of Mr. Hamilton in his communication to the Senate of January 20, 1795 (citing 3 Hamilton's Works, 518, 519), that " when a government enters into a contract with an individual, it deposes, as to the matter of the contract, its constitutional authority, and exchanges the character of legislator for that of a moral agent, with the same rights and obligations as an individual. Its promises may be justly considered as excepted out of its power to legislate unless in aid of them. It is in theory impossible to reconcile the idea of a promise which obliges, with the power to make a law which can vary the effect of it."

be not the practice of economy, but an act of repudiation."

The argument in favor of the Joint Resolution, as applied to government bonds, is in substance that the Government cannot by contract restrict the exercise of a sovereign power. But the right to make binding obligations is a competence attaching to sovereignty.[3] In the United States, sovereignty resides in the people, who act through the organs established by the Constitution. *Chisholm* v. *Georgia,* 2 Dall. 419, 471; *Penhallow* v. *Doane's Administrators,* 3 Dall. 54, 93; *McCulloch* v. *Maryland,* 4 Wheat. 316, 404, 405; *Yick Wo* v. *Hopkins,* 118 U. S. 356, 370. The Congress as the instrumentality of sovereignty is endowed with certain powers to be exerted on behalf of the people in the manner and with the effect the Constitution ordains. The Congress cannot invoke the sovereign power of the people to override their will as thus declared. The powers conferred upon the Congress are harmonious. The Constitution gives to the Congress the power to borrow money on the credit of the United States, an unqualified power, a power vital to the Government,— upon which in an extremity its very life may depend. The binding quality of the promise of the United States is of the essence of the credit which is so pledged. Having this power to authorize the issue of definite obligations for the payment of money borrowed, the Congress has not been vested with authority to alter or destroy those obli-

---

[3] Oppenheim, International Law, 4th ed., vol. 1, §§ 493, 494. This is recognized in the field of international engagements. Although there may be no judicial procedure by which such contracts may be enforced in the absence of the consent of the sovereign to be sued, the engagement validly made by a sovereign state is not without legal force, as readily appears if the jurisdiction to entertain a controversy with respect to the performance of the engagement is conferred upon an international tribunal. Hall, International Law, 8th ed., § 107; Oppenheim, *loc. cit.;* Hyde, International Law, vol. 2, § 489.

gations. The fact that the United States may not be sued without its consent is a matter of procedure which does not affect the legal and binding character of its contracts. While the Congress is under no duty to provide remedies through the courts, the contractual obligation still exists and, despite infirmities of procedure, remains binding upon the conscience of the sovereign. *Lynch* v. *United States, supra,* pp. 580, 582.

The Fourteenth Amendment, in its fourth section, explicitly declares: " The validity of the public debt of the United States, authorized by law, . . . shall not be questioned." While this provision was undoubtedly inspired by the desire to put beyond question the obligations of the Government issued during the Civil War, its language indicates a broader connotation. We regard it as confirmatory of a fundamental principle, which applies as well to the government bonds in question, and to others duly authorized by the Congress, as to those issued before the Amendment was adopted. Nor can we perceive any reason for not considering the expression " the *validity* of the public debt " as embracing whatever concerns the integrity of the public obligations.

We conclude that the Joint Resolution of June 5, 1933, in so far as it attempted to override the obligation created by the bond in suit, went beyond the congressional power.

Third. The question of damages. In this view of the binding quality of the Government's obligations, we come to the question as to the plaintiff's right to recover damages. That is a distinct question. Because the Government is not at liberty to alter or repudiate its obligations, it does not follow that the claim advanced by the plaintiff should be sustained. The action is for breach of contract. As a remedy for breach, plaintiff can recover no more than the loss he has suffered and of which he may rightfully complain. He is not entitled to be en-

PERRY *v.* UNITED STATES. 355

riched. Plaintiff seeks judgment for $16,931.25, in present legal tender currency, on his bond for $10,000. The question is whether he has shown damage to that extent, or any actual damage, as the Court of Claims has no authority to entertain an action for nominal damages. *Grant* v. *United States,* 7 Wall. 331, 338; *Marion & R. V. Ry. Co.* v. *United States,* 270 U. S. 280, 282; *Nortz* v. *United States,* decided this day, *ante,* p. 317.

Plaintiff computes his claim for $16,931.25 by taking the weight of the gold dollar as fixed by the President's proclamation of January 31, 1934, under the Act of May 12, 1933 (48 Stat. 52, 53), as amended by the Act of January 30, 1934 (48 Stat. 342), that is, at 15 5/21 grains nine-tenths fine, as compared with the weight fixed by the Act of March 14, 1900 (31 Stat. 45), or 25.8 grains nine-tenths fine. But the change in the weight of the gold dollar did not necessarily cause loss to the plaintiff of the amount claimed. The question of actual loss cannot fairly be determined without considering the economic situation at the time the Government offered to pay him the $10,000, the face of his bond, in legal tender currency. The case is not the same as if gold coin had remained in circulation. That was the situation at the time of the decisions under the legal tender acts of 1862 and 1863. *Bronson* v. *Rodes,* 7 Wall. 229, 251; *Trebilcock* v. *Wilson,* 12 Wall. 687, 695; *Thompson* v. *Butler,* 95 U. S. 694, 696, 697. Before the change in the weight of the gold dollar in 1934, gold coin had been withdrawn from circulation.[4] The Congress had authorized the prohibition of the exportation of gold coin and the placing of restrictions upon transactions in foreign exchange. Acts of March 9, 1933,

---

[4] In its Report of May 27, 1933, it was stated by the Senate Committee on Banking and Currency: " By the Emergency Banking Act and the existing Executive Orders gold is not now paid, or obtainable for payment, on obligations public or private." Sen. Rep. No. 99, 73d Cong., 1st sess.

48 Stat. 1; January 30, 1934, 48 Stat. 337. Such dealings could be had only for limited purposes and under license. Executive Orders of April 20, 1933, August 28, 1933, and January 15, 1934; Regulations of the Secretary of the Treasury, January 30 and 31, 1934. That action the Congress was entitled to take by virtue of its authority to deal with gold coin as a medium of exchange. And the restraint thus imposed upon holders of gold coin was incident to the limitations which inhered in their ownership of that coin and gave them no right of action. *Ling Su Fan* v. *United States,* 218 U. S. 302, 310, 311. The Court said in that case: "Conceding the title of the owner of such coins, yet there is attached to such ownership those limitations which public policy may require by reason of their quality as a legal tender and as a medium of exchange. These limitations are due to the fact that public law gives to such coinage a value which does not attach as a mere consequence of intrinsic value. Their quality as a legal tender is an attribute of law aside from their bullion value. They bear, therefore, the impress of sovereign power which fixes value and authorizes their use and exchange. . . . However unwise a law may be, aimed at the exportation of such coins, in the face of the axioms against obstructing the free flow of commerce, there can be no serious doubt that the power to coin money includes the power to prevent its outflow from the country of its origin." The same reasoning is applicable to the imposition of restraints upon transactions in foreign exchange. We cannot say, in view of the conditions that existed, that the Congress, having this power, exercised it arbitrarily or capriciously. And the holder of an obligation, or bond, of the United States, payable in gold coin of the former standard, so far as the restraint upon the right to export gold coin or to engage in transactions in foreign exchange is concerned, was in no better case than the holder of gold coin itself.

In considering what damages, if any, the plaintiff has sustained by the alleged breach of his bond, it is hence inadmissible to assume that he was entitled to obtain gold coin for recourse to foreign markets, or for dealings in foreign exchange, or for other purposes contrary to the control over gold coin which the Congress had the power to exert, and had exerted, in its monetary regulation. Plaintiff's damages could not be assessed without regard to the internal economy of the country at the time the alleged breach occurred. The discontinuance of gold payments and the establishment of legal tender currency on a standard unit of value with which " all forms of money " of the United States were to be " maintained at a parity," had a controlling influence upon the domestic economy. It was adjusted to the new basis. A free domestic market for gold was non-existent.

Plaintiff demands the " equivalent " in currency of the gold coin promised. But " equivalent " cannot mean more than the amount of money which the promised gold coin would be worth to the bondholder for the purposes for which it could legally be used. That equivalence or worth could not properly be ascertained save in the light of the domestic and restricted market which the Congress had lawfully established. In the domestic transactions to which the plaintiff was limited, in the absence of special license, determination of the value of the gold coin would necessarily have regard to its use as legal tender and as a medium of exchange under a single monetary system with an established parity of all currency and coins. And in view of the control of export and foreign exchange, and the restricted domestic use, the question of value, in relation to transactions legally available to the plaintiff, would require a consideration of the purchasing power of the dollars which the plaintiff could have received. Plaintiff has not shown, or attempted to show, that in relation to buying power he has sustained any loss whatever. On the contrary, in view of the adjustment of the internal economy to the single measure of value as established by the legislation of the Congress, and the universal availability and use throughout the country of the legal tender currency in meeting all engagements, the payment to the plaintiff of the amount which he demands would appear to constitute not a recoupment of loss in any proper sense but an unjustified enrichment.

Plaintiff seeks to make his case solely upon the theory that by reason of the change in the weight of the dollar he is entitled to one dollar and sixty-nine cents in the present currency for every dollar promised by the bond, regardless of any actual loss he has suffered with respect to any transaction in which his dollars may be used. We think that position is untenable.

In the view that the facts alleged by the petition fail to show a cause of action for actual damages, the first question submitted by the Court of Claims is answered in the negative. It is not necessary to answer the second question.

Question No. 1 is answered " No."

MR. JUSTICE STONE, concurring.

I agree that the answer to the first question is " No," but I think our opinion should be confined to answering that question and that it should essay an answer to no other.

I do not doubt that the gold clause in the Government bonds, like that in the private contracts just considered, calls for the payment of value in money, measured by a stated number of gold dollars of the standard defined in the clause, *Feist* v. *Société Intercommunale Belge d'Electricité*, [1934] A. C. 161, 170–173; *Serbian and Brazilian Bond Cases*, P. C. I. J., series A., Nos. 20–21, pp. 32–34, 109–119. In the absence of any further exertion of governmental power, that obligation plainly could not be satisfied by payment of the same number of dollars, either specie or paper, measured by a gold dollar of lesser weight, regardless of their purchasing power or the state of our internal economy at the due date.

I do not understand the Government to contend that it is any the less bound by the obligation than a private individual would be, or that it is free to disregard it except in the exercise of the constitutional power " to coin money " and " regulate the value thereof." In any case, there is before us no question of default apart from the regulation by Congress of the use of gold as currency.

While the Government's refusal to make the stipulated payment is a measure taken in the exercise of that power, this does not disguise the fact that its action is to that extent a repudiation of its undertaking. As much as I deplore this refusal to fulfill the solemn promise of bonds of the United States, I cannot escape the conclusion, announced for the Court, that in the situation now presented, the Government, through the exercise of its sovereign power to regulate the value of money, has rendered itself immune from liability for its action. To that extent it has relieved itself of the obligation of its domestic bonds, precisely· as it has relieved the obligors of private bonds in *Norman* v. *Baltimore & Ohio R. Co.,* decided this day, *ante,* p. 240.

In this posture of the case it is unnecessary, and I think undesirable, for the Court to undertake to say that the obligation of the gold clause in Government bonds is greater than in the bonds of private individuals, or that in some situation not described, and in some manner and in some measure undefined, it has imposed restrictions upon the future exercise of the power to regulate the currency. I am not persuaded that we should needlessly intimate any opinion which implies that the obligation may so operate, for example, as to interpose a serious obstacle to the adoption of measures for stabilization of the dollar, should Congress think it wise to accomplish that purpose by resumption of gold payments, in dollars of the present or any other gold content less than that specified in the gold clause, and by the re-establishment of a free market for gold and its free exportation.

There is no occasion now to resolve doubts, which I entertain, with respect to these questions. At present they are academic. Concededly they may be transferred wholly to the realm of speculation by the exercise of the undoubted power of the Government to withdraw the privilege of suit upon its gold clause obligations. We have just held that the Court of Claims was without power to entertain the suit in *Nortz* v. *United States, ante,* p. 317, because, regardless of the nature of the obligation of the gold certificates, there was no damage. Here it is declared that there is no damage because Congress, by the exercise of its power to regulate the currency, has made it impossible for the plaintiff to enjoy the benefits of gold payments promised by the Government. It would seem that this would suffice to dispose of the present case, without attempting to prejudge the rights of other bond-holders and of the Government under other conditions which may never occur. It will not benefit this plaintiff, to whom we deny any remedy, to be assured that he has an inviolable right to performance of the gold clause.

Moreover, if the gold clause be viewed as a gold value contract, as it is in *Norman* v. *Baltimore & Ohio R. Co., supra,* it is to be noted that the Government has not prohibited the free use by the bondholder of the paper money equivalent of the gold clause obligation; it is the prohibition, by the Joint Resolution of Congress, of payment of the increased number of depreciated dollars required to make up the full equivalent, which alone bars recovery.

In that case it would seem to be implicit in our decision that the prohibition, at least in the present situation, is itself a constitutional exercise of the power to regulate the value of money.

I therefore do not join in so much of the opinion as may be taken to suggest that the exercise of the sovereign power to borrow money on credit, which does not override the sovereign immunity from suit, may nevertheless preclude or impede the exercise of another sovereign power, to regulate the value of money; or to suggest that although there is and can be no present cause of action upon the repudiated gold clause, its obligation is nevertheless, in some manner and to some extent, not stated, superior to the power to regulate the currency which we now hold to be superior to the obligation of the bonds.

MR. JUSTICE McREYNOLDS, MR. JUSTICE VAN DEVANTER, MR. JUSTICE SUTHERLAND, and MR. JUSTICE BUTLER dissent.   See below.

In the four preceding " Gold Clause Cases," viz., Norman v. Baltimore & Ohio R. Co., and United States v. Bankers Trust Co., ante, p. 240; Nortz v. United States, ante, p. 317; and Perry v. United States, ante, p. 330, a single dissenting opinion was delivered, immediately after the handing down of the opinion in the Perry case.   It is as follows:

MR. JUSTICE McREYNOLDS, dissenting.

MR. JUSTICE VAN DEVANTER, MR. JUSTICE SUTHERLAND, MR. JUSTICE BUTLER and I conclude that, if given effect, the enactments here challenged will bring about confiscation of property rights and repudiation of national obligations.   Acquiescence in the decisions just announced is impossible; the circumstances demand statement of our views. "To let oneself slide down the easy slope offered by the course of events and to dull one's mind against the extent of the danger, . . . that is precisely to fail in one's obligation of responsibility."

Just men regard repudiation and spoliation of citizens by their sovereign with abhorrence; but we are asked to affirm that the Constitution has granted power to accomplish both. No definite delegation of such a power exists; and we cannot believe the farseeing framers, who labored with hope of establishing justice and securing the blessings of liberty, intended that the expected government should have authority to annihilate its own obligations and destroy the very rights which they were endeavoring to protect. Not only is there no permission for such actions; they are inhibited. And no plenitude of words can conform them to our charter.

The Federal government is one of delegated and limited powers which derive from the Constitution. "It can exercise only the powers granted to it." Powers claimed must be denied unless granted; and, as with other writings, the whole of the Constitution is for consideration when one seeks to ascertain the meaning of any part.

By the so-called gold clause—promise to pay in " United States gold coin of the present standard of value," or " of or equal to the present standard of weight and fineness "—found in very many private and public obligations, the creditor agrees to accept and the debtor undertakes to return the thing loaned or its equivalent. Thereby each secures protection, one against decrease in value of the currency, the other against an increase.

The clause is not new or obscure or discolored by any sinister purpose. For more than 100 years our citizens have employed a like agreement. During the War between the States, its equivalent " payable in coin " aided

in surmounting financial difficulties. From the housetop
men proclaimed its merits while bonds for billions were
sold to support the World War. The Treaty of Versailles
recognized it as appropriate and just. It appears in the
obligations which have rendered possible our great undertakings—public-works, railroads, buildings.

Under the interpretation accepted here for many years,
this clause expresses a definite enforceable contract. Both
by statute and long use the United States have approved
it. Over and over again they have enjoyed the added
value which it gave to their obligations. So late as May
2, 1933 they issued to the public more than $550,000,000
of their notes each of which carried a solemn promise to
pay in standard gold coin. (Before that day this coin
had in fact been withdrawn from circulation, but the
statutory measure of value remained the gold dollar of
25.8 grains.)

The Permanent Court of International Justice interpreted the clause as this Court had done and upheld it.
Cases of Serbian and Brazilian Loans, Publications P. C.
I. J., Series A, Nos. 20–21 (1929). It was there declared:
" The gold clause merely prevents the borrower from
availing itself of a possibility of discharge of the debt in
depreciated currency," and " The treatment of the gold
clause as indicating a mere modality of payment, without
reference to a gold standard of value, would be, not to
construe but to destroy it."

In *Feist* v. *Société Intercommunale Belge d'Electricité*,
(1934), A. C. 161, the House of Lords expressed like
views.

Gregory v. *Morris*, (1878) 96 U. S. 619, 624, 625—last
of similar causes—construed and sanctioned this stipulation. In behalf of all, Chief Justice Waite there said:

" The obligation secured by the mortgage or lien under
which Morris held was for the payment of gold coin, or,
as was said in *Bronson* v. *Rodes,* 7 Wall. [1869] 229, ' an

agreement to deliver a certain weight of standard gold, to be ascertained by a count of coins, each of which is certified to contain a definite proportion of that weight ' and is not distinguishable ' from a contract to deliver an equal weight of bullion of equal fineness.' . . . We think it clear, that, under such circumstances, it was within the power of the Court so far as Gregory was concerned, to treat the contract as one for the delivery of so much gold bullion; and, if Morris was willing to accept a judgment which might be discharged in currency, to have his damages estimated according to the currency value of bullion."

Earlier cases—*Bronson* v. *Rodes,* 7 Wall. 229; *Butler* v. *Horwitz,* 7 Wall. 258; *Dewing* v. *Sears,* 11 Wall. 379; *Trebilcock* v. *Wilson,* 12 Wall. 687; *Thompson* v. *Butler,* 95 U. S. 694—while important, need not be dissected. *Gregory* v. *Morris* is in harmony with them and the opinion there definitely and finally stated the doctrine which we should apply.

It is true to say that the gold clauses " were intended to afford a definite standard or measure of value, and thus to protect against a depreciation of the currency and against the discharge of the obligation by payment of less than that prescribed." Furthermore, they furnish means for computing the sum payable in currency if gold should become unobtainable. The borrower agrees to repay in gold coin containing 25.8 grains to the dollar; and if this cannot be secured the promise is to discharge the obligation by paying for each dollar loaned the currency value of that number of grains. Thus, the purpose of the parties will be carried out. Irrespective of any change in currency, the thing loaned or an equivalent will be returned—nothing more, nothing less. The present currency consists of promises to pay dollars of 15 5/21 grains; the Government procures gold bullion on that basis. The calculation to determine the damages for failure to pay in gold would not be difficult. *Gregory* v. *Morris* points the way.

————

Under appropriate statutes the United States for many years issued gold certificates, in the following form: " This certifies that there have been deposited in the Treasury of The United States of America One Thousand Dollars in gold coin payable to the bearer on demand. This certificate is a legal tender in the amount thereof in payment of all debts and dues public and private."

The certificates here involved—series 1928—were issued under § 6, Act Mar. 14, 1900, 31 Stat. 47, as amended. See U. S. C. Title 31, § 429.[1]

In view of the statutory direction that gold coin for which certificates are issued shall be held for their payment on demand " and used for no other purpose," it seems idle to argue (as counsel for the United States did) that other use is permissible under the ancient Act of March 3, 1863.

By various orders of the President and the Treasury from April 5 to December 28, 1933, persons holding gold certificates were required to deliver them, and accept "an equivalent amount of any form of coin or currency coined

————

[1] In his Annual Report, 1926, 80, 81, the Secretary of the Treasury said: " Gold and silver certificates are in fact mere ' warehouse receipts ' issued by the Government in exchange for gold coin or bullion deposited in the one case, or standard silver dollars deposited in the other case, or against gold or standard silver dollars, respectively, withdrawn from the general fund of the Treasury. . . . Gold certificates, United States notes, Treasury notes of 1890, and Federal reserve notes are directly redeemable in gold." In his letter with the Annual Report, for 1933, 375, he showed that on June 30, 1933, $1,230,717,109 was held in trust against gold certificates and Treasury notes of 1890. The Treasury notes of 1890 then outstanding did not exceed about $1,350,000. Tr. Rep. 1926, 80.

or issued under the laws of the United States designated by the Secretary of the Treasury." Heavy penalties were provided for failure to comply.

That the holder of one of these certificates was owner of an express promise by the United States to deliver gold coin of the weight and fineness established by statute when the certificate issued, or if such demand was not honored to pay the holder the value in the currency then in use, seems clear enough. This was the obvious design of the contract.

The Act of March 14, 1900, 31 Stat., c. 41, 45, 47, as amended, in effect until January 31, 1934, provided: " That the dollar consisting of twenty-five and eight-tenths grains of gold nine-tenths fine, . . . shall be the standard unit of value, and all forms of money issued or coined by the United States shall be maintained at a parity of value with this standard," and also " The Secretary of the Treasury is authorized and directed to receive deposits of gold coin with the Treasurer . . . in sums of not less than twenty dollars, and to issue gold certificates therefor in denominations of not less than twenty dollars, and the coin so deposited shall be retained in the Treasury and held for the payment of such certificates on demand, and used for no other purpose." See U. S. C., Title 31, §§ 314, 429.

The Act of February 4, 1910, 36 Stat., c. 25, p. 192, directed " that any bonds and certificates of indebtedness of the United States hereafter issued shall be payable, principal and interest, in United States gold coin of the present standard of value."

By Executive Orders, April 5, and April 20, 1933, the President undertook to require owners of gold coin, gold bullion, and gold certificates, to deliver them on or before May 1st to a Federal Reserve Bank, and to prohibit the exportation of gold coin, gold bullion or gold

GOLD CLAUSE CASES. 367

certificates. As a consequence the United States were off the gold standard and their paper money began a rapid decline in the markets of the world. Gold coin, gold certificates and gold bullion were no longer obtainable. "Gold is not now paid nor is it available for payment upon public or private debts" was declared in Treasury statement of May 27, 1933; and this is still true. All gold coins have been melted into bars.

The Agricultural Adjustment Act of May 12, 1933, 48 Stat., c. 25, pp. 31, 52, 53—entitled "An act to relieve the existing national economic emergency by increasing agricultural purchasing power, to raise revenue for extraordinary expenses incurred by reason of such emergency, to provide emergency relief with respect to agricultural indebtedness, to provide for the orderly liquidation of joint-stock land banks, and for other purposes," by § 43 provides that "Such notes [United States notes] and all other coins and currencies heretofore or hereafter coined or issued by or under the authority of the United States shall be legal tender for all debts public and private." Also, that the President by proclamation may "fix the weight of the gold dollar . . . as he finds necessary from his investigation to stabilize domestic prices or to protect the foreign commerce against the adverse effect of depreciated foreign currencies." And further, "such gold dollar, the weight of which is so fixed, shall be the standard unit of value, and all forms of money issued or coined by the United States shall be maintained at a parity with this standard and it shall be the duty of the Secretary of the Treasury to maintain such parity, but in no event shall the weight of the gold dollar be fixed so as to reduce its present weight by more than 50 per centum."

The Gold Reserve Act of January 30, 1934, 48 Stat., c. 6, p. 337, 342, undertook to ratify preceding Presidential orders and proclamations requiring surrender of gold but prohibited him from establishing the weight of the gold dollar "at more than 60 per centum of its present weight." By proclamation, January 31, 1934, he directed that thereafter the standard should contain 15 5/21 grains of gold, nine-tenths fine. (The weight had been 25.8 grains since 1837.) No such dollar has been coined at any time.

On June 5, 1933, Congress passed a "Joint Resolution to assure uniform value to the coins and currencies of the United States." 48 Stat., c. 48, p. 112. This recited that holding and dealing in gold affect the public interest and are therefore subject to regulation; that the provisions of obligations which purport to give the obligee the right to require payment in gold coin or in any amount of money of the United States measured thereby obstruct the power of Congress to regulate the value of money and are inconsistent with the policy to maintain the equal value of every dollar coined or issued. It then declared that every provision in any obligation purporting to give the obligee a right to require payment in gold is against public policy, and directed that "every obligation, heretofore or hereafter incurred, whether or not any such provision is contained therein or made with respect thereto, shall be discharged upon payment, dollar for dollar, in any coin or currency which at the time of payment is legal tender for public and private debts."

Four causes are here for decision. Two of them arise out of corporate obligations containing gold clauses—railroad bonds. One is based on a United States Fourth Liberty Loan bond of 1918, called for payment April 15, 1934, containing a promise to pay "in United States gold coin of the present standard of value" with interest in like gold coin. Another involves gold certificates, series 1928, amounting to $106,300.

As to the corporate bonds the defense is that the gold clause was destroyed by the Resolution of June 5, 1933; and this view is sustained by the majority of the Court.

It is insisted that the agreement in the Liberty Bond, to pay in gold, also was destroyed by the Act of June 5, 1933. This view is rejected by the majority; but they seem to conclude that because of the action of Congress in declaring the holding of gold unlawful, no appreciable damage resulted when payment therein or the equivalent was denied.

Concerning the gold certificates it is ruled that if upon presentation for redemption gold coin had been paid to the holder, as promised, he would have been required to return this to the Treasury. He could not have exported it or dealt with it. Consequently he sustained no actual damage.

There is no challenge here of the power of Congress to adopt such proper "Monetary Policy" as it may deem necessary in order to provide for national obligations and furnish an adequate medium of exchange for public use. The plan under review in the *Legal Tender Cases* was declared within the limits of the Constitution, but not without a strong dissent. The conclusions there announced are not now questioned; and any abstract discussion of Congressional power over money would only tend to befog the real issue.

The fundamental problem now presented is whether recent statutes passed by Congress in respect of money and credits, were designed to attain a legitimate end. Or whether, under the guise of pursuing a monetary policy, Congress really has inaugurated a plan primarily designed to destroy private obligations, repudiate national debts and drive into the Treasury all gold within the country, in exchange for inconvertible promises to pay, of much less value.

112536°—35——24

Considering all the circumstances, we must conclude they show that the plan disclosed is of the latter description and its enforcement would deprive the parties before us of their rights under the Constitution. Consequently the Court should do what it can to afford adequate relief.

What has been already said will suffice to indicate the nature of these causes and something of our general views concerning the intricate problems presented. A detailed consideration of them would require much time and elaboration; would greatly extend this opinion. Considering also the importance of the result to legitimate commerce, it seems desirable that the Court's decision should be announced at this time. Accordingly, we will only undertake in what follows to outline with brevity our replies to the conclusions reached by the majority and to suggest some of the reasons which lend support to our position.

The authority exercised by the President and the Treasury in demanding all gold coin, bullion and certificates is not now challenged; neither is the right of the former to prescribe weight for the standard dollar. These things we have not considered. Plainly, however, to coin money and regulate the value thereof calls for legislative action.

Intelligent discussion respecting dollars requires recognition of the fact that the word may refer to very different things. Formerly the standard gold dollar weighed 25.8 grains; the weight now prescribed is 15 5/21 grains. Evidently, promises to pay one or the other of these differ greatly in value, and this must be kept in mind.

From 1792 to 1873 both the gold and silver dollar were standard and legal tender, coinage was free and unlimited. Persistent efforts were made to keep both in circulation. Because the prescribed relation between them got out of harmony with exchange values, the gold coin disappeared and did not in fact freely circulate in this country for 30 years prior to 1834. During that time business transactions were based on silver. In 1834, desiring to restore parity and bring gold back into circulation, Congress reduced somewhat (6%) the weight of the gold coin and thus equalized the coinage and the exchange values. The silver dollar was not changed. The purpose was to restore the use of gold as currency—not to force up prices or destroy obligations. There was no apparent profit for the books of the Treasury. No injury was done to creditors; none was intended. The legislation is without special significance here. See Hepburn on Currency.

The moneys under consideration in the *Legal Tender Cases,* decided May 1, 1871, 12 Wall. 457, and March 3, 1884, 110 U. S. 421, were promises to pay dollars, " bills of credit." They were " a pledge of the national credit," promises " by the Government to pay dollars," " the standard of value is not changed." The expectation, ultimately realized, was that in due time they would be redeemed in standard coin. The Court was careful to show that they were issued to meet a great emergency in time of war, when the overthrow of the Government was threatened and specie payments had been suspended. Both the end in view and the means employed, the Court held were lawful. The thing actually done was the issuance of bills endowed with the quality of legal tender in order to carry on until the United States could find it possible to meet their obligations in standard coin. This they accomplished in 1879. The purpose was to meet honorable obligations—not to repudiate them.

The opinion there rendered declares—" The legal tender acts do not attempt to make paper a standard of value. We do not rest their validity upon the assertion that their emission is coinage, or any regulation of the value of money; nor do we assert that Congress may make anything which has no value money. What we do assert is, that Congress has power to enact that the government's promises to pay money shall be, for the time being, equivalent in value to the representative of value determined by the coinage acts or to multiples thereof." What was said in those causes, of course, must be read in the light of all the circumstances. The opinion gives no support to what has been attempted here.

This Court has not heretofore ruled that Congress may require the holder of an obligation to accept payment in subsequently devalued coins, or promises by the Government to pay in such coins. The legislation before us attempts this very thing. If this is permissible, then a gold dollar containing one grain of gold may become the standard, all contract rights fall, and huge profits appear on the Treasury books. Instead of $2,800,000,000 as recently reported, perhaps $20,000,000,000, maybe enough to cancel the public debt, maybe more!

The power to issue bills and "regulate values" of coin cannot be so enlarged as to authorize arbitrary action, whose immediate purpose and necessary effect is destruction of individual rights.[2] As this Court has said, a "power to regulate is not a power to destroy." 154 U. S. 362, 398. The Fifth Amendment limits all governmental powers. We are dealing here with a debased standard, adopted with the definite purpose to destroy obligations. Such arbitrary and oppressive action is not within any congressional power heretofore recognized.

---

[2] "It may well be doubted whether the nature of society and of government does not prescribe some limits to the legislative power; and if any be prescribed where are they to be found if the property of an individual fairly and honestly acquired may be seized without compensation." Chief Justice Marshall in *Fletcher* v. *Peck*, 6 Cranch 87, 135.

The authority of Congress to create legal tender obligations in times of peace is derived from the power to borrow money; this cannot be extended to embrace the destruction of all credits.

There was no coin—specie—in general circulation in the United States between 1862 and 1879. Both gold and silver were treated in business as commodities. The Legal Tender Cases arose during that period.

CORPORATE BONDS—

The gold clauses in these bonds were valid and in entire harmony with public policy when executed. They are property—*Lynch* v. *United States,* 292 U. S. 571, 579. To destroy a validly acquired right is the taking of property—*Osborn* v. *Nicholson,* 13 Wall. 654, 662. They established a measure of value and supply a basis for recovery if broken. Their policy and purpose were stamped with affirmative approval by the Government when inserted in its bonds.

The clear intent of the parties was that in case the standard of 1900 should be withdrawn, and a new and less valuable one set up, the debtor could be required to pay the value of the contents of the old standard in terms of the new currency, whether coin or paper. If gold measured by prevailing currency had declined, the debtor would have received the benefit. The Agricultural Adjustment Act of May 12th discloses a fixed purpose to raise the nominal value of farm products by depleting the standard dollar. It authorized the President to reduce the gold in the standard, and further provided that all forms of currency should be legal tender. The result expected to follow was increase in nominal values of commodities and depreciation of contractual obligations. The purpose of § 43, incorporated by the Senate as an amendment to the House Bill, was clearly stated by the

Senator who presented it.[3] It was the destruction of lawfully acquired rights.

In the circumstances existing just after the Act of May 12th, depreciation of the standard dollar by the Presidential proclamation would not have decreased the amount required to meet obligations containing gold clauses. As to them the depreciation of the standard would have caused an increase in the number of dollars of depreciated currency. General reduction of all debts could only be secured by first destroying the contracts evidenced by the gold clauses; and this the Resolution of June 5th undertook to accomplish. It was aimed directly at those contracts and had no definite relation to the power to issue bills or to coin or regulate the value of money.

To carry out the plan indicated as above shown in the Senate, the Gold Reserve Act followed—January 30, 1934. This inhibited the President from fixing the weight of the standard gold dollar above 60% of its then existing weight. (Authority had been given for 50% reduction by the Act of May 12th.) On January 31st he directed that the standard should contain 15 5/21 grains of gold. If this reduction of 40% of all debts was within the power of Congress and if, as a necessary means to accomplish that end, Congress had power by resolution to destroy the

---

[3] He said—" This amendment has for its purpose the bringing down or cheapening of the dollar, that being necessary in order to raise agricultural and commodity prices. . . . The first part of the amendment has to do with conditions precedent to action being taken later.

" It will be my task to show that if the amendment shall prevail it has potentialities as follows: It may transfer from one class to another class in these United States value to the extent of almost $200,000,-000,000. This value will be transferred, first, from those who own the bank deposits. Secondly, this value will be transferred from those who own bonds and fixed investments." Cong. Record, April 1933, pp. 2004, 2216, 2217, 2219.

GOLD CLAUSE CASES. 375

gold clauses, the holders of these corporate bonds are without remedy. But we must not forget that if this power exists, Congress may readily destroy other obligations which present obstruction to the desired effect of further depletion. The destruction of all obligations by reducing the standard gold dollar to one grain of gold, or brass or nickel or copper or lead, will become an easy possibility. Thus we reach the fundamental question which must control the result of the controversy in respect of corporate bonds. Apparently in the opinion of the majority the gold clause in the Liberty bond withstood the June 5th Resolution notwithstanding the definite purpose to destroy them. We think that in the circumstances Congress had no power to destroy the obligations of the gold clauses in private obligations. The attempt to do this was plain usurpation, arbitrary and oppressive.

The oft repeated rule by which the validity of statutes must be tested is this—" Let the end be legitimate, let it be within the scope of the Constitution, and all means which are appropriate, which are plainly adapted to that end, which are not prohibited but consistent with the letter and spirit of the Constitution, are constitutional."

The end or objective of the Joint Resolution was not " legitimate." The real purpose was not " to assure uniform value to the coins and currencies of the United States," but to destroy certain valuable contract rights. The recitals do not harmonize with circumstances then existing. The Act of 1900 which prescribed a standard dollar of 25.8 grains remained in force; but its command that " all forms of money issued or coined by the United States shall be maintained at a parity of value with this standard " was not being obeyed. Our currency was passing at a material discount; all gold had been sequestrated; none was attainable. The Resolution made no provision for restoring parity with the old standard; it established no new one.

This Resolution was not appropriate for carrying into effect any power entrusted to Congress. The gold clauses in no substantial way interfered with the power of coining money or regulating its value or providing an uniform currency. Their existence, as with many other circumstances, might have circumscribed the effect of the intended depreciation and disclosed the unwisdom of it. But they did not prevent the exercise of any granted power. They were not inconsistent with any policy theretofore declared. To assert the contrary is not enough. The Court must be able to see the appropriateness of the thing done before it can be permitted to destroy lawful agreements. The purpose of a statute is not determined by mere recitals—certainly they are not conclusive evidence of the facts stated.

Again, if effective, the direct, primary and intended result of the Resolution will be the destruction of valid rights lawfully acquired. There is no question here of the indirect effect of lawful exercise of power. And citations of opinions which upheld such indirect effects are beside the mark. This statute does not " work harm and loss to individuals indirectly," it destroys directly. Such interference violates the Fifth Amendment; there is no provision for compensation. If the destruction is said to be for the public benefit, proper compensation is essential; if for private benefit, the due process clause bars the way.

Congress has power to coin money but this cannot be exercised without the possession of metal. Can Congress authorize appropriation, without compensation, of the necessary gold? Congress has power to regulate commerce, to establish post roads, &c. Some approved plan may involve the use or destruction of A's land or a private way. May Congress authorize the appropriation or destruction of these things without adequate payment? Of course not. The limitations prescribed by the Constitution restrict the exercise of all power.

Ling Su Fan v. *United States,* 218 U. S. 302, supports the power of the legislature to prevent exportation of coins without compensation. But this is far from saying that the legislature might have ordered destruction of the coins without compensating the owners or that they could have been required to deliver them up and accept whatever was offered. In *United States* v. *Lynah,* 188 U. S. 445, 471, this Court said—" If any one proposition can be considered as settled by the decisions of this court it is that although in the discharge of its duties the Government may appropriate property, it cannot do so without being liable to the obligation cast by the fifth amendment of paying just compensation."

GOVERNMENT BONDS—

Congress may coin money; also it may borrow money. Neither power may be exercised so as to destroy the other; the two clauses must be so construed as to give effect to each. Valid contracts to repay money borrowed cannot be destroyed by exercising power under the coinage provision. The majority seem to hold that the Resolution of June 5th did not affect the gold clauses in bonds of the United States. Nevertheless we are told that no damage resulted to the holder now before us through the refusal to pay one of them in gold coin of the kind designated or its equivalent. This amounts to a declaration that the Government may give with one hand and take away with the other. Default is thus made both easy and safe!

Congress brought about the conditions in respect of gold which existed when the obligation matured. Having made payment in this metal impossible, the Government cannot defend by saying that if the obligation had been met the creditor could not have retained the gold; con-

sequently he suffered no damage because of the nonde-
livery. Obligations cannot be legally avoided by prohibiting the creditor from receiving the thing promised. The
promise was to pay in gold, standard of 1900, otherwise to
discharge the debt by paying the value of the thing promised in currency. One of these things was not prohibited.
The Government may not escape the obligation of making good the loss incident to repudiation by prohibiting
the holding of gold. Payment by fiat of any kind is beyond its recognized power. There would be no serious
difficulty in estimating the value of 25.8 grains of gold in
the currency now in circulation.

These bonds are held by men and women in many parts
of the world; they have relied upon our honor. Thousands of our own citizens of every degree, not doubting
the good faith of their sovereign, have purchased them.
It would not be easy for this multitude to appraise the
form of words which establishes that they have suffered
no appreciable damage; but perhaps no more difficult for
them than for us. And their difficulty will not be as-
suaged when they reflect that ready calculation of the
exact loss suffered by the Philippine government moved
Congress to satisfy it by appropriating, in June 1934, $23,-
862,750.78 to be paid out of the Treasury of the United
States.[4] And see Act May 30, 1934, 48 Stat. 817, appro-

---

[4] AN ACT relating to Philippine currency reserves on deposit in the
United States.

*Be it enacted by the Senate and House of Representatives of the
United States of America in Congress assembled,* That the Secretary
of the Treasury is authorized and directed, when the funds therefor
are made available, to establish on the books of the Treasury a credit
in favor of the Treasury of the Philippine Islands for $23,862,750.78,
being an amount equal to the increase in value (resulting from the
reduction of the weight of the gold dollar) of the gold equivalent at
the opening of business on January 31, 1934, of the balances maintained at that time in banks in the continental United States by the

priating $7,438,000 to meet losses sustained by officers
and employees in foreign countries due to appreciation of
foreign currencies in their relation to the American
dollar.

GOLD CERTIFICATES—

These were contracts to return gold left on deposit;
otherwise to pay its value in the currency. Here the gold
was not returned; there arose the obligation of the Government to pay its value. The Court of Claims has jurisdiction over such contracts. Congress made it impossible for the holder to receive and retain the gold promised him; the statute prohibited delivery to him. The
contract being broken the obligation was to pay in currency the value of 25.8 grains of gold for each dollar
called for by the certificate. For the Government to say,
we have violated our contract but have escaped the consequences through our own statute, would be monstrous.
In matters of contractual obligation the Government can
not legislate so as to excuse itself.

These words of Alexander Hamilton ought not to be
forgotten—

"When a government enters into a contract with an
individual, it deposes, as to the matter of the contract, its
constitutional authority, and exchanges the character of
legislator for that of a moral agent, with the same rights
and obligations as an individual. Its promises may be

Government of the Philippine Islands for its gold standard fund and
its Treasury certificate fund less the interest received by it on such
balances.

Sec. 2. There is hereby authorized to be appropriated, out of the
receipts covered into the Treasury under section 7 of the Gold Reserve
Act of 1934, by virtue of the reduction of the weight of the gold
dollar by the proclamation of the President on January 31, 1934, the
amount necessary to establish the credit provided for in section 1 of
this Act. Approved, June 19, 1934.

justly considered as excepted out of its power to legislate, unless in aid of them. It is in theory impossible to reconcile the idea of a promise which obliges, with a power to make a law which can vary the effect of it." 3 Hamilton's Works, 518, 519.

These views have not heretofore been questioned here. In the *Sinking-Fund Cases,* 99 U. S. 700, 719, Chief Justice Waite speaking for the majority declared: " The United States are as much bound by their contracts as are individuals. If they repudiate their obligations, it is as much repudiation, with all the wrong and reproach that term implies, as it would be if the repudiator had been a State or a municipality or a citizen. No change can be made in the title created by the grant of the lands, or in the contract for the subsidy bonds, without the consent of the corporation. All this is indisputable."

And in the same cause, (731, 732) Mr. Justice Strong, speaking for himself, affirmed: " It is as much beyond the power of a legislature, under any pretence, to alter a contract into which the government has entered with a private individual, as it is for any other party to a contract to change its terms without the consent of the person contracting with him. As to its contract the government in all its departments has laid aside its sovereignty, and it stands on the same footing with private contractors."

Can the Government, obliged as though a private person to observe the terms of its contracts, destroy them by legislative changes in the currency and by statutes forbidding one to hold the thing which it has agreed to deliver? If an individual should undertake to annul or lessen his obligation by secreting or manipulating his assets with the intent to place them beyond the reach of creditors, the attempt would be denounced as fraudulent, wholly ineffective.

Counsel for the Government and railway companies asserted with emphasis that incalculable financial disaster would follow refusal to uphold, as authorized by the Constitution, impairment and repudiation of private obligations and public debts. Their forecast is discredited by manifest exaggeration. But, whatever may be the situation now confronting us, it is the outcome of attempts to destroy lawful undertakings by legislative action; and this we think the Court should disapprove in no uncertain terms.

Under the challenged statutes it is said the United States have realized profits amounting to $2,800,000,000.[5] But this assumes that gain may be generated by legislative fiat. To such counterfeit profits there would be no limit; with each new debasement of the dollar they would expand. Two billions might be ballooned indefinitely—to twenty, thirty, or what you will.

Loss of reputation for honorable dealing will bring us unending humiliation; the impending legal and moral chaos is appalling.

---

[5] In a radio address concerning the plans of the Treasury, August 28, 1934, the Secretary of the Treasury, as reported by the Commercial and Financial Chronicle of September 1, 1934, stated:

"But we have another cash drawer in the Treasury, in addition to the drawer which carries our working balance. This second drawer I will call the 'gold' drawer. In it is the very large sum of $2,800,-000,000, representing 'profit' resulting from the change in the gold content of the dollar. Practically all of this 'profit' the Treasury holds in the form of gold and silver. The rest is in other assets.

"I do not propose here to subtract this $2,800,000,000 from the net increase of $4,400,000,000 in the national debt—thereby reducing the figure to $1,600,000,000. And the reason why I do not subtract it is this: for the present this $2,800,000,000 is under lock and key. Most of it, by authority of Congress, is segregated in the so-called stabilization fund, and for the present we propose to keep it there. But I call your attention to the fact that ultimately we expect this 'profit' to flow back into the stream of our other revenues and thereby reduce the national debt."

index